MW01285911

"Gary Dorrien is the greatest Christian ethicist since the legendary Reinhold Niebuhr. Yet his working class origins, deep philosophical probing, and especially his genuine roots in the Black prophetic tradition take him beyond Niebuhr in serious and substantive ways. This precious memoir lays bare his powerful and painful wrestling with forms of death, dogma, and domination. What a great intellectual and spiritual gift his life and book are to us in these grim times!"

—Cornel West, *Dietrich Bonhoeffer Professor of Philosophy and Christian Practice, Union Theological Seminary*

"Dorrien artfully weaves his life story together with an intellectual history of progressive political movements (secular and religious) and their interface with socially engaged theologies. He takes us on a dazzling tour! One encounters Dorrien's intellectual and political trajectory unfolding from his earliest years and an honest account of his life's pain, struggle, and joys. Like his previous works, this fascinating memoir manifests Dorrien's soaring intellect and comprehensive grasp of modern theo-political history, and his fierce commitment to scholarship that advances progressive political movements aligned with democratic socialism."

—Cynthia Moe-Lobeda, *Professor of Theological and Social Ethics, Pacific Lutheran Theological Seminary and Graduate Theological Union Core Doctoral Faculty*

"Gary Dorrien is likely the master church historian of his generation. His large corpus of books attests to his capacity for prolific, incisive, generative thinking. Now he has written a new history book, this one a thoughtful account of his life, vocation, and moral passion. It is a probing commentary on the ongoing battles for social justice in our society, battles that Dorrien joined with relentless passion, courage, and wisdom."

—Walter Brueggemann, *William Marcellus McPheeters Professor Emeritus of Old Testament, Columbia Theological Seminary*

"If historicism is the notion that all things are fashioned by their histories and contexts, then *Over from Union Road* is a deeply historicist work. This riveting and beautiful book is the remarkable story of how Gary Dorrien became Gary Dorrien, how a shy athlete from rural Michigan became the foremost religious historian and theological ethicist of our time. With his signature blend of genealogical detail, comprehensive analysis, and gripping storytelling, Dorrien chronicles the events and experiences, ideas and struggles, and loves and losses that indelibly shaped his spirituality, his activism, and his progressive Christian worldview. Along the way, the reader encounters an intriguing cast of characters, from philosophers and theologians and political organizers, to colleagues and friends and family members, as Dorrien gracefully narrates their lives and how they are intertwined with his own. Part personal memoir and part intellectual and social history, *Over from Union Road* brilliantly exemplifies what Dorrien once called "theology as biography." It is the long-awaited account of the making of Gary Dorrien—and the movements, traditions, and relationships that made him."

—Demian Wheeler, *Sophia Associate Professor of Religious and Theological Studies, United Theological Seminary of the Twin Cities*

Also by Gary Dorrien

*Anglican Identities: Logos Idealism, Imperial
Whiteness, Commonweal Ecumenism*

The Spirit of American Liberal Theology

A Darkly Radiant Vision: The Black Social Gospel in the Shadow of MLK

American Democratic Socialism: History, Politics, Religion, and Theory

In a Post-Hegelian Spirit: Philosophical Theology as Idealistic Discontent

*Social Democracy in the Making: Political and
Religious Roots of European Socialism*

*Breaking White Supremacy: Martin Luther
King Jr. and the Black Social Gospel*

The New Abolition: W. E. B. Du Bois and the Black Social Gospel

*Kantian Reason and Hegelian Spirit: The
Idealistic Logic of Modern Theology*

The Obama Question: A Progressive Perspective

Economy, Difference, Empire: Social Ethics for Social Justice

Social Ethics in the Making: Interpreting an American Tradition

*The Making of American Liberal Theology: Crisis,
Irony, and Postmodernity, 1950–2005*

Imperial Designs: Neoconservatism and the New Pax Americana

*The Making of American Liberal Theology: Idealism,
Realism, and Modernity, 1900–1950*

*The Making of American Liberal Theology: Imagining
Progressive Religion, 1805–1900*

The Barthian Revolt in Modern Theology

The Word as True Myth: Interpreting Modern Theology

Soul in Society: The Making and Renewal of Social Christianity

The Neoconservative Mind: Politics, Culture, and the War of Ideology

GARY DORRIEN

OVER FROM UNION ROAD

MY CHRISTIAN-LEFT-INTELLECTUAL LIFE

BAYLOR UNIVERSITY PRESS

Cover and book design by Elyxandra Encarnación
Cover photograph: Gary Dorrien, 2526 West North Union Road, Bay County, Michigan, 1955. Courtesy of the author.

The Library of Congress has cataloged this book under ISBN
     978-1-4813-2241-6.

Library of Congress Control Number: 2024940134

For my trinity of beloveds,

Virginia Catherine Hank Dorrien
Sara Biggs Dorrien-Christians
Eris Benzwie McClure

And in loving memory of Brenda

CON

List of Images

1 Over from Union Road

2 Alma College

3 Harvard–Union–Princeton–Brenda

4 Albany Activism

5 Kalamazoo Heartbreak

6 Over from Kalamazoo

7 Into the Obama Era

8 Twilight Surge

Notes

Acknowledgments

Index

ENTS

ix

1

29

57

95

123

161

201

229

277

299

303

LIST OF IMAGES

1   Jack Dorrien, DeTour High School; DeTour, Michigan, 1949.

2   Virginia Hank, DeTour High School; DeTour, Michigan, 1949.

3   Gary Dorrien (GD), Midland Trailer Park; Midland, Michigan, 1953.

4   GD, Midland Trailer Park, Midland, Michigan, 1954.

5   GD, Forest School; Bay County, Michigan, 1958.

6   GD, Greg Dorrien, Jack Dorrien, and Andy Dorrien; Bay County, Michigan. Father's Day, 1959.

7   The Dorrien brothers at Alma College: from left, front: Eric and Mike; back: GD, Greg, and Andy; Alma, Michigan, 1972.

8   Jack and Virginia Dorrien; Midland, Michigan, 1978.

9   GD and Brenda L. Biggs, with Bishop Wilbur E. Hogg; ordination at St. Andrew's Episcopal Church, Albany, New York, 1982.

10   Dorrien-Biggs ordination gathering: from left, Greg Dorrien, Jack Dorrien, Virginia Dorrien, Eric Dorrien, GD, Brenda Biggs, Anson Biggs, Grace Biggs, and Mike Dorrien; Albany, New York, 1982.

11   Sara B. Dorrien and Brenda Biggs; Kalamazoo, Michigan, 1988.

12   GD with Jürgen Moltmann, Kalamazoo College; Kalamazoo, Michigan, 1988.

13   GD with Brenda Biggs and Skipper; Kalamazoo, 1998.

14   Sara Dorrien singing "Maybe," Kalamazoo Children's Chorus, 2000.

15   GD with Sara Dorrien on the Brooklyn Bridge, New York City, 2010.

16   GD with Eris McClure on the Brooklyn Bridge, New York City, 2010.

17   Seminary graduation: from left, Eris McClure, Sara Dorrien, GD, Robyn Hampton Dorrien, Virginia Dorrien, and Greg Dorrien, Columbia Theological Seminary; Decatur, Georgia, 2011.

18   GD Grawemeyer Award Lecture, Louisville, Kentucky, 2017. Photograph by Jonathan Roberts, Louisville Theological Seminary.

19   GD with Cornel West, Nkosi Du Bois Anderson, and James Cone, Union Theological Seminary; New York City, New York, 2017. Photograph by Adam Crocker.

20   Eris McClure and GD, sunset in Traverse City, Michigan, 2018.

21   Baptism of Nicholas: from left, front: Patty Christians, Sara Dorrien-Christians, baby Nicholas Christians, and Eris McClure; back: Will Christians and GD, 2019.

22   Front: Clara Christians, Nicholas Christians, and Evie Christians; back: Sara Dorrien-Christians and Will Christians, 2023.

1

OVER FROM UNION ROAD

I am nine years old and have retreated once again to our backyard in semi-rural Bay County, Michigan. The day began with another failed attempt to rustle up a summer baseball game. My nearest neighbor, David Sczepanski, said to come back for him if I got something going. His across-the-road neighbor said it would take more players than I corralled last time for him to join us. There are three Owen boys—John, Bill, and Rick—so their reply is make-or-break. When the Owen boys say no, it's pointless to keep trying, and they never say yes more than once per week. Sometimes they invite me inside to watch television, but I hardly ever do that. I head to the backyard of our home on Union Road with a baseball glove, all the baseballs I've found scouring through fields and ditches, a football that I bought with my winnings in a school literary contest, and a sleeping bag.

I throw the bag over our clothesline and pitch the baseballs to it. Periodically I throw the football to imaginary receivers or kick it. This goes on for most of the day, interrupted only by my mother's call to help with one of our toddler boys or the baby boy. In the fall my dad takes me to a Friday night spectacle, a Midland High School Chemics football game, which provides the goal of my youth, to play quarterback for the Chemics. In the winter I shovel snow off the lawn to keep throwing. Many strikeouts are racked up and touchdowns scored in my solitude.

We live two miles outside Midland on a dirt road. To the right are the shacks and trailers of West North Union Road; to the left are the working-class homes of my baseball buddies on Flajole Road. Somehow, we must move at least two miles west for my Midland football dream to come true. A railroad track near our home services long freight trains with a smattering of wide-open empty cars. I have a recurrent fantasy of whisking far away on a train, which feels perfectly normal to me. I also fantasize about throwing myself in front of a train, which always unleashes a cascade of shame: think what that would do to your mother! But I do not think only of sports and flight. In the backyard I ponder that God is everywhere, that Jesus was hideously executed on a cross, and that I cannot catch the "I" in saying, "I am myself."

If God is everywhere then God must not be a discrete something out there somewhere. Over my bed I post a satellite picture of Earth on which I scrawl at the bottom, "Creation," which names the feeling of belonging to a cosmic order that the picture stirs in me. I yearn to relate to something beyond Bay County. My parents shake their heads that I cannot be dragged past either of Midland's Catholic churches—St. Brigid's downtown, or Blessed Sacrament on the east side of town. Attending Mass with my family at Blessed Sacrament or often hitching a ride with David's family, I am caught by the image of the crucified Jesus overhanging the altar. What kind of religion portrays the God-figure in tortured suffering and death on a cross? The crucifix strikes me as inexplicably strange, repelling, fixating, and true. It breaks through to me like nothing else, long before I learn any atonement doctrine. It is some kind of religious ideal transcending the flat everydayness of Bay County while I wait to play for the Chemics.

"I am myself" lacks the emotive force of the cross, but it strikes me first while walking home from a talent show rehearsal at Forest School Number Two. I turn this sentence over and over in my mind, saying it aloud, punching the first word, then the second, then the third, then the second half of "myself," then two-word combinations of the phrase, trying to catch hold of the "I" of self-consciousness. It puzzles me that I cannot do it. How can my self—this immediate "I" who spends so much time alone with his thoughts and baseballs—be so elusive? I feel the slippery problem of identity, but have no language for it and do not try to discuss it with anyone. These experiences are glimmers of the unlikely Christian Left intellectual that I became.

My father, John Ellis (Jack) Dorrien, grew up in the port village of De Tour, Michigan, on the eastern tip of the Upper Peninsula, sixteen miles from the rural Goetzville home of my mother, Virginia Catherine Hank. Jack Dorrien was slurred throughout his youth as a "half-breed" for having a Native American mother. The abuse scarred him, making him someone who shied away from emotional entanglements. His father, Ellis Dorrien, had an English and Scottish lineage by way of Canada, growing up in vagabond flux in little towns of southern Michigan, where his father, William Dorrien, had scraped a nomadic existence since leaving home at the age of thirteen. Ellis Dorrien trekked up and across Michigan in search of work, finding it in the lumber camps of De Tour and Drummond Island, later telling vivid stories of eating leaves off the trees to keep walking. In 1915 he married Anne Rice, raised by her two grandmothers in De Tour's lighthouse, where three families resided on the western shore of the St. Mary's River. Her home was a beacon for the freighters passing from Lake Superior to the lower Great Lakes or the other way around.

Anne Rice Dorrien descended from Cree, English, and French forebears. She raised her six children in her Roman Catholic faith and maintained a spotless home for them and her husband, who made his living as a De Tour dockworker tying up boats passing into and out of the North Channel. Ellis Dorrien was a buoyant charmer, bristling with masculine physicality, self-confidence, opinions, and an eye for beautiful women. He adopted his wife's religion, overwhelmed his four sons, hurt two of them badly, wounded my father more subtly, and raised two feisty daughters. My father was the baby of the family, so a great deal of Dorrien history had gone down when my parents were married in November 1950. Much of this story was a whispered tale of betrayal and enmity revolving around Ellis Dorrien.

He talked earnestly about things that no one else in my youth discussed—trade unions, the Depression, the class struggle, and strikes. Ellis Dorrien had repudiated local bigotry against First Nation descendants by marrying one, and he voted several times for Socialist presidential candidate Norman Thomas. But the bigotry wore him down, making him ashamed of his children, and he blew up his family by treating his daughters-in-law as harem candidates. Grandpa Dorrien told friends that the treatment he received for marrying a Cree was unbearable. He chafed that his children could not pass for White, and he was thrilled when my dad started up with my mother: "Don't blow it, kid; this is the great break of your life." Which it was, except not why Grandpa Dorrien thought so.

My mother got a strong dose of her father-in-law's hypermasculinity, opinions, racial anxiety, and handsy sense of entitlement upon marrying into his family. Her pale beauty excited him; surely, she would produce passably White Dorriens. When I was born, my father and his father had the same crestfallen reaction: "Oh no, what a shame; he's too dark!" Two months later, Anne Dorrien died of heart disease, to put it charitably. Upper Peninsula Michiganders call themselves "Yoopers" and were long inclined to believe that Lower Peninsula hospitals were too distant and alien for them to use. Ellis Dorrien believed it stubbornly, so Anne Dorrien lay in her bed upstairs until she died. For years afterward, my father occasionally said to me, wistfully, "I wish you had known my mother." This lament was sincere, but he had to be dragged to get-togethers with Dorrien relatives, and he cut us off from his mother's family.

Virginia Hank's family of seven people somehow got by in a two-room stub of a house planted amid a vast forestland. It had no bathroom or living room until my mother was in high school; later it got electricity. Sometimes the family rented a house for the winter months in De Tour, where my grandfather Edward Hank plowed roads for Chippewa County. Virginia Hank was strong-willed like her mother, Mary Jane (Moore) Hank, and her older sister Charlotte Hank. She loved her mother and Charlotte but battled them fiercely throughout her childhood while tenderly loving her father, another wounded type who hid from his family. Mary Jane Moore hailed from an Irish clan of Presbyterians and Anglicans that trickled to the Upper Peninsula from Ontario. She joined the Catholic Church upon marrying Edward Hank, the son of a Polish sawmill engineer on Drummond Island. My mother, the second of five children, was raised Catholic for eleven years until her mother followed her brother Milt Moore into Baptist fundamentalism. Mary Jane Hank grilled the Catholic pastor of St. Stanislaus Church, Goetzville many times at her kitchen table, pressing for biblical answers to her questions about infant baptism, purgatory, limbo, the pope, and the like. Then she joined the Baptists—the great catastrophe of my mother's youth.

Now she and her siblings were hauled to Raber Bible Baptist Church in nearby Raber and evangelized aggressively. My mother loathed evangelical Protestant religion, the Reverend Ralph Crandall, and his Bible-quoting sermons. To her, fundamentalism was degrading and stupid; at least the Catholic Mass had dignity. Her refusal to be re-baptized was a daily affront to her mother. Edward Hank never converted, either, though he made no fuss about it. He just wanted to be left alone in his shed and garage with his tools, hunting rifles, violins, roadside discoveries, and junkyard treasures.

Mary Jane Hank had two voice tones for her husband. Mostly she barked at him—"Edward!" It embarrassed me that she constantly denigrated him, never encouraging my brothers and me to do otherwise. But sometimes she called to him in a soft voice, "Dad?" "Edward!" was a recluse with a fifth-grade education who had gotten her pregnant out of wedlock, had a drinking problem as a young man, cast off the Polish-English mishmash of his childhood home, and did not let on that he might not be a Hank. "Dad" earned whatever respect he accrued at home by fathering five children and providing for them as a road worker and sometime mail carrier.

My mother's empathy for her father felt odd to me as a youth, since Grandma Hank was a forceful presence in our lives and Grandpa Hank was almost no presence at all. Grandma Hank was devoted to her grandchildren, looked out for us, could readily name my four brothers and me, and sent us $3 birthday checks. She had strong opinions about many subjects, especially dispensationalist eschatology, often sealing a disputed point with a reproach: "You don't know your Bible." Grandpa Hank rarely uttered more than a half-sentence to us. He hunted with his grandsons David Firack, Dan Firack, and especially Leon Hank, but we five Lower Peninsula boys were an alien breed to him.

My mother and her mother were strange concerning our Hank heritage. They waxed lyrically about being Irish Moores but got weird when I asked about Grandpa's family, conveying that something was off. Finally, my mother yielded the secret: when she gave birth to my brother Andy, she was warned by Grandma not to let any of her boys marry a McDonald because Edward Hank's real father was a De Tour Post Office official named Jim McDonald. We Dorrien boys, it turned out, were not really Hanks. This issue gave my mother and Charlotte something else to quarrel about, as Charlotte refused to believe her mother, for once, and my mother, as usual. My mother did not hold it against Ed Hank that their family was poor, strapped, and isolated. They never starved, so it could have been worse, and at least he didn't impose his opinions on her. Grandpa Hank was, in fact, no less intelligent than his forceful wife, with music in him. The story of my mother's life was her battle with a mother who disapproved of her, and the playing out of her fateful decision to quit college after one year.

My mother was a stunning blond beauty who evoked gaping stares from men well into her seventies. I heard it throughout my growing up and long afterward: "Your mother is a knockout," or, "Your mother is unbelievable." As a youth she befriended a Cree neighbor named Gary. In high school her only boyfriend, my dad, was the only dark male in her class. Her looks undoubtedly intimidated other candidates. Many relatives and high school classmates implored my mother not to waste her beauty and future on "the Indian," which stoked her defiance. My dad was a three-sport athlete in high school and my mom was a home-coming queen who played alongside him in the school band. He was prone to exaggerate the cultural gap between De Tour and Goetzville. On this view, she moved up by marrying him, an interpretation they sharply debated for seventy years. She retorted that their senior class trip to Washington, DC in 1949 took him out of Michigan for the first time, though Canada is plainly visible from De Tour; what could be more provincial than that? Both came from families that suffered the death of a young boy, and neither family produced a college graduate, not that anyone thought anything of it, except my mother.

For one year my mother attended Northern Michigan College of Education in Marquette, later renamed Northern Michigan University, in the Northwest UP, having won a scholarship for prospective teachers. At a raffle, she won a car that ironically robbed her of the freedom she should have had in Marquette. Her roommate Blanche McGinnis had a boyfriend in Drummond Island, so every Friday my mother was strong-armed into driving Blanche home across the state, never experiencing a college student weekend. Meanwhile my father learned the barbering trade at Green's Barber College in Detroit just before North Korea invaded South Korea in June 1950. He was very clear that the war in Korea did not compare to World War II. My dad's older brothers Kenneth and Ralph Dorrien served in the Pacific Theater during World War II and were emblems of family pride—however briefly—for doing so. Jack Dorrien had been taunted in his youth that he should prove his Americanism by serving in the war. He countered, in a story he often told, that he was thirteen years old. When he came of age during a side-show war, he took no interest in striving for war-service respect in a village that had shamed him.

My mother returned to Marquette in the summer of 1950 for the concluding year of her two-year teaching program, while my father hooked on with a barbershop on Main Street in Marquette. She took an office job and loved Marquette, feeling liberated by its college-town, port-city atmosphere. He was rudely treated in Marquette and loathed the city. It was their crucible moment, the subject of countless references and arguments for decades. My mother wanted to stay in Marquette, keep her job, get married, and finish her degree. My father wanted to move to Midland, Michigan, where Ken Dorrien worked for the Dow Chemical Company. She said she would leave Marquette only as a bride, and my dad was fine with that, anxious anyway to improve his odds of avoiding the Korean War.

Jack Dorrien knew he was way-out-there lucky to have attracted Virginia Hank. Everyone said so, especially his parents. My mom skipped an exam in the spring of 1950 because my dad showed up unexpectedly in Marquette. This event was the subject of sharp exchanges between them throughout their marriage, with wounded pride on both sides. He said that she failed her classes anyway, so she didn't give up anything by marrying him. He stuck to this version for seventy years even though it always enraged her and wasn't true. In November 1950 they wed at Sacred Heart of Jesus Catholic Church in De Tour. I exist because Britain lost the War of 1812, depriving Native Americans of the homeland in Michigan-Ohio-Indiana that Britain promised to them, the United States provided ninety percent of the United Nations military force backing South Korea, and my mother caved on college and Marquette.

Grandma Hank had conceived Charlotte before she was married, and Charlotte had given birth to her son David two years before she was married. My mother—the one who was not saved, the one whom Grandma and Charlotte berated for being a rebellious heretic destined for hell—carried an edgy moral pride at not replicating their record. She tolerated only so much chastisement from them on the righteousness theme after she married the right way in the Roman Catholic Church. Young women of her time were supposed to get married and bear children as soon as possible. Everyone said so. My mother's college classmates urged her to marry the dark young man who came all the way to Marquette to see her; evidently, he was the one marked out for her! On the way to Midland, where my father briefly worked for Dow, he made her promise to tell absolutely no one that he was part-Indian. She was incredulous: "They're going to know! You don't look *that* different from your sisters and Ralph, who are obviously Indian! What am I supposed to tell people when they ask?" He replied that people from France are sometimes pretty dark. He was French, that's all. Just stick to it.

When I came along in March 1952, I received a name that registered my mother's quiet dissent. She was proud of marrying a man with a Cree heritage and he was ashamed of it. Naming me after her childhood friend reflected that she disliked the passing strategy but accepted it. People stopped her on the street to ask whose baby she was tending; surely this little guy was not hers. It surprised her that they were so forward about it. We lived in a tiny trailer in the Midland Trailer Park on Buttles Street, where my dad's chain-smoking damaged my lungs. Then we moved to Union Road in Bay County in time for me to join the kindergarten of Forest School Number One.

The shacks to the right of us on Union Road reeked of poverty, bad plumbing, and chaos. I grew up with strict rules about consorting only with the working-class families on Flajole Road. No one in our neighborhood talked about going to college or having a "career." I grew up White working-class and have never claimed any other racial identity. My "race," whatever that was, was surely White. It puzzled me that neighboring parents questioned me on this point and that UP relatives made caustic remarks about it. Every July we made a vacation beeline to Grandma Hank's—the only kind we ever took. Some of the Hank relatives hung racist names on me, including the n-word, warning my mother that I was far too dark. I laughed it off, thinking it strange that they thought there was some issue at stake.

The story of my life was not about that, except for having a wounded father. My earliest memories are of sitting on the couch with my mother while she pored over the pages of her college yearbook. I often crawled up next to her after she had begun. She would turn the pages slowly, telling me about her classmates, classes, professors, Marquette, and the excitement of college life. The stories did not change, except for updates about classmates who graduated or got married. At some point her voice would quiver and she would begin to cry. It wasn't any specific person or story that predictably triggered a surge of regret. It felt like any part of this ritual remembrance was a potential trigger. My mother grieved intensely at giving up her chance to graduate from college. She said it every which way, her voice trembling with pain and anger, brushing away tears, moving to a declaration: "And when *you* grow up, *you* will go to college, and *you will finish college!*"

Her pained volatility and immense love and flashes of rage rolled together as the central reality of my life. I was her project and had to be perfect, as she often said. There was no predicting when she would lash out at me, beating me with a sharp-edged wooden stick that she kept on the washing machine. This went on until I grew old enough to break free from her grip and run away. My brother Greg was born when I was four years old; Andy came along eleven months later; Andy's difficult birth prefigured traumas that consumed my family for many years; and I felt like a little adult by the age of seven, a third parent available for childcare. Soon I was proficient at changing cloth diapers held together by safety pins with large pink heads.

My father was laid off at Dow and opted for a barbershop in downtown Midland, where he took over the third chair. We knew the Hank relatives intimately and barely knew the Dorrien relatives. Every summer, after a few days in Goetzville, I would push for visits to Grandpa Dorrien and other Dorrien relatives, wanting to know them. My dad never wanted to go. He respected his father but was uneasy with him and his new wife, an English immigrant. My father flatly refused to visit Ralph Dorrien, had to be dragged to visit his sister Gladys Lee, and even resisted visiting the one relative with whom he felt comfortable, his sister Edna Geyer. We knew these people only because my mother dutifully stayed in touch with them and I sometimes deposited myself on their doorstep—hello, would you like to talk to me? The Dorrien family was long on whispered cautions about who no longer spoke to whom. Grandpa Dorrien was sexually aggressive with women who attracted him, which included any woman who married one of his sons, my glamorous mother above all. He went for her when she was alone, and she had to repel him. There were strained and broken relationships throughout my father's family, and most had an origin story involving predatory behavior by Grandpa Dorrien with the wives of his sons.

My uncles Ken and Ralph were kind, gentle, and genial. They must have missed their mother terribly but didn't talk about her. They didn't talk about their war experiences, either, unless I pleaded for it. Grandpa

Dorrien hurt them by coming on to their wives, wreaking collateral harm across the family. My dad sometimes repeated his father's claim that these female in-laws were bad characters, but my mother would cut him off whenever he said it, countering that the bad character was the bristling charmer that De Tour admired. My father never came to terms with his father's predatory behavior. I instigated several awkward encounters between feuding Dorriens, refusing to take leave-it-alone for an answer, until I was old enough to understand what had to be left alone. My father had caused none of the estrangement in his family but was never one to mediate a conflict. He just slunk away.

Gladys Lee and Edna Geyer qualified for different degrees of exception. Gladys had an imperious air, a mordant wit, a fount of opinions, and could be uproariously funny, eager to dish. She walked like no one else, with a pronounced strut, her wagging head held impossibly high. My dad sort of liked her, and so did I, so we sometimes visited her together, without my mother, who had been stung too often by Gladys' put-downs. In the world according to Gladys, my mom could not be beautiful *and* smart; she had to be a dumb blond, readily exposed by Gladys' rapier wit. Gladys was only a partial exception, however, to my father's unease because she stung him too. The one person on earth with whom he fully relaxed was Edna Geyer. She was wiry, scrappy, wily, funny, wisecracking, close to my dad's age, and no less sarcastic than Gladys. Edna's children came faster than ours, and they outnumbered us by one. With Edna, once we dragged my dad to her house, he was comfortable in his skin and with the world. He teased her lightheartedly, and playfully welcomed back-at-you teasing. I never saw him that way with anyone else. He ran through the roll of former classmates, seemingly eager to hear about them, at least from her.

Edna lived with her husband, Glenn Geyer, and children in the basement of a half-built house. I vaguely remembered my cousin Judy Geyer from the toddler years, as we were the same age. The first time we visited them in my preadolescence is a prime memory for me. There were empty beer bottles strewn across the floor, dishes piled in the sink up to here, bags and clothes and half-eaten sandwiches thrown wherever, and the same foul smell as the forbidden shacks on Union Road. The yard was not landscaped and had no grass; it was a hilly mass of mud. I sat frozen in a corner, repelled by all of it, resisting the tug of my friendly, outgoing

Geyer cousins. They seemed to be happy, and I appreciated their buoyancy but felt sorry for them.

It wasn't their fault to be born into alcoholic chaos. I had a vivid sense of their unfair fate, which they lacked entirely in those years. A few years later I burst out crying when Grandpa Dorrien told me that my cousin Marybeth had to forego high school to take care of her brothers and sisters. She never lost her generous, outgoing, affectionate personality, despite sacrificing so much. All three of our visits to the Geyer family during these years were traumatizing for me. Over and over, I thought to myself: "I came this close to living like this." Only my fiercely proficient mother, scrubbing her floors to shiny-clean and dressing us like little princes, separated us from living like this. My father put it differently in one of his scrappy arguments with my mother: "At least I don't drink my income at the Overpass Bar like Mac next door." The image of that frightful possibility stuck in my head through our later years on Union Road.

My dad played briefly on a softball team, listened half-attentively to Detroit Tigers broadcasts, and cheered heartily on Sundays for the Detroit Lions. I loved to watch him play and joined him in watching the Lions. He never learned the x-and-o complexities of football, usually just yelling at Milt Plum, who had seemed great when he quarterbacked for Jim Brown's Cleveland Browns, but who descended swiftly to mediocre for us. In softball and baseball, my dad was a big believer in taking a level swing and swinging for a single. To see him clearly in the outfield, I would crawl cautiously up the stairway of the spectator stands, to the top, trying not to fear the height. One night he sprained his ankle while rounding second base, and I was alarmed. My dad is hurt! In the car, gingerly pressing the gas pedal, he told me it was nothing: Athletes get hurt all the time; it's part of being an athlete.

But he did not return to the softball diamond. The father of the Owen boys, Bud Owen, took him golfing, and our world changed. My dad set upon the great passion of his life, buying his first golf clubs, joining a Wednesday night league, and filling his weekends with golf foursomes. At the dinner table he talked a blue streak of golf: "Ben [Hogan] says to keep your left arm stiff on the backswing. . . . Arnie [Palmer] says to turn your hip through the swing." He would jump to his feet to demonstrate. There were golf magazines brought home from the barbershop, new drivers and putters tried out, and golf buddies calling to arrange tee times. He bought a set of clubs for my mother, who played one summer in a weekday league but never took to it. It was his obsession and now she was a golf widow. My dad played catch with me a single time during my years of backyard throwing, and only then because my mother goaded him. She was always willing to play catch on the rare occasions that she had time for it. She had a simple policy about playing catch with her sons, which she maintained through all five of them. She was agreeable right up to the point that you teased that she threw like a girl; then she was done with playing catch with you.

Greg was sweet-tempered and a bit vague in his early years, needing a second pass at the first grade, before he woke up dramatically in junior high school to become ebulliently social Greg. Andy was a happy toddler who began shortly afterward to show signs of emotional turmoil. He had a volatile temper, got frustrated easily, and his troubles became the consuming issue in our family. Our schooling in Bay County was as poor as the neighborhood, and we knew it. The better teachers stayed for a year, and we were left with the ones who couldn't get a job anywhere else. In a third-grade spelling bee pitting the boys against the girls, I ended up alone against thirteen girls and won the contest, being an assiduous reader who pictured big words in his head. The boys rushed upon me with jubilation; our gender is vindicated! But I believed, like them, that school is for girls. Only the girls were good at it; they even seemed to like it. I hated the endless days at Forest School, struggled to listen to the teachers, and resented that I quickly burned through the school's meager library.

Bay County schools went down to half-days, and my parents dug down deep. They couldn't afford to leave Bay County, but subjecting their children to these schools was out of play. I was vehement on this theme. We moved just inside the eastside city limit of Midland, where the schools were better, there were sports leagues for youths, and my parents dug further down to finance piano lessons for Andy. Our right to inherit one of Grandpa Hank's roadside rescue treasures, an upright piano, had not been established until my mother made a fervent plea for it for her third son. At Chestnut Hill Elementary School, I fought off twelve new classmates who pummeled me for over an hour in a field near the school—welcome to Midland! I also served as an altar boy at nearby Blessed Sacrament Church and loved Midland for its sports leagues.

As a seventh grader at Northeast Intermediate School, I was planted by Coach Tom Roberts on the ninth-grade team. I validated his decision by winning the batting title but paid for it from ninth graders who stuck my head down several toilets and violated me with sexual assaults locally called "greasing." They got their revenge, and I realized anew that something about me evoked the bully impulse in bullies. In basketball I had to play the point because I was too small to be a two guard, the only concession of its kind I ever made. In football I struggled to see over the line-players as a quarterback, so I ran a lot of rollouts and bootlegs. All my brothers played baseball, and my mother dragged my dad to countless games. Son number four, Mike, played the least of us, destined for a succession of rock bands. Number five, Eric, was in many ways the most total-jock of our bunch, having the best physique for it and embracing the family jock-legacy handed down to him. All of us could pick out our father's voice in the crowd, especially after we swung and missed: "Ok, we've seen your home run swing. Now let's see your single swing!" But the only way to know him was to caddy for him at the golf course. I was the only one to do it.

I caddied for my dad many times on Saturdays and Sundays. He was quiet, steady, and polite, complimenting his competitors when they hit a good shot, never throwing a club or raging loudly. He muttered a curse when he hit a bad shot and emitted a fleeting "Yes!" when he holed a long putt. He had no friends, but always had a crew of golf buddies. The mainstays were Dale Bouck, a quirky newspaper staffer with a jerky swing; Earl Sanders, a lanky musical-theater singer and jewelry store owner who hit prodigious drives; Charlie Waite, a portly civil engineer with a puckish personality and a scrappy game; Dick Klimpel, a friendly Dow scientist and math whiz with no athletic talent but married to my mother's friend Charlene Klimpel; and a bit later, Ken Gay, a construction company heir who played minor league baseball for several years and ended his baseball playing days on the same semi-pro team as me.

My dad bantered with them on the fairways in the same low-key, no-drama, nothing-too-personal fashion in which he conversed with his barbershop customers. They did not talk about their feelings, gossip about their wives, or venture into politics. They talked about Jack Nicklaus, Lee Trevino, the Tigers, the Lions, the Chemics, the weather, and where the golf buddies took their vacations. On things political my dad was a middle-roader, usually voting for Democrats, but quietly in Republican Midland. The only time he ever fervently backed a political candidate was in 1952, when Tennessee U.S. Senator Estes Kefauver routed the field of Democratic presidential candidates in the primaries but was denied the nomination by party bosses. My dad vowed to never again set himself up for political disappointment. He was skilled at deflecting partisan talk on the golf course, a site of pleasant civility to him. I didn't regard golf as a real sport, since no strenuous exertion was involved, and very old people could play it. But after a while I wanted to play. We developed a ritual in which I teed up on the eighteenth hole and finished the round with my dad's group. It surprised me that they chose the eighteenth hole, since we could be seen from the clubhouse; the kid who didn't pay is swinging a club. By the age of fifteen I was playing in the group on Saturday, or Sunday, or sometimes both.

I practiced assiduously, taking a few clubs and my dad's shag balls on my bike to an open field near the Tittabawassee River, where I hit many hundreds of iron shots. In those years my dad was a low-80s player. He was good off the tee, pretty good with mid-range irons, and very good with short-range irons. He could not hit a two-iron and tended to slice a three-iron, so he choked down on a three-wood and sometimes carried a four-wood, while waging love-and-hate affairs with a succession of putters. At fifteen I whaled a driver and a two-iron, and by the next year I outscored everyone in my dad's group, which delighted him. People opined that he must have felt jealous, but he never showed any trace of it, and more than once I heard him tell a barbershop customer, "My kid shoots in the seventies." Friends warned that I would be lost to the baseball team, unable to disappoint my golf-obsessed father. There was something to that, but he never pressured me to choose golf over baseball. This dilemma was of my own making.

These were the years of feeling that I won my dad's attention, or at least was gaining it. I bantered with him in the same sports-talk fashion as the golf buddies, rarely venturing a personal word about the life we shared at home, partly because that included Andy's turmoil. Playing for the Northeast Vikings, and later the Midland Chemics, and golfing in my dad's group separated me from the lives of Greg, Andy, Mike, and Eric. They interacted with each other and were impacted by each other. Greg and Andy were paired as nearly the same age, while Mike and Eric caught downstream turbulence as the younger brothers.

In the years before I followed my dad to the golf course, our family had a Saturday afternoon grocery store ritual. He worked in the morning and came home for lunch, we packed into the car and drove him to the golf course, and the rest of us headed to Kroger, where my mother nearly always declared, "Wait in the car." Dear God, here we go again. It's hot out here, and Andy never cooperates. As soon as my mother is out of ear-shot, Andy bails out of the car, heading toward the Circle shopping district. Every time this happens, it's an impossible choice, though I always make the same one: leave the others in the car and go after Andy. This is nothing compared to what my brothers went through with Andy. I never suffered the brunt of his acting-out like they did, and he knew that I loved him. But caddying for my dad relieved me of big brother responsibilities on many weekends, which my mother accepted.

She poured herself out for the troubled son. Andy had temper tantrums, clashed with classmates, scared the neighbors, and anguished at his own rage and confusion. My mother devoted constant loving care to him, making special provisions for him, and defending him when he got into trouble. There were therapists who didn't help and school officials who had to be appeased: "Please don't expel my son." He lashed at my mother, and she calmed him down: "You will be fine, I will always love you, I will never stop being here for you." My mother gave Andy everything she had, while letting go of her own volatility. She loved all her boys fiercely, doing whatever she could for them, but one needed her most and she gave her overflowing utmost to him.

She rode Andy to practice the piano, until it wasn't necessary. All of us were musical, like Jack Dorrien, who sang for fourteen consecutive winters in musical theater productions. One year the show was *West Side Story*, and the Broadway album enthralled me—fabulous music like nothing I had heard. There was a lot of competition in our family for the title of who sang the best, who held one's part the best, and who had truly perfect pitch. We played cards and board games the same way, often ganging up against my dad to prevent him from singing the song we dreaded: "Will everyone here kindly step to the rear and let a winner lead the way?"

Andy played piano with cascading up-and-down emotional power. His strong, brooding, tender, tempestuous playing resounded through our home. He brought out the feeling in Elton John songs he loved, especially "Yellow Brick Road," and obligingly launched into the swashbuckling "MacArthur Park" whenever we asked, which was every day. We held fast to the hope that piano and my mother would save him. When trouble erupted at home and someone flared hotly at Andy, my mother would declare that she was ready to take him with her and leave the rest of us behind. It never felt like an idle threat. This was the needing-her-most reality playing out. Whoever said the offending word usually took it back, knowing that my mother would stop at nothing to save her number three son.

In my first two years at Northeast, the only teacher who broke through to me was an ebullient Southerner named Mrs. Dry, who told us that science is the most important subject, so we had better pay attention in her class. I had no trouble listening to her for an hour per day. Northeast had a few male teachers, but no male teacher who was not a coach got my attention. I was an alienated kid absorbed in his own thoughts who scoffed at America-the-greatest propaganda, and a shy kid who clung to a wall at school dances and always left early. The teachers did not like me, since I clearly projected don't-want-to-be-here. What caught my attention was the heyday phase of the Civil Rights Movement. The disturbing images of police dogs attacking protesters in Birmingham, Alabama had lodged in my mind in grade school. Then the shocking television coverage of Black demonstrators bludgeoned on the bridge in Selma, Alabama in 1965 drove me to a book-reading fixation: What was the Civil Rights Movement? My teachers were nervously coy on this subject, not wanting to be quoted. I ransacked the Northeast library and the Midland Public Library for literature that explained how the protests began, why children had marched in Birmingham, why the March on Washington was historic, and who was Martin Luther King Jr.?

In the ninth grade, I read what became a touchstone book for me, L. D. Reddick's insider biography of King, *Crusader without Violence* (1959). It described King's upbringing in Atlanta as the child of a Baptist pastor; his studies at Morehouse College, Crozer Theological Seminary, and Boston University School of Theology; and his leadership of the Montgomery Movement in Montgomery, Alabama. There were eight pages of family album and newspaper pictures that I lingered over, having pored similarly for years over the artwork in our Catholic Family Bible, a wedding present that no one else in my family struggled to fathom.[1]

Reading the Bible seemed impossible to me—what were you supposed to do with the sprawling mass of whatever it was? Start at Genesis and just keep reading? That approach broke down twice. The artwork, however, was another matter entirely, reinforcing my fixation with the cross, as our Family Bible had artwork depicting the stations of the cross. Reddick was long on narrative and mercifully short on intellectualism, which was not how I experienced King's book *Stride toward Freedom* (1958). His chapter on what he studied at college and seminary sailed far above my head, a parade of Walter Rauschenbusch, Karl Marx, Friedrich Nietzsche, Mohandas Gandhi, Reinhold Niebuhr, and some personalist philosophers and theologians. This book planted the seeds of who I became, while exposing the limits of my autodidacticism. My head filled up with arguments by thinkers who never came up in ninth grade classes and whose names I mispronounced.[2]

Meanwhile the war in Vietnam escalated to a very big deal. Mrs. Virginia Braden brought it home to our speech class in the spring of 1967 by assigning a debate question: Should the United States escalate its bombing of North Vietnam? Lyndon Johnson's war architects had claimed in 1965 that Operation Rolling Thunder would boost the morale of the Saigon regime in South Vietnam, slow the insurgency in South Vietnam, destroy the industrial base and transportation system of North Vietnam, and halt the flow of guerrilla fighters into South Vietnam. Two years later it had failed to achieve any of these ends. Mrs. Braden gave us two weeks to study the war and assemble our debate arguments. To me, this assignment was the first truly interesting thing to happen at Northeast not on a sports field. It broke through my alienated distraction, triggered interesting class discussions, and contained an element of spectacle, the debates. I put together an anti-argument and lucked out in the first two rounds. In round three my team drew the pro-side and I tried to beg off, asking Mrs. Braden to replace me with a classmate. She sharply admonished me that debates have two sides. By then I wished that she had chosen a different question. I made a lackluster case for the pro-side out of loyalty to my teammate, and for a few days Mrs. Braden went back to disliking me. Then she asked me to write a paper on why I thought the pro-side was impossibly wrong. Intermediate school is miserable even when nothing bad happens. Mrs. Braden redeemed three years of classroom misery for me.

The coaches were wary of me in the fall of 1967 when I moved up to Midland High School, having heard that I might be too much a loner to be coachable. Four junior high schools funneled baby-boom students to Midland High School, creating a huge, overcrowded school with power-house sports teams. We had study halls that warehoused 300 students per hour in an annex. We had coaches teaching American history because it's a required subject and we had too many students. I paid slight attention in class and never took home a schoolbook; evenings were for reading my own books. The United States incinerated Vietnam with napalm made by Dow in Midland, turning entire villages into lakes of fire. Three speak-ers came to our American history class to promote the war. An Army recruiter said America had to defeat Communism in Vietnam, and was doing so, winning every battle. A Republican official said we had to beat the Communists in Vietnam before they invaded the United States. A Dow official said we should be proud of the great contributions that Dow and Midland made to the war. I stared out the window and implored the clock to move faster.

On April 4, 1968, Dr. King was cut down in Memphis. His assassi-nation staggered me, wounded me, and worked on me. I knew stretches of the Reddick biography by heart, having read it three times in the ninth grade and once the following year. King was my lodestar of a meaningful life, the key to whatever meaning there might be beyond my jock world of mid-Michigan. I read a story about the death threats that King had lived with for years, needing to talk about his death, the article, and my feelings. But my friends were jocks who cut me off when I lapsed into earnest talk, and my teachers managed only a few mum-bled words about MLK. I tried to tell my baseball coach, Keith Carey, what King meant to me. It seemed to surprise him that his stammering pitcher had an inner life; somehow, we bonded. Any idea that I had about what you're supposed to get out of Christianity, aside from the crucifix and the sacred atmosphere of Catholic sanctuaries, I got from King. At the end he became a Jesus figure who died for us. The crucifix story and the King story folded together in my mind and feeling. That was the crux of whatever theology I held at the end of my high school years; all these years later, it still is.

I found my way by reading my own books, not by listening to teach-ers or the pedestrian homilies at Blessed Sacrament Church. What to read after I had twice read *Stride toward Freedom* and the journalistic histories of the time was evident from the sensation that James Baldwin set off with *The Fire Next Time* (1963). The title glossed the lyric declaration in the spiritual "Mary Don't You Weep" that God would send the fire next time, not the water and the rainbow sign given to Noah. I absorbed Baldwin's searing account of growing up in Harlem and being battered by what he called the governing principles of White American society: Blindness, Loneliness, and Terror. Baldwin was especially blistering about the racism of White Christianity. I moved on to his novel *Go Tell It on the Mountain*, and tried to move up to his essay collection *Nobody Knows My Name*, which for some reason carried on about Ingmar Bergman and Norman Mailer, whoever they were, and William Faulkner, a name mentioned by some English teacher. The teachers coped with overcrowded classrooms and pegged me as unreachable. My senior year English teacher David Petrina was the lone exception. I wrote an overlong paper for him on a book I treasured, John Steinbeck's *Grapes of Wrath*, and he said, "To be honest, I never cared for that book. I prefer *East of Eden*." For a moment, I was crestfallen, until I realized that he was provoking a real conversation, caring what I thought. My favorite teacher at Midland High School couldn't have cared less about the touchdowns I scored for the Chemics.[3]

We had many coaches, and I curried their good opinion of me. A few were politically conservative, and the rest were cagey and evasive about such things. Hardly anyone in White, Republican, company-town Midland felt free to hold a dissenting view. You either mouthed Midland's pieties about itself or kept your views to yourself. My top five high school coaches were Frank Altimore, Gary Jozwiak, Jeff Hartman, Robert Stoppert, and Keith Carey. Altimore, an ebullient personality, was fresh out of Michigan State University; I was the first quarterback of his long career in Midland. Jozwiak, a model of deep decency who later won the head coaching job in football, regaled us with his memories of playing running back for the Chemics. Hartman had been Midland's greatest footballer ever before his lack of a left eye canceled his scholarship at Michigan State University, so he played for the University of Wyoming; I had vivid memories of watching him run roughshod over high school opponents. Stoppert was so venerable as the head coach in football and baseball that we players mistakenly assumed he was elderly. Carey, a former professional basketball player, longtime basketball coach, sometime baseball coach, and pillar of gracious dignity, ended his career as our vice principal.

I spent two years lurching back and forth between baseball and golf, missing baseball desperately whenever I tried to choose golf. My parents never expressed an opinion about what I should do, just wishing I could decide. None of my golf teammates were athletes, aside from golf, and some grew up at the country club. Eventually I chose baseball and my baseball friends Ron Blust, Duane Burtch, Andy Donaghy, Windle LaFever, Randy Leigeb, Bill Linde, Jim Parker, Clark Spraetz, Glenn Spraetz, and Greg Weckesser, all but three of whom also played football.

My class was the last one to consist of students from the entire city, before Dow High School graduated a class the succeeding year. We knew what that meant for our sports teams: we're the last Midland class that will benefit from being so big. We had high expectations for my senior football season, vowing that only a state championship would count as success. I led summer workouts that coaches were prohibited by state statute from attending. Every week I exhorted my teammates to obey the training rules and thus stay eligible for our championship run.

But we lost to our archrival Bay City Central, which went on to win the state title. We mounted a comeback near the end of the game that fell short when I overshot a receiver near the end zone with the game on the line. I relived that play in my head for years to come, never thinking about the games we won. There was a crowning irony: if my family had stayed in Bay County, I would have played for Bay City Central. Half the season remained to be played when we lost to Bay City, but it was a depressing exercise in play-out-the-string. We had failed, especially me. I had spent my entire adolescence anticipating a football season that ended prematurely—this was before Michigan had a football tournament. In the gloomy weeks that followed, my gang of jock friends began to disperse, I regretted my lack of a girlfriend, and I gave free rein to my reflective, Baldwin-reading, inchoately spiritual bent, no longer apologizing for it.

Ron Blust had conferred a name, "the Brotherhood," on four football players—himself, Bob Brown, Tom Drake, and me—plus Glenn Spraetz. The fiction that we were a band of brothers did not survive the dissolution of our football dream, as we splintered into different directions. Meanwhile I found myself newly ready to risk some girlfriend pain. I had been graced in my junior year with my first girlfriend, a wonderful, perky, vivacious girl named Roxanna Burke who came from the far west side of Midland, cultural terrain much like Bay County. The few months that I had with her were sublime, the happiest of my high school days. Roxanna liked jocks more or less, but she preferred the artsy types who played guitar and got invited to parties. She made plans to spend the summer in England, telling her friend Karen Morrissey that she would clear the way for summer fun by dropping me. Karen relayed this plan to her boyfriend Glenn Spraetz, who announced it to me in front of half the baseball team, adding public humiliation to my disappointment. That was enough girlfriend pain for me until we lost to Bay City Central.

I started up with a blond cheerleader from Dow High, Carolee Trapp, who could have been my mother's lookalike daughter, except Carolee lived in the rich part of town. We had a lovely platonic relationship in which she politely endured the spiritual explosion occurring to me and I politely allowed her father to evangelize me on the glories of free market capitalism. Her father, Walter Trapp, was a chemist at Dow, but his passion was a libertarian manifesto by Henry Grady Weaver, *The Mainspring of Human Progress* (1953). Weaver sought to rescue right-wing libertarianism from the anti-religious objectivism of Ayn Rand and Nathaniel Brandon, contending that the concept of enlightened self-interest underlying libertarianism is Christian. The mainspring of Western progress is enlightened self-interest, but it came from Christianity. Mr. Trapp perceived that I was on a spiritual journey and that something good might come of it if he could deflect me from my terrible politics. We walked through the argument of *Mainspring*, week by week, consuming quite a lot of my datetime with Carolee. She had zero interest in her father's worldview or mine and was probably relieved when graduation season approached for me, and we drifted apart.[4]

As a shy loner, with a moralistic streak, who read too much, I would have been marked out for social ostracism had I not been a high-profile athlete in a sports-factory school and community. Then our football season went bust and I drifted from my ostensible band of brothers. Duane Lehman, a Dow chemist and Reformed Church layperson, had invited me for two years to join Young Life, an evangelical youth fellowship. He had a kindly heart for lonely kids finding their way; he was an evangelical with no trace of bully-dogmatism; and he later told me playfully that he always recruited the quarterback. At Young Life I deepened my friendship with a studious Lutheran, Jim Metcalf; met a brilliant student from Regina Catholic High School, Nancy Nugent, who broke my heart; and became reacquainted with a former baseball teammate, Bruce Darwin, who advised me to read *Mere Christianity*, by C. S. Lewis, because Lewis was thoughtful, and *Basic Christianity*, by John Stott, because Stott was biblical. These two books were the foundation of the Intervarsity Christian Fellowship empire, and both were authored by British Anglicans, strange as that felt to many American evangelicals. I never went through an evangelical phase, but I am one of countless people who owe a debt to a genial evangelical who cared about kids.[5]

The only theologians I knew anything about were the ones that King mentioned. The public library did not have their books, or any theology section at all, and I grasped that Lewis was a literary critic, not a theologian. There wasn't much of a philosophy section either, but I remembered that for one week of sophomore English class, Ralph Waldo Emerson caught my attention. So I went back to him. It was Emerson's Transcendentalist description of his spiritual sensibility that caught me and did so again. I liked the style of his religious philosophy, especially his discussion of the Oversoul, which resonated with my slightly churched spiritual bent. For as long as I could remember having thoughts, I had yearned for a worldview. Emerson led me to the icons of American pragmatism, William James and John Dewey, partly because they occupied nearby shelf space. James' classic, *The Varieties of Religious Experience* (1902), expounded vividly on healthy-minded religiousness, the religion of the sick soul, and the first-hand experiential character of vital religion. Meanwhile I began to pay attention in class, discovering that school is less miserable that way.[6]

In the spring I pitched and played outfield for the Chemics, and we won the state baseball title. The closer I drew to a perfect season in pitching, the more Coach Stoppert roasted me for having dithered with golf. He kept it up at our awards banquet, with my dad in the audience. "You can play golf for the rest of your life," Coach said, glaring at my father. As it was, in his telling, I had nearly missed the high point of my life because my dad was obsessed with golf. That put the blame on the wrong person; I cringed for my dad as the room rocked with laughter at his expense.

This sweet season was laced with poignancy and irony. I had returned to baseball partly because I missed my baseball friends, but by the spring of 1970 we had changed enough to be awkwardly self-conscious with each other. We were becoming strangers to each other, though a few of us sustained the baseball joy through a glorious summer of American Legion Baseball, playing for Midland Berryhill Post 165. We romped through a loaded schedule, I pitched a bunch of shutouts, and the *Midland Daily News* reported after I threw a no-hitter that "he lowered his microscopic earned run average to 0.23." That earned me a teasing nickname that stuck, "Micro." It was a double-entendre marking the incongruity that the shorty who mixed electric fastballs and curveballs had stopped growing in the seventh grade.[7]

My reading habits were constant fodder for similar teasing. Near the end of the season, I lugged a copy of G. W. F. Hegel's *Phenomenology of Mind* to a tournament in Manistee, Michigan, having read too many references to Hegel not to be curious. The book was totally incomprehensible. Yet I persisted through the lengthy preface, the introduction, and the chapter on consciousness, figuring that if this book was so famous and influential, any time spent with it would be rewarded. Whatever it was about would seep into me sooner or later. Since I was accustomed to being razzed about reading too much, I didn't catch the outlandishness of hauling Hegel to a baseball tournament. A month later I enrolled at Alma College in Alma, Michigan, where my baseball playing continued, while I also played in two semi-pro leagues.[8]

A few of us from the American Legion team played the following year for Midland Lincoln-Mercury in the Northeastern Michigan Baseball League, teaming with older guys we had looked up to for years. I also pitched for a semi-pro team in Clare, Michigan. Several of us had viable shots at Major League careers. We enjoyed being teammates in the summer leagues after playing against each other in college leagues, where the play was at a high level, but not this high. Meanwhile I took up paddleball, soon becoming a tournament player. I relied exclusively on a power game until a middle-aged man beat me in the finals of a tournament with an exquisite arsenal of lobs and kill shots, which impelled me to master a few finesse shots. The perennial national paddleball champion, Steve Keeley, held court at nearby Michigan State University in East Lansing, Michigan. He and I sparred several times, he drubbed me most of the time, and raised my game. I won numerous paddleball tournaments and realized that I was done with golf. Golf only mattered to me as time with my dad. It bored me to play with anyone else, and it took too long.

At the end of our Northeastern Michigan Baseball League season in 1971 we played a best-of-three weekend tournament against Tawas for the league title. They beat our ace, Vern Ruhle, in the first game. The next day I pitched four shutout relief innings to win the second game and pitched the entire third game, which we won 6–1. On the way home, Vern proclaimed that two of us were surely headed to the Show, the name that minor league players conferred on the Major Leagues. Our teammates cheered good-naturedly, and Vern *was* headed to the Show. But I thought concerning myself, "I doubt it."

Baseball had lit me up before I went to college. A year later I could barely remember the feeling, and I had pitched too many games with a hemorrhaging arm. A scout for the Chicago White Sox pithily told me, "Young man, you've got a Major League arm, on a Little League body." That was spot-on concerning my athletic fate. The following year I hurt my arm and would have needed rehabilitation to continue with baseball. I shocked my teammates by deciding not to bother with rehab. I was too depressed to care. Some other person, who needed help, had emerged, who never considered asking for it.

Shortly after college began, I had a shattering experience of romantic heartbreak. I had fallen deeply in love with Nancy Nugent, who was far out of my league but didn't seem to realize it, so I hung on long enough to be crushed. Nancy came from an upper middle-class, intensely Catholic family that sent her to a Catholic girls' school to keep her pure and protected. Years later she repudiated all of it, but when I knew her, she was puckish about her family heritage and half-accepting of it.

We had sparkling conversations that hopped from subject to subject. Her mind was a luminous wonder, along with the looks and charm that won the Miss Midland pageant; she howled with laughter at pictures of her riding on a parade float. My jock reputation didn't faze her, once it turned out that I could keep up with her. Nancy would elicit an opinion and take the other side just for the joy of thrashing out an argument. She also scared people and had a mean streak, so I was her first boyfriend. She went off to St. Mary's College in South Bend, Indiana, planning to transfer to Notre Dame two years later when it went coed. We had an idyllic friendship through our pre-college summer and into the fall until the day I told her that I hoped to be with her forever. That set off her psychic alarm, and a week later she dumped me.

The agony of losing her devoured me. I grieved intensely without telling anyone what I was going through. Telling someone never felt like an option. It was stunning how bad the torment got—wildly raging pain that wouldn't shut off, a knot in my stomach with constant emotional ache. I had just moved to a new place, Alma College, where I had no friends. Alma was geographically isolated in mid-Michigan and very Greek. There was no social life to be had if one did not join a fraternity or sorority, or at least own a car. The two fraternities with a jock culture approached me briefly but readily accepted my no-thanks reply. I didn't realize that my despair would only worsen if I did nothing to alleviate it. Feeling worse seemed impossible, until I spiraled into it. This was the full-blown breakdown that had long been waiting for me, but that was not what I thought. I thought I was suffering the over-a-cliff catastrophe of losing my soulmate.

Paddleball brought up a demon from far down. I was respectful and considerate toward other players, but sometimes I would slam my head with the paddle. Our best players at Alma—Dave Chapin, Herb Taylor, and Jim Woolcock—were startled by the head-slamming, which seemed to come from nowhere: "Why do you do that?" I didn't do it to cause some effect. I was just furious with myself and had to express it. On one occasion in a semi-final round I broke the paddle and was reduced to finesse shots. Sometimes I wondered if I played this sport just to smash myself on the head.

I had been normal enough in high school to have three wonderful girlfriends, a horde of jock friends, and some late-coming religious friends. Now reclusive-wounded pain fed on itself, turning me into some other person—the last to leave the library before the lights were turned out; friendless, except for friendly professors and dormmate Kenny Foster; embarrassed at my emotional state and too ashamed to tell anyone; washing dishes at a restaurant to pay for bus fare and music; yearning for activist movements that didn't exist in Alma; and brutally depressed. On many Saturday nights, after the library closed, I walked to the Strand Theater in downtown Alma to see what film was showing. Only once did I go in, to see *The Concert for Bangladesh*, which was magnificent. The rest of the time the film did not seem worth the two dollars in my pocket. Heading back to campus, I consoled myself that at least the trip consumed an awkward hour.

In my room I wore out my music albums. As a high school senior, I had co-hosted a weeknight jazz program with elderly jazz musician Karl Hawkins on WQDC-FM radio in Midland, beginning as an intern and working up to paid staff. At first, he bridled at being paired with a jock helper. Then it surprised him that I loved his stories about Sidney Bechet, the pioneer of soprano saxophone jazz; Louis Armstrong, the genius of the Jazz Era; Coleman Hawkins, whose tenor sax built upon Bechet and Armstrong; and Dizzy Gillespie, whose trumpet virtuosity and scat singing lifted bebop in the 1940s to prominence. Mr. Hawkins lived in a rich cultural world. It grieved him that jazz was so marginal in 1970, routed from the field by rhythm and blues and rock and roll. He knew many of his jazz favorites personally and could still thrill at records he had played hundreds of times. He would break off a conversation to hear a favorite run, transported: "Listen to this!" He rolled his eyes at phone callers asking, "Isn't that the quarterback?" He fretted that the station would shut down, which it did just before I graduated. My last paycheck was the album section of my choice.

I went for the bluesy jazz that we played on "Jazz with the Hawk," stocking myself with Coleman Hawkins, Billie Holiday, and Sarah Vaughan. My almost-favorite rock groups, Led Zeppelin and the Rolling Stones, had an obvious blues base, and my favorite rock group, Crosby, Stills, Nash, and Young, had a deeper blues influence via Stephen Stills, though it was harder to hear in that foursome. I also loved the Motown songbook from Smokey Robinson to the Temptations to Martha and the Vandellas. WQDC had most of it, and no rock and roll section. In my room at Alma College, I stewed in music-soaked pain that hardly anyone noticed, a mysterious loner jock who pored over notoriously difficult books and stole away to paddleball matches.

For four years of college and my first four years of graduate school, I had no romantic life whatsoever, unable to ask a classmate, "Would you like to go out with me?" Who would want to be with me? I could barely stand it.

2
ALMA COLLEGE

College is the place to make a better life possible, reinventing yourself if necessary. This emphatic message was my earliest memory and belief. It was burned into my psyche in Bay County, after which Mr. Petrina told me I should go to a liberal arts college to get a liberal arts education. Liberal arts colleges are strewn across the Midwest because every Christian denomination of the 1830s sought to plant a flag in the expanding Western frontier. My senior high school baseball season was underway when Mr. Carey settled the issue of which college I would attend. He had played for Alma College in the early 1940s before he played professional basketball for the Midland Dow A.C.s and commenced his coaching career at Midland High School. He met with the Harold Baker Foundation in Midland and with Coach Butch Cantrell at Alma College, landing the scholarship that took me to Alma.

Alma was a tiny town in mid-Michigan touting its location at the crossroads of two state highways and its Presbyterian college. The student body was long on valedictorians and salutatorians plucked from small high schools across Michigan. The faculty had no scholar stars but many teaching stars. Nearly everyone on the faculty was White and male, including the recent hires. Wesley Dykstra and Roger Haverfield in philosophy, David Lemmon in sociology, Louis Toller in physics, and Joseph Walser and Ronald Massanari in religious studies were my mainstays. Some had to be waited for while I completed the distributive requirements. The godsend introductory course for me was on the history of Western philosophy, taught by Dykstra.

He was a bearded, pipe-smoking, elbow-patched brother of another philosopher, Ivan Dykstra, who taught at Hope College in Holland, Michigan, where the brothers played mental chess for fun. Dykstra took us on a fabulous tour mediated by the first two volumes of W. T. Jones'

A History of Western Philosophy, at the time a four-volume work in a new edition. Jones said it is better to understand a few major philosophers than to learn a little about many philosophers. He devoted one-third of his text to primary source passages, presenting the idioms, method, and problems of major thinkers, and supplied judicious commentary not lacking an edge. Dykstra had taught the first edition several times and was delighted with the 1969 edition, which added discussions of axiomatic geometry, Greek skepticism, and Gnosticism. We ran through the Pre-Socratics, Plato, Aristotle, Democritus, the Epicureans, the Pythagoreans, a sampling of Stoics, and Sextus Empiricus, all of it fascinating to me. I loved Plato's idea that things are what they are because they participate in the Forms that correspond to their distinct properties or kinds. Plato broke through the world of appearances, conceiving the Forms as abstract objects knowable only to the mind. We took up Aristotle too soon for me, but I appreciated that one could construe lower-cased forms on realist terms, conceiving each form as the form of some thing, not as existing independently of things. We plunged into the Christian world of volume two, surveying Paul, John, Plotinus, Augustine, John Scotus Eriugena, Abelard, Thomas Aquinas, Duns Scotus, and William of Occam, plus Averroes, much of it less comfortably to me. Did too much Platonism—actually, Plotinus-style Neoplatonism—seep into Christianity? If a Christian doctrine comes off as bad philosophy, does that refute Christianity? I filled the margins of volume two with reasonings marked "Dorrien's view," defending my improvised Christian worldview from W. T. Jones.[1]

Dykstra was the son of a pacifist, book-writing, Reformed pastor, so he understood students who approached his field through their religious concerns. He had graduated from Western Theological Seminary in Holland, Michigan, undertaken doctoral study at Union Theological Seminary in New York, and refused to revise his dissertation, so he had no doctorate. He parried my questions by advising me whom to read, rarely telling me what he thought. We bonded over my surprising knowledge of James and Dewey, and I told him I had also wrestled that summer with Hegel, which broke his decorum. Dykstra was the epitome of a professorial professor, always in character. The Hegel reference was too much; he burst out with a guffaw, shaking his head. Jones argued that the central problem of modern philosophy is how to understand the reality of value in a world of facts. Dykstra concurred that human beings are distinctly valuing creatures, and that modern philosophy began with the turn to the knowing subject inaugurated by Descartes. I took his second-term course on the problem of value in modern philosophy and got my first dose of Immanuel Kant (1724–1804).

Dykstra conveyed the same high regard for Kant that he otherwise reserved for Plato and Aristotle. He said almost nothing about Kant personally, or Kant's lifelong context in Königsberg, East Prussia, except that Kant was extremely exacting in his devotion to thought, order, and the good. We read excerpts from Kant's *Groundwork of the Metaphysics of Morals* (1785) and the *Critique of Practical Reason* (1788), usually called the Second Critique, where Kant elaborated his supreme principle of practical reason, the categorical imperative. The primary version was that one must act only on maxims that deserve to be universalized, asking what everyone should do in a given situation. Another version was that one must never treat a person as a mere means to an end. Kant argued that freedom and the categorical imperative are reciprocally implied in each other, for freedom implies that we are subject to the categorical imperative, and the categorical imperative implies that we must be free.[2]

Our class sorted out different kinds of principles and applications, including Kant's complex discussion of hypothetical imperatives, and his crucial distinctions between analytic and synthetic reasoning, and heteronomy and autonomy. Analytic reasoning is instrumental and conditional, framed by "if this, then that." The categorical imperative is synthetic, providing an *end* that all rational agents must adopt. Heteronomy is the imposition of an external authority, which cannot justify itself, and autonomy is self-governance, the rule of reason that Kant prized. I appeared to be more excited than my classmates to acquire these ideas. But as the weeks flew by, I learned something else about myself: I have a genealogical bent that needs to know the origins of things. Otherwise, I feel adrift in the stream of wherever I happen to be.

Kant argued in the Second Critique that pure practical reason is not as circumscribed as pure theoretical reason and thus holds primacy over it. Practical reason can be pure, proceeding from a priori principles, or empirical, driven by desires or sensible evidence. However, only *pure* practical reason can rationally determine if we are free, whether God exists, and how we should act. Kant's prior, colossal, epochal work, the

Critique of Pure Reason (1781), established his theory of the faculties of reason. Our philosophy majors advised me not to bother with the First Critique, a badly written nightmare of logic-chopping abstraction that was impossible to understand. One major told me he got as far as Kant's discussion of time and space in the Transcendental Aesthetic—seventeen pages past the prefaces and introduction.[3]

I didn't doubt that the First Critique was severe and sprawling. But I couldn't imagine going further with modern philosophy without studying its foundational work. Kant built his towering stature on it. In his early career, Kant had not believed in freedom, because Isaac Newton's mechanical laws of physics left no room for it, unless one swallowed G. W. Leibniz's theory of infinite soul-like monads. Like his great rationalist predecessors Leibniz, Baruch Spinoza, and Christian Wolff, the early Kant tried to rehabilitate metaphysics on a mathematical model making no appeal to experience. Then Kant set on the path that produced the First Critique—still accepting Newton's mechanical universe, rejecting systems based on Aristotle, wrestling with David Hume's skeptical contention that there are no links between facts in the world of experience, and believing that his own powerful sense of moral obligation must imply some degree of moral choice. The First Critique cleared room for practical reason by redefining metaphysics as the science of the limitations of theoretical and practical reason. In the summer preceding my sophomore year I read it straight through, vowing to keep an open mind and not stop reading. Some sections were reasonably intelligible, Kant's horrible writing style notwithstanding, but how his transcendental aesthetic, logic, analytic, and dialectic fit together, I had no idea.

Kant sought to solve the mystery of the pure thinking of reason, asking how a priori concepts relate to objects. Unlike empirical representations, a priori concepts are not the effects of objects given in experience, but unlike mathematical concepts, neither do a priori concepts create their objects in the act of conceiving them. There is nothing in a mathematical concept that is not in its object. Kant granted that mathematicians justly construct axioms a priori because they work with pure intuitions about lines and triangles and the like. But philosophy is restricted to the analysis of concepts, lacking any right to assume a priori intuitions about metaphysical realities. So how do a priori concepts correspond to objects? What can be known on an a priori basis apart from experience? Kant pursued these questions with relentless transcendental logic, making an intricate argument about twelve transcendental categories of understanding and two pure forms of sensibility. The categories sort into subcategories of quantity, quality, relation, and modality, and the forms of sensibility are time and space.

I entered my sophomore year with a patchwork of abstract arguments in my head that didn't fit together and were difficult to describe in conversation. Kant told a story about the modern debate between rationalism and empiricism leading to him, but the empirical aspect of his argument was hard to see because he waxed at length about transcendental idealism. Moreover, I knew from the Second Critique that he cared above all about the freedom-morality couplet. It just didn't seem that way amid the logical grinding of the First Critique.

Kant said we cannot prove that freedom is real, or even possible. All we can do at the level of pure reason is recognize the impasse-contradiction between the mathematical antinomies of a limited temporal-spatial world and the whole consisting of indivisible atoms. The same thing is true of the two dynamical antinomies: spontaneous causality and the existence of God. Pure reason cannot prove or disprove that the world has a beginning, any composite thing in it is made up of simple parts, freedom exists, or a necessary being exists. On Kant's account, the dynamical antinomies are adjudicated only by pure practical reason. Scholastic and modern rationalist systems wrongly alienated human beings from their freedom, projecting the source of morality into a world transcending human power.

I wanted to do an independent study with Dykstra that produced a thesis representing what I understood thus far. Now that I could talk about the connections between the First and Second Critiques, I felt that I understood the Second Critique better than I had in Dykstra's class. He gently declined to authorize an independent study, especially on this subject. "You're only a sophomore," Dykstra said. "Once you start on independent work, maybe next year, wouldn't you rather write about Kant's moral religion?" No. I respected Kant's contention that religion has no warranted claim to knowledge apart from its connection to moral truth, and that religion must help people to be good, otherwise it is an instrument of bondage. But Kant's argument about religion surely was not as important as the position—whatever it was—that he expounded in

Critique of Pure Reason. I fixed too literally on the metaphysical problem, still the Catholic boy who scrawled "Creation" on a picture of the Earth. Dykstra tried to soften the blow of refusing me by remarking that he saw an earlier version of himself in me. This statement floored me, lacking any capacity to hear it; he's a philosophy professor and I'm a bumpkin jock. I feared that I may have crossed a personal line that I didn't understand, and now I was left too much on my own not to plunge even further into deep water by going back to Hegel.

Hegel's name kept coming up, Kant led naturally to Hegel, Dykstra advised me to steer clear of Hegel, but Kant's legacy in philosophy and theology apparently ran through Hegel. So I took my first sustained plunge into Hegel, returning to the copy of Hegel's *Phenomenology of Mind* that I had bought as a high schooler at the Michigan State University bookstore. It was the J. B. Baillie translation that wrongly rendered Hegelian *Geist* as "mind," a monument to a venerable English misunderstanding of Hegel that did not prevent me from reading Hegel more creatively than I read Kant.[4]

The textbooks said that Hegel developed a closed pan-logical system based on Kant's transcendental ego, Aristotle's final causation (the explanatory priority of the final cause over the efficient cause), and a logical mill identifying thought with sense and being. The Marxian Left-Hegelian school contended that Hegel was an atheist who only played with religion, perhaps in proto-Marxian fashion. These were the dominant interpretive options when I read Hegel in college. The closed system view had a Right-Hegelian theological school, and the Left-Hegelian view was favored by French Marxists. But Hegel would not have caught me had I believed that he expounded a closed system or that he only pretended to care about religion. His *Phenomenology* obviously built upon Kant's strenuous attempt to unite reason and experience. It also had the severely formal language of Kant, but the *Phenomenology* was a panoramic romp through familiar subjects that Kant didn't consider. The too-literal seriousness that I applied to Kant I did not apply to Hegel. Hegel raced through methodological debates, epistemology, religious beliefs, stories, smart-aleck asides, ethical theory, Greek tragedy, medieval court culture, modern science, pseudoscience, Romanticism, and much more. Always he probed for the spirit within his prolix array of subjects. The *Phenomenology* was a wild, puzzling, obscure, rollicking monster of a book that hooked me like no other philosophical text I ever read. Much of it seemed incomprehensible, but I enjoyed deciphering chunks of it. More important, I felt the power of Hegel's interpretation of Christianity as a picture story about Spirit embracing the suffering of the world and returning to itself.[5]

Hegel brilliantly described Spirit redeeming the world by desiring, sundering, suffering, reconciling, and coming to know itself. I had no idea if Hegel's *Science of Logic* was a logical mill like the textbooks said, but I knew what caught me in the *Phenomenology:* the expansive vision and the Christian tropes. At Alma I thought that Hegelian *Geist* was the idea of Mind in general, and that Hegel extended Kant's transcendental framework. I caught only a glimmer of the Hegel who discovered social subjectivity while theorizing about restless dialectical negation. But Hegel riveted me for reasons I half-comprehended and wanted to understand better. His dialectical idealism lifted me above the sense plane of my despair, much like Platonism did, except Hegel employed Christian doctrines to color the world religiously.[6]

I bought a copy of Kant's *Critique of Pure Reason*, placing it on my desk alongside the *Phenomenology* and a picture of my family. This pair of books stayed there through my years at Alma. I was in over my head and too much on my own, pulled into the notoriously abstruse problems of German idealism. If Kant and Hegel were fundamental to everything that mattered in modern philosophy and theology, as I believed, it felt only right to get *to* everything else through them.

Roger Haverfield tried to dissuade me. He was a young analytic philosopher still writing his dissertation at Michigan State University. Roger held stronger negative views about Kant's Hegelian legacy than about Kant himself. To him, Kant was the progenitor of an unfortunate idealistic obsession with subjectivity that yielded Hegel's misguided absolute idealism, which nearly ruined British philosophy in the late nineteenth century. British absolute idealists F. H. Bradley and Bernard Bosanquet fashioned a dominant school contending that all relations are internal, and everything is logically connected to everything else. The whole is individual and universal, a concrete universal containing all things.[7]

Roger loved to tell the story of how three Trinity College Cambridge philosophers—Bertrand Russell, Ludwig Wittgenstein, and G. E. Moore—put philosophy on the right track by refuting the idealistic doctrine that relations are properties of the nature of things (internal relations). Russell refined the predicate calculus of Gottlob Frege, which greatly expanded the range of sentences that can be parsed into logical form, though Russell discovered while writing *Principles of Mathematics* (1903) that a set will be a member of itself only if it is not a member of itself. His grappling with this paradox yielded two versions of a theory of types that logicians strenuously debated and rejected; meanwhile Russell developed a theory of logical atomism contending that all truths depend ultimately upon a foundation of atomic facts. His leading protégé, Wittgenstein, argued in *Tractatus Logico-Philosophicus* (1922) that language presents logical pictures of facts, which are called thoughts; words are names; propositions are meaningful only if they can be defined and pictured in the real world; and we must keep silent about all ostensible realities that do not fit these conditions. Properly speaking, ethicists and artists do not speak language! Roger gave Moore his due as a founder of analytic philosophy, mostly for defending Russell, but Russell and Wittgenstein were the heroes of this story, developing systems of logical atomism that sought to create an ideal language for philosophical analysis. Then came the logical positivism of Rudolf Carnap and the Vienna Circle, which employed formal logic to develop an empiricist account of knowledge, followed by A. J. Ayer's landmark *Language, Truth, and Logic* (1936), a punchy English rendering of Carnap and logical positivism. A meaningful statement, on this account, is either analytic or is capable of being verified by experience. Metaphysics, by definition, is meaningless.[8]

I pleaded to Roger that it cannot be right to reduce the glorious field of philosophy to language analysis and logic. He replied that there were plenty enough differences among logical atomists, logical positivists, logical realists, commonsense realists, ordinary language analysts, and logical behaviorists to keep philosophy departments going for another century. Moreover, the field would surely always teach its history, including the later Wittgenstein's refutation of his picture theory of language. I devoured Wittgenstein's posthumously published *Philosophical Investigations* (1953), which sketched a use-theory of language that wonderfully introduced the concept of a language game. But this book did not assuage my shrinkage aversion. Somehow, philosophy was still reduced to a fraction of its former concerns.

I asked Roger to read something I had written on Kant's First Critique, and he groaned with mock despair. On his view, I struggled too strenuously to make Kant intelligible, because Kant isn't intelligible. Kant was surely a genius—after all, at the age of thirty-one he came up with the nebular theory of the creation of the solar system. But Roger said the *Critique of Pure Reason* is a patchwork mess of abstraction that birthed Hegel's ridiculous system; he quoted verbatim the ridicule that Russell and other analytic founders heaped on Hegel. Philosophers must stick to verifiable facts while helping students in every field to make sound arguments. No philosophy department should be judged by how many majors it attracts, because philosophy is the ultimate service field. He admitted to respecting nineteenth-century English titan John Stuart Mill, so I wrote a thesis with him comparing the moral philosophies of Mill and Moore, which reminded Roger of what he *didn't* like about Mill. Mill was too much like Dewey and Russell, trying to save the world, writing his least impressive work when he tried. Roger said that was a loser for a philosophy field that had to justify its existence to academic administrators.[9]

The latter issue hung over nearly every discussion I held with him. Roger seemed, at first, prematurely melancholic to me, until he introduced me to his world of All-But-Dissertation anxieties, grumpy thesis advisors, philosophy conferences, term appointments, and tenure requirements. His senior colleague had molded a respected academic career while lacking a doctorate, but Roger knew that would not be possible for him. He could see the writing on the wall, once telling me that philosophers make excellent carpenters, did you know that? His wife, Carol Haverfield, also taught philosophy at Alma as an adjunct, so they would need *two* jobs to forge careers in this embattled field. Roger's appointment at Alma ran only as long as my time there, his academic career ended, and its sadness lingered with me long afterward, my first acquaintance with the busted dreams that pervade academic life.

Dave Lemmon was another ABD from Michigan State University. He had an encyclopedic knowledge of sociological theory, teaching me its canon, and dwelt on his favorites: Emile Durkheim, Max Weber, and Karl Mannheim. He had entered graduate school with a boyish undergraduate enthusiasm for Weber and was deflated by his mentor's insistence that he master the structural-functionalist social action theory of American sociologist Talcott Parsons. Parsons wiped out Dave's enthusiasm for sociology, the academy, and finishing his dissertation. By my junior year at Alma, Dave was my closest friend. We hung out together, shot basketball hoops, shared our similar record collections, and talked shop about sociological theory. Dave confided that he longed to hunt and fish in Upper Michigan, not to teach sociology. He got this far into the academy only because he happened to be good at school. He guided me to political economists, especially Karl Marx and Karl Polanyi, and was intrigued that I anticipated a career in social justice activism and perhaps the ministry, not the academy. Dave had only considered the academy when it mattered, now with regret. His marriage broke up, he moved out of his house, and his ex-wife invited me over for—I don't know what. I was shy, nervous, and clueless, drumming up friendly conversation as much as I could, while she grew angry. Perhaps she invited me to fulfill some revenge fantasy? Or wanted incriminating information about him? I never found out. Driving me back to Wright Hall, she seethed all the way, and I was confused and humiliated. I never told Dave about it since both of us were embarrassment averse.[10]

Dr. Toller was a teaching legend at Alma who befriended me before I took courses with him. One day he plopped down next to me in the cafeteria, announcing that he sought to determine if Dykstra had perhaps exaggerated about me. Dr. Toller was wonderfully ebullient, with an impish sense of humor and a true academic calling, a born teacher who loved to banter with students. He would ask a question about whatever I was reading just to run with it, emoting, "I'm getting smarter all the time!" In his courses on light and sound, he persuaded me that nothing on earth is more wondrous than light, except maybe light theory. He grieved for the many students whose fear of mathematics prevented them from accessing his field. Sometimes he told them there was still time for them to overcome it, whereupon they could become better math teachers than the ones they experienced. One day he brightened with delight at discovering the source of my confusion about virtual images: "You don't know what virtual means! It doesn't mean real!" Indeed, I was from Bay County, where we thought that virtual and real were interchangeable terms.

The iconic teacher at Alma College was Joe Walser, a Hebrew Bible scholar who won the teaching award every time he was eligible for it, every third year. He was a Presbyterian protégé of John Bright at Union Theological Seminary in Richmond, Virginia, earned his doctorate at Duke, and was six years into his teaching career at Alma in 1970 and prematurely balding when I got there. Walser gave bravura lectures on the Bible in Alma's largest classrooms, making the biblical stories come alive, with historical critical commentary. He wanted to use Bright's *History of Israel*, but Bernhard W. Anderson's *Understanding the Old Testament* recounted biblical history in the sweeping epic-narrative fashion that Walser taught it, which mesmerized generations of Alma students. Walser was a pastor to many of them, deeply kind, and friendly to all. Someone had to teach world religions, so he did so amiably. It was endearing to watch this master teacher fumble with note cards when he taught about samsara, karma, and the four noble truths of Buddhism. Walser *was* Alma College at its best, sometimes doubling in later years as the chaplain or provost, often taking students on his summer archaeology digs in Israel near Beer Sheva and Arad.[11]

Ron Massanari was my foremost teacher at Alma, though I took only one regular course with him. His first day there was also mine. He had grown up Mennonite in Champaign, Illinois, graduated from Goshen College, liberalized at Garrett Evangelical Seminary in Chicago, and sailed through the doctoral program at Duke in three years, graduating in 1969. Walser invited him to our introductory class, so students would meet the new professor. Massanari unleashed a torrent of intellectual talk about something called Marxist/Christian philosophy of hope and something else called death-of-God theology.

These were the two hot trends in theology, he said. German philosopher Ernst Bloch fused Hegel, Marx, and a bit of Christian eschatology to argue that humans are inherently utopian beings and that society must be liberated from the bondage of capitalist estrangement. According to Massanari, German theologian Jürgen Moltmann wrote the most important theological work of the 1960s, *Theology of Hope* (1964, English 1967), by appropriating Bloch. Moltmann argued that the Bible does not hypostatize divine reality above or before the world in the fashion of Hellenized Christianity. The God of the Bible holds together the present and the future; Christianity is inherently eschatological, revolutionizing the future through its kingdom-focused hope. Massanari said this idea of the divine as the power of the future working into the present was the only one that he could accept. The God-is-dead theologians whom he planned to teach—Thomas J. J. Altizer and William Hamilton—were correct in contending that the hypostatized God of classical theism is dead.[12]

This was harder-edged than Walser expected, at least as first-day introduction. He read the room, reaching out to students who were red in the face, assuring them the Religion Department was not anti-religious. But he also said it was a great thing for Alma College to have a high-powered theologian. Massanari did not aim for Walser-like legend status at Alma. He was there to provoke students, challenge them, and subvert their provincialism, telling them their mothers were not the greatest cooks in the world.

I attached myself to Massanari from the beginning, quizzing him about theology and theologians. He was razor-sharp about both. I read all the books that he assigned to his classes, we engaged in weekly shoptalk about them, and he teased me that Dykstra and Walser handled too gently the papers I wrote for them, allowing me to prattle about my beliefs and feelings: "I don't care what you believe, and I don't care about your feelings either. I'm here to mess with your head." We developed a ritual; I would hand Ron a paper and he would say, "I'm going to tear the hell out of this one." He was a great thrasher of papers, and he became a treasured friend. Ron steered me away from his classes, so the only one I ever took was on major theologians from Friedrich Schleiermacher (1768–1834) to Rudolf Bultmann (1884–1976), in my junior year. But he facilitated two independent projects and a thesis with me in my junior and senior years, and for four years he was the faculty epicenter of my intellectual journey.

Ron believed that modern theology was expiring. He taught superbly about its glory era from Schleiermacher to Ernst Troeltsch (1865–1923), commending the old German liberals for grappling creatively with modern disbelief. Schleiermacher launched the modern era of theology by reasoning that all doctrines are attempts to make sense of religious experience. Spiritual feeling is the wellspring of religion; external authority cannot compel a credible belief; God is the "whence" of the human experience of dependence and freedom; whatever is religiously true must pass the muster of critical reason and experience. Troeltsch was the last great figure of the German liberal tradition, calling for a thoroughly historicist theology that does not privilege Christian questions. Ron said the dialectical theologians who overturned the liberal establishment in theology after World War I—Karl Barth, Paul Tillich, Emil Brunner, and Rudolf Bultmann—kept theology alive for a half-century by refashioning shards of the old orthodoxies. Now the end of the line had come, which Altizer and Hamilton poignantly described. Perhaps theology could wrangle a future as a post-theistic form of cultural studies and political theology.[13]

Ron had a soft spot for Walter Rauschenbusch, because of his religious socialism, which reminded me of King's discussion of Rauschenbusch in

Stride toward Freedom. Maybe there was something in Rauschenbusch worth retrieving. Altizer and Hamilton made me skeptical about delving further into theology. If that was where theology was going, I was inclined to stick with Kant and Hegel. I didn't belong to a church, so there was nothing holding me to theology except Jesus crucified and MLK. In my sophomore fall term, however, I read Rauschenbusch and James Cone on my own.

Rauschenbusch's social gospel classic, *Christianity and the Social Crisis* (1907), enthralled me. He described the prophetic strain of biblical teaching as a message of radical social transformation. Christianity, he argued, obscured the revolutionary spirit of the gospel, but it was not too late for the church to adopt the way and spirit of Jesus. The church is supposed to be a new kind of community that transforms the world by the power of Christ's kingdom-bringing Spirit. The idea of the indwelling and growing commonwealth of God is not merely part of Christianity; it's the central thing holding everything else together. Christianity is a kingdom movement that carries God into everything you do. In a concluding chapter with a Leninist title, "What to Do," Rauschenbusch made a scintillating case for democratic socialism.[14]

His liberal theology and radical politics were equally compelling to me. I turned the pages exclaiming that this was what Christianity should sound like. For years I had felt that King laid hold of something in Christianity that the rest of the church somehow missed—something inspiring movement idealism and a real surge for social change. Rauschenbusch had arguments about what was missing, expressing brilliantly the vision of a liberationist Christianity. The books that I read about the social gospel said it was an idealistic understanding of Christianity that briefly influenced liberal Protestantism before it was discredited by the neo-orthodox reaction, especially Barth and Reinhold Niebuhr. Reading Rauschenbusch, I could see various problems. He loved idealistic rhetoric, said almost nothing about racism, and was proudly, stridently, vehemently anti-Catholic. But for grasping and expressing the prophetic core of the gospel, Rauschenbusch soared above everyone except King.

Cone published his searing book *Black Theology and Black Power* the year before I started college, and he followed it up the next year with *A Black Theology of Liberation.* I read both books spellbound over one weekend. Reading Kant, Hegel, and Marx on my own did not faze me because

I didn't get frustrated when they were incomprehensible. I just kept reading. With Cone, I wanted to understand every blistering sentence, but I knew almost nothing about the Black nationalist tradition that influenced him, nothing at all about the Martinique psychiatrist-author Frantz Fanon who also influenced him, and I puzzled at Cone's reliance on Barth for key parts of his argument. As far as I could tell, Cone applied to theology the insights of James Baldwin and Malcolm X, the two pertinent figures I had read, with help from Barth and Tillich. I needed to talk to someone about Cone; fortunately, religion scholar Tracy Luke taught an upcoming course on Black American literature.[15]

Cone's electrifying prose was ringing in my head when the college held an event for students and administrators. I got planted next to the president, radiating awkward shyness, but he was a Presbyterian minister named Robert Swanson who had taught at McCormick Theological Seminary in Chicago before he came to Alma, so I asked if he had read these books by Cone. Dr. Swanson said he regretted that being a president prevented him from keeping up with theology. I said he should make an exception for these books, and he surprised me by replying, "Let's invite Professor Cone to campus." He sent me to confer with Luke, and a few months later James Cone himself was speaking at our little college.

Cone rocked our campus with a fusion of his two books, a brief excursus on a song by the Rascals, and a stunning concluding section that was just for us. He talked about slave ships and auction blocks and lynching. He explained that Black theology interprets Christianity and the American experience from the perspective of oppressed Black Americans. He said very hard things about White liberals, White Christianity, White conceits, and King, describing White Americans as racists who couldn't imagine giving up their White privilege. He lightened the mood for a moment with a song that everyone knew, "All the world over, so easy to see! People everywhere, just wanna be free." Then he held up a copy of Alma's course catalog and ripped it to shreds from a standpoint that no one had ever heard at Alma College: We were being taught White theology, he said, and White philosophy, White sociology, White psychology, and White everything else as though nothing but White thinking counted as thought. And all of it was paraded in the name of universality and the liberal arts.

Cone was the founder of the revolutionary turn in theology that interpreted Christian doctrines through a Black Power conception of blackness. He taught me, even more than Baldwin, to view U.S. American history through the lens of the Black American struggle against racism. He employed the term "Black" in a twofold sense marking the cultural identity of a specific people and a symbol of liberation for all oppressed people, confirming at Alma that the second meaning was important to him, though Cone was still several years from accepting that feminist criticism was similarly legitimate or that Black theology needed an economic critique. Reading and meeting Cone was the highlight of my sophomore year. Being a loner spared me from much of the offended feeling he stirred on campus; I wasn't at the frat parties that carried on about it. He said he came to Alma only to learn if we had any Black students, learning that we had twenty-eight. Many years later he told me that the thing he most enjoyed in his career was his lecture touring of the early 1970s.

The lowlight of my fall-term junior year was the 1972 presidential election, my first experience in organizing. U.S. Senator George McGovern won the Democratic nomination as a mildly progressive opponent of the Vietnam War who rallied the reform forces in the Democratic Party after the catastrophic election of 1968 put Richard Nixon in the White House. I worked hard for McGovern, canvassing in residential neighborhoods, handing out leaflets at the grocery store, working the campaign telephones, and catching bitter flak.

It was a harsh experience. People didn't just oppose McGovern in Alma. They hated him for calling America to come home from the war. How in God's name could the Democrats nominate a pinko-Communist for president? How dare they suck up to those despicable kids who rioted at the 1968 Convention? We heard a lot of that. I went door-to-door by myself until two doorstop encounters teetered on the edge of violence, which taught me the importance of pairing up. I tried to enlist Thomas Hill, an extroverted psychology major, to go door-to-door with me. Tom and I had friendly debates about how his department taught psychology and what is worth pursuing in political activism. Alma College categorized psychology as a natural science, a coveted status that the psychology department won by reducing its field to physiological psychology, the behavior analysis and operant conditioning of Harvard psychologist B. F. Skinner, and a pinch of social learning theory. Classic theories of personality got a one-off dismissal in a single course that debunked all the options except the cognitive-affective theory of Walter Mischel and the social learning theory of Albert Bandura. This was like the positivist issue in philosophy, except psychology was a strong major at Alma that sent many students to graduate school.[16]

Tom was destined to be one of them, accepting that his department stripped the psyche out of psychology. Meanwhile he urged me to bail out of McGovern campaign purgatory: "Why are you wasting your time on McGovern? He's a mere liberal, not even close to us politically, and he's going to be crushed anyway!" Since this was my first experience in organizing, I didn't know the answer. I was learning early lessons about politics and myself. My friend Kenny Foster took the opposite tack: "Gary, you can't change the world. Try to enjoy yourself for a change." That was a non-starter for me. Kenny was a Yooper from Newberry, two hours from De Tour. He never settled on a major, dropped out of Alma to join the Navy, and already had a gentle grace, which deepened in later life after he graduated from the Navy and Michigan Technological University. I stuck with the Dems to the bitter end in a campaign that later became for me a baseline reference point, the place where I established what kind of political Lefty I was and am: a democratic socialist who doesn't disparage liberals, social democrats, and ethically sincere conservatives.

The two towering theologians of the twentieth century, Barth and Tillich, and the preeminent social ethicist Reinhold Niebuhr, still loomed over theology, though Barth and Tillich had passed on, and Niebuhr died in 1971. They had written the massive systematic works that framed the field. To study modern theology was to engage their vast writings. Barth dethroned liberal theology in the 1920s with a slashing, eschatological, dialectical theology shot through with existentialist tropes borrowed from Søren Kierkegaard, especially in Barth's second edition of *The Epistle to the Romans* (1921) and his collection *The Word of God and the Word of Man* (1928). Then he set upon the multivolume *Church Dogmatics* in the 1930s, developing a neo-Reformation theology based on the faith and idioms of the Reformed Confessions. Barth held stringently to the Reformation principles that the Bible alone must be the rule of faith (*sola scriptura*) and that sinners are justified by grace through faith alone (*sola fide*). He blasted everything smacking of cultural theology, employed philosophy minimally and eclectically, and dropped Kierkegaard.[17]

"Neo-orthodoxy" was a bad name for his approach, which Barth hated, but it stuck, especially in the United States. Very few neo-orthodox theologians were politically radical like Barth, or personally stormy like Barth, or even carried out his extreme version of *sola scriptura* biblicism. Barthians didn't write about the ways that Barth was not a Barthian or neo-orthodox. They described Barth as the savior of modern theology who ranked with John Calvin and Thomas Aquinas. On Christmas break of my sophomore year, I took my dish-washing savings to McCandless Bookstore in downtown Midland to order the first two volumes of Barth's *Church Dogmatics* and the first two volumes of Tillich's *Systematic Theology.* The books arrived at McCandless a few weeks later, my mother transported them to the home of my high school and college classmate Anne DeBoer, who delivered them to me. I was overjoyed to receive them, while Anne charitably stifled a giggle at how strange I had become. By the following year, when I finally took a Massanari course and commenced independent projects with him, I had memorized ample chunks of Barth and Tillich.

Tillich's theology and his legacy in theology were very different from Barth's. Both were democratic socialists who practiced the yes-and-no approach of dialectical method. Both conceived faith in Pauline terms as a gift of grace, and both despised the Ritschlian Culture Protestantism in which they were trained. But Tillich protested that Barth's neo-supernaturalism and strict adherence to *sola scriptura* were impossible, a form of pretending. Liberal theology had gone bad by baptizing German nationalism, not because it started with Kant and Schleiermacher, engaging modern disbelief. Tillich said he would have no interest in God if he did not believe that God was part of himself. Steeped in German idealism, he espoused a post-Kantian form of it, developing a theology of culture disciplined by his dialectic that the conflict between orthodox heteronomy and critical autonomy yields the religious ideal, "theonomy." Another version of the same dialectic pitted sacramentalism against rationalism, yielding Tillich's religious socialism. His three-volume *Systematic Theology* offered religious answers to cultural questions, exactly what Barth said theologians must not do.[18]

Tillich became spectacularly famous in the United States in the 1950s, twenty years after he fled Nazi Germany to teach at Union Theological Seminary in New York. Two generations of Union students passed through Union with no idea that Tillich had ever been a radical socialist. This was the Tillich that we inherited in the early 1970s, the one who wrote a massive theological system and seemed to replace his neo-Marxian socialism with depth psychology. I had no inkling at Alma College that Tillich's German political past would soon become important to me. At the time it was enough to plow through his system, the crowning achievement of his storied American career. American scholars failed to explicate the vast intellectual debts that Tillich owed to Friedrich W. J. Schelling and Martin Kähler, so Tillich got credit for originating concepts that he repurposed. His debt to Hegel was similarly obvious if one knew Hegel, but even the Hegel influence passed mostly unremarked. We thought in the early 1970s that Tillich's star was fading after he had magnificently dominated American theology in the 1950s. Then some of us recovered the Tillich of the pre-Nazi period.[19]

Reinhold Niebuhr's place in this story of inheritance was harder to gauge. He was best known as the theologian of Cold War realism who achieved icon status in mainline Protestantism and the Democratic Party. Since Niebuhr's long run as the foremost theologian of the Cold War had only recently passed, it overshadowed all other aspects and periods of his career. He had argued in the 1950s that Communism is distinctly evil because it is a perverted religion. Unlike fascism, it could not be smashed directly; Communism had to be defeated by a united democratic West with patient, sufficient, persistent counterforce. Niebuhr was a pillar of the liberal mainstream of the Democratic Party, urging the Kennedy and Johnson administrations to defeat Communism in Vietnam, until 1966, when a despairing Niebuhr called the nation to end its apocalyptic disaster in Vietnam. Five years later, when Niebuhr died, the United States still had 157,000 troops in Vietnam.[20]

All of this was too current in the classrooms of my college years to read Niebuhr through the historical lens that we applied to Barth. The Barth story was the founding narrative of twentieth-century theology, so we historicized Barth. Niebuhr was deeply implicated in our present situation, so we did not linger over what he said in 1932, even though *that* Niebuhr was the American Barth who redirected American theology. Whatever he had first said to become famous, Niebuhr was now a symbol of the Democratic Party establishment that created a catastrophe in Vietnam.

Youthful graduates of the New Left and the founders of liberation theology contended that Niebuhr was a chief apologist of the American Empire not deserving the title of a prophet. Neoconservatives countered that America needed the Niebuhr of the 1950s who called America to fight against Communism and anti-Americanism. Neoconservatism was an intellectual-political backlash against the antiwar, Black Power, and feminist movements of the 1960s. I pored over the periodicals section of the college library every week, reading assiduously the journals in politics, philosophy, sociology, and theology. In the first week of every month, I anticipated with appalled fascination the new issue of *Commentary*, the tribune of an ascending neoconservative movement. *Commentary* was not stodgy, Waspy, or middle-brow like most magazines of the Right. It skewered the political Left with highbrow polemics that conveyed an inside-knower feeling of betrayal.

The 1972 presidential election was the movement takeoff, as most of the neoconservatives came from the Max Shachtman wing of the Socialist Party and the Cold War wing of the Democratic Party. They loathed the liberal insurgency in the Democratic Party that nominated McGovern for president. They celebrated Nixon's reelection, even though many still called themselves socialists. Two things caught my attention about the rise of the neoconservatives: the conversion story and the Niebuhr angle. The articles and the extensive letters section of *Commentary* bristled with repudiations of former allies. *Commentary* blasted feminism, the antiwar movement, Black Power, secular liberals, liberal Jews, and liberal church leaders ferociously. It did not say that some feminists went too far; it said that all feminists were pathetic and ridiculous. *Commentary* editor Norman Podhoretz wrote snarky polemics condemning liberals for supporting affirmative action, failing to defend middle-class values, going wobbly on Zionism, and turning anti-anti-Communist. The magazine was about demolishing opponents, not dialoguing with them. The fascinating thing was that nearly everyone who wrote for *Commentary* was a former lefty or still claimed to be one.

The neoconservatives denied that they had changed. They said American liberalism had changed, not them. Calling them conservatives of any kind was insulting, at least at first. On their telling, the new liberalism of the Democratic Party was balefully idealistic, moralistic, feminist, anti-American, obsequious to Black Power accusation, near-pacifist, mealy-mouthed on Zionism, and self-righteous—all things Niebuhr hated. They wailed that even the Socialist Party—the original home of hardline anti-Communism in the United States—sprouted a squishy wing calling America to come home from Vietnam. Neoconservative founders Michael Novak, Irving Kristol, Paul Ramsey, Richard

John Neuhaus, and Ernest Lefever hailed Niebuhr as their role model. They recycled his blistering attacks on antiwar idealists of the 1930s and soft-on-Communism idealists of the 1950s. Their only regret about Niebuhr, they said, was that he ended badly, repenting of urging Johnson to fight the Communists in Vietnam.[21]

Certainly, the neocons had a basis for claiming an affinity with Niebuhr, and some had known him personally. But Niebuhr belonged to the political Left throughout his career, first as a social gospel liberal, later as a Socialist Party partisan who ridiculed social gospel liberals, and later as a Democratic Party mainstay who scorned Republicans. The neocons who lionized him, by contrast, streamed into the political Right, heaped ridicule on every social justice movement of their time, and rode into power in the administrations of Ronald Reagan, George H. W. Bush, and George W. Bush. I was past Alma College before I fathomed how profoundly the neocons misused Niebuhr. Grasping Niebuhr whole was impossible in the early 1970s; it would be like trying to see the Empire State Building from across the street.

In the spring of my sophomore year, our Vice President for Development, Guile Graham, told me the college was seeking to rekindle its relationships with numerous Presbyterian congregations in Michigan. Was I willing to preach at Sunday services representing the college? I wrote a sermon on the role of myth in religion, the Bible, and Christian faith, giving due credit to Tillich. Pure myth, I said, is the history of the gods; myth is the natural language of religion, and the mythic impulse is essentially unifying. Like all scriptural traditions, the Bible contains ample mythic material, which doesn't mean that these parts should be denigrated or cast aside. We must break open the myths of the Bible to recover the spiritual truths buried in them. In conservative Christian colleges, I said, you cannot speak this plainly about Christian myth; at Alma College, we study theologians who write honestly about such topics. Theology is not about pretending to believe something unbelievable. "Religion" is a name for the ways that individuals and communities name and ritualize their ultimate concerns. Faith is the state of being ultimately concerned, a gift of grace. Theology helps to clarify which concerns deserve to be ultimate. For the three years that I preached for Alma College, I updated the illustrations periodically, but the core was usually this page from Tillich. It was a species of cultural apologetics geared to represent the college. Mr. Graham and I were warmly received wherever we went, though occasionally a pastor let on that he (they were all he) preferred Barth over Tillich.

Every summer of my college years, I worked on a street repair crew for the City of Midland. We worked normal day shift hours except in July, when we labored in the wee hours in the dark. The men with whom I worked came from the same class terrain in which I grew up. Most thought it was fine that I defected to college-world, though my boss Gene resented it. He baited me by spraying the n-word, matched my angry comebacks with emotional heat of his own, and inveighed against the hippie professors he imagined. Yet every summer he took me back when he could have said no. In Gene's view, the only reason to attend college was to have access to college girls. He plied me each summer on this subject, incredulous that I wasted another year of access. On that subject he was right, though I never told him what happened to me with Nancy. Gene was the last person I would have trusted with a secret about heartbreak. One day, driving down Main Street in our big yellow truck, he lunged out the window to leer at a blond beauty on the sidewalk, wailing, "Oh my God, can you imagine being with that?" It went on, got more graphic, finally the fantasy ended, I counted to five, and replied, "That was my mother." For a moment he was stunned. Then he said he didn't believe it, so I asked her to deliver my lunch at the shop. Gene flushed red in the face, stammered it's-nice-to-meet-you, and muttered for weeks afterward at the unbelievable luck of my father.

My father was accustomed to hearing it. The first time that my mother attended one of his musical theater cast parties, she set off a flurry of fevered speculation about who the hell was married to her. My dad let it play out for half the evening before letting on that he was the answer. One summer day at noon he called me at the shop: "Son, did you hear? You got number 280." He was choking up as he said it, the only time I had ever heard him do so, reporting my draft lottery number. I would not have gone to Vietnam anyway. But on one lucky draw I got the avoidance opportunity that had required him at my age, with a low draft number, to get married and beget me.

Back at college I wrote senior theses on Marx and German Jesuit Karl Rahner while continuing my autodidactic grappling with Kant and Hegel. Lemmon had a textbook-sociology acquaintance with Marx and no direct acquaintance with Marx's *Capital* (1867), so I was mostly on my own with Marx. I had to learn Rahner because he was the foremost Roman Catholic theologian of the twentieth century and every theologian in my head was liberal Protestant, neo-orthodox Protestant, Black liberationist Protestant, or post-Christian. If I studied only one modern Roman Catholic theologian, better make it the best one. Massanari did not know Rahner's work but was willing to read a thesis on how Rahner appropriated the existential phenomenology of his teacher at the University of Freiburg, Martin Heidegger. On the side I worked through a blue-and-gold book titled *Teach Yourself German*, refusing to spend precious course time on language courses. To read German was obviously imperative for me; to speak it seemed wholly unnecessary, since I really was a bumpkin.[22]

Hegel should have led me to Kant's argument about intellectual intuition in the Third Critique, the *Critique of Judgment*, but I was too fixed on the puzzles of the First Critique to get there. Robert Paul Wolff and Norman Kemp Smith stood out among analysts of Kant's epistemology. Wolff interpreted Kant as a pure subjective idealist, rendering the Kantian categories as objects within experience. Smith contended that Kant incoherently patched together subjective idealism with an argument for objective idealism that rendered the Kantian categories as conditions of experience. Roger Haverfield told me that Smith refuted Smith's own claim that Kant deserved his towering stature in philosophy. Much as I disagreed with Roger, I did not peer beyond the Kant scholarship of Anglo-American philosophy, since most of it was untranslated in a language I was hurrying belatedly to read.[23]

It was trendy in the 1970s to say that the Marx we need is the early humanist Marx who wrote about alienation, not the later economist Marx who wrote the unreadable *Capital*. I gave the early Marx his due for his insight that individual persons distinguished themselves from animals by producing their means of subsistence and thus indirectly producing their material life. But I pushed back against the way that Lemmon and Massanari taught Marx, countering that Marx substantiated his thesis only in *Capital:* the problem of alienation is distinctive to capitalist society. Wherever capital predominates, it changes everything. I interpreted Marx's *Contribution to the Critique of Political Economy* (1859) as the overture to *Capital*, fixing on the first three chapters of *Capital*, which summarized the theory of value and money that Marx developed in *Critique*. Marx followed Adam Smith and David Ricardo in explicating the concepts of supply and demand, competition, and the market, but Smith and Ricardo moved straight to quantitative formulas about market relations and the flow of exchange value. Marx employed Hegelian dialectics to unveil the essential-what behind the phenomenal appearances of market relations. In *Critique*, he explored the seemingly simple question of where the value of a commodity comes from. In *Capital*, he argued that capitalist production and exchange renders human labor literally inhuman by turning commodities into fetishes.[24]

I dug into his landmark contention that commodities are mysterious. Marx showed that the exchange process turns a commodity into something as strange and subtle as scholastic metaphysics—stamping the social character of human labor upon the product of labor *as an objective character*, while presenting the relation of the producers to the sum of their labor as a social relationship *between the products of their labor*, not between the producers. Capitalism renders the social relations between who makes what, who works for whom, and the production time required to make a commodity as economic relations between objects, the value of a given commodity when compared to another commodity. Here was the upshot of Marx's humanism—his demonstration that the market exchange of commodities obscures the human relations of production. Under capitalism, the previously undisguised human relation of laborers to their work through the process of production, exchange, and consumption is veiled through institutions shrewdly dubbed "the free market" and "private property." Relations between people are replaced by purported relations between things, which Marx scathingly called *Verdinglichung*, reification.

Plunging into Rahner was pointless without acquiring some understanding of Thomas Aquinas and Heidegger. The Catholic issue was perplexing because I realized that no Catholic school would have allowed me to pass straight to Rahner, but I had time for only one modern Catholic thinker. I tried to repair my first deficit by studying the first forty-nine questions of Thomas' *Summa Theologica*, leaving off at the angels. Then I waded through Heidegger's fantastically obscure *Being and Time* (1927), which broke from the entire Cartesian project of modern philosophy and Heidegger's mentor, Edmund Husserl, by arguing that Husserl's phenomenology began in the wrong place. Instead of asking how objects are constituted in our consciousness, philosophy must inquire into the mode of being in which the world constitutes itself.[25]

Being expresses itself through human being(s), so Heidegger argued that phenomenology is rightly a method of access to being that begins with an analysis of Dasein—human existence. He tried to say it without replicating the anthropocentrism he sought to surmount, which turned out to be impossible. The early Heidegger described Dasein (literally, "being-there," *da-sein*) as essentially temporal, constituting a tripartite ontological structure of existence, thrownness, and fallenness in a world of past, present, and future. Rahner showed that you didn't have to be Protestant like Tillich and Rudolf Bultmann to theologize Heidegger's phenomenological ontology. Belgian Jesuit Joseph Maréchal construed the Thomist analogy of being within Kant's transcendental framework: to recognize a cognitive limit is to transcend it. Maréchal's Transcendental Thomism was Kantian in focusing on the subject who knows, not the object known, but it was Thomist in its realism and its concept of the human intellect as an active power. Rahner refashioned Transcendental Thomism by wedding the Thomist concept of dynamic mind with Heidegger's analysis of being-in-the-world (Dasein), arguing that the acting intellect becomes a faculty of willing through the act of reaching for its object. I wrote a 120-page thesis that analyzed Rahner's Heideggerian metaphysic and briskly recounted his career: embattled in the early 1930s at Freiburg for departing from neo-scholastic orthodoxy, teaching at the University of Innsbruck until the Nazis took over the university in 1939, working at a pastoral institute in Vienna from 1939 to 1949, developing his signature theme that whoever reaches out for truth and the holy is under the influence of divine grace, and vindicated at Vatican Council II, where his influence was strong and historic.[26]

I carried Rahner in my head as a possible model, the Catholic Schleiermacher, for a remote possibility, a Catholic future. Theologically I identified with Schleiermacher, Hegel, Rauschenbusch, Tillich, King, and Cone, yet on Sundays and most weekday mornings I attended Mass at St. Mary Church, realizing I had a Catholic soul. Dave chided me to go on a date before I graduated from college, never quite recognizing that my depression exceeded his. Ron said I had a bad case of "intellectual masochism," plunging headlong into impossible systems. He meant Kant and Rahner, not Marx, since Marx was worth the struggle. Dave asked a question that changed my life.

I had bored into Marx's primary texts, but where did I place myself in contemporary scholarship on Marxism? Specifically, Dave asked, "Do you know Michael Harrington? He thinks like you do!" No, I did not know Michael Harrington. But by graduation week I had read all five of his books and found a North Star. Dave was right: on things political, I thought very much like Harrington. He had won a splash of fame with his book on American poverty, *The Other America* (1962). His book *Toward a Democratic Left* (1968) expounded his signature vision of a progressive-Left Democratic Party. I devoured his big book, *Socialism* (1972), identifying with his political history of democratic socialism. It turned out that Harrington had recently written a memoir, *Fragments of the Century* (1973), so his personal history became part of my intellectual landscape. It had a chapter on his battle with the neoconservatives, whom he had named as an act of dissociation. They were not the right wing of the political Left, as they believed; they were the Left wing of the political Right, a chasm-difference. I agreed emphatically with that.[27]

Harrington told his story of growing up in St. Louis, Missouri; attaining a Jesuit education in high school and college; joining Dorothy Day's Catholic Worker community in New York City; trying to believe in Day's anarcho-pacifism, church, and God; joining a Marxist sect in New York City, which involved dropping anarcho-pacifism, Catholicism, and God; teaming with Black activist Bayard Rustin to drag the Socialist Party into the Civil Rights Movement of the 1950s; writing *The Other America*; blowing his chance to mentor the New Left of the early 1960s; suffering an emotional breakdown; and failing to hold together the Socialist Party of Eugene Debs and Norman Thomas, because it was overtaken by Socialists for Nixon. Most of this narrative was new to me in the spring of 1974, and some of it was unfathomable. I judged from the beginning that Harrington strained too much to make Marx sound like himself, an occupational hazard for apologists. But I wanted to know more, including what became of the scrappy little group he described on the next-to-last page. He had founded it in February 1973 after the Socialist Party imploded but did not name it. Perhaps his publisher forbade him from naming this new hope of the democratic Left?

The summer of Richard Nixon's downfall flew past as I prepared to enter Harvard Divinity School. Nixon had stoked White resentments and sabotaged the Vietnam peace talks of 1968 to win the presidency. Then he solidified the Republican takeover of the former Dixiecrat strongholds, kept the war going, and tried to lie and obstruct his way out of Watergate, so his downfall was a relief. It was hard to appreciate at the time that he opened the door to China and came closer than any president to obtaining universal health insurance. We did not know that Nixon was the last Republican who would care about universal health care.

My friend Jim Metcalf and I prepared differently for seminary: Hebrew and advanced Greek for him; W. E. B. Du Bois and teach-yourself-Greek for me, with help from Jim. Unlike me, Jim was headed toward ministry in an actual church, the Missouri Synod Lutheran Church, having completed his undergraduate studies in the Concordia Seminary system. In our senior year of college, I had written a long letter to him filled with the names and signature arguments of biblical scholars and theologians. Jim, befuddled by all of it, asked his theology professor for a translation, who assured him there was nothing whatsoever in this letter that he needed to know. One day in the summer of 1974 my dad remarked out of the blue that I could readily return to playing golf: "You still have your swing, son! It wouldn't take long for you to beat us again!" I had read piles of books during the weekends that I might have spent on a golf course. My dad did not fathom that I had never cared about golf, my assiduous practicing notwithstanding; I had cared only about being with him, until "I am myself" acquired an individuated meaning for me.

A week before I flew to Boston on my first flight anywhere, I rounded up my sports trophies and scrapbooks and pitched them into several trash cans. I didn't make a thing of destroying the trophies; I just threw them into the cans, and some of them broke. I did, however, rip the pages of the newspaper scrapbooks until I tired of it and threw the rest away. It didn't feel dramatic or any such thing to me. My adolescent sports days were over, I was moving far away to graduate school, and I didn't want my brothers to have to look at my trophies, so I discarded whatever I wouldn't be taking to Cambridge. My brother Andy, however, seeing the trash cans on the street awaiting pickup, was stunned. He gathered the trophies that weren't broken and the pages that weren't ripped apart, taking them to his room.

"Mom," he asked, "why did he do that?" She didn't know, so he asked me next, now focusing on the newspaper clippings: "Why did you rip up the pages?" Perhaps it made some sense to him that trophies are cumbersome, and perhaps also that at some point they become embarrassing. But he pressed for an answer about the pages—the record of all those years of teams and games. Did I not care about any of it anymore? For a moment I froze, not knowing the answer, or how to respond. I hadn't thought about my feelings until he asked. It cut me to my heart that he cared. I thanked him for caring, and for retrieving what I threw out, and for asking. Had that been our last time together, this memory would be unbearable. But it was not far from the last time.

3

HARVARD–UNION–
PRINCETON–BRENDA

On the flight to Boston in September 1974 I read an ad for a Franciscan community that gently asked readers if they might have a religious vocation. "If I flunk out of Harvard," I thought, "I can join the Franciscans; it will be all right." I expected to be less unusual at Harvard Divinity School, except in a bad way. Surely, I would compare poorly to classmates who were raised to go to Harvard. The prospect of meeting Harvard professors terrified me: they would peg me as a bumpkin, I would acknowledge it contritely, and perhaps they would cut me a break. That was the optimistic scenario; otherwise, it would be the Franciscans for me.

I didn't expect the professors at HDS to mentor or befriend me. What surprised me was that this issue hovered over HDS like a stone cloud. My classmates were highly intelligent, knew they were well prepared, and carried themselves with self-confidence. Many were graduates of fabulous schools I had never heard of: Bard College, Brandeis University, Carleton College, Claremont McKenna College, Dickinson College, Haverford College, Kenyon College, Pomona College, Smith College, Williams College, and so on, plus the Ivies. Every year, HDS admitted students like them from schools like this, where they had been personally nurtured. Every year a bunch of them were surprised and angry to discover that no such mentoring occurred at Harvard. My class had many students who reacted that way. I, however, expected to be thrown on my own and was just hoping not to flunk out.

My first week was a thrilling whirl of befriending Divinity Hall dormmates, exploring the North End of Boston, eating my first-ever restaurant meals involving silverware and waitresses, meeting professors, and reading Mary Daly's *Beyond God the Father* (1973). In college I had a simple understanding of feminism as the imperative of equal rights for women and the liberalization of gender roles. Feminism was political and cultural, having to do with the Equal Rights Amendment, sexist attitudes in American society, and social policies on childcare and parental leave. To the extent that feminism applied to religion, it was about the right of women to be ordained and accepted as church leaders. The idea of applying feminist criticism to Christian doctrine, creating feminist theologies, had just begun.[1]

Daly had written a pioneering work of feminist theology in 1968, *The Church and the Second Sex*, but it was reformist, operating within the tradition and structures of the Roman Catholic Church. I entered divinity school just as feminist theology became a movement calling for a revolution of consciousness. *Beyond God the Father* was the manifesto of radical feminist theology. Daly argued that the story of the fall in Genesis 3 is fundamentally a myth of feminine evil, an example of cosmic false naming that metamorphosed the viewpoint of women-hating men into God's viewpoint. A truly liberating feminism would indwell the metamorphic power of words and female energy, imagining ultimate reality as verb, the original surge of life, reclaiming women's elemental powers. Daly called radical feminism "the ultimate revolution" and "the cause of causes." Until women, she said, had enough physical and psychic separation from males to think out of their own existence, it was impossible to say what a radical feminist ethic would be.[2]

Beyond God the Father stopped just short of claiming that Christianity is inherently oppressive or that male evil is hopelessly unredeemable. I read it in one sitting, stunned by the book's apocalyptic ferocity. Two days later I read it again, this time catching more of its scathing Nietzschean humor. A month later I knew much of it by memory. The parallels between Daly and James Cone were obvious, but Daly's book radiated the post-Christian trajectory she was on. *Beyond God the Father* teetered on the edge of condemning maleness itself, espousing anti-political separatism as a way of life, and conjuring a new species of Gnostic dualism and otherworldliness, after which Daly dispensed with teetering on these points and left Christianity behind.

When I got to HDS it had a cluster of Daly-feminist students and a one-year history of teaching feminist theology. Rosemary Radford Ruether, in 1971–1972, had taught courses at HDS that she could not teach at her institution, Howard University in Washington, DC. At

Harvard she got rough treatment from the Daly-feminists, who said Daly was the real thing and Ruether was a reformist pretender. Some of my classmates had taken different sides of this debate, which they recounted to us newcomers in the Divinity Hall basement, the kitchen. Early in the fall semester, Ruether spoke at Boston College, where Daly taught. We made the long Green Line subway trip to the BC campus at Chestnut Hill, underestimating how long it would take, and ended up in the standing room section at the back of a lecture auditorium.

Ruether was a Catholic historical theologian trained at Claremont Graduate School, where she had studied biblical prophecy in the context of Mediterranean history, forming three conclusions: the only scholarship worth reading was liberal Protestant; biblical monotheism was commendably ethical, unlike the pagan theophanies of the gods; and Protestant scholarship was too much like the Bible in denigrating pagan religions. She liked the prophets but not their polemic against Ba'alism. She admired the Catholic synthesis of the ancient world's religious heritages, and was grateful for Vatican Council II, which kept her in the Catholic Church. In the 1960s Ruether enlisted in the civil rights movement, taught at Howard, gradually identified with feminism, and wrote a massive book manuscript on the roots of Jewish messianism in Near Eastern kingship and New Year rituals. This book, though never published, fueled for many years her prolific writings on feminism, Christology, anti-Semitism, goddess religion, and political theology. At Boston College she inserted a gist version of her signature talk into a preview of her next book.[3]

Tribal culture, she argued, mythologized a holistic worldview. The earth goddess and sky god played complementary roles, as did females and males. The salvation of the individual was not divorced from that of the community or the renewal of the earth. New year's festivals celebrated the annual death and resurrection of the cosmos. The king, personifying the community, played the role of the dying and rising god. His female counterpart—a virgin and mother, and wife and sister—rescued the dying god from the netherworld. At the end of the celebration the two united to form the divine child of the new year's life. This communal sense of a sacred cosmos did not survive the imperial invasions of the first millennium BCE that swept the peoples of the Mediterranean into alien civilizations. To the extent that the religions of the earth survived, they became private cults for individuals. Renewing earth and society was no longer the point. Salvation became otherworldly and individual; nature was an alien reality; individuals conceived their bodies as foreign to their true selves; the idea of a heavenly escape to a true home displaced the idea that the earth is humanity's home.

Ruether construed Christianity as a synthesis of the Hebrew and classical myths of redemption. The Hebrews clung to their tribal identity against a succession of imperial powers, claiming the land as a divine legacy, interpreting the earth festivals as historical events in their communal journey, and anticipating a renewal of earth and society in a messianic age. They also repressed the feminine imagery of the old religions—aside from symbolizing Israel as the bride of YHWH—which tore the cycle of death and resurrection from the sacred cosmos. Death and resurrection were refigured as historical wrath and redemption. Classical philosophy further alienated the individual from the world, viewing the body as an obstacle to clear knowledge and moral integrity. Christianity absorbed the Platonist myth of liberation to an eternal otherworld and refashioned the old myths of the new year and the virgin-mother goddess, the historical consciousness of Israel, and the anti-feminine spirituality of late antiquity, synthesizing the best and worst of late classical civilization.

Feminist theology, Ruether said, is a vision of anti-patriarchal wholeness that corrects Christianity's exaggerated and transcendent male ego. At Boston College she reported that her next book had gone to press, lacking a title. She tried out titles on the crowd, settling on *New Woman, New Earth: Sexist Ideologies and Human Liberation* (1975). Conservatives and Daly-feminists pushed back, but Ruether held her ground, reveling in the back-and-forth. She made a couple of rueful asides about her bruising year at HDS, which we rehashed on the way home. Later she recalled of her year at HDS: "To be concerned about class and race was seen as distracting from 'pure' feminism. The influence of Mary Daly was evident here." Ruether's year at Harvard clarified to her that her feminism was socialist and anti-racist, not pure.[4]

Shortly after Ruether spoke at Boston College, Michael Harrington came to Harvard to promote his new organization, the Democratic Socialist Organizing Committee (DSOC). He wore a corduroy jacket and blue work-shirt, and endured the customary introduction that always made him cringe: "Michael Harrington is the author of *The Other America*, the book that launched the war on poverty, and the successor of Norman Thomas, the great Socialist leader of the mid-twentieth century." Mike gently reintroduced himself. He said he had also written books titled *Toward a Democratic Left* and *Socialism*. Perhaps some of you would be interested in *these* books? They mattered far more to him than *The Other America*, a puffed-up version of a magazine article he had written during his Greyhound Bus years as an organizer for the Socialist Party. This book had burnished him with writer-fame as a liberal political journalist, not as the organic intellectual who learned his Marxism in the socialist movement. Mike could hear his epitaph in these introductions: "Wrote *The Other America*, downhill after that." As for succeeding Thomas, he blushed at the title. In 1974, Mike was just beginning to earn it.

Norman Thomas was the last great socialist who had ever believed the world was progressing toward justice and freedom. Gently raised in middle-class Ohio Presbyterianism, he had graduated from Princeton University and Union Theological Seminary, entered the Presbyterian ministry in 1911, served a mixed-ethnic mission congregation in East Harlem for seven years, implored his denomination not to support America's entry into World War I in 1917, and joined the only U.S. American national organization to hold out against the war—the Socialist Party. Thomas joined the party just as nearly all its intellectuals fled from it; they were not going to be trampled by the patriotic stampede to war. The party was viciously persecuted for opposing the war. Then the meteor of world Communism crashed into the Socialist movement and blew it apart. Thomas inherited the shattered wreck of the Socialist Party, at first believing that democratic socialism synthesized the cultural progress of modern society and was destined to become the basis of a world government.

The rest of his life, in his telling, was a succession of terrible disillusionments that made him evermore miserable—down, down, down, down. The Socialists failed to get a Farmer-Labor-Socialist-Progressive party off the ground; Thomas ran for president six times to spread the message of democratic socialism; Franklin Roosevelt stole 90 percent of the Socialist program to build the New Deal; Thomas tried various approaches to the Communist problem, and all were disastrous failures. In countless union and activist struggles, Thomas teamed with Black union organizer A. Philip Randolph and was a spiritual godfather to the four socialists who organized the March on Washington in 1963: Randolph, James Farmer, Bayard Rustin, and Martin Luther King Jr. They loved Thomas for keeping the Socialist Party going and for imploring the New Left of the 1960s to wash the flag, not burn it. King called Thomas one of the bravest persons he ever met and the foremost advocate of a just society. Randolph said Thomas had no personal faults; none whatsoever.[5]

I joined DSOC at Harrington's Harvard lecture. To my generation of democratic socialists, Thomas registered as the last idealist. He must have had more shortcomings than our elders let on because look at the pitiable state of our movement! Soon there were chapter meetings and actions to organize, and meetings with Boston DSOC, where a venerable lion of the Jewish Labor Committee, Julius Bernstein, was our leader. We showed up for solidarity support wherever a local union was on strike. Our university chapter had a charismatic undergraduate leader, Nick Minard, who picketed for the Harvard printers' union and passed out leaflets in Harvard Yard asking students to think about the poverty and powerlessness of miners. Nick suffered the suffering of people he never met. In January 1975 he threw himself off the William James building, plunging to his death. We were left with a stricken sorrow at a brilliant life tragically cut short and a cautionary example of holding unbearable burdens too closely.

Meanwhile I worked the midnight-to-eight shift on weekdays as a security guard for Harvard University, patrolling its grounds and buildings, changing clothes in a restroom before entering class. Being seen by professors and classmates in my uniform would have been mortifying. My first year at HDS was a blur of struggling to stay awake through classes. I was there to be a student, not to work for Harvard, but my student debts were escalating and I needed a job for living expenses. Forrest Church, a doctoral student in church history, picked me out in the wee hours outside his Holden Green residence. He was highly personable and a quick study, typing me after a few questions. Forrest was not actually empathic, but he thrived on conversation, regaling me with stories about HDS professors. I asked if he was related to U.S. Senator Frank Church of Idaho, which launched him on a run of political storytelling that began with his father and resumed the next night. Forrest had the kind of brilliance that could have been channeled to any field. He had managed one of his father's election campaigns and could have gone into politics, but that was his father's field. He was planning an academic career, but was already dubious of the small-world insularity of most academic careers. Forrest had chosen religious studies because Frank Church wasn't religious. Then All Souls Unitarian Church in New York City surprised him with the offer of a public pastoral stage, where he had a long run as the most visible, prolific, and controversial figure in American Unitarian Universalism.

I forged close friendships with four students at HDS—H. John McDargh, Robin Lovin, Mary Ellen Ross, and Ken Baynes—who put up with my constantly blurry tiredness and weird hours. John, a graduate of Emory University, was a doctoral student in religion and psychology who wasn't sure what approach he should take to this field, studying under William Rogers. Then he discovered the object-relations tradition of psychoanalytic theory pioneered by Harry Stack Sullivan, Melanie Klein, Donald Winnicott, Harry Guntrip, and Ronald Fairbairn, which enthralled him. John waxed excitedly on the object-relations theme that human beings are driven fundamentally to secure personal relationships, not to satisfy the drives of a homeostatic Freudian ego-self. He was deeply kind, sensitive, conflictedly Catholic, and gay, an outreaching type for whom object-relations theory aptly described the story of his life. John was my first friend to negotiate the social politics of coming out as gay, and the first to show me what it looks like to be in the throes of a consuming intellectual passion. Coming out was a perilous endeavor when he entered the job market; I greatly admired him for it. Meanwhile, to be his friend was to catch second-hand his immense learning, as it occurred, in object-relations theory, including the strain of it that inquired into how human beings internalize images of the divine. His dissertation on this subject featured the research of a Boston psychoanalytic theorist, Ana-María Rizzuto, after which John embarked on a distinguished teaching career at Boston College and joined the Episcopal Church.[6]

Robin Lovin was a graduate of Northwestern University, a dedicated United Methodist minister, a Somerville apartment roommate of John's, and a doctoral student studying under social ethicist Preston Williams. He bantered with ease about Aristotle, moral theory, the history of Christian ethics, political philosopher John Rawls, Methodist scuttlebutt, and legal theory. He lit up when he talked about legal theorists H. L. A. Hart and Lon Fuller, and what Rawls took from Hart. One night, Robin explained to me that Hart separated law from morality, contending that different types of norms combine to form the structure of a legal system; Fuller rejected Hart's legal positivism, espousing a secular version of natural law; and Rawls elaborated Hart's principle of fair play, which somehow refurbished Kantian liberalism. I lost the thread somewhere, but it was fascinating.

Robin was on a path to becoming the foremost interpreter of his generation of Reinhold Niebuhr, but back then, he was not a Niebuhr guy. Niebuhr was just one of the people in his wheelhouse, and Robin hadn't read much Niebuhr before Williams told him he should. To the extent that the early Robin had a Christian ethical canon, it was German Lutheran theologian Dietrich Bonhoeffer and American Roman Catholic theologian John Courtney Murray. Bonhoeffer caught Robin before he enrolled at Harvard; then Robin studied what Murray said about religious freedom, the U.S. American experiment in it, and religious pluralism. Robin later contributed to the Murray renaissance of the mid-1980s, by which time he was well into his career at the University of Chicago Divinity School and known for other things.[7]

I had three clues about Robin's turn toward Niebuhr, aside from the influence of Williams. The first was related to the rise of neoconservatism in the mid-1970s. The neocons said it was possible to win a nuclear war, and the United States should achieve the nuclear superiority that serves this objective. I walked Robin through the argument, he got red in the face and said, "It's so ridiculous. This has nothing to do with Reinhold Niebuhr." Two things struck me. I had never seen Robin agitated, and, apparently, he had feelings about Niebuhr. Later that year, when we talked about Black theology and James Cone, Robin said that Cone helped him to appreciate Niebuhr, especially *Moral Man and Immoral Society*. The third clue was that much of the Murray discussion about public theology referenced Niebuhr, which Robin took up. Robin kept up with me long after it seemed that I would never be an academic. A year after he graduated from Harvard, he won the ethics job at Chicago. It thrilled me that a friend of mine was teaching at the University of Chicago. It felt like he zoomed from zero to ninety overnight. In his first class at Chicago, Robin was a little nervous, the lecture seemed to go well enough, and he was starting to relax when someone asked him how to reconcile what he had said with Kant's *Critique of Judgment*. Robin had two thoughts as he felt the panic surging through him. One, he had not read Kant's Third Critique in many years. Two, is this what Chicago is going to be like?

Mary Ellen Ross was my film and music buddy. Until I met her, I knew nothing of the French and Italian cinematic traditions and had never seen an Ingmar Bergman film. She had graduated from Pomona College in Claremont, California, and was destined to complete a doctorate in ethics under William Schweiker and Robin at Chicago before undertaking her teaching career at Trinity University in San Antonio, Texas. Mary Ellen introduced me to films that she knew by heart, always willing to watch one of her favorites with me and discuss it. She classified films by their directors, another new concept for me, comparing Bergman, Vittorio De Sica, François Truffaut, and Federico Fellini as readily as I talked about philosophers. I took a deep plunge into the soaring, spiraling, enthralling symphonies of Ludwig van Beethoven, ever-after my gold standard; adored the symphonies of Johannes Brahms for fusing mid-Romantic harmonies and Classical structures; and cringed at loving the wildly gorgeous symphonies of Gustav Mahler until Mary Ellen said I was too easily shamed by haughty music critics. It is wrong to apologize for loving anything beautiful! We had shimmering conversations that started with films, morphed into music, politics, theology, feminism, Boston, our classes, and the academy, and interspersed our personal histories. Evenings flew by in Mary Ellen's company because I was blissfully happy in it. She might have been The One for me had I been willing to risk losing her Platonic friendship. Our classmate Bill French, not shy or Platonic, and later her classmate at Chicago, struck up a romance with her and I was happy for them.

Ken Baynes was my philosophy buddy. A graduate of Gordon College in Wenham, Massachusetts letting go of his evangelical theology, he was on a post-Christian path without knowing it. Neo-Calvinist philosopher Nicholas Wolterstorff, in *Reason within the Bounds of Religion* (1976), rejected the standard academic conception of inquiry as the unrestricted pursuit of truth guided by wherever the evidence leads. He argued that it is legitimate for a Christian scholar to be constrained by Christian doctrine because no one possesses a perfectly certain core of certainties on which all valid knowledge claims must be made. This anti-foundationalist apologetic briefly held Ken in Christianity, where he combined Barth and philosopher Hans Georg Gadamer, reasoning that the truth of grace is prior to any method of inquiry. Ken and I caught that Hegel's attempt to track the movement of spirit in history was another way of describing the priority of grace over method. Barth, to the extent that he could be described philosophically, was a quasi-Hegelian witness to the Wholly Other God of grace, the One Who Loves in Freedom. How, exactly, Hegel and Barth should be understood in relation to Kant was a prior question of daunting complexity on which we looked for help.[8]

Harvard's philosophy department was a strongly analytical outfit headed by Willard Van Orman Quine, who said there is no mind-body problem because minds are not real. Many Harvard philosophy students shared Quine's view that everything is physical—more precisely, that physical predicates are sufficient for describing things as they are, though Quine allowed himself a loophole for numbers and other select abstract objects. Harvard philosophers Stanley Cavell and John Rawls lamented that their students dismissed German idealism as inscrutable metaphysical phantasmagoria about subjectivity, and therefore could not pass an exam on it. Cavell and Rawls surmised that if anyone could make classic Continental philosophy intelligible to their students, it was Heidelberg philosopher Dieter Henrich, a specialist on Kant, Hegel, and the post-Kantian tradition. They invited Henrich to Harvard to try.[9]

Ken and I were thrilled. Henrich was wrapped in a full-length fur coat on the day I tracked him down in Harvard Yard for his permission signature. He gave profusely detailed lectures that unveiled the systematic structure of post-Kantian thought, seeking to bridge the chasm between Continental and Anglo-American philosophy. He packed lecture halls with philosophy students and a few Divinity School students that included Mark C. Taylor, later an eminent postmodernist; David S. Pacini, later an historical theologian at Emory; and Stephen Dunning, later a philosopher of religion at Penn, all of whom engaged Henrich directly. Pacini shared with me his notes on lectures that Henrich gave on Kant before I got there. Ken and I were too lowly to approach an exalted German professor, but we defended him against snarky local derision and helped each other decipher what he said. I could appreciate why neuroscientists dismissed the concept of mind or reduced it to unfathomed neural firings in the brain, but I never quite got over that so many budding philosophers waved off their minds and selves and freedom and the unity of their consciousness.[10]

Our heads were bursting with strands of philosophy and theology known only to us. Ken befriended Harvard theologian Arthur C. McGill, an eclectic prober who gave riveting lectures on theodicy, suffering, and death, and I befriended Harvard theologian George Rupp, a young neo-Hegelian already plotting his move into academic administration. George was the only teacher I ever had who specialized in the German post-Kantian theological tradition. Many years later, when George served as president of Rice University and Columbia University, his lectures rang in my head as I wrote books analyzing aspects of the German tradition. My book *The Word as True Myth* (1997) might have waxed less expansively on the first left-Hegelian theologian, David Friedrich Strauss, had George not taken us up and down the wild ride that was Strauss' career and legacy. At Harvard, Ken and I grappled with Henrich's pathbreaking lectures on how Kant's system fits together and why the *Phenomenology of Spirit* similarly has an integral unity. I fastened on Henrich's thesis that Kantian idealism is about the realization of truth in free self-determination, while Ken worried more about how this idea showed up in Hegel.[11]

In the Second Critique, Kant said that freedom is the only idea of speculative reason whose possibility we know a priori. We do not understand this idea, yet we know it as the condition of something we know, the moral law. If we had no freedom, we would not be able to grasp the existence of the moral law within us. To Kant, the concept of mind as a subject of knowledge was impossible lacking the idea of a world governed by laws. No concept of mind as a subject of knowledge is possible lacking the idea of a world governed by laws. In any concept of mind, some concept of the world is implied; otherwise, there would be no self-understanding of the mind. Henrich showed that Kant used different metaphors of reason in the First Critique, the Third Critique, and near the end of his life to explain what his system was about, each time describing the actual multi-dimensionality of his vaunted dualism. In the First Critique he described reason as an organic totality that coordinates the dualistic structural distinctions between sensibility and understanding, reason and understanding, and reason and judgment. Each cognitive faculty exists for the sake of the others and for its own sake. Reason, more broadly than the specific faculty of reason that is distinct from experience and understanding, embraces all cognitive faculties, aiming at a totality that makes experience complete. Every part of pure theoretical reason exists for the sake of all the others and its own sake.[12]

Kant's famous distinction between reason and understanding yielded his distinction between the intellectual world and the sensible world, but reason cannot be a unifying principle if it does not aim for a totality of combination that completes experience. Henrich argued that Kant needed a feedback loop between his ontological system and his theory of how the various faculties of mind combine with each other. Platonic dualism ran deep in Kant's thought, but even Kant needed a basis for defining what his philosophy was about. Schelling and Hegel devised post-Kantian systems that were strong on this point, repudiating Kantian dualism. Henrich stressed that Kant's epistemology was a philosophy of mind, beginning with the self and its mental activities, not a formal theory of rules about logical or objective realities. Kant derived his idea of the two worlds from his theory of an active self, which requires something given. His idea of something given yielded his distinction between the unknowable *noumena* (the thing-in-itself) and the knowable *phenomena*, two worlds constituting Kant's ontological framework. However, once Kant put into play the theory of two worlds, he could not return to the self, because it could not be construed as a member of one world or the other, and Kant could not conceive the self as a relation between two worlds if it was merely a subject that combines what is given to it.

In the First Critique, Kant said he tried to solve the problem of metaphysics. In the Third Critique, he said he demonstrated the continuous transition from acts of understanding to reason to practical reason, including the apprehension of beauty. Henrich observed that the second boast was larger; Kant claimed to theorize the achievements of mind before Hegel took on the same project. Near the end of his life, in his essay on the progress of metaphysics since G. W. Leibniz and Christian Wolff, Kant took a third pass at explaining his system, arguing that reason has a destination, which his thought was structured to justify. Rightly conceived, philosophy swings on two hinges, like a door. One is the ideality of time, the pure form of inner sensibility through which external things and pure concepts of the mind are related. The other hinge is the idea of freedom.[13]

The destination of reason is the idea of freedom. Kant went back to his theme in the Second Critique that reason is a vault whose keystone is freedom. All other ideas, he reflected, gain stability and objective reality only by attaching themselves to the idea of freedom. Henrich pressed the Kantian verdict that if we do not insert the keystone to the vault of reason, the vault will not work. When we insert the keystone of freedom, the vault becomes self-supporting. Kantian idealism is a theory about the connection between the principles of the intellectual world and the sensible world through practical reason and freedom. But Kant never quite said that he needed a feedback loop from his onto-logical framework to the principles of his system, so he never explicitly said that he found it in freedom—the link between the intellectual and sensible world and the unity of the self. Thus, Hegel tagged Kant as a dualist who failed to press his own doctrine of intellectual intuition to its logical conclusion. Henrich refined Kant's explanation of his system and similarly interpreted Hegel's *Phenomenology* as an integral argument correlating the development of mind and the development of concep-tions of the world. On Henrich's pioneering account, Hegel took over Friedrich Hölderlin's idea that love—not Kant's transcendental unity of apperception—is the golden principle of synthesis, and Kant is best interpreted as a theorist of freedom.[14]

These arguments helped to build the bridge that Cavell and Rawls had imagined, establishing a new conception of the post-Kantian tradi-tion. Peter Dews, Michael Dummett, Manfred Frank, Jürgen Habermas, John McDowell, and Hilary Putnam were prominent in the 1980s among those who called for bridgework, often citing Henrich. My encounters with philosophy departments might have gone better had they occurred a decade later. As it was, when I later wrote theses at Union Theolog-ical Seminary and Princeton Theological Seminary on post-Kantian idealism, I had to scrounge for faculty readers at Columbia University and Princeton University, where the analytic versus Continental divide was very much in place. Meanwhile at Harvard I lugged Hegel's *Sci-ence of Logic* to Fenway Park several times, strenuously marking it up while cheering on the Boston Red Sox, undeterred on one occasion by an incredulous fan who asked, "Why don't you just spray paint that book?"

University of Innsbruck Jesuit theologian Josef Sudbrack taught spiritual theology at Harvard for one year. I wrote a paper for him that criticized Rudolf Bultmann for interpreting the gospel through Heidegger's privatizing existentialism, albeit stripped of Heidegger's

atrocious Nazi politics. Fr. Sudbrack called me to his office: "If Bultmann is so wrong, why write about him?" I said I took for granted that
Bultmann is a towering figure in theology; it didn't seem necessary to
build him up before the slashing commenced. Fr. Sudbrack asked for
specifics about Bultmann, and I rattled on about his biblical scholarship until Fr. Sudbrack had heard enough: "Sehr gut! Sehr gut! Bultmann is a great man! You can't just say no to Bultmann!" He turned to
my extensive footnotes and bibliography, shaking his head quizzically:
"So many books! How can you read so many books?" Fr. Sudbrack
leaned forward, peering at me intently, wagging his finger: "Read *one*
book and know it inside and out!" He and I worshiped with the Jesuit
community at nearby Weston School of Theology, where one week he
asked me teasingly if I had found my one book. I confessed that I was
still racing through piles of books; meanwhile a Weston Jesuit pressed
me too aggressively about becoming a Jesuit and I pulled back from
the Weston community.[15]

Cambridge had a leftover outpost of the once-vital University
Christian Movement, so I joined it. They asked me to organize a weekend conference, and I knew who we should get: Ruether. She gave a
sisterhood-is-powerful talk that roared against sexism, racism, militarism, and other oppressive isms, sometimes breaking a heavy feeling in
the air with a caustic expletive. She described women as the original and
ultimate proletariat, admonished a churchy dissenter that God created
a world, not a church, and exhorted women not to settle for whin-
ing; feminism was a revolution, not a pity-party. Ruether bristled with
non-pious self-confidence, rebuffing the students who asked to be nurtured—would they have expected a male theologian to nurture them?
I was thrilled to be in the same room with her. Ruether teased me that
HDS had no feminist theologians, and I agreed that Harvard's lack
of one was incredible. She repeated something she had said at Boston
College—that feminist theology was "the next great revolution" in theology and religion. "Next" seemed surprisingly modest to me since the
revolution was well under way. Several years passed before it occurred to
me that she could not have been as confident as she seemed, which was a
clue to "next." For feminist theology barely existed anywhere in the mid-
1970s, and even Ruether, for all her books and speaking engagements,
had almost no experience of teaching it.

My Divinity School classmate John Rolander, who also studied at the Business School, had a job as a superintendent of an apartment building owned by renowned architect Eduardo Catalano. I filled in for Rolander for two weeks while he took a Christmas vacation, which yielded a job offer. Mr. Catalano asked me to maintain an apartment building he was converting to condos on 9 Chauncy Street in Cambridge, near Harvard Law School. Swiftly I was delivered from the midnight shift and its dreary exhaustion. I had regretted that paddleball was little known in Boston. Now, restored to normal hours, I became a runner, taking ninety minute runs up and down the magnificent Charles River and around Fresh Pond. Two of our condo buyers were incoming law students Winthrop Gardner Minot and Spencer Abraham. Win was a New England blueblood by any of his names, later going into corporate law; Spencer came up from an immigrant business-family background in East Lansing, Michigan to become a conservative Republican U.S. Senator. Both were skittish that the guy who shoveled their parking lot and fixed their plumbing was a fellow student, but I was thrilled to have a job providing an apartment and discretionary time.

My family seized this opportunity in the summer of 1975 by driving out to my two-room flat. They were joyous and joyously received. They had begun to take lake vacations not involving the UP, a lifestyle change made possible by my mother's work as a legal secretary, but this was my first time with any of them on a non-UP vacation. They chortled that I owned a single fork, spoon, knife, plate, and bowl, using the oven only to warm up leftover grinders, otherwise called heroes or hoagies on my next two stops. I took them to Fenway Park and through the Freedom Trail, exhausting my sparse knowledge of Boston cultural sites. This was the fabulous Boston Red Sox summer in which Fred Lynn and Jim Rice were rookies. Even my diehard Detroit Tigers family enjoyed the magic of that Red Sox summer.

One night it was time for the secret: Andy had disappeared that spring, made his way to Grandma Hank's house, and tried to kill himself by consuming a bottle of pills. He and my mother pulled me aside to tell me that he had narrowly escaped dying. I was shocked, fighting back tears. It terrified me to think that he had nearly died, but I struggled to keep my composure, aware that an overreaction might trigger him. I told him that I knew something about wanting to kill yourself, because

I had felt that way many times. He was surprised by this news, but also curious, asking, what did you do? I blurted out the truth, lacking the time to think about it: whenever I got close to it, I remembered that I should first give sunny California a try. Maybe my longtime fantasy about moving to California meant something. Maybe he had a similar fantasy that could work for him?

HDS theologian Harvey Cox enlisted me in his inspired idea for a new course on Tillich. Andover Library at HDS possessed Tillich manuscripts from the 1920s that had not been translated into English, though some were currently being translated. Harvey asked me to read whatever Andover had in the basement as preparation for enrolling in his course. Few Americans besides James Luther Adams knew much about Tillich's religious socialist writings of the 1920s. We were overdue for courses on Tillich that didn't focus wholly on his American career. I befriended Harvey by saying yes, poring over the Andover manuscripts, conversing with him about them, and recruiting him to DSOC. Harvey gave sparkling lectures explicating Tillich's conception of religious socialism, sometimes calling on classmate Ron Marstin or me for commentary. Tillich astutely contended that Marx's critique of commodity fetishism is the best part of Marxism, and that socializing the economy is not the essence of socialism. Socialism must replace the predatory will to power of capitalism with a liberating spiritual ethos; otherwise it merely rationalizes alternative forms of hubris, power worship, and dehumanization. Harvey and I agreed that *that* was Tillich at his best.[16]

In December 1976 my four impacted wisdom teeth had to come out, so my mother flew out to be with me for the surgery. We had a lovely day in Boston interspersed with a Lina Wertmüller film, and I bought my first bottle of bourbon, wisely informed that I would need it. The procedure went badly, lasting twice as long as expected. For five days I consumed only broth and bourbon. John and Robin came for visits, bantering easily with my mother, to my delight. That week I read *Up from Communism: Conservative Odysseys in American Intellectual History* (1975), by John Patrick Diggins, and discovered that I loved this genre, a fusion of political and intellectual history. The story that Diggins superbly told was the 1940s forerunner of the neoconservative drama currently playing out. All four of the figures that he discussed—Max Eastman, John Dos Passos, Will Herberg, and James Burnham—had moved straight from the political Left to the political Right without passing through liberalism. I was so enthused about this book that I couldn't stop talking about it, never mind that my mouth was carved up and I was supposed to rest. At week's end my mother flew home, and John undertook his comprehensive exams, which at Harvard are taken together in a two-hour block. Theologian Richard R. Niebuhr, one of John's examiners, declared, "We believe that you have done very well." John was ecstatic, we went out for ice cream to celebrate, and it struck me that it took only a few words of understated commendation from these professors to thrill us.[17]

When I returned home from the ice cream, the phone was ringing. My mother was on the other end, crying: "Honey, we've lost Andy. They say he killed himself, with the shotgun." Blackout. I remember nothing of the next ninety minutes. "They say" registered my mother's disbelief, but I don't know if I caught it. I must have called John or Robin, because they came, as did my boss Deborah Forsman, who came with Mr. Catalano, who pressed three $100 bills into my hand for the flight. I also remember clutching the bourbon. The following morning, I had my first solid food in a week, a bit of chili on the flight, and arrived home.

Eric had come home from school to find Andy blown apart outside his bedroom in the basement. We sat in the spot where shots had been fired into his chest and head. My father wept, a surreal sight to me. Eric was frozen in traumatized silence. I learned that Greg had flipped his car on the state highway racing home; we nearly lost Greg the same day as Andy. Some of our questions assumed a suicide premise, which my mother vehemently disputed, which stymied what could be asked or said.

We stared at each other with a mute realized terror. Andy had sold small quantities of pot for a dealer from Saginaw, had been caught by the police officer who lived in our neighborhood, and had identified the dealer to the police. Then he feared for his life, telling my mother that the dealer was going to kill him. She had come home at lunchtime to urge him not to miss a job interview. At noon, Andy had been fine. Two hours later he was shot twice. There was evidence of a physical struggle, with broken light fixtures and damaged furniture; then the police compounded the damage by ripping apart ceilings and closets in search of nonexistent drugs. They called his death a suicide, which kept the lid on their investigation of the Saginaw drug ring. A few months later, the police got the bust that Andy's testimony enabled. My brothers and I never compared notes on who believes the suicide story—one measure of the fraught trauma that has gripped my family ever since.

For two months I stayed with my family in this nightmare state, through the funeral, the cards from friends and relatives, the evenings of poring over photograph albums with my mother, and the searing recollections of Andy's life. All those years that she poured herself out for him had come to this cruel ending. My brothers had conflicted memories of Andy's impact upon them, but my mother's feelings trumped everything for us, so it took many years for the memories to trickle out. Our tenuous Catholicism came to an end. My mother was done with church observance and God, my father and brothers followed her lead, and Christmas became a memory of the catastrophe of December 1976.

We had never been a family that discussed religion, unless Wilbert Schremp came for Thanksgiving or Christmas dinner. He was married to my mother's younger sister Lorraine, managed a chain of evangelical Protestant bookstores, and adopted a succession of fundamentalist and conservative evangelical theologies. Will was a restless seeker without realizing it, as I told him. For many years he believed there must be one true form of Christianity; he just hadn't found it. Meanwhile my family dropped its nominal religion. Any kind of God-talk, in our situation, would have felt boorishly offensive. I sympathized with this feeling without adopting it. My spiritual temperament had led me to a Schleiermacher-Tillich-MLK worldview that I had no desire to relinquish. Growing up tenuously Catholic in a spiritual wasteland had inoculated me from wanting to be free of religion. At the same time, I realized that the intellectual theologies that fed me were utterly foreign and meaningless to my family.

We made furtive attempts to look ahead. Greg was at Delta College, Mike was at Midland High School, and Eric was at Northeast Intermediate. Greg whisked Eric into his extroverted gang of game-playing, party-going friends, looking out for him. Ken Baynes filled in for me at 9 Chauncy Street while I began to realize that I needed to be alone. Staying in Midland was out of the question, but so was returning to Cambridge, because I had friends there. I didn't want to be with people who knew I was suffering. I especially didn't want to talk about it, so I had to be among people who didn't know me. I called Union Theological Seminary on the phone and was put through to the acting dean of the faculty,

Robert Handy, who told me not to worry about transcripts or any such thing. Just come, he said; we have a place for you.

A week later I flew back to Cambridge and packed my books into a U-Haul. Ken took my job and I drove to 3041 Broadway in New York City, beholding the picturesque Collegiate Gothic buildings by which Union marked its kinship with Oxford and Cambridge, not Wittenberg or Paris. I unloaded my books in a second-floor room of McGiffert Hall, deposited the U-Haul downtown in Chelsea, took my first subway ride on the 1-train back to Union, and met the kindly Dr. Handy, who turned my hodgepodge of Harvard theology and philosophy courses into two years of Union transfer credits. He decreed unilaterally that Union's Master of Divinity requirements in preaching, fieldwork, and practical theology could be waived, but I would need to load up on biblical studies and take some church history. That was fine with me, because Raymond E. Brown taught Bible at Union and Handy taught church history. If I could keep my brain occupied with distributive requirements while the rest of me shut down in reclusive depression, so be it.

HDS dean Krister Stendahl was an iconic figure in theological education. He had swung Christian Testament scholarship away from its conception of Paul as an angst-ridden individual struggling with his conscience, and later served as bishop of Stockholm in the Church of Sweden. During my first year at HDS, Stendahl had taken a sabbatical to write the Anchor Bible commentary on Paul's letter to the Romans. When he returned, Stendahl said he had read enough of Brown's massive work on the gospel of John to decide that if that was the new model of an Anchor commentary, he would not be writing the commentary on Romans. Brown's encyclopedic command of the history of biblical interpretation raised the bar on what constitutes a Bible commentary. He extensively summarized what scholars said before him while delivering his own strong, clear, cogent analyses and judgments. His classes were showcases of exegesis and interpretation, always sprinkled with a literature review.[18]

Ray was an orthodox Roman Catholic priest (Sulpician) who preached on weekday mornings across the street from Union at Corpus Christi parish. I heard him preach many times on weekday mornings before hearing him lecture the same morning. He invited me to his apartment, accepted that I didn't talk about myself, and told me what it was like for him in his early career, a priest ordained in 1953 who lacked any inkling that Vatican II would occur. The first Catholic theologians to get an exemption from the anti-modernist encyclicals of Leo XIII and Pius X were biblical scholars. In 1943, Pius XII's encyclical *Divino afflante Spiritu* called for new translations of the Bible into vernacular languages using early manuscripts instead of the Latin Vulgate, which legitimized textual criticism, permitting use of the historical-critical method within boundaries drawn by Catholic doctrine. Ray said he clung for over a decade to *Divino afflante Spiritu*. It was just enough to legitimize his scholarship, until Vatican II issued the dogmatic constitution *Dei verbum* in 1965, which opened the door to a non-inerrancy doctrine of biblical infallibility: Scripture is infallible for its saving purpose, not in its reportage of incidental details. The first volume of Ray's historic *Gospel According to John* came out the following year.[19]

Form criticism, a method developed by German scholars Hermann Gunkel, Martin Noth, Martin Dibelius, and Rudolf Bultmann, classifies units of scripture into distinct literary patterns such as poetry, proverbial saying, legend, and the like, investigating the oral transmission of each type to identify the original genre. Redaction criticism focuses on the process by which editors shape texts to achieve distinct theological or ideological purposes. German scholars Günther Bornkamm, Hans Conzelmann, and Willi Marxsen developed the redaction critical method of comparing accounts, analyzing recurrent motifs and themes, and dissecting editorial word choices and styles. In the classroom Ray paid due respect to form critics but specialized in redaction criticism, often finding the hand of a redactor in the most innocuous-looking text. The latter discoveries could be unsettling. A few times they took my breath away, as I thought: "Oh my God, it's all made up. It's fiction all the way down." But there was Ray, at the lectern in his clerical collar, delivering another load of editorial redaction, while prizing his Catholic orthodoxy and the *imprimaturs* that bishops stamped on his books. In the Society of Biblical Literature, which he served as president during my year at Union, Ray occupied the middle ground, exactly where he wanted to be.

I was a sponge for his immense learning, appreciating that he loved the work. I kept to myself during quiet evenings in the library, took a job at an educational institute for food money, audited lectures by Cone and visiting theologian Gustavo Gutiérrez, and showed up for meetings and actions called by New York DSOC. Cone had recently published his major theological work, *God of the Oppressed* (1975), which responded to critics of his early work and surprisingly adopted MLK's doctrine of redemptive suffering. Gutiérrez had founded Latin American liberation theology on the argument that theologians must privilege the questions and experiences of oppressed people of faith. Acts of solidarity and praxis come first; liberation theology is secondary reflection shaped by the voices of oppressed people. One day, Gustavo told his class that he had spent the past week reading Walter Rauschenbusch, a revelation to him—why don't you Americans talk about this American treasure? That emboldened me to approach him after class, telling him what Rauschenbusch meant to me. To me, Gustavo was the Rauschenbusch of our time, with the difference that Gustavo inaugurated a theological revolution that spoke to the condition of millions in the Global South.[20]

In October 1977, Robin Lovin attended a conference in mid-town, knocked on my door, and introduced me to Cornel West, who had joined the Union faculty the previous year at the age of twenty-three. I had previously seen Cornel holding forth to a sidewalk crowd at Harvard but had not met him. He had grown up in Sacramento, California, and heard the gospel at Shiloh Baptist Church. He cut his teeth politically at Black Panther meetings, admired Malcolm X and MLK, was hooked by Kierkegaard's struggle with melancholia and mortality, and sailed through Harvard in three years. He entered the doctoral program in philosophy at Princeton, studying under Richard Rorty and Sheldon Wolin, and adopted Rorty's pragmatic historicism. Wolin persuaded him to drill into the Hegelian Marxist background of the Frankfurt school, so Cornel started with a dissertation on British neo-Hegelian T. H. Green. At Union he switched to the Aristotelian aspects of Marx's thought and switched again to the ethical values underlying Marx's critique of capitalism and morality, meanwhile politely enduring critics who told him he didn't deserve his faculty position. Cain Hope Felder, later a prominent biblical scholar, was a leading chastiser of Cornel; church historian James Washington, the dearest friend Cornel ever made in the academy, was his rock and ally. In my room, Cornel headed straight for the Kant and Hegel section. He pulled down the brand-new English edition of Hegel's *Phenomenology* translated by A. V. Miller, remarked on my marginal scribblings, and asked, "Is it any good?" He meant the translation, not the *Phenomenology.* "Yes," I said, "it's wonderful, so much better than Baillie, though Miller doesn't understand the master-slave parable; he thinks it's pro-colonial apologetics." Cornel burst out laughing and I thought, "Thank you, Robin; I have met Cornel West." I knew I would savor the memory for a long time, with no thought that I would ever climb anywhere near Cornel's world.[21]

Mike Harrington spoke at Columbia that year to promote his book *The Vast Majority* (1977), which drew a good crowd but hardly any new members for DSOC. I was surprised and Mike was used to it. He did not ask why I had turned up in New York; I was relieved that I didn't have to tell him, or anyone at DSOC. In those years, DSOC was a player in New York City politics and in mid-term national Democratic Party politics, compensating for its tiny membership by attracting high achievers in the unions, the academy, social activism, and the Democratic Party. We were in the Democratic Party because we had internalized the humiliation of the Norman Thomas years. We accepted Mike's vision of a realigned Democratic Party, a progressive labor party in disguise, where we worked on the left wing of possibility. Two things enabled us to play an outsized role in the party: We were better than liberals at defending the welfare state, and we had major union leaders: American Federation of State, County and Municipal Employees (AFSCME) national president Jerry Wurf, AFSCME New York president Victor Gotbaum, UAW president Doug Fraser, and Machinists president Bill Winpisinger. Mike was proud that he recruited them to democratic socialism. For years afterward, when someone at a National Board meeting declared that we should move out of New York City, I smiled at the naivete of believing it was possible. Many DSOC leaders could not imagine living anywhere else, and Mike was one of them.[22]

Jimmy Carter had won the White House just as the post-World War II economic boom ran out and the bill came due for years of farming and factory overproduction. Factories retooled for computerized production while coping with unsold inventories. The Organization of Petroleum-Exporting Countries (OPEC) pulled off an oil embargo, the workforce changed from blue to white collar, and standard Keynesian tools no longer flattened economic cycles to keep the economy on a steady growth course. DSOC and the labor movement seethed that Carter did almost nothing to stem a tidal wave of layoffs, plant closings, and union busting. Mike despaired over Carter's bad luck and failure but realized that both reflected the structural crisis of the welfare state. Rational-choice Marxism had its heyday during this period, explaining the combination of stagnation and inflation that blighted the Carter years. G. A. Cohen, John Roemer, and Jon Elster described welfare state capitalism as a structural conflict in which capitalists, state managers, and workers rationally maximize their material interests. State managers provide public services and impose regulations up to the point that capitalists allow, but capitalists have the upper hand because the legitimacy of the managers depends on the health of the economy. State power is exercised within class configurations that condition how it is exercised. Mike resisted the vogue of rational-choice Marxism because it tied the interests and behavior of classes and state managers to capitalist structures. Rational-choice theory was great for importing Marxism into the academy, but it stripped Marxism of its distinct power—dialectic, the new reality trying to burst forth from the tensions of the class struggle.[23]

Political economist James O'Connor, in *The Fiscal Crisis of the State* (1973), was more helpful to us. He argued that the growth of the state sector is a cause of the expansion of monopoly capital and an effect of its expansion. The state sector causes monopoly industries to expand, *and* the state expands as an effect of monopoly growth. As technology advances and production becomes specialized, big firms swallow small ones, creating an economy that is much more difficult to regulate, facilitate, support, clean up, and bail out than the economy of smaller enterprises it replaced. Against conservatives, O'Connor showed that the growth of the state is indispensable to the expansion of capitalism, especially the monopoly industries. Against liberals, he denied that the expansion of monopoly industries inhibits the growth of the state.

As monopoly capital grows, so do social expenses. The more that social capital grows, so does the monopoly sector. The more the monopoly sector grows, the more the state expends on social expenses of production. O'Connor argued that this accumulation of social capital and social expenses is a contradictory process yielding the fiscal crisis of the modern state. The state socializes capital costs without appropriating the social surplus. Welfare state capitalism is about capitalists socializing their losses and keeping the profits. The fiscal crisis of the state is the upshot of the structural gap between state expenditures and state revenues.[24]

This analysis and a similar Germany-based account by Claus Offe got us through the 1970s. Marx famously described the democratic state under capitalism as the executive committee of the bourgeoisie. Offe and Harrington said this is a true insight into the function of the state under late capitalism, where the state plays the indispensable role of articulating a unifying national interest and ideology that transcends all business rivalries. In the U.S. the state sustains the functional illusion that all Americans have equal opportunity, freely choose their work, and freely choose their rulers. We Harrington-socialists refused to follow O'Connor on one point, believing that he exaggerated the co-optation of the organized working class. O'Connor said that monopoly capital had completely bought off the unions. Autoworkers, steelworkers, and other big unions had no place in the next Left; any plausible resistance to capitalism must rely on alliances of teachers and administrators, transport workers and transit users, welfare workers and welfare recipients, and the like. We refused to believe it, though we recognized that the case for fatalistic resignation was very strong. The game is rigged, and the welfare state is deeply implicated in it. But Mike insisted that the welfare state is more dialectical and complex than O'Connor said. It mattered that progressive unions existed. Almost nothing that the democratic Left wants in the economic arena is achievable without them. Universal health insurance, price controls on oligopolies, quality education, full employment, redistribution of wealth and income, and a minimum guaranteed income are out of reach if big labor rests content with sharing the spoils of monopoly capitalism.[25]

Running in Central Park was almost as enjoyable for me as the Charles River had been, just before running became a mass activity. It stunned me, years later, when I ran my old routes in Central Park alongside hundreds of others. New York City was battered, dangerous, and reeling in 1977, but all of it was new and interesting to me. I often took the subway to some distant site and ran home, learning the city by running through it. Sometimes I ran past huge piles of rubble, city blocks lacking a single building that hadn't been torched. One night the lights went out. By the time that I gingerly descended the stairs at Columbia's Butler Library, I could see buildings on fire and stores being pillaged. New York had careened far out of control, but I understood why my DSOC comrades loved the city; I loved it too. At the end of my year at

Union, I ransacked the Columbia philosophy and religion departments for a primary reader of my thesis on the Kantian basis of Hegelian idealism. Philosopher of religion James Alfred Martin Jr. mercifully came to my rescue, urging me to publish an article version featuring the Henrich arguments. UTS Methodist theologian Christopher Morse, my second reader, was intrigued by my quasi-Barthian glosses at the end, and skeptical of my solidarity organizer identity. He said he doubted that a person who thought constantly about Kant, Hegel, Tillich, and Barth did not have an academic calling.

Had I stayed for another degree at Union and Columbia, I would have done it with Martin, Morse, Cone, and West. But I identified Union with the trauma that brought me there, needing to make a new beginning somewhere else. My frightening school debt was ironically a reason to enroll somewhere, putting off the financial reckoning. Princeton Theological Seminary was nearby, philosopher Diogenes Allen was on the faculty, and enrolling at Yale Divinity School would have required me to borrow twice as much as at PTS, so in January 1978 I rented a U-Haul in Chelsea and drove through a snowstorm to Princeton, hustling the van back to Chelsea in time for the one-day rate. That night I lay awake in my bare former room in McGiffert Hall, vowing to join a church, perhaps an Episcopal church, get on an ordination track, find a job in organizing, and break out of my loneliness: "It's my own fault that I'm so lonely."

The Episcopal hunch rested on no personal acquaintance whatsoever aside from reading William Temple, and I barely paid off the U-Haul, needing a job as fast as possible. I landed one at Princeton Hospital, working the midnight shift on weekends and three weekdays, where my first task was to insert the deceased body of a three-hundred-pound man into a freezer. Working on weekends and lacking a car thwarted my church search, especially since the Episcopal congregation across the street from the seminary wouldn't take me. At the seminary, Allen was my first faculty mainstay, telling me that I should have mastered Leibniz before busting my head on Kant and Hegel. Unlike Kant, who went off on his own, Leibniz reconciled modern philosophy with Plato, Aristotle, the Scholastics, and Renaissance humanism.

Allen justly taught that Leibniz was the greatest of the rationalist Descartes-Spinoza-Leibniz trio. Descartes held that the essence of body is extension, so matter is infinitely divisible. Spinoza was a sublime cosmic materialist and pantheist lacking the mathematical genius of Leibniz. Leibniz grounded metaphysics on the principles of contradiction and sufficient reason: a proposition cannot be true and false at the same time, and everything has a reason (there is no effect without a cause). These two rational foundations yielded, for Leibniz, the principles that God always acts for the best, the predicate in all true affirmative propositions is always included in the subject, two things that share all properties are identical, and there is an actual infinity in things. Allen said modern philosophers and theologians would have done better to adopt Leibniz's harmonious Lutheran rationalism than to impale themselves on Kantian problems. He favored Anglican neo-Thomist Austin Farrer among recent thinkers and sought to train Presbyterian seminarians to think like Farrer and Leibniz.[26]

Everything that Allen taught was more philosophical than many PTS students thought was necessary, and he could be tough on them. There was seminary lore about him throwing erasers at students and imploring them to think for once. Allen urged me to brush aside Kant and start over; he also exhorted me to take no courses with liberation theologian Richard Shaull, controversial at PTS for turning radical. I was steeped, however, in Latin American liberation theology, and Shaull was the one North American whose name was all over it, having served as a Presbyterian missionary in Colombia, taught theology in Campinas, Brazil, and co-authored with Gutiérrez a state-of-the-art text, *Liberation and Change* (1977).[27]

I bonded with Dick as soon as we met. We had Left politics and solidarity organizing in common, and a friendship with Gustavo. Dick described his life as a succession of shattered dreams. He had been a PTS graduate and missionary who believed his nation's rhetoric about being a champion of democracy and freedom. Later he joined a forerunner of the liberationist base communities in Campinas, still believing that the United States could be an ally to social justice struggles in Brazil. By the time of Brazil's military coup in 1964, it appalled him that he had ever believed that U.S. American power might benefit anyone in Brazil except the economic and political elite. Returning to the United States, Dick realized that he could have known better all those years ago if he had paid attention to the oppression of Black Americans. Now he was near the end of his career, and deeply alienated. Dick offended PTS administrators and faculty by urging students to renounce their dreams of success in a corrupt society and church. I was striving not to be prematurely alienated, so most of our conversations revolved around what is pointless and what is not. DSOC, he thought, was probably pointless; too many professors and high-brass union leaders there.

Theologian Daniel Migliore and social ethicist Gibson Winter taught at PTS. I luxuriated in Dan's wonderfully detailed lectures on Barth's *Church Dogmatics*, appreciating that he guided Princeton students through the intricacies of Barth's theology. Gib had come from the University of Chicago Divinity School to build up social ethics at PTS, having written a landmark text in the field, *Elements for a Social Ethic* (1966). I audited his course on liberationist political theologies, which he based on Spanish theologian Alfredo Fierro's recent book *The Militant Gospel* (1977). I liked and respected Gib very much; years later my one regret about my PTS years was that I didn't spend more time with him. But he had entered his third phase by 1978, fashioning an arcane theory of symbolic hermeneutics based on the hermeneutical theorizing of Paul Ricoeur and Hans-Georg Gadamer. I didn't want to tell Gib that I preferred his phase-one work on church and society, and his phase-two work on reuniting social ethics and social theory, to his current fixation. So we met occasionally for lunch and shoptalk, and I majored in an unexpected field.[28]

The special teacher at PTS was psychologist of religion James E. Loder. I had no real interest in his field. Once at a DSOC meeting in Manhattan, someone asked if anyone knew of a good therapist. No one said yes, and a few of us chuckled self-consciously; we're solidarity organizers who feel we're at war with the navel-gazing culture of self-obsession. But Loder was said to be really good, don't miss your chance to take him. I saw it immediately. For the first class, he assigned Kierkegaard's *Point of View for My Work as an Author* (1859) but said nothing about Kierkegaard. We were there to study transformation, he said—a word morphing like a butterfly out of its cocoon-like biblical word, metamorphosis, the rooted true form, as distinguished from the mask, a false form. Transformation is about a change into true form. Loder admired the specificity of the behavioral sciences and the willingness of theology to risk ontological statements about human nature. He proposed to draw upon both fields to describe the nature of the human spirit and the work of the Holy Spirit in human experience. The following week there was finally a word about Kierkegaard, who said the point of his vast authorship was to provoke and explore the inner contradictions in his readers, vanishing afterward to let them find their own truth before the Truth.[29]

That described Loder's project and his debt to Kierkegaard. He had grown up in a non-religious family in Lincoln, Nebraska, cherishing his father, a humanistic high school principal, and his mother, an artist, both of whom puzzled over Loder's metaphysical streak. He graduated from Carleton College in Northfield, Minnesota in 1953 with a degree in philosophy, enrolled the following year at PTS to become a Presbyterian minister, and fixed on Athens (reason) versus Jerusalem (faith). His father died and Loder had his first searing encounter with "the Void," as he later called the relentless drive of existence toward nothingness. In despair he called God to do something, and soon felt a warm flow of liquid heat rising through his body, his first such spiritual experience. He picked up Emil Brunner's book *The Scandal of Christianity* and devoured it, not so much reading it as recognizing the spirit of it. Every Loder student knew this story, and the maxim from Martin Luther that Loder attached to it: theologians are made not by studying books, "but by living and dying and being damned."[30]

After seminary he undertook clinical training at the Menninger Foundation and earned a doctorate in 1962 in philosophy of religion at Harvard, writing a dissertation on Freud and Kierkegaard on religious consciousness. Freud represented Athens and psychoanalysis, and Kierkegaard represented Jerusalem and faith. Loder's former Christian Education teacher at PTS, D. Campbell Wyckoff, lured him back to PTS, never mind that he had no degree in Christian Education. Whatever he was putting together would be good for Christian Education. Loder judged that Wyckoff's field could use a strong dose of Kierkegaard. The kindly Wyckoff and his equally revered colleague at PTS, Freda Gardner, taught the foundational courses, leaving Loder free to cook his stew of psychoanalysis, Kierkegaard, theology, social theory, and theories of language and culture. From the beginning he had strong ideas and a loner style, attracting large enrollments in courses that nobody had to take and which many complained were impossible to understand. For all the complaints, they kept coming for the show.[31]

Loder's second transforming experience occurred in 1970 on the New York State throughway in a camper driving north toward Albany, in the company of his wife, Arlene, and daughters Kim and Tamara. Near Kingston he spotted two women struggling to change a tire by the side of the highway. He crawled under their car to help with the jack, a sleeping truck driver crashed into the car, and Loder was crushed and dragged under it. Arlene rushed to the front of the car, prayed before momentarily losing consciousness, pulled on the bumper, and the car lifted high enough for Loder to scramble out. He had five broken ribs and a punctured lung, and his thumb was ripped off. But he felt a surge of life rushing through him. It reminded him how much he loved his daughters and Arlene; amid a chaotic scene on I-87, he told them not to worry, "This has a purpose." Afterward, he tried for two years to return to his book manuscript correlating Jean Piaget's structuralism and Maurice Merleau-Ponty's phenomenology and failed. Something in his psyche refused to be repressed—the memory of the life that poured into him after the accident. This life, he had felt, was not his own. His well-being came from some source beyond his natural strength. He was being lived by a gracious Power exceeding the power of the accident to harm or kill him. Finally, Loder realized that he needed to teach and write about *that*, in something like the spirit *of* his experience. When I got to PTS, he had been doing it for five years.

"We're going to really pray in here," he told classes. Loder would really do so, taking us up and down the oscillations of his inner life. He riffed on his canon of Kierkegaard, Freud, and Piaget no matter the subject, and favored Barth, Barthian theologian Thomas F. Torrance, and Anglican philosophical theologian John Macquarrie when he waxed theological. Many students, not grasping why Loder loved Kierkegaard, puzzled that he preferred the atheist Freud over the religion-friendly Carl Jung. Loder judged that Jungian spirituality sacralizes normal human development, so it isn't saving. Normal human development is a road to despair, ruin, and hell. What we get from normal productivity is approval. What we need is love, to be transformed to true form, which cannot be earned. On Loder's view, Jung's spiritualization of the unconscious warded off the Void, blocking the Holy Spirit. Freud, at least, compels readers to confront the meaningless absurdity of their lives.[32]

He began to call me out for comments on philosophical and theological points. This is how most PTS students who learned of my existence did so, except for the activists I befriended in the South African divestment campaign at the university. Loder labored on a sprawling, disjointed, oversized manuscript titled "Transformations of the Human Spirit." It ran more than a thousand pages, a mass of rambling headlong brilliance and too many frameworks. One day he lugged it to class and plopped it on my desk in front of fifty students. "Maybe you can find the book in here," he said. We had weekly meetings and I told him there were two books in there, and perhaps three, depending on his willingness to focus the first one on his argument about experiences of transformation within the dynamics of human development.

"Transformations of the Human Spirit" was too unwieldy to be a book, but everyone who took Loder's courses knew what mattered to him: his account of the four dimensions of human experience and his theme that experiencing the Holy One creates the self as spirit. He took from Macquarrie the semi-Heideggerian conception of being as the implicit assumption behind all that is—that which is so universal that it cannot be classified *and* is so close to us that it cannot enter explicit awareness. We cannot talk about being without shrinking it to the units and structures of grammar, which renders it as a being among others, so we must read "being" metaphorically. Loder set aside the investigation of being-itself, working up to it through the four dimensions of human being—environment, selfhood, the possibility of not being, and the possibility of new being. The environment comprises a lived composition, all possible worlds taken collectively, and God's re-composition of it, which Loder distinguished respectively as "world," *world*, and *World*. The self transcends the embodiment of being human to repeatedly re-compose its lived "world." Both dimensions of human being are weak and tenuous compared to the possibility of annihilation, the Void of nothingness toward which all experiences of nothingness point. We experience new being—the Holy—when being is explicitly manifest as being-itself.[33]

Loder ran long on the psychological dynamics of building up and losing the capacity to compose a world, the situational context in which transformation occurs. He had two lodestars on the self, Kierkegaard and Wilder Penfield, a neurosurgeon who founded the Montreal Neurological Institute. Penfield induced memory recall during surgery by electrically stimulating the temporal lobes of subjects. He discovered that when he touched a part of the brain that made a subject move a limb or recall a childhood experience, the subject would say, "You did that, *I* didn't." His research yielded the concept of a memory tape, but Penfield could not find the "I" with his electrical probe. Loder invoked Penfield's research as evidence of the dual nature of the self-relatedness packed into the symbol, "I." The self *is* a body and *has* a body. To the extent that it says "I," it is embodied, but to the extent that it creates new meanings, or declares, "You did that, *I* didn't," it *has* a body which it uses to express its transcendent purposes. Penfield did not philosophize about the self, or why it is not an entity. For that, Loder leaned on Kierkegaard, who reasoned that the self is a *relationship* entirely unique in relation to its worlds. The self as a positive relationship is a relation that relates itself to itself, knowing *within* and together *with* oneself. To Loder, breaking open the mind-brain connection was essential to being human. *Everything* in life, he said, is meaningless and absurd, devoured by the Void, unless, as Kierkegaard said, the self becomes grounded in the Power that posits it. All proximate forms of nothingness, including harm, absence, loneliness, and death, drive toward the Void. The self becomes *itself* only when it expresses being-itself as that which enables flourishing.[34]

The two-dimensional world that ordinary human development strives so intently to sustain comes to nothing whatsoever. Loder pressed hard on the point that the meanings by which we live in a two-dimensional world are meaningless and absurd. Every self is a body of death headed toward death in a material universe that is itself destined to silence. The Void pervades the self and the world, a nihilating reversal of creation vaster even than the definitive metaphor of the Void, death. Loder refused to believe that anyone *lives* in three dimensions. French existentialists Jean-Paul Sartre and the early Albert Camus claimed to embrace their nihilistic absurdity but did so too vehemently to be believable. Encounters with the Void, Loder argued, are deadening. To let the Void wash over you is not to write philosophical books about privileging the questions of existence. It is to fall into despair, identifying with an overpowering aggressor. Loder judged that Sartre was too fascinated by the Void to truly identify with it. If Sartre believed, as he claimed, that nothingness haunts being like an unholy ghost, his awed fixation with it was really a negative surrogate for the Holy.[35]

Loder told his personal stories of feeling the presence of the Holy One after his father died and after the truck driver smashed into him. In both cases, the presence of the Spirit re-created his self as spirit, a new spiritual life that expressed and disclosed the inner life of being-itself. He piled up arguments that there is an analogical relationship between the human spirit and the Holy Spirit, the likeness is established by the logic of transformation, and reality is fundamentally relational and bipolar. I helped him lop off entire chapters and hundreds of pages, stressing that nothing we cut would go to waste. Loder kept whittling for two years past my time at PTS, yielding his book *The Transforming Moment* (1981).

He urged me to stay for a second degree at PTS that would convert to advanced standing in the doctoral program. I said there was no reason for me to earn a doctorate because I was not going to be an academic; I was an organizer committed to economic democracy and the abolition of White privilege and male privilege. But I agreed to hang on for another year and degree, working with him. To Loder, that made me persuadable, and someone who should call him Jim. He was formal enough with me that he never asked about my story; our friendship was based on my comprehension and appreciation of his project. I chose an extra year with him with no thought of it leading to anything—whittling his manuscript, joining his doctoral seminar, and befriending his brilliant teaching assistant Laura Inglis and her partner, Peter Steinfeld. Laura, a Gib Winter doctoral advisee and Quaker whom we lost much too soon, was a purer Kierkegaardian than Loder—so pure that I could imagine Kierkegaard not condemning her plans for an academic career. Many years later, teaching Kierkegaard to college students, I thought of Laura, imagined how she would channel Kierkegaard to these students, and flushed with shame at my pitiful efforts.

Princeton had a DSOC group that didn't do anything except talk, so I stayed involved in New York City DSOC. I joined the anti-apartheid campaign at Princeton University calling the university to divest from South Africa, where I befriended my PTS classmate Christian Iosso. We made our first connection by recognizing each other from the seminary as we marched around Nassau Hall in March and April 1978. How Chris and I were alike was obvious from where we were, plus we both grappled constantly with Reinhold Niebuhr arguments. How we were not alike was soon evident: He was extroverted, had grown up in a historic Presbyterian congregation in nearby New Providence, New Jersey, and was very much at home in mainline Protestantism. Meanwhile I tried to join Trinity Episcopal Church, across the street from PTS. My Catholic sensibility was a factor, and I was vaguely aware that Anglicanism somehow had the richest tradition of Christian socialism. Above all, I had devoured William Temple's seminal Anglican work, *Nature, Man, and God* (1934), a synthesis of Logos theology, Hegel, democratic socialism, and philosopher Alfred North Whitehead that enthralled me. I planned to explain all this to the clerics at Trinity Church but was cut off by a secretary who told me that Trinity did not accept PTS students planning to seek ordination. I meekly accepted this disappointing information, which left me stranded in Princeton, since I lacked a car and I worked anyway on Sundays at the hospital. I had only one reason to remain in Princeton for an extra year and degree, Jim Loder. In his office I met Brenda Louise Biggs.[36]

Jim was Brenda's therapist. She was a pistol—irreverent, extroverted, wisecracking, big-hearted, volatile, intense, and opinionated, with a ready laugh, erupting in delight at good jokes and bad ones. She was tiny in size and huge in personality. She smoked three packs of cigarettes per day, cussed like a sailor, called out b-s instantly upon hearing it, had a radiant ebullience, and frankly told her friends that she never found at the seminary the kind of spiritual fellowship that had impelled her to seminary. I had just begun to go on dates, attending two films with two of Brenda's residence hall neighbors, when she asked me outside Jim's office, "Would you like to see another movie?" Our first date was in Brenda's room in Alexander Hall, a television series about Harriet Tubman and the Underground Railroad, *A Woman Called Moses*. It evoked earnest discussion. What would you give your life for? To what are you devoting your life now? We talked all night, telling our stories, and were still talking at breakfast time, so Brenda drove me to her favorite diner on Route One.

She had grown up in the upper middle-class of Bethlehem, Pennsylvania. Brenda spent summers at the country club swimming pool, campaigned for Nixon in 1968, and became an anti-war Democrat in 1970 at Hood College in Frederick, Maryland. As an English major she read depressing novels that repelled her; Brenda vowed that when she got past college she would read no more so-called high literature. Returning to Bethlehem, she taught first grade and burned through what she called "my *Looking for Mr. Goodbar* years." For four years, Brenda was a nurturing teacher by day and a cruiser of rough bars at night, taking home some of the worst guys she met. This phase ended with an abortion, a tentative visit to an evangelical Bible fellowship at First Presbyterian Church of Bethlehem, and her conversion. Two progressive evangelicals who later joined the *Sojourners* community, Ginny and Rob Soley, were ringleaders of the fellowship group. Brenda formed deep friendships with them and found a new life.

Evangelical feminism was then in its heyday, a fledgling wing of evangelicalism boasting young scholars Virginia Ramey Mollenkott, Nancy Hardesty, and Letha Dawson Scanzoni. It was a lodestar for women like Brenda and Ginny who prized the spiritual intensity of evangelical religion and loathed the sexism of evangelical leaders. The way to a better evangelicalism was for women like Brenda to become pastors. Ginny and Rob urged Brenda to accept her obvious pastoral calling, First Presbyterian Church supported her in it, and in 1976, Brenda enrolled at PTS.

She liked and respected most of her professors, yet for two years, PTS was a disappointment to her. It was nothing like the life-changing experience that had propelled Brenda to seminary, falling short of what she expected seminary to be. Biblical criticism drained the Bible of its spiritual power. Theology courses featured arguments that only academics cared about. PTS felt churchy and nerdy to her, a launchpad for smug males with "Big Steeple Pastor" stamped on their foreheads who patronized her. She missed the fellowship she had experienced in the group with Ginny and Rob. Brenda's conversion story elicited shaming glances from classmates, and she nearly quit seminary, but a summer assignment in Clinical Pastoral Education at Rush Memorial Hospital in Chicago reminded her that she had a call to ministry.

Brenda had extraordinary gifts for ministry. Many ministers are too introverted and awkward to be someone you would want to be visited by in the hospital; I later became one of them. Brenda was nothing like that. She breezed into hospital rooms, bantered easily with patients and hospital staff, and teased the patients she knew. Outward-reaching care came naturally to her, as did blunt honesty. When we met, she had just watched the film version of *Looking for Mr. Goodbar* (1977) for the third time, drawn to its bar-cruising protagonist "like a moth to the flame," she said. "It's something I discuss with Loder. And I sure as hell don't call him Jim." Loder, she reported, had said nothing particularly insightful to her, except this: "I just wish your lion and your lamb could lie down together." That was spot-on, which Brenda recited for the rest of her life. With typical Brenda-bluntness, she told me that she had never been attracted to a nice boy and couldn't stand jocks either. Yet near the end of our first date, out on Route One, she declared, "You're going to like my dad. He's a conservative Republican, but he's such a sweetheart."

For the next three weeks I heard a great deal about Anson Biggs and Grace Sorenson Biggs. Anson's family was Scot on his Arnett side and Welsh on his Biggs side. The Biggses were Presbyterians with many civil engineers; Anson's father had worked for the Federal Trade Commission in Washington, DC; and Anson was the youngest of six children, carrying on the family tradition of graduating from the University of Maryland. During World War II, Anson served in the Corps of Engineers in George Patton's Third Army, building and destroying bridges. He came down with tuberculosis and was sent to Fitzsimmons Hospital in Denver, where one of his nurses was Grace Sorenson, an Iowa Lutheran farmgirl whom he married in 1945. Anson was as kindly and conservative as Brenda said, an accomplished patent engineer at Bethlehem Steel whose life was a web of family commitments, professionalism, Lutheran church committees, and civic projects. His steadfast love for his daughter was her emotional rock.

It was painfully otherwise between Brenda and her mother. Like Anson, Grace was the baby of her family, with elderly parents, so she clung tightly to her two brothers and three sisters. There were tragedies in Grace's family past that marked and haunted her. She taught school for five years in Iowa, later worked as a nurse in Denver and Bethlehem, and raised two children, John and Brenda. Brenda waited for me to ask about her mother, replying: "When I was a kid, I had the best mother in the neighborhood. Everyone thought so, including me. Our house was the one they wanted to go to. Today my mother drives me nuts. We fight all the time, and it can get very ugly." She paused, adding: "Of course, you'll have to take my side."

So I was warned. Grace had an anxious, disapproving edge that perpetually triggered Brenda and for many years alienated John from the family. She also worked harder than Anson at making things go right and making me feel welcome. We had a getting-acquainted dinner foursome in Princeton at which Brenda disclosed that I read the *New York Times* every morning and watched the *CBS Evening News with Walter Cronkite* every weekday evening before dinner. She said it with comic Brenda incredulity, but her parents were impressed. They watched Walter Cronkite too; meanwhile Grace and I bonded by swapping hospital midnight-shift stories. Brenda began to join me for the evening news in the TV room at the seminary student center. We watched the fall of the Iranian monarchy and she began to imagine a future with a Lefty intellectual and activist who belonged to no church, lacked middle class manners, and had no comprehensible career plan. Shortly before Brenda and I graduated from PTS, she was ordained to the Presbyterian ministry in a service at First Presbyterian in Bethlehem. The service ran long; afterward we had a four-person receiving line: Brenda, standing with Anson; and Grace, with her arm around me, telling every person who came through: "And now I'd like you to meet my future son-in-law." Later that night, back at the house, Grace said to me, "I will never have a better night than this one." That prediction held up until grandchildren began to arrive.

Brenda and I had dated for four months when we had to decide about marrying. Even that timeframe got squeezed by the demands of applying for positions in the Presbyterian ministry. The first time that we said, "I love you," was the night before I drove Brenda in her car to Lancaster, Pennsylvania, where she interviewed for a ministry position. There were several more interviews spread over her last two months of seminary. We could lament the shortness of our courtship, but that wouldn't change anything. Brenda was heading into the ministry and couldn't show up with me if we were unmarried. She was all-in and adamantly certain, ready to marry me and to begin her ministerial career. She pressed me for a decision, and I was stunned at how quickly my life had changed. I loved her as much as she loved me. This fact alone probably would have carried me to yes, but in my case, it was accompanied by a recognition: meeting Brenda was the best thing that had ever happened to me.

4

ALBANY ACTIVISM

Albany, New York was a blank space to me, a disappointment, and a blessing. It was initially a blank space because First Presbyterian Church in Albany was the one job interview of Brenda's that I had missed. She and Chris Iosso drove there together to interview for the same job, Chris on the chance that Brenda turned it down, which was never a possibility. First Presbyterian was the jewel that Brenda wanted. Albany disappointed me for lacking community organizing, but it became a home of abundant community, friendships, activism, and flourishing for us.

Shortly after Brenda and I graduated from PTS, I received a message at Princeton Hospital that my brother Greg had been in a terrible car accident in Sanford, Michigan. Both drivers were killed, and Greg's heart was punctured. He was rushed to Midland Hospital, where they saved his life by realizing that they couldn't save him, so he was rushed two hours away to Henry Ford Hospital in Detroit, where he barely survived. Brenda and I had planned a sweet summer of moving to Albany and getting married. Instead, I quit my job and flew to Detroit, and she moved by herself to Albany.

There were dreadful days of painful procedures in Detroit, including one where Greg lost twenty pounds of fluid bloat in five minutes. There were grueling days of trying to clear his lungs; on one of them, Brenda's thirtieth birthday, Greg and I watched Jimmy Carter give his derided "malaise" speech and I made a tender birthday phone call. Most nights I slept on the floor of Greg's room—whenever he said, "Please don't leave tonight." I had grabbed only two books on the way to the Newark airport—*The Portable Nietzsche* and *Basic Writings of Nietzsche*. Then I regretted these choices. Nietzsche was as entertaining and brilliant as I expected, but his proto-Nazi celebration of dominating will-to-power repelled me. A decade later I remembered this intense revulsion as two kinds of Nietzsche-quoting deconstruction swept the academy—the extension of Nietzsche's attack on subject-centered reason carried out by disciples of Martin Heidegger and Jacques Derrida, and the ingenious critique of power fashioned by Michel Foucault. Meanwhile in Detroit, there were halleluiah-days when Greg began to walk the floor and tease the nurses and venture outside. He went home in August, and I returned to Princeton to U-Haul my books to Albany, finding myself in a lovely two-room brownstone apartment with high ceilings on Willett Street, down the street from Brenda's congregation. So this is the middle class!

Our tiny August wedding was to consist of Grace and Anson, Brenda's seminary friends Lisa and Billy Darling (officiating), and my friends John McDargh and Ken Baynes. Two days before the wedding, I prevailed on my mother to leave Greg for two days to attend the wedding: "You'll regret it if you don't come." No one in my family had met Brenda, who began her wary dance with my strong-willed mother. Our wedding group had plenty of room around a table at Jack's Seafood Restaurant downtown. The next day we took an afternoon honeymoon to Saratoga, and the following day Brenda headed back to work while I plunged into Albany seeking an organizing position.

The organizing situation was not what I expected of the state capital. Gamaliel and the IAF (Industrial Areas Foundation) had no history in Albany, while PICO (Pacific Institute for Community Organizations) was still a regional outfit in 1979. No group in Albany operated on the community organizing model of multi-congregational activism focused on community interests and building power. My work in DSOC pointed to a possible career in labor organizing, but that would have taken a while, beginning with a job in a unionized enterprise that led to a job in a union hopefully linked to DSOC. There was no DSOC chapter in the Albany region, which had to be remedied, and the leading organizing group aside from public employee unions was NYPIRG, the New York section of Ralph Nader's Public Interest Research Group. It did not appeal to me, radiating an ethos of White, middle-class, Nader-style, consumer politics based on the idealism and availability of college-graduate organizers like me.

I took a job as a teacher in a school for emotionally disturbed youths, the Parsons Child and Family Center. The name felt ironic to me because most of our students were resident wards of the state lacking a family.

We were their family, helping them cope with heartbreaking psychiatric illnesses and the ravages of sometimes horrid parental abuse. On my first day arrival, my boss Brian Aylward was blocking the doorway, restraining a violently acting-out twelve-year-old, pinning him to the floor. There was a lot of screaming and kicking. As I gently stepped around them, I thought, "I'll hang on until lunch, and then slip out this door." Instead, I stayed for three years, until Bishop Wilbur E. Hogg hatched another plan for me. My fellow teacher and friend Clifford Brothers told me sagely that Parsons was evidence that one can grow accustomed to anything with enough practice. He virtually adopted me, reading my first publications and arranging speaking venues for me. The work at Parsons felt brutally difficult to me until I bonded emotionally with my students, too closely in some cases, wanting to adopt two of them. I was lucky to be married to someone who understood the importance of emotional boundaries. Brenda talked me down both times: "We're just starting out, Gary. Try to make a rational decision! Picture our own children!"

She made a splash in Albany with sparkling sermons and her exuberant, direct, wisecracking personality. Growing up in mainline Protestantism enabled Brenda to skillfully navigate its culture. This sense of familiar belonging was invaluable to her because her boss was gone much of the time. Robert C. Lamar was in the last four years of his thirteen-year campaign to unite the two largest Presbyterian denominations—the Presbyterian Church in the United States (mostly Southern) and the United Presbyterian Church in the United States (majority-Northern). The stretch drive of this historic enterprise to create the Presbyterian Church USA put him on the road, often in tandem with his Southern counterpart Randy Taylor. Bob had graduated from Yale Divinity School, taken over at First Presbyterian Albany in 1958, and served as moderator of the United Presbyterian Church in 1974. He was my first exemplar of what mainline Protestantism must have been like in the 1950s, when half the U.S. population was mainline Protestant and the annual conventions of the National Council of Churches (NCC) routinely received page one attention in the *New York Times.*

Bob cast a large shadow in Albany civic life. Ecumenism in Albany was old-style and institutional like the NCC, not the community organizing model, but it crossed the Protestant-Catholic divide. Bob was tall, hulking, personable, and highly able, bristling with Gene Hackman-like masculinity and self-confidence, a skilled orator and French horn player who golfed in the high-70s at the country club. He prized his close friend-ship with Albany Catholic bishop Howard Hubbard, who had served as a street priest in Albany's South End and made bishop in 1977, at the age of thirty-eight. Hubbard's youth and justice-ministry background made him a godsend to the social justice community. The people he appointed to peace and justice ministries organized much of the local activist work related to immigration rights, poverty, the Nestlé boycott, and the religion-labor movement.

I befriended everyone in this network, especially Maureen Casey, Jay Murnane, Liz Nolan, and Brian O'Shaughnessy. Maureen and Liz had personal sway with the bishop through their commission work for the diocese, while Jay and Brian leveraged their clerical standing as priests. We had no inkling of the clerical sexual abuse in the diocese of Albany that later engulfed Hubbard and the diocese. Many years later, Hubbard was forced to resign for decades of quietly recycling predator priests and being accused himself of sexual violations. This outcome was unimag-inable to us in the early 1980s. We were feminists who took for granted that the struggle for feminist reforms in the Catholic Church was a long-term enterprise. The bishop's office was our bedrock ally on core social justice issues that soon included Central American solidarity politics.

The year 1980 set off a fire alarm for the Left. Jimmy Carter had alienated the entire liberal-Left flank of his party, Ronald Reagan won the Republican nomination for president on a far-Right agenda, and U.S. Senator Edward Kennedy challenged Carter for the Democratic nomination. Harrington and Kennedy were close friends who idealized each other, so DSOC went full bore for Kennedy, who ran a strange, timid, vacuous campaign that devastated DSOC and failed to unseat Carter. DSOC refused to slink back to Carter; Mike could not muster his usual appeal about the lesser evil and holding your nose. He was too disgusted with the odd, isolated, tone-deaf Carter to try, and too deflated by how close he came to achieving his fantasy of riding into a Kennedy administration. One month after the election of November 1980 put Reagan in the White House, historian Larry Wittner and I co-founded an Albany chapter of DSOC.

Larry was a young scholar working toward tenure at State University of New York (SUNY-Albany). His first book, *Rebels against War* (1969), a history of the American peace movement from 1941 to 1960, was esteemed on the Left when we founded DSOC. Then he expanded the second edition at both ends, 1933 to 1983, which allowed a book-ending peek at the history we were living. His new partner, Dorothy Tristman, helped us fathom the residual sectarian mentality of the New York Socialist culture we had entered, as Dorothy was a veteran of the Young People's Socialist League. Two months after Larry and I rounded up all the likely Left-liberal types who might join DSOC, my Catholic activist friends and I co-founded a local chapter of the Committee in Solidarity with the People of El Salvador (CISPES).[1]

Salvadoran Catholic Archbishop Óscar Romero had denounced the military dictatorship of General Carlos Humberto Romero in El Salvador, declaring in 1978 that he was ready to sacrifice his life for the redemption of his nation. On March 24, 1980, he was assassinated by a right-wing death squad while saying mass at the chapel of Hospital de la Divina Providencia. On December 2, 1980, Maryknoll Sisters Maura Clarke and Ita Ford, Ursuline Sister Dorothy Kazel, and lay missionary Jean Donovan were raped and murdered by five members of the Salvadoran National Guard. These events convulsed our peace and justice community, and changed it, throwing us into solidarity activism supporting the viciously persecuted people of El Salvador and Guatemala, and in defense of the revolutionary Sandinista government in Nicaragua, where four liberationist Catholic priests held cabinet posts.

Reagan set off the greatest surge of progressive activism since the mid-1960s. He spewed racist attacks on "welfare queens" of his imagination, slashed government aid to the poor, delivered a massive tax cut to the rich and the corporations, heaped an extra increase on Carter's escalated last military budget, and threatened to invade Nicaragua, impelling an alarmed reaction in formerly sleepy churches, unions, and college campuses. I served as president of Albany DSOC while Wittner served as secretary and newsletter editor. Within a year we had a bustling local of 165 members consisting mostly of professors, students, social workers, union officials, and state government bureaucrats. The ethos of Albany DSOC was middle-class, bookish, deeply civil, pro-union, and policy oriented, fostering strong personal and political connections to AFSCME, ACTWU, and the Public Employees Federation.

CISPES was completely different, consisting of young radicals fresh out of college, way-left-of-DSOC academics, and religious activists. I failed to persuade almost anyone in either organization to join the other one. In DSOC, "organizing" meant labor organizing and the political work that we undertook mostly in the left wing of the Democratic Party. In CISPES, labor unions were beyond the pale, except for a couple of us and our Trotskyite faction, and so was the Democratic Party, except for a few of us. A cultural chasm divided DSOC from the Central American solidarity organizations of the 1980s, notwithstanding that DSOC actively opposed Reagan's policies in Central America.

I spoke every week for CISPES, raising medical aid money and contending against Reagan's right-wing policies toward El Salvador and Nicaragua. Albany CISPES had an emergency mentality; Salvadorans were being killed and we felt compelled to stop it. Albany DSOC met once per month and averaged three major events per year. We provided solidarity support for other groups and striking unions but made no attempt to match the intensity of CISPES. My friends in CISPES did not regard DSOC as radical or an ally. We in DSOC reeked, to them, too much of Old Left anti-Communism, with too many tenured professors, public officials, and union bosses. I was reduced almost to begging when my fellow founders of the Social Justice Center in downtown Albany balked at allowing DSOC to join. In DSOC we believed that democratic socialism linked us to all social justice and anti-war struggles. My friends on the Social Justice Center steering committee roundly disagreed, razzing me for months after they barely let DSOC join. To them, DSOC was like the Nuclear Freeze movement and the National Organization for Women—middle class, wonky, and careerist. DSOC, to them, exemplified the New Left maxim that social democrats are not radical.

My friendships within and across these organizations were wondrous blessings to me despite the lack of crossover. I had never lived at so high a pitch, bonding with an exotic brew of personalities. Three young CISPES activists—April Brumson, Darby Penney, and Francie Traschen—and one young peace activist, David Miller, were especially dear friends to me. April had the strongest commitment to Central America of all of us, based on her friendships with Salvadorans and Guatemalans; one of Brenda's later sermons had a wonderful reminiscence about atheist-Lefty April coming forward for Communion at my ordination service. Darby called herself an "urban guerrilla," grumbled that CISPES had too many pacifists, and went on to a productive career as a mental health activist. Francie was our youngest member and best activist, a luminous flower child who could settle a group dispute simply by stating her feelings on the matter. David was a movement workshop leader and consultant with a buoyant personality who bluntly told his Quaker clients that they would never grow beyond their decorous White pacifist culture because they prized it too much.

CISPES burgeoned from the inroads that we made into churches and college campuses. Soon the Sanctuary Movement morphed from being a flank of Central American solidarity activism into a significant enterprise of its own. Brenda enlisted me to teach adult education courses at First Presbyterian, the one part of her job description she didn't like, and at a coalition of downtown churches called the Focus Institute. She observed several times that I was overdue to join a church, just so I didn't join her church. No Episcopal church played any role in local social justice activism. I was crestfallen to discover that Albany had one of the most right-wing, insular, anti-feminist Episcopal dioceses in the country. My activist friends shrugged off this problem as something they took for granted, but William Temple was a lodestar figure to me, so I kept looking for a viable congregation in an Episcopal diocese that was itself deeply alienated from the liberalizing drift of its denomination.

Many clerics had flocked to Albany to avoid having to deal with female clergy. My search for a congregation failed until I entered St. Andrew's Church on North Main Street. Anywhere else in the Northeast, it would have been a mainstream Episcopal congregation. In Albany it was a dissident oasis. The rector of St. Andrew's, Bruce Gray, was a dozen years older than me and a product of nearby Troy, New York. He had studied at a liberal seminary, Episcopal Theological School in Cambridge, Massachusetts, and was enrolled in the Doctor of Ministry program at Virginia Theological Seminary in Alexandria, Virginia. To the extent that Bruce was influenced by any theologian, it was American historical theologian John E. Booty, a gatekeeper of the Anglican *via media* between Catholicism and Protestantism. But there were not many theologians on Bruce's bookshelves. He was happiest when he hung out with firefighters, eventually as chaplain to the Albany Fire Department.

Bruce welcomed me, befriended me, supported my application for ordination candidacy, and encouraged me to bring all my activism and intellectualism to St. Andrew's. He asked me to teach a Wednesday night course on modern theology and was delighted when we had to move it to the sanctuary, growing too big for our classrooms. I introduced my new Episcopalian friends to Paul Tillich, James Cone, Rosemary Radford Ruether, and Jürgen Moltmann, and featured the only two Anglicans in my wheelhouse, Temple and John Macquarrie.

Temple was the foremost Anglican theologian and church leader of the twentieth century, having ended his storied career as Archbishop of Canterbury during World War II. I became an Anglican almost entirely on the strength of his intellectual and spiritual influence on me. He was a neo-Hegelian and a democratic socialist with a Catholic spiritual bent just like me, though he grew up in English castles. He was eloquent, gifted, and spiritually deep, a social justice stalwart, and buoyant, a light to many. In seminary I had been hooked by his magnum opus, *Nature, Man, and God* (1934). Now I bought his corpus of books at the Anglican Bibliopole bookstore outside Saratoga and read them in sequence. Temple's early books refashioned traditional Anglican *logos* theology in Hegelian terms: Spirit is the nature of the Supreme Reality that created all things, a real source and cause of process. The will of Christ is one with the will of God and expressive of it, but not identical with it. Will and personality are ideally interchangeable terms. "Socialism" is a modern name for the Christian conviction that cooperation is the moral law of the divine order.[2]

Temple expounded these themes as an Oxford fellow and cleric on his way to a global stage as an ecumenical leader. *Nature, Man, and God* consisted of the Gifford Lectures he delivered from 1932 to 1934, blending neo-Hegelian theology with the new organic metaphysics of philosopher Alfred North Whitehead, an expert in relativity physics. Whitehead taught that feeling is the essential clue to being and that things are complexes of motions that possess within themselves their own principle of motion. The universe is a creative advance into novelty, and "God" is a name for the ordering factor in the process of creativity. Temple reasoned, with a favorable gloss on Whitehead, that the mind emerges through the process of apprehensions and adjustments that it apprehends. The fact that the world gives rise to minds that apprehend the world tells us something important about the world—there is a deep kinship between mind and the world. The world has a relation of correspondence to mind, something that every rational being experiences in discovering oneself to be an occurrence within the natural process with which one recognizes kinship. Mind and matter, he argued, are related dialectically. Matter does not generate thought, nor does thought generate matter. The world of matter, always a relative flux of forms, lacks a self-explanatory principle, while mind has the principle of purpose or rational choice. Since there is no materialist explanation for the emergence of mind, and because mind contains a self-explanatory principle of origination, it is reasonable to believe that mind contains the explanation of the world-process. If mind is part of nature, nature must be grounded in mind; otherwise, nature could not contain it.[3]

The world-process as such stands in need of explanation—the point at which Temple took leave of Whitehead, who distinguished between God's primordial nature (the universe of creative possibilities, a unified actual entity), and God's consequent nature (the accumulated actualization of the choices of self-actualizing entities, the completion of God's nature into the fullness of physical feeling). Temple denied that God's primordial nature is the explanation of the world-process as the ground of possibility—a claim holding no more explanatory value than to say that the ground of possibility is the ground of possibility. To be sure, Whitehead said beautifully poetic things that sound like Christian theology. His concept of the primordial God might be construed as an impersonal stand-in for the Eternal Word. His concept of creativity might be construed as an impersonal substitute for God the Creator. But Whitehead excluded personality from his description of organism in process, so his lovely description of God as the fellow-sufferer who understands had no basis besides Whitehead's poetic feeling.

Temple conceived the world-process as the medium of God's personal action and God's active purpose as the determinant element in every actual cause. To half believe in God, he said, is pointless. The concept of divine personality must be taken in earnest, conceiving God's purposive Mind as the immanent principle of the world process. The world has an immanent reason, a *Logos*. If this principle is impersonal, it is a principle of logical coherence. If it is personal, it is purposive, moral, spiritual, and a principle of variation, for personality, whether human or divine, is immersed in the world process at the level of immanent reason.

Temple pointed beyond the flux of the world process to the divine personality itself transcendent. God immanent is a principle of adjustment, but God transcendent is eternally self-identical. This dialectic, Temple argued, not Whitehead's scheme of God and world, is at the heart of things. God transcendent is the eternal "I AM" of Exodus 3:14; God immanent is the divine self-expressed in which the world is implicit. I embraced Temple's argument that Chalcedonian orthodoxy merely described the problem of Christology without solving it—how was Christ one person in two natures? Greek theology, Temple said, was paralyzed by its assumed doctrine of substance, so it missed the crucial point that matter is dead while spirit is irreducibly charged with powers of life. Instead of lowering Christology to a claim about the sameness of substance between Christ and God, Christology should operate at a spiritual level, identifying spirit with will. Christ was divine identically, not generically, and was human inclusively, not generically, united to God by sharing God's will. I disliked Temple's idealistic tendency to override the world slaughterhouse of tragedy, suffering, and oppression, but otherwise I treasured his thought and example. If he was an Anglican theologian, let alone the gold standard Anglican theologian, I could ask the diocese of Albany to consider me as an ordination candidate and accept the consequences.[4]

Bruce had dreadful stories about how bad it could get in the Albany diocese, and some of our diocesan insiders at St. Andrews had worse stories, cushioning me for the letdown. But the ordination process begins with a congregation's recommendation of a candidate to the bishop. Our bishop was a saintly, pastoral, high-minded graduate of Brown University and the U.S. Army chaplaincy named Wilbur Hogg. His staunch conservative-traditionalism at St. Luke's Cathedral in Portland, Maine qualified him for the Albany diocese; then he was elected in 1974 for his saintly qualities and his emphasis on bridging the Evangelical versus Anglo-Catholic chasm in Anglicanism. Bishop Hogg was an evangelist on the theme that the rivalry between these two wings of Anglicanism is baleful for the church. The remedy was not the liberal inclusiveness of the Broad Church tradition; it was for the two kinds of orthodoxy within Anglicanism to find common ground in the gospel and the sacraments.

He liked to scrap about theology but was frustrated that his clerics couldn't do it, or at least wouldn't do it with him. He told me so in our first meeting after deciding that he liked me. Nothing in my very public record of solidarity activism put him off. Bishop Hogg said he looked forward to arguing with me about feminism and gay sexuality, and he knew all about my involvement in CISPES and DSOC; no problem. I thought I might zoom through the roof. Not in my wildest fantasy did I imagine this meeting going so well. We met many times afterward, he treated our get-togethers as theology bull-sessions, and I never held back. Bishop Hogg had a sermon in his head for every Sunday of the three-year lectionary cycle. I would ask what was coming the following Sunday, we conducted back-and-forth over his answer and the scholarship we drew upon, and occasionally he would say, "Maybe I need to rethink that one."

The chair of the Commission on Ministry, Fr. Robert Pursel of St. Paul's Church in Troy, similarly befriended me upon assigning himself to me. I was awaiting my first appearance before the commission when he bounded into the hallway, grabbed my hand with both hands, and exclaimed, "Gary, I'm so happy to meet you! Until now, I was the only intellectual in this diocese!" Fr. Pursel was a scholarly Anglo-Catholic Anglophile with a theology doctorate from Trinity College, Toronto. We marched through the canon of Anglican history and theology, meeting once per month for entire afternoons, beginning with Richard Hooker, lingering over the Caroline divines, disposing too swiftly of Joseph Butler, and accelerating through the Oxford Movement and Broad Church liberalism. Most of it was new to me, and Fr. Pursel loved talking about all of it except Butler, whose subtle philosophical mind did not suit him.

For a while he loaned me out to a fellow enthusiast of Caroline moral theology, Fr. Ray Donovan, who reinforced Fr. Pursel's line about the true identity of Anglicanism. On this telling, Lancelot Andrewes pioneered in the 1590s the distinct moral theological ethos rooted in the prayerful spirituality of the Church Fathers that defines true Anglicanism. The Anglican *via media* as expounded by William Laud, Jeremy Taylor, and other divines of the Caroline era was a positive approach of its own, not merely a compromise between the High Church and Low Church wings of the Church of England. I pushed back against abstracting an idealized "Anglicanism" from the history of the Church of England's royal absolutism, racism, and imperialism. Fr. Pursel admonished me to adhere to the "higher things," at least with him, and I risked our friendship by explaining that that was not an option for me. I had come through the door of solidarity activism and was schooled in various strategies of theological whitewash. If I was to be ordained in this tradition, I had to grapple with the blood on its hands, not take refuge in an idealized claim about the essence of Anglicanism. I tempered his disappointment by discovering that the strongest anti-imperialists in late nineteenth-century Anglicanism were Anglo-Catholic socialists such as Charles Gore, Scott Holland, Charles Marson, and Conrad Noel. Meanwhile the doyens of Anglican liberalism, Hastings Rashdall and W. R. Inge, were racist bigots who touted their supposed cultural superiority. I wrote a paper on this subject that Fr. Pursel might have liked, but he abruptly resigned from St. Paul's amid a controversy at the congregation, my tutorials ended, and I was fast-tracked to ordination.

Had the Albany diocese operated more democratically I would have had no chance of being ordained. As it was, one supportive bishop and two supportive rectors were almost all I needed to skate to the diaconate in one year. Three members of the Commission on Ministry obsessed over my feminist Presbyterian clerical spouse; they couldn't imagine how this marriage would work out. My friend Nancy Rosenblum, a Commission member and deacon who worked, like her Jewish spouse, for the state government, mercifully declared that there would be no further queries along this line, which removed my last roadblock to ordination. I was maxed-out on an emotionally demanding job, leadership in two activist organizations and the Social Justice Center, teaching adult education classes for Brenda and St. Andrew's, and ordination requirements. Then in 1982 my structure of obligations shifted. Bishop Hogg planted me at an ecumenical prep school, the Doane Stuart School, for $10,500 per year, and Bruce paid me $2,000 to be his associate at St. Andrew's Church.

Doane Stuart, located on the campus of the Roman Catholic Sisters of the Sacred Heart, was very important to Bishop Hogg, who had co-founded it in 1975 as a merger of an Episcopal school and a Roman Catholic school. I taught six classes per day, conducted a weekly chapel service, and provided pastoral counseling. This was not high school as I remembered it, though I won the teaching award in my second year. The students came from well-off families, many drove expensive cars to school, unlike their car-pooling teachers, and some students exuded the kind of worldly sophistication I had first encountered at Harvard. The ornate chapel connected the school to a nursing home where Sacred Heart Sisters spent their last days. Sometimes an overhearing nun interrogated me on a sermon point. One insisted that I must be wrong about the doctrine of the Eucharist in Anglican Christianity—how can several different views be permissible? Another sister grieved at my story about rocker Bob Seger. I had heard the Bob Seger System twice as a teenager at Daniel's Den in Saginaw. Later it delighted me when Seger made it big, whereupon he said that during the ten years when he played at little dumps in Michigan, he didn't worry about achieving a big success because he was doing what he loved, making music. I thought this was a nice story about finding and embracing what you love. Sister was appalled to learn that I had spent entire evenings of my youth immersed in the "gutter depravity" of rock music.

Doane Stuart was more progressive than its predecessor schools had been, though its ecumenism was bounded by Catholic plus Anglican. I befriended an extraordinary teacher, Paul Loatman, whom students called "Doc" for his Ph.D. in American history. Paul bristled with knowledge, opinions, and extroversion. A product of working-class Catholicism in nearby Lansingburgh, New York, he had a commanding presence in the classroom, prowled the hallways with a sharp eye for transgressions, especially pot transactions, and teased his four children as they passed by. In class he pushed students hard, drilling them on historical facts, challenging them to earn his respect. At lunchtime he and I chewed over the news of the day. We started with whatever graced page one of the *New York Times*, ranged over politics and culture, and finished with jock talk. Paul loved the Catholic tradition of social teaching, the Boston Red Sox, and Bruce Springsteen's music. He sparred with me over feminism and was a stout defender of the Walter Mondale mainstream of the Democratic Party, except when the Democrats let him down, which was often. He and I scrimmaged the varsity basketball team and were justly accused of competing too strenuously. In Paul's case, "no blood, no foul" was a cardinal rule, whereas I knew that my best shot at reaching many of these students was through sports, not religion. After a long day of teaching and chaplaincy at Doane Stuart, I would strap on my clerical collar to make pastoral calls at hospitals and nursing homes, often meeting with Brenda at a cheap restaurant before we headed to our evening meetings.

DSOC never scaled up to what we wanted it to be. Always there were anxieties about our image, our position, and Harrington's limitations. Were we too close to Kennedy, the liberal Democrats, and the big unions? How could we cut back on union speakers at our conventions when they paid for everything? DSOC had very few people from the generation slightly older than me. In 1980 most of our members were either older than forty or younger than twenty-five. At two national board meetings we discussed this problem uncomfortably. Some of us had friends who wanted to join a democratic socialist organization, but not DSOC. They were not going to hang out with Social Democrats and Harrington's union buddies. Harrington took this problem personally; there seemed to be no end to paying for his long-bygone clashes with Students for a Democratic Society (SDS) and the New Left. His Old Left anti-communism had repelled the youth of the 1960s. After SDS imploded in 1969, a handful of its refugees founded the New American Movement (NAM) to carry on the best traditions of the New Left—socialist feminism, grass-roots direct action and anti-corporate activism, socialist schools in church basements, and Antonio Gramsci's cultural Marxism.

NAM activists Barbara Ehrenreich and Judith Kegan Gardiner expounded the socialist feminist argument that was fundamental to NAM: Marxism is a theory of economic exploitation, contending that inequality arises from social processes that are intrinsic to capitalism as an economic system, and feminism is a theory about the universality of sexual oppression, contending that male rule rests on the fact of male violence. Ehrenreich said it was fine to combine Marxism and feminism as a hybrid but better to aim for a synthesis. The promise of socialist feminism, yet to be realized, was to be the common ground between Marxism and feminism, synthesizing class and sex, and capitalism and male domination. NAM ringleaders Stanley Aronowitz, Carl Boggs, and Richard Healey contributed mightily to the Gramsci boom of the 1970s and '80s, expounding the classic Gramsci contention that capitalism exercises hegemony over people where they live in schools, civic organizations, religious communities, newspapers, media, and political parties. Hegemony is the cultural process by which a ruling class makes its domination appear natural. Gramsci argued in the 1930s that the Left had to contest capitalism at the cultural level; otherwise, it was wasting its time. This argument swept much of the socialist Left in the 1980s, especially in the academy. The academy had never played an important role in the Left until socialists of my generation embarked on academic careers, from which I was a holdout.[5]

NAM looked down on the social democracy of DSOC, conceiving itself as the democratic socialist real thing. But DSOC was far more accomplished than NAM, so Healey pushed for a merger. The only significant opposition to it came from the right flank of DSOC, which bore grudges from the battles of the 1960s. Why should DSOC bond with SDS exiles and pro-Communists who trashed Socialists for years, indulged Communists, turned Communist, and destroyed their own movement? Exaggerated things were said at the 1981 DSOC convention in Philadelphia about the supposed anti-Israel stance of NAM. A tone of anger I never heard previously in DSOC raged in factional caucuses that were also new to DSOC. Harvey Cox gave an address at the convention and pressed me to explain the seething atmosphere, wondering if maybe this was not his group. NAM called for recognition of the Palestine Liberation Organization (PLO), but so did most parties of the Socialist International. NAM had only a handful of pro-Palestinian activists, a group outnumbered by its Jewish Zionist former Communist flank in the orbit of *Jewish Currents*, edited by Zionist NAM stalwart Morris Schappes. In the end the two organizations agreed to support negotiations with the PLO *and* U.S. military aid to Israel. This was the only issue on which DSOC demanded a specific commitment. It was a marker that no issue confounds and convulses the Left like Israel-Palestine.

The unity convention of 1982 in Detroit founded Democratic Socialists of America (DSA) on my thirtieth birthday. Harrington chaired the new organization, NAM members Ehrenreich, Healey, Roberta Lynch, and Manning Marable were named to the national board, and I thrilled at watching DSOC stalwart Deborah Meier risk a personally reflective talk to this convention of hardcore socialists. DSA soon became a better organization than DSOC had been, with only a slightly larger membership. Basically, it was an umbrella for activists primarily devoted to feminism, anti-racism, LGBTQ activism, anti-militarism, labor, Third World solidarity, religious socialism, and environmentalism. We muddled through the Israel-Palestine trauma by clinging to the hope of a two-state solution marked approximately by the Green Line, the pre-1967 border. At its best, DSA stressed that all justice issues are interconnected. Cornel West blessedly joined DSA, explaining that he needed to belong to some organization that cared about everything he cared about. That was the best argument for DSA, but there were never enough people who felt that way. In Albany the merger did not yield a synergistic surge of new members or activism. We held our own with pretty much the same group we had previously.

My ordination to the priesthood on December 18, 1982, was a gala affair for the activist community of Albany. A lot of our folks were colorful types who wore their ideological and sexual identities on their clothing and bodies, plus they sat together, so they stuck out from the church folk. We had a strong contingent from the Albany diocesan chapter of the Episcopal Peace Fellowship (EPF), another group that I founded and led, which linked me to peace activists in numerous Episcopal congregations. My entire family came to Albany for the service, as did Grace and Anson. Bishop Hogg, surveying surely the wildest crowd of his episcopacy at the luncheon reception, began with an apt observation: "People hear the gospel in different ways." It became one of my maxims. Our lives were abundantly rich in friends, community, and work that we treasured. Brenda and I went full blast in the interim, interrupted by a wounding miscarriage, a devastating second miscarriage, and two breakdowns that mocked the reality of our situation: Brenda was a magnificent pastor, and I was a one-skill imitation of a pastor, but she went through hell in Albany, which made her stronger, while I sailed by on my one skill.

Our first miscarriage was a first trimester sorrow that came two years after we married. It scared us more than we let on, and it taught me something important about Brenda. As soon as she was pregnant, she banished cigarettes and alcohol from her life and stuck to it. Nothing could break her from chain-smoking, or cause her to try, until she was pregnant; then she swung completely the other way. Harming her baby was out of the question. As soon as she miscarried, Brenda went back to three packs per day and red wine. This experience prepared us hardly at all for the emotional devastation of the second miscarriage, a second trimester nightmare entailing two days in the hospital, Brenda's almost unbearable heartache and loss, and nurses who insisted on calling me "Dad." That was exactly what I had just lost; I winced every time they said it. The only thing to be said for this experience was that it brought out the best in Brenda's congregation. Her friends Harriet Seeley and Sheryl Sheraw, both social workers, love-bombed her with caring attention, and we ate church casseroles for weeks.

Intertwined with these traumas were the conflicts that Brenda endured with a handful of her congregants who didn't like her. Four were prominent: two men who recoiled at her feminist sermons and wisecracking, and two women for whom no amount of personal attention from Brenda was ever enough. These four people acquired a presence in our lives far beyond anything they deserved. They wielded the power to hurt Brenda, were keenly aware of it, and did so frequently. They were classic clergy killers; it was just Brenda's bad luck that they had joined Bob Lamar's congregation. Sometimes she would come home, hurl her purse across the living room, and scream with all the pent-up pain and rage that were in her. On two occasions she had breakdowns that required formal leaves negotiated with Bob. He was caring, sympathetic, and a true friend both times, grasping that three of these characters treated Brenda in a way they never treated him. He was also humbled by an impending divorce that was mostly his fault. The first time that Brenda took an emergency leave, she opted to go home to her parents, a mistake we sorely regretted afterward.

Brenda basked in her father's company and very much not in her mother's company. When the four of us were together, I was content to say nothing about politics, and Anson felt the same way, knowing that I had terrible politics. Brenda, however, could never resist teasing Anson on this subject. She could go for weeks without talking about politics, but put her in the same room with her father and suddenly she was a fire hydrant of political opinions, all of them designed to needle him. Anson never took the bait or got angry or offended. He loved Brenda so much that he enjoyed all her teasing, which he understood was a form of affection. Grace told me, "You know, he's not such a teddy bear on that subject; you should hear him." But with his spirited daughter, Anson took the razzing and loved her back.

Grace and Brenda had said very harsh things to each other from Brenda's teenage years onward. The mutual resentments were piled high, and the two of them clashed whenever we got together. The only question was how long it would take. Sometimes the sparks would fly within ten minutes of greeting. At other times we got through a couple days of simmering civility before the explosion came. Brenda suffered over this issue and Grace was philosophical about it. Whenever one of their fights turned insulting and explosive, Brenda would plunge emotionally; sometimes she apologized the next day. Grace did not plunge or apologize. The closest she came to apologizing was to say, "Let's move on and forget it." A few months after I entered this family, Grace told me: "Gary, there are certain things that Brenda and I are always going to hold against each other. She is not the daughter that I wanted, and I am not the mother that she wanted. But she knows deep down that I love her." Which was true. On occasion, when the feuding got bad enough, Brenda would ask Anson to take her side, always a mistake. Anson unfailingly had Grace's back in our presence, and Grace never asked me to take her side against Brenda. On occasion she told me, "I love you for taking care of my girl."

Brenda wished for a mother who took care of her, but she was going to struggle with depression no matter what Grace did. Her first emergency leave did little good because Grace got in the way and was there to be blamed. The next time that Brenda reached a breaking point, it was fortunately almost summertime, so getting away was not the public spectacle that the previous episode had been. We combined vacation time with a leave in the Vermont mountains, had wondrous days of healing at Killington Peak, and Brenda read a book that changed her life: *Born to Win: Transactional Analysis with Gestalt Experiments*, by Muriel James and Dorothy Jongeward. It supplemented the transactional analysis of Eric Berne with therapeutic experiments shaped by the gestalt theory of Fritz Perls.[6]

The transactional and gestalt approaches focus on the present situation, accentuating the difference between achievement and authenticity. Authentic persons, James and Jongeward argued, do not conceive life as a challenge to achieve expectations or ideals. They do not give scripted performances or try to manipulate others to play a given role. Authentic persons are aware of their uniqueness, actualize it, are grateful for it, and appreciate the uniqueness of others. A few years earlier, had we read alongside our seminary fare the James/Jongeward appropriation of "games people play" that Berne made famous, we probably would have scoffed at simplistic self-help discourse. In the Vermont mountains, Brenda called Sheryl Sheraw, asking if she knew anyone who conducted therapy employing the *Born to Win* approach.

Facing down her dread of group work was Brenda's last obstacle to being helped by the transactional-gestalt approach. She arrived for her first session, walked out just before it began, stewed about it for two weeks, protested that group work should be optional, cringed at the thought of baring her soul to strangers she didn't trust, and joined the group that made the rest of her extraordinary ministry possible. Brenda would come home burbling about not setting herself up to fail and not letting toxic people get to her. One blessed day she came home with an announcement: "I am done with social activism. I can't take the criticism and conflict that come with it. It's not me. It's not my calling. It's your calling. I have to concentrate on being a pastor to people who don't like my politics."

It made a huge difference in her life and ministry. Brenda disengaged from fighting with smarter-than-you types who always had to be right. Doing so relieved her of having to spend her evenings reading about the history of El Salvador and the politics of the nuclear arms race. Most of her congregation would have been surprised to learn about her struggle. They loved her spunky, fiery, outgoing charisma from the beginning; they appreciated that she was deeply caring and an outstanding preacher; and Brenda roared for feminism before and after "It's not my calling." Feminism was wholly *her* with no need to ruin her evenings by reading books about it. She teased me for keeping up with trends in feminist theory: "Do you really need to read about something so obvious?"

Brenda was a special friend to people who struggled with depression. She told them she had coped with it her entire life and knew how terrible it was. She was skilled at getting people to open up about personal things and perceptive in analyzing what came out. Her sermons were jewels of expository preaching, always drawing from her deep well of feeling and insight. Often, she began with a pairing-hook that caught listeners right away, using me as a foil. One of them practically wrote itself after the opening sentence: "Gary likes films; I like movies." Her congregation laughed gleefully as she spoofed my favorite films. Another sermon in this genre expounded on friendship as grace: "I have friends; Gary has admirers." This was the opening line to a luminous sermon that she preached at every congregation she later served. She said I was one of those people who must be good all the time, and I attracted activist types who liked me for it. But true friends, she advised, share their deepest vulnerabilities and fears with each other. Deep friendships are occasions of grace that enable friends to be candid, unprotected, bawdy, boisterous, intimate, and flawed with each other. Christianity is about being saved by grace, not about saving the world or being good all the time.

I tried to learn ministry from Brenda; certainly, she was my role model, however little it showed. Three of the worst things that a cleric can do in a hospital call were routine occurrences for me. When I made a hospital visit, especially to someone I didn't know, I had to walk past the room three or four times to work up the nerve to enter. Eventually I entered with all my earnestly shy awkwardness, setting off immediate discomfort in the patient and whoever else was present. After a while, the visit usually went surprisingly well, so I stayed too long upon relaxing, losing track of the time and wearing out someone who needed rest. Finally, it was time to exit. I felt guilty about leaving, so to justify my departure, I declared, "I'll see you tomorrow." I'll see you tomorrow! Now I had to repeat this performance the next day. Brenda tried to help: "For God's sake, Gary, what is wrong with you?" But she understood that I will-power myself through my deficiencies and traumas. People loved Brenda's breezy, friendly, direct pastoral calls, and she never had to apologize for leaving.

She grew in wisdom during her years in Albany. Brenda got a spiritual director, and later became one, helping others discern the presence of God in their lives. She preached beautiful funeral sermons that people cited for months afterward. She decided that weddings were like social activism, something not for her. Wedding rehearsals were magnets for obnoxious groomsmen who showed up drunk and thought it was uproariously funny that this church had a lady minister. They amused themselves by disrupting the rehearsal, and one day Brenda said, "To hell with that." We knew plenty of ministers who were willing to do weddings, and she didn't need to be one of them. We belonged to a gang of associate pastors from the downtown churches that Brenda dubbed "the Ass-Passes." She let them perform the weddings, making exceptions only for friends who were certain not to inflict their boorish friends on her.

The only activist groups in Albany that forged real bonds of trust and activism with Black Americans were the mainstream establishment groups: the Capital Area Council of Churches, the Democratic Party, and select trade unions. I annoyed my Lefty friends by pointing this out with some frequency. We thought that our politics made us more anti-racist than the establishment groups, but no snapshot of our meetings would have borne us out. All the working-class and middle-class Black people I knew in Albany were people I met through the Council of Churches, which had two annual anchors, the Martin Luther King Jr. Memorial Service and the CROP Walk. I performed dutiful service in both enterprises each year, always regretting that they did nothing to change the status quo. These were ritualized occasions at which ecu-menical Christians sang the songs and linked arms and felt better. Since DSA operated selectively in the left wing of the Democratic Party, we were positioned, in theory, to play a role in ordinary party functions, but of course we mostly didn't. Being seen as regular Democrats would have been mortifying to us.

Our best opportunity to change the organizing realities occurred when Jesse Jackson ran for the 1984 Democratic nomination for pres-ident. I volunteered for campaign duty and was told to recruit mem-bers of my own organizations. My organizations didn't endorse electoral candidates—DSA was the exception—and some of my friends were anarcho-liberationists who didn't believe in voting anyway. So I mostly trolled for individual volunteers. Our DSA union leaders went all-out for former Vice President Walter Mondale, and I argued that there were rea-sons why DSA was so White. Here was a rare opportunity to change what kind of organization we were, building relationships with people who didn't trust us and had no reason why they should. I had nothing against Mondale; I fully expected to work for him once he was nominated. I also respected that Mondale had strong support among mainstream Black Democrats. This wasn't about that, at least during primary season. To me, the issue was to change the organizing reality on the ground. Enough of us went for Jackson that Albany DSA made no endorsement, but Jackson campaigners did not regard DSA as an ally, because we weren't. Maybe next time, I thought, would be different; I took for granted that Jackson would run again in 1988.

Every morning except on Sundays I ran at sunrise before Brenda awoke. I pounded ten miles per day in sixty minutes, and when the weather turned too cold to run outside, I ran on a tiny basement track at the YMCA, where it took twenty-four laps to reach a mile. The constant turning at a hard pace chewed up my ankles, which didn't stop me from running, or even slow me until my forties. In my forties I still ran ten miles per day, but at a jogger's pace with injured ankles, and not in the morning, as I lost the discipline for sunrise exertion. Through my fifties and sixties, I ran in the early evenings or late at night, needing the time to feel up to it. Running was immensely joyful to me, even with banged up body parts. I never regretted the bodily toll, the price of running. On the road, once my empty-nest years came, I was always eager to see a new place by running through it. My lecture circuit memories are long on college campuses, forest roads, beaches, and mountain vistas, but topping them all is the memory of my thirties, when sunrise running felt as natural as breathing.

I did not expect to become an academic. In Albany I wrote articles and books covering my range of subjects and did not, for seven years, reconsider my decision about the academy. Brenda and our friends persistently questioned this position, and ironically it was the very work of organizing that pushed me into the academy. Organizing consists mostly of small-bore meetings, canvassing, and showing up to support allied groups; meanwhile the next big event must be planned. Often it features an academic who recently wrote a book on the issue that defines the group. On several occasions, especially in CISPES, we devoted months to organizing a big event and were treated rudely by a speaker who didn't bother to eat a meal with us, spend any time with us, or ask who we were. The boorish speakers tended to give bad lectures, too. Two such back-to-back episodes propelled me in an unexpected direction. The first time, nursing our bruised feelings at a bar, my friends planted a seed by lamenting that I should have been the speaker. The next time the speaker arrogance was the worst ever. I sat in the front row thinking, "I could give a better lecture than this, on this topic, right now. Maybe I need to become an academic. If I do, I will never treat people the way we are being treated."

That is how I became an academic. I could have combined church ministry, organizing, and independent scholarship for the rest of my days and been content. What changed my career path was experiencing the relevance of the academy to organizing. My book *The Democratic Socialist Vision* (1986) mixed the Old Left and New Left history I had inherited with the solidarity organizing of my experience. It was steeped in Norman Thomas Socialism and the DSOC-NAM dialogues that produced DSA, describing economic democracy as common ground for liberationist movements. It ran long on soon-outdated critiques of Reagan's policies, waxed too earnestly on economic dependency theory, and built up to my argument for a mixture of cooperative and public ownership featuring public banks that could be funded by an excess profits tax. I did not call my position a Left-communitarian proposal or refer to the burgeoning communitarian movement in political theory. I was devoted to making a case for democratic socialist policies regardless of what happened in the academy.[7]

But the communitarian upsurge caught my attention. Communitarians criticized the liberal devotion to individual rights and the egocentrism of U.S. American culture, upholding the importance of character-forming institutions. Notre Dame moral philosopher Alasdair MacIntyre, in his landmark book *After Virtue* (1981), contended that modern individualism is an assault on the very idea of virtue. The following year, Harvard political theorist Michael Sandel set off the communitarian gusher in *Liberalism and the Limits of Justice* (1982), a critique of the individualistic conception of the person undergirding liberal theory from Kant to John Rawls. Sandel argued that liberalism strips individuals of the moral grounding they need to make good decisions about rights and justice. If liberal democracy is to survive the deracinating logic of liberal theory, some conception of the good life rooted in moral communities must trump the freedom of the self to choose its own values and ends. MacIntyre and Sandel pressed a similar argument about the importance of moral experience, but MacIntyre was dour, pessimistic, anti-feminist, and contrarian, a conservative who retained strains of his earlier Marxism, while Sandel wrote gracefully eloquent prose about saving liberal democracy from itself.[8]

Communitarians retrieved Aristotle on justice as a community bound by a shared understanding of the good, Hegel on justice as recognition, and John Dewey on democracy as the project of continuously recreating the public. They wrote scores of books describing civic republicanism as a third-way alternative to welfare state liberalism and throwback hyper-capitalism. They spread across a wide political spectrum ranging from democratic socialists (Robert Bellah, Harry C. Boyte, Rosemary Ruether, Philip Selznick, William Sullivan, Michael Walzer), to moderate progressives (Sandel, Amitai Etzioni, William Galston, Jane J. Mansbridge, Charles Taylor), to conservatives (William Bennett, Robert Nisbet, Christina Hoff Sommers). Bellah co-authored a landmark civic republican bestseller, *Habits of the Heart* (1985). Walzer developed a lodestar pluralistic theory of equality keyed to the critique of domination in multiple spheres. Etzioni built a movement organization geared to his centrist politics. Boyte founded a communitarian caucus in DSA but soon judged that DSA was not his home base.[9]

Harry Boyte cut his activist teeth in the Black freedom movement. His father, Harry G. Boyte, was MLK's first paid White staffer in the Southern Christian Leadership Conference, and the younger Harry Boyte served as a field secretary of SCLC during his college student years at Duke, 1963 to 1967. King assigned Harry to organize poor Whites; Harry worked on SCLC's voter registration and community organizing campaigns through the 1960s; and he was scarred by the internal wars of the New Left and the death of King. In the 1970s, Harry was a leading player in NAM's attempt to build something from the ruins of the New Left. When I first met him, he was urging his fellow NAM activists to merge with DSOC. Then he sought to build a communitarian base in DSA, urging DSA to replace its Socialist myth with his Left-communitarianism. But that proved frustrating, and Harry concluded that he was still too ideological, like DSA. He rethought what he had learned in the Black freedom movement: it had taught him to value a type of politics that transcends political parties, ideology, and partisanship, which he called citizen politics.

IAF national senior organizer Gerald Taylor and Princeton political theorist Sheldon Wolin were crucial influences on Harry's concept of citizen politics. Taylor trained thousands of clerics, lay leaders, union staffers, government officials and others for nearly thirty years as the Southeast Regional Director of IAF. Wolin wrote extensively about participatory democracy, the primacy of the political in public life, and the problems of bureaucracy and elitism in liberal democratic states. Harry developed the idea of a politics of *public work* shorn of ideological over-commitments. Citizen politics, as he described it, is grounded in everyday life, deals with the world as it is, and embraces Dewey's idea that democracy is about reinventing the public sphere to create a more just and inclusive society. Harry worked with feminist philosopher Elizabeth Minnich, political theorist Benjamin Barber, and social theorist Colin Greer at Union Institute in Cincinnati, a consortium of twelve colleges and universities now branching out on its own. He wrote a dissertation that superseded his prolific previous writings. The book version, *CommonWealth: A Return to Citizen Politics* (1989), launched a new era of community organizing scholarship. He labored over it during the period that I contemplated an academic turn. Harry didn't persuade me to bail out of DSA, but I followed him into the Union Institute to work with Minnich, Greer, Mark Rosenman, and him.[10]

Minnich was a protégé of political philosopher Hannah Arendt, a scholarly specialist on Arendt's thought, and one of the founders of women's studies. She wrote insightfully about pedagogy, puzzling that many academics never think about *how* they teach. Greer was occupied at the time with editing an essential movement magazine, *Social Policy*; later he headed the New World Foundation. Rosenman was a social theorist committed, like Boyte, Minnich, and Greer, to radical democracy and interdisciplinary scholarship. All of them teased me for publishing what might have been my dissertation just before I entered the doctoral program; who does that? I shucked off the teasing, since I regarded *The Democratic Socialist Vision* as a prequel to the book I needed to write, on the Christian socialist wellspring of liberation theology. The dissertation poured out of me shortly after our lives were transformed by the coming of Sara Biggs Dorrien.[11]

Sara arrived on January 2, 1986. I babbled some kind of announcement on the phone to Anson, who had one question, as I told Brenda, who knew what it was: "He just wanted to know how *his* girl was doing." Exactly. Sara's birth was joyously celebrated across our spectrum of Albany communities. The *Albany Times-Union* ran a picture declaring, "For unto us a child is born, unto us a daughter is given." There were nice receptions at the Social Justice Center and Doane Stuart, and outsized, over-the-top receptions at First Presbyterian and St. Andrew's. There were visits from both sets of grandparents, Brenda surprised herself by tiring of her job, the summer months came, and I wanted only to walk through parks with Sara strapped to me.

Our last year in Albany was poignantly strange. Our friends could feel us pull away, chiding that we weren't the first couple to have a child; remember your friends! Foremost in that category were my dearest friends from St. Andrew's Church and the Episcopal Peace Fellowship, Margaret and David Hannay. Margaret taught English at Sienna College, David taught computer science at Union College, and their daughters Deborah and Cathy were my students at Doane Stuart. We told them long before anyone else that our Albany phase was ending. Brenda was doing the minimum at a job she no longer wanted, while I looked for a position in college chaplaincy. My favorite kind of ministry, I had learned, was to help students find their way in their coming-of-age years. In 1987 I spotted an Episcopal chaplaincy opening at Western Michigan University (WMU) in wonderfully named Kalamazoo—a

Potawatomi term of unknown origin perhaps meaning "boiling water." The Potawatomi were still there in Southwest Michigan in the 1830s when settlers from New England barged in.

The eight-member committee appointed by the Diocese of Western Michigan had three ringleaders: Ernst Breisach, a noted intellectual historian at WMU; E. Rozanne Elder, a prolific historian of medieval monasticism at WMU; and Franklin Presler, a political theorist at Kalamazoo College. Ernst was a cultural and political conservative who took warranted pride in his theological erudition. Rozanne was a feminist scholar just beginning to create her vast editing corpus of Cistercian Studies. Franklin, temperamentally a conservative who thought his way to liberal Democratic positions, had grown up in a missionary family in India. They whittled down to one candidate and invited me to come for two days of discussion, which were wonderful. We ranged over theology, politics, the church, the 1980s generation, the academy, and WMU. They were eager to hire me, pressing this point when Bishop Howard Meeks joined our group on the second day.[12]

A leader in the Cursillo charismatic movement, he was in his third year as bishop, and was the only grumpy person in the room. No one appeared to be comfortable with him, so it was hard to figure how he made bishop. Shortly after I departed, Meeks blistered the committee for wasting his time: "I am not going to bring a Left-wing intellectual into this diocese! What were you thinking?" The committee members took turns pleading my case, to no avail. They made a power move, issuing an ultimatum, which Meeks accepted eagerly, abolishing the committee. It was the luckiest stroke of my career. Franklin called me that night, asking why I had not applied for the Dean of Stetson Chapel position at Kalamazoo College—a far better position, with a faculty appointment and a higher salary, what were you thinking?

I had missed the announcement of this opening and hadn't known that Kalamazoo College was in the last stage of a search process. Franklin felt obligated not to tell me about it until the WMU committee was terminated. He didn't have to sell me on Kalamazoo College, which the locals called "K College" and the college community called "K." It was the most selective liberal arts college in Michigan, the only one with a national reputation, and known for its pioneering study abroad program. I had visited the campus once, in 1971, pitching for Alma. A group of players from the losing team and their friends had chanted a sing-song farewell to us as our bus rolled out of the parking lot: "We-e-e're still smar-r-r-ter!"

We Alma players had no doubt of that. Had I bothered to apply to K in 1970, I would not have remotely qualified for admission. Now Franklin submitted my resume to the search committee at the eleventh hour. K president David Breneman, an economist, had to approve paying for an extra candidate, later telling me he would have refused but couldn't resist grilling me about political economist Oskar Lange. My interview with him revolved around market socialism, just before I gave an idealistic lecture on "Religion and the Common Good." The first draft intertwined splinters of my current book project with four splashes of humor, and my sermon the next day was a variation on "be not be conformed to this world, but be ye transformed by the renewing of your mind" (KJV, Romans 12:2). Brenda shrewdly told me to make only two humorous runs: "They need to see that you have comic timing and a sense of humor, but you don't need to show them four times. Think about the humorless types who might be on the committee." That helped me to bank on earnest sincerity. I bonded with world religions scholar J. Mark Thompson and biblical scholar Waldemar Schmeichel, who later told me it was fortunate that Brenda didn't tell me to cut *all* the humor. On my departure I locked eyes with Franklin as we shook hands, two introverts who conveyed more to each other with a long look than with the mumbled words we managed.

My friends on the WMU committee chortled with delight at my happy ending, spreading the word that I was coming to Kalamazoo anyway. They had imaginings of Bishop Meeks flushing with embarrassment at my presence, which didn't really occur during the brief time he had left as a bishop. He got in trouble and was forced to resign from the ministry. The Episcopal Diocese of Western Michigan got a second chance at getting it right, and did so winsomely, bringing Edward L. Lee Jr. to Michigan two years after I settled into chaplaincy, teaching, and liberal arts programming at the formerly Baptist college on Academy Street.

5

KALAMAZOO HEARTBREAK

The academy had played only a marginal role in the political Left before my generation poured into the academy and brought the social movements of the 1970s with it. I was unusual in my generation for coming late to the academy and for being as deeply influenced by the Old Left as by the New Left. My identification with Martin Luther King Jr., Norman Thomas, and the past century of Black freedom struggle, Christian social ethics, and democratic socialist politics marked me when we moved to Kalamazoo College in 1987. The Cold War was fading, neoliberalism hollowed out the United States' industrial base, Jesse Jackson was running again for president, the communitarian movement surged, gay activist Larry Kramer founded the AIDS Coalition to Unleash Power (ACT UP) to fight the HIV epidemic, the tidal wave of French deconstruction washed over the academy, and the debate over multiculturalism heated up. I arrived in Kalamazoo with a little girl who was erupting into speech, a spouse who mistakenly thought she wanted time off from ministry, and a nearly complete manuscript on the theology and politics of Christian socialism.

I carried Sara on my shoulders to the dining hall and other gatherings, where she bloomed into a radiant hyper-articulate charmer. She enthralled me. It was the purest joy I had ever experienced. I took her to every meeting and event that I thought should be able to handle the presence of a talkative little one. We set precedents in several cases, and some colleagues grumbled about it. Brenda told friends that Sara would need to get her moral character from her mother, since her father thought she walked on water. When Sara liked a movie, she had to watch it a hundred times, which I was happy to do, enjoying her delighted immersion in the characters and songs. Fortunately, she was pluralistic about parks, so we tracked down all the parks in the metropolitan area and made rounds of them. My $28,000 salary was not enough for us to buy a second car, but some of our favorite parks were mercifully nearby in our K College–Western Michigan University (WMU) neighborhood.

The luckiest stroke of our Kalamazoo years occurred simultaneously with our arrival, as our seminary classmates Jan and Vaughn Maatman also moved to Kalamazoo. They had wed as undergraduates at Hope College in Michigan and were classmate friends of Brenda's at Princeton Seminary. Jan had served as a chaplain at Bowling Green State University in Bowling Green, Ohio, and Vaughn had worked as a residence hall administrator at the University of Chicago. In Kalamazoo Jan took a ministry position at a Presbyterian shelter, Ministry with Community, before moving into nonprofit organizational leadership, while Vaughn served as director of residential life at K College. We bonded with Jan, Vaughn, and their sons Micah and Joseph. Brenda had never lacked one or two intensely close friendships. Then she renewed a friendship with Jan transcending all others that carried her to the end of her days. My life was so overflowing with absorbing work and family love that I could have gotten along with no friends. As it was, I acquired a bounty of them that Brenda described as one of God's mysteries.

I banged out the last pages of my dissertation on the manual typewriter I had bought in seminary, setting off howls of hilarity from chapel secretary Gilda Cekola and chapel music director Paula Pugh Romanaux. I was well into the succeeding book before their teasing drove me to employ a word processor, though I still wrote the first drafts of chapters longhand in composition books. My dissertation spun a Christian socialist thread running from Walter Rauschenbusch and Paul Tillich to three renowned theologians of the present—Jürgen Moltmann, Gustavo Gutiérrez, and Argentine liberationist José Míguez Bonino, building up to my liberal-liberationist position and its affinities with Cornel West and Rosemary Radford Ruether.[1]

Rosemary and I similarly described a mosaic of intersecting justice struggles as pre-figurative pieces of an unrealized collective vision, and Cornel and I shared the Council socialist vision of interlinked self-determined worker guilds. But I did not invoke Councilism to disparage democratic socialism as Cornel did, because Social Democracy has real-world achievements and organizations, whereas council socialism exists only in the heads of Marxists, Lefty dreamers like Cornel and me, and guild-nostalgists. I noted that Cornel's writings of the mid-1980s tacked in the direction of the democratic socialism he criticized; Michael Harrington had influenced him during the lecture tours they conducted together for DSA. In May 1988, the Congress on Religion and Politics held a three-day conference at the University of Chicago. I gave two lectures spun from *The Democratic Socialist Vision* and the dissertation, and took my last walk with Mike, who rebuffed introspection as usual, pumping me for details about the speaker lineup. Mike bravely battled esophageal cancer until his death in 1989. In his last years he insisted on speaking first at conferences, since he didn't know how much time he had left. That night he preceded Rosemary and Cornel, the crowd gave Mike a standing ovation before he said anything, he responded characteristically that he had no idea how to respond, so here were the three points he planned to make. The only book of Mike's that I ever assigned at Kalamazoo College was *Socialism: Past and Future* (1989), but I often taught books by Rosemary and Cornel.[2]

Jesse Jackson was running again when we moved to Kalamazoo. Many of us who worked in his campaigns did not conceive the Rainbow Coalition as merely the vehicle of Jackson's desire to be president or vice president. To us it was a revival of MLK's crusade to abolish racism, severe inequality, and militarism. Jackson went to places where people had lost their farms and manufacturing jobs. He talked about companies moving to low-tax havens, laid-off workers searching for jobs, poorly paid domestic workers taking the early bus, and millions of people lacking health insurance. He connected with angry, anxious, hurting crowds of people, often turning them into standing throngs imploring him to win this time. Reaganism was a party, Jackson said—a roaring splurge of tax cuts for the rich combined with mindless military spending that created fantastic debts while gouging the middle class, the working class, and especially the poor. Those who enjoyed the party should pay for it. Those who were not invited should not have to pay for it.[3]

Jackson advocated a fifteen percent cut in the Pentagon budget, an immediate freeze on the development and deployment of nuclear weapons, and negotiations with the Soviet Union for disarmament. He said the United States should stop punishing drug users with harsh mandatory prison sentences and start punishing money-laundering bankers. He called for a single-payer system of universal health care, ratification of the Equal Rights Amendment, reparations for slavery, and New Deal-type programs supporting family farmers. He contended that South Africa should be declared a rogue nation and the United States should help to create a Palestinian state. His positions forced his mostly centrist Democratic rivals to declare themselves on subjects they preferred to muddle. Frontrunner Michael Dukakis explained more candidly than he wanted that Jackson's positions would not end up in any platform supporting his candidacy.

Kalamazoo was a progressive college-town anomaly in the southwest region of Michigan dominated by very conservative, Republican, evangelical Grand Rapids. My introduction to Kalamazoo's vibrant left-liberal community occurred through the Jackson campaign. Larry Alcoff, a union organizer and Marxist, and Linda Alcoff, a feminist social philosopher beginning her academic career, moved to Kalamazoo at the same time as me. Larry threw himself immediately into the Jackson campaign, helping to build a local powerhouse from a modest network left over from 1984, sweeping his spouse and me into his marathon workdays. Kalamazoo had most of the base Rainbow groups, especially Black churches, ecumenical White churches, antiwar activists, feminists, blue-collar unions, teacher unions, students, and academics. I soon befriended two social justice stalwarts, WMU social work professor Don Cooney and WMU sociologist Ron Kramer, who exemplified what constructive, ethical, community-oriented, best-practices activism looked like in southwest Michigan.

Jackson ran first or second in sixteen of the twenty-one Super Tuesday contests, the race narrowed to Jackson versus Dukakis, and Michigan's upcoming caucus of March 1988 began to feel like a big deal. Jackson filled our largest venue, Miller Auditorium at WMU. He was intensely low-keyed, determined, serious, and long, intertwining set pieces with current events, telling us to believe what we were seeing—this thing was real. We could win in Michigan. He won Michigan by running up the vote in Detroit, Flint, Lansing, and Kalamazoo, the magical evening of the 1988 campaign.

The friendships I made through the Jackson campaign were my activist base for the next eighteen years. Very few of my activist friends spoke the arcane deconstructionist language of Jacques Derrida and Michel Foucault that swept the academy, or even knew it existed. My two friends who knew it best, French scholars Kathy Smith and Jan Solberg, were K College academics not involved in activism. But the rise of the cultural Left in the academy vastly enriched how the political Left conceived justice, challenging the Marxian and social democratic emphasis on economic justice. Academics intensely debated what counted as justice and essentialism. I welcomed the opportunity to convene conversations about multicultural politics and education, taking advantage of the fact that I directed the area's leading lecture venue.

The Liberal Arts Colloquium Credit program (LACC) at K had been founded by my predecessor at Stetson Chapel, Bob Dewey, to boost the college's handful of endowed lectureships. On my watch it ballooned to 120 speakers each year. There were constant airport runs, hospitality arrangements, dinners, discussion groups, speaker introductions, and lectures. I tried to represent every academic field every quarter, offering students the opportunity to hear noted scholars in their major, and I struggled to integrate the LACC into K's Study Abroad program, in which most students spent their junior year abroad. K was a pioneer in the field of international education. We built much of our curriculum around a junior-year experience of cultural immersion, though we fretted that some of our programs were too short to achieve it, and we put up with the year-round demands of the quarter system to facilitate the Study Abroad program. A failed attempt to switch to trimesters had ended shortly before I joined the K faculty. Classes typically met three times per week, and a full-time teaching load was two courses per quarter for three quarters per year. The faculty got a quarter off every year, but I spread my courses over all four quarters, since I had to be there anyway to run Stetson Chapel and the LACC program. K had a handful of kindly, erudite, liberal, elderly professors who went out of their way to befriend me: Conrad Hilberry in English, Romeo Phillips in education, David Scarrow and the recently retired Lester Start in philosophy, and J. Mark Thompson in religion. Only Conrad wrote much for publication, but all were eloquent teachers of the liberal arts, as were two other friends who were closer to my age—Jan Solberg and anthropologist Marigene Arnold. I treasured them all.

Teaching was exceedingly enjoyable to me. I taught elective classes that filled our largest classrooms and sometimes topped one hundred students, still the organizer eager to reach as many people as possible, teaching courses ranging across modern theology and social ethics. "Theology" I defined as any discourse that makes claims about what is religiously true. I employed all the methods of the religious studies approach to religion—comparative, phenomenological, analytical, historical, theoretical, and evaluative—but regarded them as secondary to what matters: What is it all about? What have the greatest religious thinkers said about what is religiously true and good? The first time that I taught a senior majors course on Modern Jewish Thought, I almost took a strictly religious studies approach, except the books bored me. At the last minute I changed the reading list, opting for books by theologians Martin Buber, Franz Rosenzweig, Abraham Joshua Heschel, and Judith Plaskow, which were far from boring.

I conducted a weekly interfaith chapel service on Fridays and pastoral counseling on three days per week between classes and LACC planning. There were weddings on most weekends, and some that I conducted were union services for gay and lesbian couples, which sparked angry demands to defrock or fire me. Bishop Edward Lee guarded my back in the church, and K president Lawrence D. Bryan, arriving in 1990, deflected protests from some of the same people. Both were stellar friends to me. Sara accompanied me to many weddings and union services, after which she conducted her own services in our backyard, where she was always the presiding cleric, never a bride. These were the years of funerals for gay men who died of HIV-AIDS, and of colorful, new, ballooned rituals to defy the desperate grief and fear. It was also the period when colleges like K instituted new codes of conduct against sexual harassment and assault. Dean of Students Marilyn La Plante and I handled all the college's disciplinary cases involving students, faculty, and staff. Some were terrible, and most began for me with a phone call from Marilyn: "Gary, I've got bad news for you." Marilyn and I developed a deep mutual trust and respect that carried us through thirteen years of this grueling work, until she retired in 2000. The cases involving charges against faculty colleagues were especially wrenching for me; we had two other cases that inflamed the entire campus that turned out to be completely fabricated; and our worst cases stuck in my head as nightmare material long after I departed K.

The LACC program grew into a sprawling monster that never ceased, took time off, or allowed any illusion of control. It exacerbated the relentless demands of the quarter system and was no less unforgiving. I was always overstretched, plus fearful of forgetting someone at the airport. Were there enough programs about the cultures of our Study Abroad sites? How should we reintegrate the returning students? Were we making good use of the quarter system, or did it ensure our failure? I chaired committees that wrangled over these questions constantly.

All of it was redeemed by my opportunity to bring every social-political theorist and theologian on my fantasy list to Kalamazoo. In my early years at K, the social theorists and political philosophers included sociologist Arjun Appadurai (University of Chicago), political philosopher Ronald Dworkin (New York University), philosopher Nancy Fraser (Northwestern University), political theorist Amy Gutmann (Princeton), Black feminist theorist bell hooks (Oberlin College), political theorist Nancy L. Rosenblum (Brown University), conservative icon Russell Kirk, and political philosopher Michael Walzer (Institute for Advanced Study). My first three theologians were Langdon Gilkey (University of Chicago), Jürgen Moltmann (Tübingen University), and José Míguez Bonino (Instituto Superior Evangelico de Estudios Teologicos). I tried and failed several times to lure Cornel West to K, but he advised me to invite one of his doctoral students, Michael Eric Dyson, who rocked our crowd like no one else.

Arjun Appadurai had authored only one book at the time, on religion in British colonial South India, but he bristled with the brilliance that later produced his pioneering works on migration, media, technology, money, and ideology, the five dimensions of global cultural flows. He helped us interrogate our roiling faculty debate over multiculturalism, chiding us that for a school with a distinguished tradition of international education, we were surprisingly provincial. bell hooks had entered the second realm of her takeoff phase when she came to K. Her books *Ain't I a Woman* (1981) and *Feminist Theory* (1984) were landmarks by the late 1980s. hooks gave us a taste of what became her most personal book, *Talking Back* (1989), not so much delivering it, lecture-style, as performing it, unforgettably, stressing her signature theme that education either integrates students into the regnant system of domination or is a practice of freedom that seeks to transform the system. She said she was a Black feminist, not an Alice Walker-womanist, because she lacked the womanist piety about grandmothers and Southern Black communal female culture; nobody policed what she thought. A White male student asked a cringey question about affirmative action and hooks generously engaged him in a conversation about the kind of college community he should want to join.[4]

One of my book-models was Amy Gutmann's *Liberal Equality* (1980), which made a grand tour argument that liberal theory espouses equal opportunity to participate *and* the equal distribution of economic goods. I asked her to reprise her argument and its implicit critique of communitarian theory. She did so splendidly, telling me captivating stories about her Harvard mentors Michael Walzer, John Rawls, and Judith Shklar. I invited Nancy L. Rosenblum to similarly complicate the fashionable anti-liberalism of the time, reprising her book *Another Liberalism* (1987). She conceded that liberal theory usually wards off everything personal, affective, and expressive, promising an impersonal government. But liberal theory, she said, also has a romantic side. The anti-liberalism that launched the communitarian rocket was one-sided and overwrought, not describing her own liberal romantic sensibility. Rosenblum expounded her perspective in spirited fashion, also with great stories about mentors, in her case Samuel Beer and Judith Shklar.[5]

Linda Alcoff told me about her friend Nancy Fraser, so we promptly invited her. Fraser had not yet published her first book, *Unruly Practices* (1989). I could see coming what she soon became, the foremost socialist-feminist theorist of her generation. At the time, however, Fraser's visit taught me a chastening lesson. Linda gave her a strong introduction, the students warmly welcomed her, and within fifteen minutes they had turned her off. Fraser made no attempt to relate to them, reading a paper loaded with gnarled jargon. Near the front, the students were reasonably polite; in the middle, they grew angry and restless; in the back near me, they loudly mocked her words and tone of voice, entertaining each other. They were offended, plus blunt in showing it. I tried futilely to shush them to silence. As soon as Fraser ended, entire rows bolted for the exit, spurning the discussion period. I learned something important about where I was. If my Alma classmates and I had heard this lecture, we would have endured it compliantly, some of us feeling humiliated by our intellectual inferiority. This crowd was not like that. It was long on high achievers who expected to be treated with respect. They didn't know field jargon because they were not in graduate school. They were not going to listen to someone who didn't address them. From that evening onward, I self-censored. There were some big-name scholars on my fantasy list whom I knew to be poor speakers. I crossed off all of them. Running this program was going to be hard enough with good speakers—which Fraser later became.[6]

Ronald Dworkin gave us two days of his shimmering mind and company, regaling us in raconteur fashion before he turned all-business, placing his watch on the podium before he launched. He braided the critique of legal positivism he developed in *Taking Rights Seriously* (1977) with his chapter on liberalism in *A Matter of Principle* (1985) and the legal framework he propounded in *Law's Empire* (1986), making his signature argument that positivists are wrong about the lack of right answers to difficult legal questions. There are right answers to find if one uses sufficient critical reason and imagination. Dworkin glossed his case for a left-liberal extension of what he called "the New Deal package," lamenting that conservatives and Marxists attract far more attention in the academy than they deserve. We caught a glimpse of his thesis that an adequate conception of law undergirded by an adequate political theory might yet unite, or at least hold together, the spheres of morality, legal justification, and political legitimacy. He wove this symphonic argument concisely, not seeming rushed, yet mindful of the time, driving to his conclusion at the stroke of fifty minutes, when he reaffixed his watch and invited questions. I thought as he awaited the first question, "That's the gold standard." On the way to the airport, he had a realization: "You're the guy who wrote *The Democratic Socialist Vision?* But you're a chaplain." The airport was too nearby for me to explain myself to him.[7]

Russell Kirk was a prolific "man of letters" of the old school and the author of the classic *The Conservative Mind*. We spent two splendid days and an afterglow evening together, along with his radiant spouse, Annette Kirk. Russell gave a talk on the indispensability of natural law reasoning, we compared notes on authors that he and I treasured, and we fixed on Joseph Butler, Samuel Taylor Coleridge, and Reinhold Niebuhr. Russell said he had radar for people who were more conservative than they realized. Niebuhr was a good example, on his view, and so was I. There was no way, he claimed, that a true Lefty could know and admire Butler like I did. He teased me that the Episcopal Church was plummeting like a rock, until he stopped in mid-stream to say there was nothing funny about losing the Episcopal Church. I prattled about Coleridge's post-Kantian idealist metaphysics until Russell opined that that was the only bad part of the later Coleridge. Russell knew Niebuhr well enough to appreciate that Niebuhr loved the United States as much as he did. He was committed to the view that the formerly almost-Marxist Niebuhr progressed almost all the way to the eighteenth-century father of modern British conservatism, Edmund Burke. We stayed in touch, in 1993 I wrote a book on neoconservatism, and Russell wrote a vintage-Russell blurb for it. By then he was fading, and we lost him the following year. I savored the memory of hearing him joyfully expound on the permanent things.[8]

Michael Walzer was a source of pride to us in DSA despite his opposition to the DSOC-NAM merger. His first book, *The Revolution of the Saints* (1965), had classic status as a study of the Puritan origins of radical Anglo-American politics. His storied career at Princeton and Harvard had led to academic nirvana in 1980, joining the School of Social Science at the Institute for Advanced Study in Princeton. Three years later he published the book version of his Harvard classroom debate with libertarian philosopher Robert Nozick. In *Anarchy, State, and Utopia* (1974), Nozick expounded a Lockean state-of-nature case for a minimal state based on the rights to safety and property. In *Spheres of Justice* (1983), Walzer expounded a Left-communitarian theory of complex equality: just equality is never about only one thing, various goods must be distributed according to their social meaning, and political theory should be grounded in the traditions and cultures of specific societies. This book was the centerpiece of my course on "Ethics and the Common Good." For two resplendent days I bantered with Walzer about the differences between *Spheres of Justice* and *A Theory of Justice* (1971), by John Rawls. Walzer appreciated that Rawls' abstract, neo-Kantian, social contract egalitarianism lifted the field of political philosophy to a new height of influence and relevance. Still, he believed, as I did, that political philosophy should operate closer to real-world ground. I had deep affinities with Walzer and yet shied away in subsequent years from approaching him. My feeling was that he was eminent and didn't need to be bothered with me. In Europe, Walzer's cautious, temperate progressivism would have put him in the mainstream of the Social Democratic parties. Gutmann aptly observed that he was the most self-contained person she ever met. I pondered the irony that some of the most individuated reasoners I knew were prominent communitarians.[9]

Langdon Gilkey's book *Naming the Whirlwind: The Renewal of God-Language* (1969) was one of my models from Alma College onward of how to craft a theological argument. Gilkey epitomized the theologians who were trained in neo-orthodoxy before they reverted to some version of Schleiermacher's approach after neo-orthodoxy crashed. He had studied under Reinhold Niebuhr and Paul Tillich at Union Theological Seminary, made his early reputation as a scholastic exponent of 1950s neo-orthodoxy, took for granted that Niebuhr was anti-liberal, and in the early 1960s lost his entire structure of certainties. All the boasts he had absorbed from Niebuhr and the Biblical Theology movement about biblical revelation, God acting in history, and being superior to the liberal tradition disintegrated. At least Schleiermacher and Troeltsch were honest about their naturalistic and historicist premises. So-called neo-orthodoxy was an anti-liberal boast about a foundation it never had. Gilkey spent the 1960s rethinking his position, which yielded his highly astute *Naming the Whirlwind* and a sequel, *Reaping the Whirlwind* (1976). He remained the protégé of Niebuhr and Tillich but shorn of Niebuhr's shooting-gallery polemics against liberal theology.[10]

I asked him to give two lectures, teach a class, speak to a clergy group, and finish with a chapel sermon. The first night, Langdon drank four glasses of wine at dinner before delivering a sparkling lecture blasting the creation science movement. He had testified in 1981 for the American Civil Liberties Union in a trial contesting an Arkansas law that required public schools to teach creation science, so this was one of his stock lectures. It was laced with jokes, including at himself. Langdon said his beatnik-assemblage was toned down from what he used to wear—the ACLU had cleaned him up for public inspection. He had a story about one-upping a *Time* magazine reporter who was astonished to learn that theologians at the University of Chicago believed in evolution. Langdon played the reporter for a laugh, rolling his eyes, but added, "Have you noticed that whenever speakers tell you about their encounters, they always win?" After the lecture, he was greatly relieved that we headed to an afterglow bar. There he held forth with stories about Niebuhr, Tillich, his University of Chicago colleagues, and his wife, Sonja Weber Gilkey, throwing back much more wine. Langdon was grateful that his secular Danish spouse had found religion and eventually joined the Sikhs, "a totally pre-critical faith," he said. She became a Sikh therapist and allowed no alcohol at home, which had already added years to his life: "Still, I live for these lectures!"[11]

Jürgen Moltmann was the world's preeminent theologian. He had been in my head since my first day at Alma College and had written half of his five-volume dogmatics when he came in 1988 to Kalamazoo. Volume two, *God in Creation* (1985), argued that God's relationship to the world is an intricate, many-layered relationship of community, not a one-sided relationship of domination, and that rethinking theology ecologically requires casting aside the Kantian analytical focus on subject and object, restoring the pre-modern concept of reason as the organ of perception and participation. Jürgen's forthcoming volume three, *The Way of Jesus Christ* (1989, English 1990), argued that Judaism and Christianity are bound together and divided by the messianic hope that Christianity got from Judaism. We heard a blend of the two books under the series title of "Hope in the Dangers of the World Today." In a class session, Jürgen came closer to embracing absolute pacifism than he had done in his books. I asked him about it, and he replied: "There is a contradiction in my life that I have never resolved. I am a pacifist, yet if I had a chance—like Bonhoeffer—to kill the tyrant who was killing others, I know that I would do it." He had survived World War II as a soldier only because he surrendered in Holland in 1944 to the first British soldier he met in the woods. Jürgen reached further down, confessing that he felt the hypocrisy of calling himself a pacifist because he had been liberated "through the suffering and violence of others who fought against Hitler." He was a pacifist who believed that violence sometimes serves the higher moral end, and that Germans like him were in a poor position to claim to be pacifists.[12]

The future-oriented works of Moltmann and University of Munich theologian Wolfhart Pannenberg sustained the appearance that Germany still produced the best theologians. Jürgen ruefully told me it wasn't true. A spirit of conformity, he said, had descended on German theology. He looked to South America, Central America, and even North America for theological leadership, while lamenting that many liberation theologians recycled warmed-over Marxism. I asked him how he would characterize his relationship to Barth; he paused for dramatic effect, declaring: "I am glad that Karl Barth was not my father!" Jürgen had feared in his early career that Barth had already said everything worth saying. Then he found the hope theme that Barth had not developed, and fixed on Barth's many deficiencies, beginning with Barth's rude treatment of critics and followers. The only LACC dinner that Brenda ever attended was the one that hosted Jürgen. She was thrilled to meet him, he graciously asked who her favorite feminist theologian was, and she said she didn't really have one, but recently she slogged through twenty pages of her husband's copy of *God in Creation*.

José Míguez Bonino headed the list of Latin American liberationists who Moltmann said relied too heavily on Marxian dialectics. He had grown up Methodist in Sante Fe, Argentina, served as a pastor in Mendoza, earned a doctorate at Union Theological Seminary in 1960 with a dissertation on ecumenism, joined the Faith and Order Commission of the World Council of Churches (WCC), and served from 1975 to 1983 as a WCC co-president. He became a leading liberation theologian by contending that Argentina's political emancipation from Spain led straight to a dependent role in Anglo-Saxon neocolonial expansionism. Míguez was the foremost theological exponent of economic dependency theory. He detailed the ravages of corporate capitalist dominance, exploitative trade agreements, aid to repressive military governments, and the promotion of cash crops for export in Latin America, appropriating dependency theory in wholesale fashion, brushing past its in-house debates over Marxist economism. I argued in *Reconstructing the Common Good* (1990) that Chilean economist Fernando Fajnzylber and Argentine economist Aldo Ferrer developed stronger forms of dependency theory than the reductionist analysis of Andre Gunder Frank on which Míguez over-relied. I also said that liberation theologians must repudiate the "Communist terror, totalitarian rule, and economic bankruptcy" that issued from the Soviet revolution, and which cursed the nations where Communist parties ruled.[13]

We bonded as soon as he landed in Kalamazoo. Míguez greeted me as a brother in the struggle and thanked me for interrogating his work: "Your book had bad timing, or, maybe, great timing!" It had gone to press just before the Berlin Wall came down on November 9, 1989. Every reviewer commented on the timing, and Míguez had read reviews that fixed on my socialist anti-Communism. I knew before we reached Hall House that this would be a special week in my life. He had no shred of defensiveness, even though he was a global figure while I was an assistant professor who had criticized two central features of his work. Most speakers were protective of their time, and sometimes they begged off from meeting with students. Míguez was the opposite. He volunteered for an extra class, and I cleared my schedule to take meandering walks with him. He wanted to know everything I knew about scholarly trends on all the subjects we held in common. He filled our largest lecture venue with a talk about Christian socialism that reflected his many years of WCC ecumenism. Míguez had co-authored major WCC statements on neo-colonialism and ecojustice, created much of Latin America's ecumenical infrastructure, and reframed how the ecumenical movement spoke its vaunted language of reconciliation. Liberation theology, he said, whatever it got wrong, is revolutionary and right to ask liberationist questions: Who calls for reconciliation? With whom do they call? Who do they oppose? For what purpose do they act? Who benefits from reconciliation?[14]

Míguez asked what I was writing; I said I had books on neoconservative politics, U.S. American social Christianity, and the myth problem in theology in my head. All were mapped out; I just needed time to write them. He gave me a gentle stare: "All these books while you run this lecture program?" I failed to see why not. I loved the work and didn't get blocked. More important, I hired a succession of friends to help me run Stetson Chapel and the LACC program: Pam Sotherland, whose husband, Paul Sotherland, taught biology at K; Laura Packard Latiolais, whose spouse, Christopher Latiolais, was my closest friend on the faculty; and a few years later, Becca Kutz-Marks, my dearest friend ever. We bonded with each other through our children, socialized together, and looked out for each other. Had I hired outside professionals with a time-clock mentality, I would have run the LACC program and myself into the ground. As it was, our office was a band of friends who enjoyed being together, trusted each other, and worked in tag-team fashion. Pam was an evangelical Episcopalian trying not to give up on mainline Protestantism, until she did. Through her I experienced the advantage of hiring a friend, so I did it two more times, adding Laura to our team until she landed a career job, and then Becca.

Brenda sorely missed ministry as soon as we moved to Kalamazoo. For a while she helped at Disciples of Christ Church in Kalamazoo, where we befriended pastor Chuck Kutz-Marks, his clerical spouse, Becca, and their children David and Marie. Becca was the ringleader of a so-called Bible Study class that studied only feminist theologians, the more radical the better. She was ebullient, totally transparent, a terrible driver, and a mama bear, looking out for her family and whoever she befriended. Brenda recharged at the Disciples Church. Then she undertook supply work at a church in small-town Allegan and proceeded to an interim pastorate in smaller-town Gobles, where we spent our Sundays. Sara and I usually made it through the sermon, and not much longer; I had radar for Brenda's non-verbal cues to exit with the restless child. Every-week preaching was a new deal for Brenda. In Albany she had averaged one sermon per month, enjoying the luxury of plotting sermons for two or three weeks, trying out drafts at the dinner table. How does this sound? What do you think? Now there was time only for a first draft and a quick review. Brenda devoted herself to what interim pastors do—keep the doors open, help the congregation survive a transition, do the rounds of pastoral care, and give the church a boost if possible.

Her favorite stewardship sermon opened by recalling hyperbolically that Anson Biggs chaired a congregational stewardship committee for a hundred years, after which he did the same thing for another century for the Lutheran Synod. Perpetually armed with magic markers, charts, and newsprint, he did not shy away from asking people to up their pledge. When Brenda enrolled at seminary, Anson gave her his favorite book on steward- ship, which had a story about an elderly man who moved into a house with an overgrown front garden. Brenda said, if you find this story too silly to tell, take it up with my father, he'll be here sooner or later. Anyway, the homeowner worked hard on the garden, turning it into the jewel of the neighborhood. His pastor came for a visit, speaking in the strangely pious idiom that some pastors think is obligatory: "My goodness, isn't it wonder- ful what you and God have done with this garden!" The homeowner drolly replied, "Well, you should have seen it when God had it alone."

Brenda played the responding laugh, confirmed that she shared the crusty feeling of the homeowner, and turned the story inside-out, waxing on the predictable tendency of churchgoing Presbyterians to take credit for the blessings of their lives. We take pride in our industrious work and achievements, she said, overlooking that none of us grows a garden, raises a child, or builds a career by our own effort. We are blessed to be a blessing to others. People don't like to hear about money in church, but Jesus talked about money more than anything else. The church is not Christian if it doesn't reach out beyond its walls in love. Brenda would follow with a challenge to give until it hurts, *being* the church—this odd group of folks who see Jesus in the faces of the poor and give God the credit for their blessings.

She consumed three mystery novels per week; when I met her, Brenda was reading one called *Knife in the Head*. She pored over letters to the editor with a similar relish, though she never wrote one, and was delighted when the grocery checkout line ran slow, so she could read the *National Enquirer*. Human foibles fascinated her, especially, people who rationalized their selfishness with moralism or ideology, and people who lectured strangers in public, above all in letters to the editor. Letter writers also conveyed their sorrows; sometimes Brenda quoted them. For three years, Brenda fixed an eye on First Presbyterian Church in downtown Kalamazoo. It was the big congregation that she wanted. Finally it came up with a quarter-time position for making pastoral visits to homebound members, and she grabbed it gleefully.

In Albany we had gone through three rounds of breast lumps, biopsies, and good news. In 1990, shortly after she joined the staff of First Presbyterian, Brenda felt another lump and was terrified. "This one is cancer," she said, "I just know it." She turned out to be right. At the clinic we gasped and cried and quaked with fear. I made a deranged call to provost Richard Cook, years later a treasured friend, but at the time a stranger to me and a newcomer to the provost's office. I babbled some hysterical message to his secretary, somehow believing I needed to call right away. Brenda and I sat frozen in fright for an hour in the clinic lobby, unable to move, think, or pretend. Our daycare provider, Kristen Kimm, was a mother of four children who took in several others. When we came for Sara, Kristen mercifully did not assault us with pious slogans. She shook as she embraced Brenda, two women bonding over a shared terror. We had stepped into another world and would need our friends more than ever.

There were years of radiation, chemotherapy, a double mastectomy, and recovery. We bought a cute little house built in 1910 and loaded with character, that was two blocks from the campus, the only house I've ever owned, and completed the transaction by obtaining a cocker spaniel named Skipper, a sweet-natured companion for a little girl who asked, "Where are my sisters?" We dodged the sister question until Sara was old enough to hear a story about miscarriages and cancer.

For months, Brenda talked a blue streak about a new acquaintance with bristling self-confidence who said he was to the right of Attila the

Hun. Brenda bantered playfully with him about his cynical a-moralism and misanthropic impulses, escalated to teasing him about his Right-wing politics, and one day called me to the dining room to tell me: "I am totally in love with him. I need him and love him, and you know it."

It was obvious by the time she said so. I emitted some strange guttural moan from hell, unable to choke out words, feeling gut-punched and cast aside. But weeks of fearing this announcement had prepared me to focus on the need in the middle and not overreact to the declaration of love. Brenda needed him; I did know it. We were immersed in the mortal threat to her life, and she needed his bawdy, irreverent intimacy to get through it. I loved her far too much even to consider leaving her: it was not a possibility. As for her love for him, it seemed to me more like an infatuation with a snarky type who made her laugh, compensating for my deficiencies. For three years we danced around her bond with him. I knew she was moving past it when she began to tease me again about not being her type: "You know, you're not my type! I never went for the nice boys. And jocks—I couldn't stand those guys. So how in God's name did I end up with a nice boy jock?" I had caught Brenda on the rebound from one of her bad boys, whereupon she had saved me, as I damn well knew.

I took for granted that her job would expand after people at First Presbyterian got to know her. Brenda was still quarter-time in 1991 when the church's adult ministry Sunday School class studied the plight of the homeless and underserved of the Kalamazoo community. This little group of Presbyterians dreamed of a free health clinic at the church to provide preventive care for those whose only health-care option was a hospital emergency room. Brenda rounded up physicians, nurses, pharmacists, and others, plus the cooperation of two local hospitals. Bill Clinton was elected president in 1992 and we ardently hoped that national health insurance would soon make the church clinic unnecessary.

That year, St. Luke's Episcopal Church, across the street from Brenda's church, had to fire its rector pronto and the congregation asked me to help for a week or two. Two weeks turned into eleven months as I adjusted to every-week sermonizing. My dear friend Paula Romanaux, who directed the music programs at Stetson Chapel and St. Luke's, declared that for however long they had me at St. Luke's, we would be singing everything that is singable. She followed through on this vow, sometimes bulldozing me into singing at Stetson too. The good folks at St. Luke's took their time appointing an interim pastor, the Presbyterians often finished their service before we did, and Brenda came over with Sara to join us. Meanwhile Brenda's health-care group plunged ahead, opening the clinic in 1993, the same year that my father retired from barbering on the day he turned sixty-two. The First Presbyterian Church Free Health Clinic became one of the jewels of the Kalamazoo community, filling a gap that the founders regretted still existed, and my dad devoted himself to golf and drinking, commencing a downward slide that could have been delayed had he heeded my mother's plea to keep working. For him, there was no case to be made for working longer than necessary.

I was holding down two full-time positions, ostensibly for an interim, with heavy committee and chair responsibilities on both sides. One of my new responsibilities was chairing the Committee on Multicultural Education; two others were chairing the Humanities Division and the Religion Department. Gingerly I asked senior professors if I might please check their syllabi for multicultural content. Some told me where I could stick the syllabus, resenting that multiculturalism decentered their expertise. We might have stalled there lacking the leadership role that English professor Gail Griffin played on our faculty. Gail was a brilliant White feminist with a big personality who keenly grasped the justice of Black feminist criticism of White feminism. She was the symbol at K of how feminism changed the old-boy cultures of colleges like K, and of why colleges like K needed committees on multicultural education.

My two-sided load was too much, and not meant to be until circumstances formalized the status quo. Theologian Paul McGlasson and I had joined the K faculty simultaneously and were both on tenure tracks when he left, after two years, to teach at Eden Theological Seminary in St. Louis. I moved up to full-time teaching, the College spent two years conducting formal searches for a new chapel dean, and I covered both positions while the searches proceeded, meanwhile taking over as the untenured chair of Humanities, the Religion Department, and multiculturalism. I was so eager to move out of the chapel that I did it literally, hauling my massive library prematurely to the Humanities building, Humphrey House. Both chapel searches, however, went bust while the college spiraled into a financial crisis. The second search failed partly because of the financial crunch. Larry Bryan terminated staff and adjunct faculty lines, broke off the salary negotiations with a chapel dean candidate, incurred bitter criticism from anxious faculty, and called me to his office.

Much deeper cuts were coming, he said, including the elimination of tenured faculty positions and entire programs. He offered a deal: if I continued my present regimen in the Chapel and the Religion Department, including the LACC program and the new academic appointments, the Religion Department would not lose one of its three faculty lines. I gasped at the thought of it. I was overstretched and wanted very much to make my home at Humphrey House. Larry was a deeply good person, a theologian expert on Dietrich Bonhoeffer, a treasured friend to me, and wounded by the incoming fire. Mark Thompson's retirement from K doubled the jeopardy of losing his position. I agreed to the deal, which wiped out my prospect of ever receiving a sabbatical. My department colleague Waldemar Schmeichel furiously condemned me as a suck-up capitulator. On his justified view, I damaged the College by befriending and enabling a president who shrank the College. Friendship, however, was not my only motivator; I was convinced that if we lost one of our three Religion positions, we would never get it back. For months I harbored the guilty knowledge that several departments would soon be losing a position while Religion would be spared because of a deal that I accepted.

We filled the third position with a specialist in South Asian Buddhism, Carol Anderson, who brought a new perspective into the Religion Department. K was a longtime outpost of the Chicago School of Theology, especially the process thought of Alfred North Whitehead and Bernard Meland, which Meland protégé John Spencer taught for twenty-two years at K with distinction, conducting seminars on Whitehead's *Process and Reality*. Our curriculum featured a careful balance of theological studies and religious studies shaped on both sides by the history of religions method. Carol believed that colleges like K should not teach theological-anything. Religion should be taught strictly as the history, sociology, and anthropology of religion, dispensing altogether with theological heritages. As long as Wally, Carol, and I were the Religion Department, it was going to sustain a balance of theological and religious studies courses. But Wally seethed at me for capitulating to the president; Carol regretted that I tied the Chapel to the Religion Department; and I hauled my library back to Stetson Chapel, never getting a term off in my eighteen years at K.

Every night I wrote into the wee hours after Brenda fell asleep. I couldn't sleep anyway while unwritten books rattled in my head. My previous books were strewn with clunky sentences reflecting that I was still honing a style. Now I wrote two doorstopper books that paid closer attention to rhythm, tone, and cadence: *The Neoconservative Mind: Politics, Culture, and the War of Ideology* (1993), and *Soul in Society: The Making and Renewal of Social Christianity* (1995). The former book dissected the neocon phenomenon that I had tracked since Alma College. Many scholars and pundits issued funeral eulogies for neoconservatism, stressing that its Cold War militarism had become moot. I argued that the neocons were building a post-Cold War future by banking on culture war and the ideology of unipolar dominance.[15]

Neocons were distinctly skilled at culture war because they were ideological warriors who believed in the power of ideas to change the world. They turned every issue into a referendum on anti-Americanism, being so proficient at it that they persuaded the Old Right foundations to finance their think tanks and magazines. Two schools of neocon unipolar ideology emerged as I wrote the book: the realists who didn't need a rationale for sustaining the United States' singular economic and military dominance, and the democratic globalists who said the United States had a mission to spread democracy throughout the world. I interviewed neocon godfather Irving Kristol, a guru of the realist view, and democratic globalists Norman Podhoretz and Michael Novak, just as the neocons retooled for a post-Cold War world. I said the "neo" still mattered in the Republican Right, and not only because many neocons were Jews who recoiled at the antisemitism and fever swamp uglies of the Old Right. "Neoconservative" did not mean "Jewish conservative," since there were many Niebuhr-quoting Catholic and Protestant neocons, although they, too, backed the right-wing Likud Party in Israel. "Neoconservative" named, above all, the foreign policy flank of the Republican Party, which made an idol of the United States' unipolar hegemony.

The reviews for *The Neoconservative Mind* yielded an attractive job offer in the land of my longtime California fantasy that would have taken me out of theology. But leaving Kalamazoo was out of play for Brenda and me, and I was already writing *Soul in Society*, eager to return to my theological homeland. This book constructively interpreted the social gospel, Niebuhrian realist, and liberationist movements in social ethics, braiding a fusion of these perspectives. I did not conceive it as a history of social ethics since it analyzed only the three major paradigms before driving to my argument that ecojustice and economic democracy must go together. The book was widely reviewed however, many social ethicists assigned it as a history of their field, and when Union Theological Seminary came for me ten years later, it was for *Soul in Society*.

James Cone assigned it at Union for its analysis of how Black liberationist, womanist, and feminist theologies transformed social ethics. Ethicist Larry Rasmussen assigned it at Union for its methodological analyses and its emphasis on ecology. Former Union president Donald Shriver wrote a wonderful review of the book, so I invited him to speak at our Baccalaureate service. Don took a side trip to Chicago and got stuck on I-94. Stetson Chapel filled to overflowing with no Baccalaureate speaker. I was well into an improvisation when Don and Peggy Shriver burst through the front door and Don marched straight to the pulpit. Afterward we decompressed at a hotel bar. Don asked if we had met when I was a student at Union and he was president, I said no, he took a deep breath, and declared: "My chief qualification for being the president of Union Theological Seminary was my immense capacity for absorbing hostility!" He reeled off four harrowing stories of the hostility he endured at Union. All had intertwining ideological, personal, and financial factors, and all had cut him deeply. But Don said he still loved Union, and he hoped very much that I would someday teach there.[16]

Soul in Society defined me in the social ethics field, where many colleagues described me as a rival-opposite of eminent Duke University ethicist Stanley Hauerwas. Stan contended that the social gospel was wrong to ascribe a social justice mission to Christianity, after which Reinhold Niebuhr espoused a social gospel stripped of idealism, after which liberationists doubled down on the social gospel mistake in radical new ways. Social justice, Stan said, is a bad idea that diverted Christian ethics from its proper starting point in the oddly distinctive, pacifist, kingdom-centered faith of Jesus. Stan and I debated our differences in various forums and forged a friendship. He wrote a history of American Christian ethics that fixed on seven White male theologians—Rauschenbusch, Niebuhr, Richard Niebuhr, John Courtney Murray, Paul Ramsey, James Gustafson, and John Howard Yoder. I implored Stan not to represent our field in this way, and he subsequently wrote a much-quoted article announcing that he would not publish the book. On his telling, the field of Christian ethics had lost its way, his own prominence in it notwithstanding. My disagreements with Stan were deep. I rejected the dichotomy between the faithful church and the pagan everything else that he borrowed from Yoder, which disparaged other religions, reduced the kingdom of God to a my-group binary, claimed "nonviolent us" status distinguished from unrighteous others, and thereby masked the oppressions named in liberation theologies. But I never regarded myself as the opposite of Stan because we shared the same basis in the gospel. He was and is a Christian brother to me.[17]

Every year I enlisted local rabbis and Holocaust survivors to help me organize a Holocaust Memorial Observance. We filled Stetson Chapel to its six-hundred-seat capacity, so I instituted a second service in the evening that also filled the chapel. Many Jewish and Christian congregants drove considerable distances to attend these services. With the survivors especially in mind, I was an assiduous gatekeeper of the rules for these occasions that famed Holocaust survivor and writer Elie Wiesel prescribed: Do not substitute your memory for that of the survivors. Let the martyrs and survivors tell their story in their words. There is plenty of testimony to draw from; it should be enough for you. Wait, at least, until the last survivor is gone before you remember them with your own memories and hang-ups.

That was my model for my first ten years of Holocaust memorials. Every year the service was completely different and always the same. The music and readings changed, but not the Wiesel definition of what it means to remember the Holocaust. We did not allow students to read their poems. We did not allow Christians to talk about themselves and their guilt. In the early years I made a liberationist point in generalized language, urging that our religious traditions must reach out in solidarity to the oppressed and dispossessed. I said it a bit stronger each year, naming the Palestinians and Kurds in a litany of the oppressed, declaring that our religious traditions are not worth saving if they do not stand for justice. My organizing team caught flak for the litanies that expanded the frame of the occasion, which caused some hurt feelings and dropouts, but this issue did not destroy the service as we were warned. The service thrived until K's Jewish students demanded to know for whom it was designed.

In 1997 they began to rebel against the Wiesel rules. Our Jewish students wanted to read their poems and talk about themselves. They were not impressed with Elie Wiesel's authority, and that first year, I was offended, thinking silently, "Who are you to ruin this service? You're nineteen years old; you grew up in a shopping mall; you've never done anything for social justice." But I gave some ground because I liked them, and I realized that generational experience cannot be replicated. Generation X had its own traumas to negotiate. The next year, our students spurned the Wiesel model and my tender feelings for the old folks who attended every year. Whom was Stetson Chapel here to serve? The year after that, they completely threw out the old service.

No, they would not read a selection from Viktor Frankl. To make this service relevant to them, our students had to take it over, and I had to face the anger and disappointment of the survivors, rabbis, and local religious communities who treasured the old model and grieved to see it end. In my last years at K, the Holocaust memorial featured the poetry and prose of K students, the crowds sharply diminished, we cut back to one service, it was modestly attended, and I recognized that the new service was better than mine in three ways. It spoke the plaintive, personal, direct language of Generation X. It allowed our students to express their grief about the Palestinian crisis and everything else that troubled them. And it taught me that I had perpetuated, for too long, the over-investment of the ecumenical movement in a remembrance model of ecumenism. The next phase of Jewish-Christian ecumenism must put liberationist faith at the center, not ritual remembrances of the Holocaust.

It grew harder to keep up with the relentless demands of the LACC program, though I appreciated the upside, hosting literary theorist Michael Awkward (University of Michigan), sociologist Orlando Patterson (Harvard), organizer theorists Harry C. Boyte (University of Minnesota) and Ernesto Cortés Jr. (Industrial Areas Foundation), sociologists Robert Bellah (UC-Berkeley) and Amitai Etzioni (George Washington University), historians Darlene Clark Hine (Michigan State University) and Martin E. Marty (University of Chicago), activist rabbi Balfour Brickner (Stephen Wise Free Synagogue in New York City), theologians John B. Cobb Jr. (Claremont School of Theology) and Daniel Maguire (Marquette University), neoconservative Catholic writer Richard John Neuhaus, and philosophers Robert C. Neville (Boston University), Hilary

Putnam (Harvard), and Ken Baynes (SUNY-Stony Brook). I shared affinities with all of them that produced treasured memories.

Awkward drew upon Black American literature to make a case for crossing cultural boundaries. Patterson argued that freedom-consciousness is rare, historically Christian, and recent, as he said in *Freedom in the Making of Western Culture* (1991). I organized workshops for community organizers to meet with Boyte, who returned twice to K, and Cortés, an iconic figure in the IAF tradition. Bellah and I conducted a wary dance. We shared progressive Christianity, democratic socialism, Tillich's concept of religion as a symbolic expression of ultimate concern, and an emphasis on moral imagination. I liked and respected Bellah immensely, commending especially his contention that the moral languages of capitalist and expressive individualism have overwhelmed the languages of biblical faith and civic republicanism in U.S. American life, to its detriment. Bellah was conservative in the same specific sense that I am, seeking to conserve the formational and liberating aspects of America's religious communities of memory. But we had a tense lunch in which I said that *Habits of the Heart* was seriously marred by its White, male, Protestant, middle-class purview. Bellah defended the book's gestural invocation of MLK; I said that rendering a dehistoricized King as an exemplar of White progressivism heightened the book's whiteness problem; and Bellah was unhappy with me. Afterwards, he and I approached each other cautiously at conferences. Etzioni had not yet plunged into communitarian movement-building when he spoke at K; later he tried to enlist me to shore up the left flank of his movement. As he envisioned it, I would be a counterweight to conservative communitarians, and he would be the Wise One in the middle.[18]

Hine spoke out of her historical research on Black nurses, and Marty gave a puckish-virtuoso talk on the ironies of postmodernism. Brickner's magnetism lit up our dinner crowd before he gave a riveting talk on being passionately Zionist and pro-Palestinian. Cobb decried the eco-crisis and the anti-intellectualism of American churches, both from a Whiteheadian perspective, and Maguire wowed our crowd three times with scintillating talks that glossed his books on social justice ethics. Neuhaus teased me that he deserved many more pages than he got in *The Neoconservative Mind*, we luxuriated outside on a park bench so he could smoke, and we vowed on the way back to the airport to keep talking, which happened several times subsequently. Neville argued that pragmatism and meta-physics go together, with or without his ontology of creative action, and Putnam, a high-flyer like Neville, similarly graced us for two days with his generosity, acumen, and expansive conception of pragmatism.[19]

Introducing Ken Baynes to Christopher Latiolais was a sweet delight for me. Ken's book *The Normative Grounds of Social Criticism* (1991) combined Rawls' theory of justice with Jürgen Habermas' theory of communicative rationality. He promptly cut to shoptalk with Chris, who had studied under Robert Pippen at UC–San Diego and with Habermas at Goethe University Frankfurt. Chris joined the K faculty through the self-sacrificing generosity of my philosophy colleague David Scarrow. We conducted faculty searches in which hiring a White male was out of the question because nearly every department's history was a parade of White males. It fell upon our generation to diversify the faculty. We lost Linda Alcoff to Syracuse, conducted a search for a feminist philosopher, and narrowed the field to three finalists, while dutifully reading other files. David remarked with a blend of pain and wonder, "Look at this Lat-iol-is guy! He is incredible!" I launched into a diversity-imperative speech, but David cut me off. He wasn't protesting; he was only registering his regret, which worked on him. At our next meeting he issued a proposal: what if he traded his retirement for a second appointment that we filled now, hiring this Latiolais guy?[20]

And so I lucked into my closest friend on the faculty, a Habermas-like polymath who taught across the entire Continental and analytical waterfront in philosophy and filled his home with antique treasures. Chris taught and embodied the Habermas thesis that rationality is best located in structures of interpersonal linguistic communication. He implored us to get as much as possible out of Kantian practical reason instead of assuming that our identities and language games are incommensurable. He and I wrangled over Habermas' turn against the Kantian transcendental frame, and he unfailingly came to my chapel talks, translating what I said into atheist philosophy steeped in Kierkegaard, Nietzsche, Heidegger, Theodor Adorno, Mikhail Bakhtin, and Habermas. He took me to his favorite antique stores, where the owners brought out silver trays that they saved for him. Brenda and Laura tolerated no philosophy talk when we gathered as a foursome, which was often. We breezed through each other's homes, I hired Laura to save us from being crushed by the LACC steamroller, and Brenda constantly teased Laura and Chris that they never adjusted to Midwest culture. They were Europeans by way of California. Sara and I often picked up Cecelia Latiolais, Marie Kutz-Marks, or Kelsey Kimm on our way to a park. Meanwhile Brenda dragged Laura to a year-round Christmas store in Frankenmuth for a weekend just to enjoy the spectacle of Laura blanching at Midwest Christmas kitsch.

In 1990, University of Chicago political philosopher Iris Marion Young published a landmark book, *Justice and the Politics of Difference*, that reframed how I taught social ethics. She contended that a theory of justice informed by liberationist movements must begin with the concepts of domination and oppression, not distribution. A sense of justice must arise from listening, not from applying purportedly universal principles of justice. Young developed a fivefold concept of oppression as exploitation, marginalization, powerlessness, cultural imperialism, and violence. Distributive injustices, she argued, may contribute to, or result from, these forms of oppression, but all involve structures and relations beyond distribution. I agreed with that without accepting her rejection of universal human rights.[21]

Young's argument played a featured role in the roiling academic debates of the 1990s over cultural leftism. Old-style social democrats in the orbit of *Dissent* magazine charged that cultural leftists like Young and Judith Butler ruined the Left by undermining its advocacy of economic justice and common dreams; sociologist Todd Gitlin and philosopher Richard Rorty were prominent in this school. Butler countered that the only significant Left to survive neoliberalism and postmodernity was the cultural Left; socialists should be grateful instead of snarling at it. She fashioned a gender-bending stew of philosophy, anthropology, literary theory, and psychoanalysis, pioneering the queer theory thesis that gender is a performance with a script and an audience. Marxists and social democrats denied that Butler's work was a contribution to Left politics; *Dissent* mocked it as a model of how not to write for *Dissent*. Young was more troubling to the socialist Left for clearly belonging to it, but she elevated cultural recognition and liberation above economic justice.

Nancy Fraser made her breakthrough in 1995 by intervening in this debate, contending that the major axes of injustice are two-dimensional. Every form of injustice is rooted simultaneously in the political economy and the status order. No struggle for justice can succeed lacking a politics of redistribution *and* a politics of recognition. Fraser charged that Butler trivialized the commitment of the socialist Left to economic justice and that Young wrongly ignored terribly real tensions that exist between the redistribution and recognition orientations. Redistribution strategies silence the most pressing causes of harm for denigrated groups, while recognition strategies try to mitigate unjust outcomes without changing the underlying structures that generate unjust outcomes. Fraser said welfare state distributive justice is inadequate and so is multicultural recognition. To make a real advance beyond them, the political Left must add insult to injury by wedding two forms of utopianism—socialist redistribution and feminist-liberationist recognition.[22]

This debate crowded into the time that my course on social ethics devoted to the complex pluralistic equality of Walzer, the common good religiosity of Bellah, and the liberationist Christianity of West and Ruether. I felt some misgiving about featuring the fractious Young-Butler-Rorty-Fraser argument, which lost the spiritual ethos of my previous emphasis on Walzer-Bellah-West-Ruether and which sometimes turned class discussions into sidebars on Foucault and Derrida. I liked Foucault's analysis of omnipresent relations of power, recognized the brilliance of Derrida's negative differential ontology, and appreciated that both influenced Butler, whose queer theory *was* a major contribution to left politics, a game-changer. But the deconstructionist heyday purveyed a nihilistic denigration of subjectivity and moral reason that I disliked very much, and I lacked a good answer for students who asked why a course centered on Young and Fraser was taught in the Religion Department. I redesigned the course several times and never felt that I got it right. I felt a similar pang about what happened to my course on liberation theologies. The early version ran long on the founders: Cone, Gutiérrez, and Míguez Bonino. It brimmed with the texts and revolutionary contexts that created liberation theology, but both felt remote in the 1990s, a nadir period so grim and depressing that no amount of updating could mask the problem: we were living amid the triumph of neoliberal globalization, which yielded predatory races to the bottom and Bill Clinton's cynical triangulating presidency. If Wall Street capitalism was completely triumphant, it was hard to persuade college students that liberation theology still mattered.

These were years of intense demoralization on the Left. DSA asked me in 1999 and 2000 if I could write an encouraging word about anything.

I could not, writing that Clinton mustered deep-down conviction and sought to change public opinion on only one issue in his entire presidency, the North American Free Trade Agreement. His so-called third way kept tacking to the right because you can't triangulate with a Left that doesn't exist. I didn't mean there was no Left. I meant there was no Left that pulled Clinton to the left or that compelled him to take it seriously. Harrington built DSOC on the conviction that democratic socialist ideas advance during periods of liberal ascendancy in solidarity with mass movements. I believed that was right, and still do, but liberalism was dead, replaced by a neoliberal counterfeit, and you had to be middle-aged to remember what a mass movement felt like.[23]

Cornel West had already been to Kalamazoo, so I failed to lure him back, but he told me about a brilliant doctoral student at Princeton whom I should invite, Michael Eric Dyson. Dyson had grown up amid Detroit's flourishing Motown cultural vitality of the early 1960s and its devastation after the riot of 1967. Born in 1958, he beheld the '67 riot with a stunned awe. A year later he was watching television when a news bulletin interrupted, announcing that King had been shot in Memphis. Dyson had never heard of King or Memphis. His first clue that this mattered terribly was that his stepfather froze with a stricken look. The television networks replayed King's mountaintop sermon of the previous night. Dyson recognized King's words about the Promised Land, which never evoked at his church the tumultuous response that King evoked. He caught that something magical was happening at Mason Temple. Dyson watched the program transfixed, somehow knowing he would never be the same.

He married early, at nineteen, preached at a Baptist Church in Detroit, studied at Carson-Newman College in Jefferson City, Tennessee, and traveled to Union Seminary to meet West, who encouraged him. Dyson won admission in 1985 to the doctoral program in Religion at Princeton, where he studied under ethicist Jeffrey Stout, religious historian Albert Raboteau, and philosopher of religion Victor Preller, before West arrived in 1988. At K, I saw immediately why West recommended him. Dyson was hyper-articulate and torrential in West's fashion, fusing his street savvy and graduate education. The backbone of his talk came from the Malcolm X section of his dissertation, from which he veered into riffs on MC Hammer, 2 Live Crew, Public Enemy, Michael Jackson, Spike Lee, and John Singleton. He described hip-hop as the CNN of Black culture, explained that the capping/belittling techniques of "dissing" rap had a history in Black oral practices, and said he loved the bawdy humor of 2 Live Crew, while rejecting its misogyny. Rap musicians were the cultural griots and street preachers of contemporary urban life, refashioning the signifying parodies of Black folk culture. For those who love hip hop, Dyson argued, it often compensates for the decline of the Black church. They hear the powerful religious message in it—oftentimes more prophetic than anything said in a local Black church.

The lecture sparkled, gyrated, teased, and soared; it felt that Dyson could have kept going for hours. Later that year he published a book version, *Reflecting Black* (1993). It marked out the three intersecting fields of his subsequent work: Black popular culture, the intersections of race, gender, sexuality, class, and politics, and Black religion. Dyson went only so far with Cone's thesis that all Black people are united by Black suffering and struggle, as epitomized by Martin and Malcolm. Dyson appreciated what Cone meant but stressed that King had more in common with Harrington than with Black conservatives like George Schuyler. "Black experience" names too much complexity and diversity to be homogeneous, or the content of a unity category. *Reflecting Black* contained previously published pieces from a stunning range of periodicals—*Z Magazine*, *Artvu*, *Tikkun*, *Cultural Studies*, *Christianity and Crisis*, *New York Times Book Review*, *Nation*, *Democratic Left*, *Emerge*, *Social Text*, and *DePaul Law Review*. I read the acknowledgments page and let the intimidating evidence wash over me: he had barely begun and had already published this widely?[24]

Dyson *was* just getting started. In 1995 I brought him back to Kalamazoo to be our Baccalaureate speaker. He was jovial through dinner but blanched at the sea of White-parent faces filling cavernous Stetson Chapel. I caught his reaction and urged him—do what you do, we don't need your imitation of a White sermon. He was still skittish until I gave an introduction that waxed long on his personal background and sampled some of his writing in *Reflecting Black* and *Making Malcolm* (1995). Dyson gave me a nod, said "ok," tucked his prepared text under his chair, and riffed for forty scintillating minutes. A student speaker and a reader had preceded him. Dyson stitched his improvised sermon around what he had just heard, strumming on the Dry Bones of Ezekiel 37. It was sensational. There were set pieces from sermons he had preached and *Making Malcolm*, but they were delivered as gold standard improvisational response. Stetson

Chapel shook from the tumultuous reaction of the graduates, and I played flak-catcher with many of their outraged parents.[25]

Afterward we decompressed in my office before heading to a sports bar and the televised National Basketball Association playoffs. I had made only a halfway transition to 1990s technology, so a manuscript of my next book, *The Word as True Myth: Interpreting Modern Theology* (1997), was parked on my desk. Michael delayed our NBA plan, riffed through the manuscript, and read chunks of it aloud. This book fortified the Tillich-Niebuhr argument about excavating the truth in myths with a quasi-Barthian argument that the Word must transform myths for their truth to be realized. In Christ, the hidden God is apprehended not by sight or in God's being, but by faith through grace and in (mythic) sign. It surprised Michael that Karl Barth was in my head to this degree. Then he admonished me: "Why are you teaching college students? You should be shaping the field at a seminary, training doctoral students." This judgment stuck in my head for nearly a decade, partly because Michael brushed off my assurance that I loved teaching college students. These books, he observed, were not aimed at college students—I was called to be somewhere else. But my beloved spouse and daughter tied me intimately and irrevocably to Kalamazoo until Sara finished high school.[26]

A lifetime of fighting depression had prepared Brenda for a decade of battling cancer. In the early years she said that cancer was nowhere near as terrible as depression. She stopped saying it after the recurrences began, meanwhile enduring all the surviving-cancer rhetoric that she could stand. Brenda appreciated that many people find solace in the institutionalized practices and piety that one encounters upon receiving a cancer diagnosis. As a pastor she was familiar with all of it before she became a cancer patient. But she had little tolerance for most of it as applied to herself, beginning with survivor talk, which she loathed. "Nobody survives cancer," she would say. Obligatory happy-talk repelled her, pious and not, especially when people imposed it on her insistently. Brenda was a Good Friday Christian even during her so-called survivor years, when she joined a Jazzercise class and loved it.

I watched her across the gym at West Hills Athletic Club while I ran on a treadmill. She bounced and emoted, yelled encouragement to strugglers, and teased the instructor. In September 1994 she preached a baptism sermon that began with a Jazzercise story: "The other night I was approached by someone who wanted to know where I preach, how often I preach, and what I preach about. All of this while we were warming up." Brenda said she tried to be succinct and encouraging, but the woman interrupted her, cutting to the real point: "Will I feel good when I leave your church? I want to feel good." Brenda replied, not so confidently, "Well," and the music began, mercifully. Her faltering "well" apparently answered the question, for the woman did not approach her afterwards or come to First Presbyterian.

Brenda clarified that she did not blame this person for wanting to feel good at church. She wanted to feel good too. But the gospel, she said, is emphatic that what human beings want from God is not what God offers. Jesus let go of his power so that a woman who had suffered pain and social isolation might be healed. He rose above his need for acceptance by consorting with the unacceptable. He wept in anguish on Palm Sunday because the crowd cheered for the wrong things and he knew where he was headed. He died on a cross and forgave those who crucified him. Brenda said we need to hear that God loves us as we are, but we also need to hear that we are supposed to participate in God's love. As long as we kill each other with guns and armies, we are invited by God to weep, and to learn the things that make for peace. As long as there is cruelty and injustice, hunger and pain, we are invited to suffer with the suffering in a way that leads to redemption. And in accepting this invitation we find our salvation.

Brenda took on a searing tragedy in her ministry shortly before her first cancer recurrence. A young mother who attended First Presbyterian drifted off to sleep, awoke with a shot of fright, looked frantically for her infant child across the bedroom and the den, through the living room, to the swimming pool, where she found her drowned son. Brenda would leave the house clutching her service book like a life preserver, groping for words. The woman swung back and forth between blaming God and condemning herself. Brenda gently urged her not to blame herself, without correcting her theology. It felt too soon to poke a hole in the worldview that might be a lifeline. Finally, after weeks of this, she took up the theology issue, cautioning her friend against blaming God. Brenda said that faith, to her, was not about explaining things: "I don't believe in a Sky Father God who makes everything happen. To me, God is the mystery of life. I think that God's heart breaks at the death of a child."

In 1995 a routine test revealed that Brenda's cancer had recurred as bone metastasis. We were crushed by this news. We camped out in her office, not ready to face Sara, someone brought us a Burger King dinner, and we cried and grieved. Brenda said, "It's a death march from here onward." She had recently received a full-time appointment at First Presbyterian, an achievement she prized immensely. Letting go of it was excruciating for her, which she prolonged for a year, squeezing all that was left of her career cruelly cut short. In 1997 we planned a fall vacation to Disney World but were told to reschedule the trip because Brenda had only a month to live. The three of us hurried to Disney World, where I wheeled Brenda to Epcot and the like in the morning, and she emoted gamely, wanting desperately to make a last good memory for Sara. At noon, Sara and I tucked Brenda into bed and undertook afternoon excursions. Every day, heading back to our room with a pounding heart, I feared that Brenda would be dead. At the end of the week, she muttered uncharacteristically, "I guess I'll go home and die."

But she did not die. Perhaps the Pamidronate (Aredia) hardened her bones, or perhaps Brenda's fierce desire to see Sara's next milestone held off her death sentence. Her doctors told me repeatedly that they had no idea how she was still alive. We tried every experimental treatment on offer, as I insisted on trying and Brenda indulged me. We made summer and Christmas visits to two hotels in Traverse City, Michigan, where Brenda suffered constantly, sites of searing memories for me. In November 1998 we returned to Disney World in a triumphant Thanksgiving flourish of sorts, along with the American Academy of Religion, the only time that AAR has ever camped in Orlando. Brenda exulted at wheeling around some of the same parks as last time, I attended no AAR events, and Sara pulled me outdoors for evening swims. Brenda began to talk about one more trip. The following March we flew to Phoenix during spring break for the winding mountainous journey to the Grand Canyon, driving through Sedona, Arizona and the stunning Painted Desert, stealing extra last memories just as NATO forces commenced air strikes against Yugoslavia.

I realized at reading the *New York Times* story about NATO bombing that I had been in a blur for two years, reading stories that didn't register. Brenda asked me to recap the NATO war, and I mumbled something about ethnic cleansing of Albanians and NATO demanding that Yugoslav forces withdraw from Kosovo. Probably anyone in the bar next door could have better explained it. Some part of my brain whirred along during these years, producing my books on evangelical theology and the anti-foundationalist aspects of Barthian theology. Writing these books during the wee hours was the only break I got from the trauma of watching Brenda being tortured to death. I could write about Barthian dialectics and keep track of Brenda's medication schedule but couldn't read a newspaper. We saw as much of the Grand Canyon as possible from a wheelchair. We tried to be thankful for being there and frantically found a medical clinic to treat Sara's strep throat. It frightened me that my thirteen-year-old girl was this close to having only me for a parent.[27]

Johann Sebastian Bach became my everyday companion, his music endlessly looped in my head as compensation and an entry to prayer. I had learned the English Cathedral tradition after becoming an Anglican and had leaned on it for fifteen years, prizing especially John Ireland's anthem "Greater Love Hath No Man," which St. Andrew's Church sang at my ordination, Edgar Bainton's ethereal "And I Saw a New Heaven," and the "Five Mystical Songs" of Ralph Vaughan Williams. Until Brenda's recurrences began, I had no glimmer of how badly I would need Bach's thrilling, complex, profoundly spiritual music. His gloriously transcendent *Mass in B-Minor* became my mainstay. I sang over and over the sublime sacred motet "O Jesu Christ, meins Lebens Licht," and two arias from the *St. Matthew Passion*, "Erbarme dich, mein Gott" and "Mache dich, mein Herze, rein."

Brenda appreciated what Bach meant to me; sometimes she indulged a motet or an aria while we drove home from chemotherapy. But she had grown up on Bach, an every-Sunday given of Lutheran worship. The music that fed her was John Rutter's lovely, colorful, accessible, modern English Cathedral classic *Magnificat*, and above all, the folk-style sacred music of the St. Louis Jesuits, a group of Jesuit composers associated with St. Louis University who moved in 1980 to Seattle. Their songs vivified the liturgical reforms of Vatican Council II, conveying biblical narratives and sayings in hymnody featuring simple, heartfelt, singable contemporary melodies and acoustic guitars. The luminous pastoral song from the *Earthen Vessels* album (1975), "Be Not Afraid," written by Bob Dufford, was one of Brenda's favorites. Her favorite was Dan Schutte's incomparable spiritual jewel "Here I Am, Lord." We sang it together countless times. All these years later, I cannot sing it or even hear it without bursting into tears, because it is beautiful and so Brenda.

On July 15, 1999, my parents drove down to Kalamazoo with my sister-in-law Robyn Dorrien and niece Hope Dorrien to quietly celebrate that Brenda made it to birthday number fifty. Brenda was too violently ill to join us, which everyone gathered understood. But Robyn's spirited voice wafted upstairs, Brenda called me upstairs to help her, she surprised herself by joining the party, and she roared with laughter at reaching fifty. In the fall we sang together her repertoire of favorite hymns, which included most of the St. Louis Jesuit songbook, and Brenda asked for stories about the ministerial characters in my first volume on liberal theology. Gradually she became less and less able to track Sara's stories about music rehearsals and performances, which frustrated her. In December, Brenda got out of bed and fell to the floor; the cancer had gone to her brain. She wearied of fighting it. In January she enlisted Laura, who had taken a position with Kalamazoo Hospice, to help her tell me that she was done with fighting. That night I shook and wept for hours in the garage.

My band of angels began to take over. Pam and Becca took control of the chapel and LACC programs, and three nurses from the church clinic—Marcia Cowell, Phyllis Curtis, and Jane Givens—relieved me at class time as I taught my Winter quarter classes. Brenda's lion and lamb never did lie down together. She had terrible anxiety attacks nearly to the end, sometimes raging and shaking for half the night, despite being highly medicated. She opted every day for me to carry her to a bath, spurning sponge baths, sagely declaring that she wanted to honor whatever body she had left. She delivered homiletic lessons, near the end telling Jan that privileged types like us will need to serve in heaven. Brenda had just endured two nights of brutal anxiety attacks, so Jan pushed back: "Surely you will get to rest and be served by others in heaven. You've been through so much in the last ten years." Brenda was adamant: "No, I've had a good life. Think of the children who never grew up, who had no parents to comfort them. Children who starved to death. We must gladly serve them."

People told me constantly how important Brenda had been to them. Some told stories about the magnificent funeral eulogies she gave for a parent or grandparent. Some recalled being startled, and then delighted, by her wisecracking bluntness. Many described her as being real in a way that they had not expected to encounter in a minister. In her last months we received a crush of cards and letters that retold the stories and said thank you, I love you, and goodbye. One day, eyeing a pile of them, Brenda asked me, "Have you written thank-you notes to these people?" "I've written a few," I offered weakly. She rolled her eyes and said, "What am I going to do with you?"

Sara bloomed as a singer in Brenda's last months. This girl who loved to sing, and who cherished her eighth-grade music teacher, Theresa Johnson, began to sing constantly after her mother entered the final phase. Sara belted torch songs in January and February 2000, repelling the looming specter of death, filling the house with her defiant voice. The gala of the Kalamazoo Children's Chorus approached, and Sara tried out for her first featured solo, singing "Maybe" from *Annie*. It's the heartbreaker song of the show in any context, and I fretted how-in-God's-name could she do it? Sara won the solo slot and began to sing the song all the time.

She sang it with stunning beauty and control, adding all the songs in the show just before Brenda faded into a semi-coma. On the way to Sara's last dress rehearsal, I told her, "Sweetie, Mommy is going to die sometime in the next few days." She quietly said, "Ok." The next night she sang "Maybe" like an angel, perfectly, with a breathtaking tender vulnerability. Most of the crowd didn't know what they were witnessing, besides a wonderful performance. Those of us who knew were undone by it. The Dorrien grandparents were there, while the Biggs grandparents readied for the trip to Kalamazoo. Anson and Grace knew they could not bear to watch their daughter die. They asked me to call for them, and John, at the very near end.

Brenda gave instructions to Jan and Laura and Becca about not letting me fall into a dark hole, and instructions to me about her funeral: "You know, there's going to be a huge crowd at my funeral. Can you give them this message? 'In lieu of flowers, please vote for Democrats.'" Shortly after midnight on Good Friday, April 21, I crawled into bed and held Brenda for the last time. She was still breathing when I drifted asleep. Two hours later, I awoke, and she was gone. I held her for an hour, putting off the necessity of awaking Sara and calling Brenda's parents. Finally, I went for Sara. She promptly walked to our bed, climbed on top of Brenda, and kissed her on the lips, saying, "Goodbye, Mommy; I love you." When they carried Brenda's body down the staircase, I unleashed some godawful unhinged scream. For a moment I was too insane to protect the feelings of my fourteen-year-old girl. At the funeral, which was as huge as Brenda expected, we did not sing her favorite hymn and mine, "Lift High the Cross," because we had many Jewish, secular, and other non-Christian friends who would not have known how to hear its love language about a crucified King:

> Each newborn servant of the Crucified
> bears on the brow the seal of him who died.
>
> Lift high the cross, the love of Christ proclaim
> till all the world adore his sacred name.

6

OVER FROM KALAMAZOO

I had never taught a class with empty rows until I lost Brenda. Then I walked into a class and counted eight students. It stunned me speechless. K students had learned belatedly of the pain I was in and steered clear of it. I got through the class only because it contained one godsend female student with an ebullient personality who refused to let me ruin it.

The Clinton years ran out, and Vice President Al Gore spent the summer of 2000 vowing to fight for the hurting people whom Bill Clinton left behind, which offended Clinton. Clinton had done some good things. He pushed through a gas tax—the last president even to try. He tried to make peace between Israel and the Palestinians, and he presided over a robust economy, running three years of budget surpluses. But he took pride in ramming NAFTA down our throats. He terminated the government's sixty-year commitment to provide income support for the poor, expanded the federal death penalty and the war on drugs, and supported the Defense of Marriage Act. He waved goodbye to manufacturing jobs with a lot of happy-talk about the blessings of neoliberalism, perfectly representing the Democratic political class that rolled over for vulture capitalism, leveraged buyouts, and stock buy-backs. Near the end he tore down the Glass-Steagall wall separating commercial and investment banking, whereby Wall Street fell in love with derivatives. I wrote articles against his triangulating opportunism and true-believing neoliberalism, but my books of that period were exclusively theological because I was too traumatized for anything else.

I taught the Senior Majors course during Brenda's last months of dying while my angel helpers Pam Sotherland and Becca Kutz-Marks ran Stetson Chapel and the LACC program. Brenda's ten-year battle had not prepared me in any way for losing her. The door closed and I was thrown into another world. For two years of grieving and grace with Sara, I had a pounding head with brain fog, the world acquired color only through Sara's ventures in it, and I fought off an overpowering aggressor, never believing that therapy might have helped, since talking about myself for fifty minutes was the last thing I could have tolerated. Then I crawled into the sunlight just in time to rally against an imperial catastrophe and to experience two years of golden beauty.

James F. Jones Jr., our president since 1996, looked out for me while he doubled K's endowment. Jimmy said the heart of a college is its faculty: administrators come and go, but the faculty defines a college and sustains it. We professors nodded approvingly while counting on him to reverse the college's recent losses. Jimmy was a buoyant personality from the business class of Atlanta, Georgia, the Georgia Military Academy, and graduate degrees at Emory, the Sorbonne, and Columbia. He had given up his career as a scholar of Romance languages and literature to build up academic institutions as an administrator, coming to us from Southern Methodist University in Dallas. Southwest Michigan was a foreign country to him. Jimmy relished the cultural challenge it posed, though a sizable chunk of our faculty never let him forget that he was an outsider with strange ways.

As an overachiever who worried about everything, Jimmy pushed himself to exhaustion while fretting about stroking out. On his watch the College created ten endowed faculty chairs, increased student scholarship and faculty development funds, and renovated five major buildings. Jimmy's many passions included opera, piano, organ, Charles-Marie Widor's "Symphony for Organ No. 5," camping, mountain climbing, fishing, Cuban cigars from Paris, jogging, the Episcopal Church, cavorting with his Irish field setters Reva and Atticus, running antique Lionel trains, and driving his antique automobiles. A reporter asked him about the cars, and he replied, "Well you know, these are little boy things." There was a lot of little boy in Jimmy, and a boy who could have taken a clerical track. He told me that he may have missed his clerical calling but wanted this presidency at K to be his ministry.

I had vowed when the faculty asked three colleagues and me to coax a resignation from Larry Bryan that I would not befriend the next president; it was just too painful. Jimmy swept me into his life, contending that we had too much in common not to be friends, and schemed with

Don Parfet to establish the College's first distinguished professorship, the Ann V. and Donald R. Parfet Distinguished Chair. Don was a prominent business executive and magnanimous civic leader who headed ten different companies over his career. The plans for the Parfet inaugural were underway when Brenda died, after which Jimmy aimed for an event in February 2001, telling me I might be able to feel something by then.

I wrote over two hundred thank-you cards and gave thanks for the women in our lives who looked out for Sara: Jan, Becca, Laura, Theresa Johnson, Janet Brody, my mother, ubiquitously called Nanny after she became a grandmother, and especially beloved Robyn Hampton Dorrien. The galley proofs for volume one of my trilogy on theological liberalism, *The Making of American Liberal Theology: Imagining Progressive Religion* (2001) arrived in the summer of 2000 and defeated me. I had entertained Brenda in her last year with my best stories about William Ellery Channing, Ralph Waldo Emerson, Horace Bushnell, Elizabeth Cady Stanton, Henry Ward Beecher, Theodore Munger, and other notables of volume one. Most were pastors and all were colorful nineteenth-century characters; Brenda regretted not having known about Beecher. Then came the galleys, which my editor Stephanie Egnotovich filled with red ink, making them unreadable to me. Stephanie tied a great many short sentences to the preceding or succeeding longer ones. The rhythms that I worked so hard to create by mixing short and long sentences, she did not like; she said it's wrong to let readers take a breath. I untangled some of the run-on sentences she created, but couldn't pay attention to her markings, and gave up. Stephanie was a dear friend to me, which made it harder to push back. She had edited my two previous books and was very high on the new one, telling me it was a highlight of her career to work on it.[1]

Sara and I went to Albany in June 2000 for a memorial service for Brenda. We were love-bombed at First Presbyterian Church, which helped a little, and toured Sara's early childhood home and neighborhood on Willett Street. Then we headed to New York City to feast on Broadway shows. When Sara took interest in a show, she learned all the songs and sang them constantly. Now our show-consciousness exploded. We didn't bypass anything we wanted to see, and we tried out shows we had never heard of. My girl knew what she liked, and I wanted only to compensate for the trauma that was her childhood. The so-called popular girls at her elementary school had treated her cruelly for being a hurting kid with a dying mother. School life improved for Sara in intermediate school mostly because of one person, music teacher Theresa Johnson.

Theresa demanded the disciplined attention of her students, taught them how to sing, and mother-loved them, ferrying chronic truants to school with her own two children in the backseat. She was a pillar of Hillside Intermediate School and of her Black Pentecostal congregation. Sara adored her, and so did I. Talking constantly about Mrs. Johnson and developing a magnificent obsession with singing were intertwined developments in Sara's life. In September 2000 she moved up to Kalamazoo Central High School, where she won all-state honors in singing four times.

The election of November 2000 and the drama of dimples and chads pretty much sailed past me. When journalists called for a quote, it surprised me to come up with anything. Volume one was showered with laudatory reviews, and Stephanie said, "I told you so!" I cringed at the run-on constructions I would not have written but didn't tell her for two years, waiting until she and I went through this dance again on volume two. Volume one bore my new Parfet title alongside the only usable picture of me from a recent publicity shoot. K College communications director Scotty Allen and photographer Keith Mumma traipsed through my house to get a decent picture and failed. I looked sick and withdrawn; there was no light in me. The publicity for the Parfet gala contained no pictures of the honoree, and the picture on the book was a distance shot with a tiny head poking out of a lawn hedge.

My Parfet lecture was a high-flyer: "Hegelian Spirit and Holy Spirit: Theology, Myth, and Divine Transcendence." There was more love in the room than I could handle, so I fixed on a spot at the back and avoided faces, expounding the category of Spirit in Hegel's intersubjective dynamic fashion, lingering at the cross in Hegel's tragic Lutheran fashion, conveying my debts to Paul Tillich on theologizing broken myth, and making my argument for liberal engagement with critical disbelief and liberationist opposition to domination and oppression.[2]

My pounding head and its fog began to worry me by the summer of 2001. I had sworn off alcohol in 1995 to reduce the depressive pressure in my life, so the first thing the grief literature commends—stop drinking—I had already done. Taking a quarter off from my job and the next book might have helped, but Becca and I were running Stetson

Chapel and the LACC program by ourselves, and the grief books didn't know that I love to write. I've never felt chained to it. So I slogged through the summer, grateful that my classes had rebounded, and wrote volume two, *The Making of American Liberal Theology: Idealism, Realism, and Modernity* (2003). It covered the first half of the twentieth century, necessitating trips to the library archives of Boston University, the University of Chicago, Union Theological Seminary, and Colgate Rochester Crozer Divinity School in Rochester, New York. K had a late September start in 2001, so Sara stayed with Becca and Marie while I flew to Rochester on September 10 for two days of immersion in the papers of Walter Rauschenbusch.[3]

I had previously given the Stanley I. Stuber Lectures at Rochester and spoken at a conference there, so I knew the city well enough to have favorite running routes. On the first day I pored over Rauschenbusch's letters in the afternoon and ran afterward. The next morning, I took an extra-long run in the radiant sunshine of that fateful day. On the way back to the hotel, I looked up barely in time to see that a driver racing through a red light was about to run me over. I leaped straight upward and landed on her windshield, startling the distracted driver. She was apologetic and I brushed it off; a bruised shoulder was not going to deter my second day in the Rauschenbusch archive. I sprinted with an adrenaline-rush back to the hotel, where a receptionist said you have a call; it was Becca telling me to turn on the television. The North and South Towers of the World Trade Center had been struck and were on fire, a stupendously surreal sight as WTC workers fled for their lives and plunged to their deaths.

The attack on the South Tower dispelled the brief illusion that the attack on the North Tower might be a freak accident. The Pentagon was hit while I hurriedly prepared to head home. I watched the South Tower collapse in a cloud of smoke and dust just before exiting the hotel, racing back to my tenth-grade girl, grateful that I had rented a car in Rochester. Otherwise, I would have hitchhiked to Kalamazoo. I did not risk the shorter route through Canada, taking instead the path around Lake Erie through New York State and Ohio, which at least involved no border controls. Between the car radio and the gasoline stops with crowds glued to television screens, I absorbed the fevered alarm and tragedy of that incomparable day. Al-Qaeda was being named as the likeliest culprit before I made my first gasoline stop, by which time the North Tower had come down. It was hard not to keep gaping at the screen. The network television commentary was restrained compared to what I heard on radio. Broad-brushed epithets about "Muslim terrorists" and cries for vengeance were standard fare. There were reports of long lines and ugly incidents at gasoline stations, so I rushed to Kalamazoo, wanting very much not to get stranded on I-90.

We held K's Convocation on September 27 on the lawn, where I gingerly addressed the world-historical moment while performing the essential work of an opening ceremony: welcome to your college experience! I added LACC speakers on Islam and the Middle East, the only subjects we were discussing anyway, and returned to the archival notes I had taken for volume two of liberalism. This book tied together the three schools of thought and their institutional homes that dominated liberal theology in the first half of the twentieth century: evangelical liberalism (Union Theological Seminary), post-Kantian personal idealism (Boston University), and ultramodern naturalism (University of Chicago), all of which were social gospel traditions. I accentuated Tillich's intellectual debts to Hegel and Friedrich Schelling and made a case for interpreting Reinhold Niebuhr as a liberal who denounced only idealistic, rationalist, and pacifist versions of liberal theology, not the indispensable project of reconciling theology with science and modern thought. Above all, I argued that the most wrongly overlooked tradition in U.S. American religious thought is the Black social gospel. Benjamin E. Mays epitomized it, exactly as MLK believed. I built up to a concluding chapter on Howard Thurman, describing him as a Black social gospel pioneer of interfaith and mystical trends in liberal theology. At conferences I said that I was not the person to write a multivolume history of the Black social gospel, but we needed very much for someone to write it.

My next go-round with Stephanie occurred in the summer of 2002. My ability to concentrate was improving despite the howling-something in my head. I asked Stephanie not to turn my short sentences into run-on constructions that wrecked my cadences, she relented as much as she could stand, I unwound some of her changes, and we settled closer to my end than to hers. That book has a few run-ons that I would not write, but I don't wince when I see people reading it, unlike volume one. Volume two of the liberalism trilogy is the book I wrote even though I cannot remember writing it, the marker that I carried on after losing Brenda.

Greg and Robyn took Sara on high-spirited getaways with their daughter Hope and their extroverted gang of friends—occasions of ineffable gratitude for me. Greg was fifteen years into his directorship of the West Midland Family Center, which he turned into a sprawling showcase of preschool, children's, high school, and adult programs and services. Every summer, Sara and I took in Broadway shows before visiting the Biggs relatives in Bethlehem. All were sweet reunions of loving affection laced with sorrow. Anson and Grace were splendid grandparents to Sara and her cousins Taryn and Ryan Biggs. Grace offered updated assessments of how Sara was exactly like Brenda, sort of like Brenda, and not remotely like Brenda. Usually, she was not far off.

Volume two came out in January 2003, and by then I had written half of volume three, which ran long on Whiteheadian metaphysical arguments about pan-experientialism, self-creating subjects, eternal objects, and various ways of conceiving God as an ordering factor in the process of creativity. But that month I pushed aside volume three, throwing myself headlong against the coming invasion of Iraq. I feared and dreaded through 2002 that President George W. Bush (Bush, or W) would smash into Iraq. Eleven of his foreign policy advisors had called upon Clinton in 1998 to overthrow the government of Saddam Hussein in Iraq, and twenty neocons held high-ranking positions in his administration. Vice President Dick Cheney was the key to this windfall of appointments. He had served as Secretary of Defense in the administration of George H. W. Bush, seethed at the *realpolitikers* who ran it, embraced the unipolar ideology of the neocons, and stocked W's administration with neocons. Deputy Secretary of Defense Paul Wolfowitz and Defense Policy Board chair Richard Perle were the leading neocon appointees. They joined Defense Secretary Donald Rumsfeld, another old hand like Cheney, in fantasizing about smashing Arab regimes, urging Bush that overthrowing Saddam would transform the Middle East.[4]

Neocons and their convert-allies like Cheney and Rumsfeld, plus the unipolar wing of the Democratic Party, had mapped out in the 1990s what was later called the Bush Doctrine, before Bush himself thought about such things. In the early months of W's presidency, he was onboard for unipolar doctrine, spurning the World Court, and achieving what neocons in the Pentagon called full-spectrum dominance. But he angered neocons by temporizing on the Middle East and by refusing to gin up a new Cold War against China. Bush held them off until 9/11 drove him to rally the nation to a perpetual war on terrorism backed by an ideology of preemptive war and unilateral overthrow. On the weekend after 9/11, he told Perle at Camp David that first he would hit Afghanistan, then Iraq. In his State of the Union address of January 29, 2002, Bush declared a "global war on terrorism," vowing to overthrow any nation that aided terrorists and describing Iran, Iraq, and North Korea as an intolerable "axis of evil."[5]

Now he was determined to smash into the Middle East at its center. Iraq was the best candidate because it was a warm-water port with a vast oil supply and seventy-two airfields in the middle of the Middle East, it was under UN sanctions, its tyrannical leader had tried to assassinate Bush's father, and Bush's key advisers had long been determined to overthrow Saddam. They convinced Bush that Iraq would break without much of a fight and a pro-American government would be readily imposed.

But all of that was very hard to talk about in a democratic republic that prided itself on invading only for noble reasons. Bush officials could not get a stampede going by calling for a new imperialist power base in the Middle East, and it would not have been credible to claim a humanitarian ground, since Saddam's fifteen-year reign of brutality had not stopped the United States from arming him against Iran, or later from inciting Iraqi Shia and Kurds to rebel against him. The United States was deeply implicated in both of Saddam's mass-killing rampages, and both were long past when Bush officials said it was an urgent necessity to invade Iraq. State Department experts warned against invading and occupying the Arab world's Yugoslavia. Wolfowitz, Rumsfeld, Perle, and Wolfowitz-Perle protégé Douglas Feith blew off State Department expertise. They had a privileged vision of what would happen and did not allow it to be challenged, never mind that they didn't even know the names of the tribes in Iraq.

To get a stampede going, the Bush administration told Americans that Saddam threatened their safety. It claimed to know that he possessed huge stockpiles of chemical and biological weapons, a nuclear weapons program, and links to al-Qaeda, while knowing very well that it lacked any real evidence. UN inspectors had spent the mid-1990s incinerating Saddam's nerve agents and monitoring his shuttered nuclear program.

The Pentagon had to create its own intelligence unit, which relied on stories from exiles, just to claim that it had some evidence. Neocons had dreamed for years of overthrowing half a dozen Middle Eastern governments. Now they demanded it, competing for toughest-guy status.

Charles Krauthammer, who named the unipolar doctrine, contended after 9/11 that as soon as Bush overthrew the Taliban government in Afghanistan, the United States needed to overthrow Syria, Iran, and Iraq. Angelo Codevilla said the next phase of the war on terrorism must overthrow Iraq, Syria, and the Palestinian Authority. Frank Gaffney said that Iraq, Iran, and the Palestinian Authority headed the list. Michael Ledeen said the toppling order should be Iran, Iraq, Syria, and Saudi Arabia. Norman Podhoretz said the United States needed to kill the regimes in Iraq, Iran, and North Korea, followed soon afterward by Syria, Lebanon, Libya, and the Palestinian Authority, and then Egypt and Saudi Arabia. All had spent the 1990s charging that Clinton wasted America's military dominance by refusing to use it. Now the neocons were riding high, powered by 9/11, Bush's anti-terrorism rhetoric, and patriotic gore.[6]

Pacific School of Religion in Berkeley, California invited me in the summer of 2002 to present the Earl Lectures of January 2003 along with Gustavo Gutiérrez. Each of us would lecture once, followed by a next-day dialogue. PSR faculty dean Delwin Brown, a prominent Whiteheadian theologian, asked me to explicate my liberal-liberation perspective in conversation with Gustavo, which I agreed to do. In the fall, Bush enlisted Congress in his march to war. My revulsion at the authorization spectacle burned off some of my brain fog, though not the pounding. Hardly anyone broke through with a counter-narrative about why the United States was preparing to invade a sovereign nation that had not harmed the United States and had nothing to do with 9/11. In December I asked Del for permission to give a talk titled "Resisting the Permanent War." He agreed and the Earl Lectures were held on January 28, 2003.

Gustavo delivered one of his stock speeches about theologizing from the standpoint of solidarity with the poor. He had given this talk many times, and was in top form at PSR, but said nothing about the world-historical crisis of the moment. The crowd grew restless, and Gustavo ran long. I began to think about shortening my talk when Del whispered to me, "Don't worry about the time. Give us exactly the lecture you planned." That was the permission I needed. I started with a tribute to Gustavo and pivoted to the upcoming invasion of Iraq, contending that it was a looming catastrophe based on manufactured evidence, outright lies, and imperialist hubris. Perhaps Saddam managed to hide some nerve agents from the UN inspectors, but we were not invading Iraq over that. This was the next phase of Bush's so-called war on terrorism. I accepted the legitimacy of UN-backed police action against al-Qaeda in Afghanistan and drew the line there. Bush's declared refusal to distinguish between terrorists like al-Qaeda and those like the Taliban who harbored terrorists was an atrocious rationale for overthrowing any government that Dick Cheney didn't like. From Saddam onward, I said, we were faced with the logic of perpetual war to which Bush had committed the United States. Bush did not select Saddam because he posed a threat to the United States. Saddam was next in line because he was not strong enough to have to be dealt with diplomatically.

The crowd was deathly quiet. I built to a close about purging our own evils and refusing to invade anyone in the Middle East. Christians who fail to repudiate anti-Jewish and anti-Muslim bigotry, Whites who refuse to confess their racism, males who fail to interrogate their sexism, and heterosexuals who denigrate LGBTQ persons perpetuate the evils of an oppressive society and church. If we swear our highest loyalty to our nation, we will perpetuate American imperialism: "Today we need a peace movement that says, 'I don't want my country to invade any nation in the Middle East. I don't want my country to be dragged into wars that don't come remotely close to being a last resort, inflaming resentments that will last for centuries. I don't want my country to plant military bases for itself anywhere in the Middle East. Not in my name do you invade any Muslim nation in the name of making America safe.'"

The crowd exploded with a passionate, loud, long roar of response to months of militaristic inundation. The following week Secretary of State Colin Powell dramatically told the UN Security Council that the United States possessed hard evidence of Saddam's weapons of mass destruction. Neocons had fretted through 2002 that Powell was not on board. He talked about coordinating international police action against al-Qaeda and working through the UN, and neocons attacked him furiously, charging that Powell was stuck in the outmoded counterterrorism of the past. Repeatedly they demanded that Powell had to accept the president's policy of unilateral war or get out of the administration. In January 2003,

Bush gave Powell the same choice, telling him to put on his war uniform. Powell made the wrong choice, making a hard-sell case at the UN. I stood among boisterous pro-war onlookers at an airport while Powell spoke; it shook me to see how bad this was getting. On February 23, I spoke to a passionate crowd at Stetson Chapel, where we launched Kalamazoo Nonviolent Opponents to War. On March 8, the *Christian Century* ran my Earl Lecture as the cover article, "Axis of One: The 'Unipolarist' Agenda," and twelve days later the United States smashed into Iraq, with cheering media thrilled at being embedded and used.[7]

The antiwar movement took over my life. I wrote a flurry of articles against the war, and in the early going I got a strong taste of the 80 percent of the public that supported invading Iraq. My calendar filled up with whoever contacted me first at Stetson Chapel. I spoke to civic groups that sometimes failed to keep it civil, to academic groups that tried to respect my academic freedom, and to many little peace groups trying to birth themselves. Most church congregations could not handle an antiwar presentation in 2003, and those that braved it usually insisted on a debate format or carefully took a neutral stance regarding my position. I wrote speeches on unipolar ideology, the perpetual war on terrorism, the Pentagon's stovepiped fake evidence, the politics of occupation, the escalating Pentagon budget, and the ironies of American Empire, riffing multiple versions of all with continual updating. Some I gave upwards of twenty times, recycling speeches for the first time since my Albany CISPES years, which embarrassed me. Some had a narrative section that I invited audiences to recite along with me if they had heard me previously.

The war to conquer Iraq went spectacularly badly, which shocked the Bush administration, forcing it to rely on reserve forces pressed into multiple tours. I wrote *Imperial Designs* (2004) in July–August of 2003. The United States had 139,000 troops mired in a horrific occupation of Iraq, another 34,000 stationed in Kuwait, and 10,000 in Afghanistan. The U.S. Army was not supposed to exceed 482,400 troops, but by the following January it exceeded that number by 10,000 with plans for more, driven by the double-or-nothing demands of conquering Iraq. I watched the public turn against the invasion it had cheered. Some groups that hated me in 2003 invited me back in a friendlier spirit. *Imperial Designs* flowed out of my road lectures, wherein I discovered the pertinent wonders of the Internet. My previous books relied on my capacity to remember articles and books I had read long ago. Now a few strokes delivered a trove of information from obscure journals I had never heard of. I gasped at glimpsing the extent of it. What will happen to scholarship when the libraries are digitized? I wondered about it during my second and third years of anti-war road-lecturing.

In the 1990s I had played a marginal role at peace and justice conferences sponsored by the National Council of Churches, where my friend Chris Iosso served as a policy staffer under NCC General Secretary Joan Brown Campbell. Once at a conference postmortem, legendary clerical activist William Sloane Coffin Jr. blistered me as the worst of my kind: "Do you know why the liberal churches are failing? Because we have no leaders. Do you know why we have no leaders? Because we have leaders like you. You're shy. You're *nice*. You're so nice I could puke. You should have spoken up today but instead you let me walk all over you." These justly scathing words rang in my head for years until Bush smashed into Iraq. Then I received periodic manna-from-heaven phone calls from Bill Coffin urging me to stay strong, hang in there my friend, don't worry about the crowds that shout you down; you're getting to them. There were also calls from Joan Campbell, now retired from the NCC, who plotted a progressive religious campaign for the 2004 election.

On May 18–19, 2004, the Clergy Leadership Network for National Leadership Change held its founding conference in Cleveland. Joan and her financial angel Al Pennybacker gave it a clunky name to signify that this outfit was an election vehicle, though it was not affiliated with the Democratic Party, though the whole point was to oppose the Republican Party and prevent four more years of Bush as president. Nothing like this organization had existed during the catastrophe election of 2000, so Joan launched a lecture tour vehicle, starting with a conference in Cleveland.

The opening program featured Riverside Church pastor James Forbes, who flashed his Pentecostal background more than he customarily did at Riverside. The next day, Jesse Jackson gave a harrowing speech on voter suppression, and U.S. Senator John Edwards, about to become the Democratic nominee for Vice President, played it safe, except when he talked about poverty. He was eloquent about the ravages of poverty. I gave a talk against imperial wars, and Obery Hendricks Jr. succeeded me, walking to the podium with a note card in one hand and a Greek New Testament in the other.

My talk was very political for a while, turned Christian in the middle, and veered back to politics. Obery was the opposite of me. There was no prefatory banter whatsoever. He started with a reading of Luke 4 that put Jesus front and center. The gospel tells us what the gospel is about, Obery said. It's right there at the beginning of Jesus' ministry. It's good news for the poor, meant as a collective identity. The point of his ministry was to struggle for radical change, the only kind that makes a difference for the poor and oppressed. Jesus said that captives are to be released—political prisoners and people whose grinding poverty landed them in jail. Jesus advocated liberation for those oppressed by the crushing weight of empire. Obery admonished against weak translations that render the oppression as mere bruising. Jesus ended by proclaiming the year of the Lord, so, his mission was, and is, good news for the poor, struggling for radical change, freeing people from jail, opposing oppressive empire, and land reform.

Obery whisked through Micah, Amos, and Matthew 25 in similar fashion, spelling out passionately what the Clergy Leadership Network needed to stand upon: *mishpat*, justice; *sadiqah*, righteousness; and *hesed*, steadfast love. The principles of Jesus and biblical faith call for the establishment of just relationships and equal rights, the righteous fulfillment of the responsibilities of relationship, and the steadfast love of God and all others, especially the hungry and hurting. With that standard in place, Obery reviewed the past four years of Bush's presidency. It was a tour de force on everything we had just lived through: the tax cuts for the rich; the campaign against the estate tax; the punitive cuts in assistance to low-income people, ranging from Medicaid to housing assistance to school programs; invading Iraq; and the naked imperialism paraded by Bush officials, especially the vice president. Obery described the celebrants of American empire as advocates of an evil vision.[8]

He told me that he had recently moved to New York Theological Seminary in New York City, which delighted me, though I couldn't tell him why. The previous week I had received a phone call at the chapel: "Gary Doran, this is Joe Hough. Gary, you need to come to Union Theological Seminary! The Reinhold Niebuhr Chair has your name on it! We all agree, and we never agree about anything!" Joe said that he had raised $40 million for Union, which had fully recovered from its financial meltdown of the late 1990s. Now it was time to spread the word that Union was back. He swung back to the Niebuhr chair: "Think about it, Gary. You need to come to Union! If you do, you'll be on the Columbia faculty too." And he hung up.

What was that? Was I just offered a job by the president of Union Seminary? Surely Union has a search committee for the Niebuhr chair? Is Joe Hough even on it? Six weeks went by with no word from Union. Finally, church historian John McGuckin called me to say that he was the chair of the Niebuhr committee, it was doing a targeted search, and I was the target. John was graciously clear: I would need to visit Union in the fall to give a public lecture and meet the Union community, but this was for the sake of process, not to decide something; the decision had been made.

The future was coming for me. I had floated the word that when Sara entered college, I would be open to a move. My last two years at K were the golden years for me. My headache subsided, Sara always had a next show or concert, glorious singing resounded in our home, the future intruded, and I found a romantic partner at St. Luke's Episcopal Church. Sara's sophomore year songs were Eliza Doolittle's lovely "Wouldn't It Be Loverly" and the big-voice "Show Me" and "Just You Wait" in *My Fair Lady*, an enormously demanding role that Sara pulled off. As a junior she fabulously belted the torch songs of Annie Oakley in *Annie Get Your Gun* and loved the character. In her senior year she sublimely sang the tender songs of *Cinderella* and hugged all the little girls afterward who lined up in their Cinderella costumes. I didn't want her high school years to end. But college visits were made, Sara graduated from high school in June 2004, and the following month I taught an intensive course at Iliff School of Theology in Denver on liberal theology.

I felt keenly pulled forward that summer. Sara rehearsed for a civic theater show in Paw Paw, Michigan while I taught at Iliff. The class was pure joy for me. All the students were grown-ups, half were pastors, and a few were doctoral students. We had rich theological discussions that far exceeded anything that was possible at a liberal arts college. I emoted gleefully about the class to my friends Sheila Davaney, a theologian at Iliff, and William Dean, a theologian who had recently retired from Iliff. They replied that there was something pathetic about my excitement. I had not, they said, lucked into an extraordinary group of students; this group was typical of Iliff.

Iliff had open positions in theology and ethics, offering me whichever one I preferred. I had a friendly luncheon with the Iliff faculty at which theologian and Osage Nation citizen Tink Tinker broke the happy-talk mood, telling me bluntly, "If you come here, I'm going to make you deal with your Native American soul." That scared the hell out of me. I blanched and thought to myself, "Dear God, I'm just entering my empty nest years. I cannot spend them confronting my soul!" But the prospect of a friendship with Tink was a big pro-Iliff factor for me. I told him that I had benefited from White privilege all my life, so I didn't deserve any part of a Cree identity. Meanwhile I envisioned a move to Denver in which I became a mountain hiker and cyclist and taught on the side at the University of Denver.

I pictured it through the fall term of 2004, savoring a summer past that had featured my first solo respite in twenty-five years, long runs in the afternoon, and wistful thoughts about my girl's imminent college years and my crossroads. I felt overwhelming gratitude for a wondrous daughter, cherished friends, meaningful work, a beloved band of brothers and parents, and coming through. A few of my friends had already left Kalamazoo: Larry Bryan to MacMurray College in Jacksonville, Illinois; Richard Cook and Terry Lahti to Allegheny College in Meadville, Pennsylvania; Pete Gathje and Jenny Case to Christian Brothers University and University of Memphis Law School in Memphis, Tennessee; Jimmy Jones to Trinity College in Hartford, Connecticut; and Paula Romanaux and Peter Hopkins first to church music positions in Grand Rapids, Michigan, and then in Philadelphia. That made it easier to let go of Kalamazoo, as did knowing that Chuck and Becca were planning a career move. My brothers were flourishing. Greg was building an outstanding community center; Mike played in a popular Austin, Texas, band called *The Recliners* that puckishly converted Top 40 hits into lounge music; and Eric worked for Republican Congressional Representative Dave Camp, a longtime friend of my mother's. More important than Iliff-versus-Union was that my friendship with Cindy Stravers had turned romantic; I was falling in love with her. When I came home from Denver, my foremost concern was whether Cindy and I had a future, either in Denver or New York.

She had grown up with a twin sister in the strongly evangelical culture of Grand Rapids. Cindy had married an Episcopal cleric, mothered three wonderful daughters named Nelleke, Xan, and Hannah, earned a degree in sociology at Western Michigan University, and endured a painful divorce. She took a position at St. Luke's Church, directing children's and family ministries, and audited one of my classes, where I called on her sometimes to mask that I was sneaking a look at her anyway. Cindy and I became friends, and I judged that she should not be preparing, as she was, to enter the permanent diaconate. If anybody had a calling to be an Episcopal priest, it was Cindy. She had a deep Sufi-Quaker-Anglican spiritual wellspring and the caring heart of a pastor. Normally I do not presume to advise people on what they should do. With Cindy, I opined persistently that she should go to seminary to become a priest. Her daughters were grown up, it was not too late for her call, and anti-war speaking had eroded my shy-away tendencies.

We had sweet months of romantic merging and of plotting possible futures. Through the fall of 2004, only Cindy, Sara, and Becca knew that I was struggling with Union versus Iliff, leaning toward Union. We ran through pro-and-con; pro for Iliff included the Rocky Mountains and that Iliff had an Anglican Studies program through which Episcopalian students studied for ordination. On October 7 I visited Union. Joe Hough enlisted doctoral students Malinda Berry and Jennifer Heckart to ferry me around, arranged a breakfast meeting at Christopher Morse's apartment, and bluntly told me that he had four things to tell me: "One, most of our students are not as brilliant as these two. Two, your apartment would not be as nice as Christopher's. Three, I cannot come close to matching your offer from Iliff. But four, Union is where you should be, Gary, and I think you know it." Joe had me figured, though I didn't decide for Union until four days before Christmas. Union faculty are assigned to required apartments and a sizable chunk of their salary is the rental value of the apartment. I preferred Denver, Iliff, and the Rocky Mountains to living in New York City with no home, but I chose Union because of its unique role and legacy in theological education.

Our usual Dorrien family Christmas at Grand Traverse Resort, near Traverse City, should have been a joyous occasion. Cindy joined us, my family warmly welcomed her, and my memories of Brenda's tortured last Christmases at this site threw me into the trauma zone. It took me three weeks of apologies to regain my pre-Christmas standing with Cindy. We announced our plan to be married, anticipating that Cindy would become a candidate for ordination and enroll at General Theological

Seminary, where she had lived previously with her seminarian husband, five miles from Union. In March 2005 we made a trip to New York on my birthday to see our apartment, making decisions about wall colors and furniture. Cindy entered our soon-to-be living room, froze in front of the window, and gasped: "Oh my God, I can't marry you. I cannot come here with you." In a moment, our plan had become terribly real to her, and frightening. We tried to talk it out, but the truth had burst forth. Cindy told me that she had ended both of her previous post-divorce romantic relationships the same way, with a suddenness that surprised her. She had hoped to regain the buoyant happiness she had felt before she was divorced. But being with me had not made her happy; it was more like the opposite.

That turned my last weeks at K College into a nightmare that couldn't end fast enough. I avoided gatherings where colleagues would have asked what happened to my engagement. All I wanted was to get away. I didn't so much bid farewell as disappear, even making an early exit from the goodbye reception. K moved on from me, hiring a chaplain with no faculty status, expunging theology from the Religion Department curriculum, and assigning the LACC program to a faculty committee. Some of my colleagues, including dear friends of mine, had long felt that my role at the College was outsized and anachronistic. This wasn't 1950 or 1890, so why should the chaplain be so central to the College? One of my senior colleagues held up a harsher mirror: "You are a super-achiever, the ultimate rate-buster. Your colleagues like you, but they will be thrilled to see you go."

That was a hurtful farewell. I had never heard the term "rate-buster," so I had to look it up, realizing it must be bad, which indeed it was—a worker who makes life worse for one's colleagues by exceeding the standard rate of output. My departure made it possible for K to wall off the Chapel from the academic program and to eliminate theology from K's mixture of theology and religious studies. The LACC program ran aground, and the College abolished it. Many years later, in 2017, K Provost Mickey McDonald asked me incredulously, "How did you run that LACC thing for all those years? We couldn't find anyone who was willing to do it." Meanwhile in 2005, my activist friends in Southwest Michigan did not allow me to disappear. They were determined to hold sentimental farewell events laced with promises of continuing to work together. These tearful goodbyes accentuated that I was relinquishing my deep involvement in human-scale democratic communities, something precious to me.

Union Seminary, not New York City, had to be my compensation for leaving Kalamazoo. Sara completed her first year at Western Michigan University and performed in a summer show. In July I gave my Nissan Altima to my mother; Sara and I drove to her last performance in her Corolla with our bags packed; and we headed to New York at sunset. For the rest of the summer, we pounded the streets, often choosing a show, sometimes for the third time, eating nearby, and walking the four miles home from Times Square. The first time that I ordered a beer at dinner, Sara was stunned. She had grown up with a teetotaling father; what happened? I had abstained only because alcohol is a depressant. Now I no longer worried that a couple of Molsons might plunge me into a bad place, just as Sara approached her legal drinking coming of age.

In August, Cindy wrote a long letter to me that lamented and blasted my failure to move past Brenda. She told me that she had dreams in which Brenda hovered over her, blocked her, and silenced her. I had not seen her, Cindy said, for who she was, which made her doubt herself when she was with me. Being with me and feeling overwhelmed by my world of intellectualism and activism had only heightened her sense of not being seen. When she was not with me, she said, "I turn cartwheels in the hallway and like myself. When I am with you, I feel sad and depressed, and don't know who I am." I burned with shame at reading this devastating letter. Cindy deserved far better than me. In 2010 I preached at her ordination to the priesthood in Norwalk, Connecticut, and she has remained a cherished friend to me.

I was keenly mindful of whom Union had just lost. The leading figure in womanist theology, Delores Williams, had retired from Union in 2004, along with my predecessor in the Niebuhr chair, Larry Rasmussen. Novelist Alice Walker famously wrote in 1983 that a womanist is a Black feminist or feminist of color who is always in charge, often considered to be willful, loves other women, is committed to survival and the wholeness of people, and loves herself. Many Black women who entered the academy in the 1980s identified with this description. Williams brilliantly infused it with theological content, contending that liberation theology does not work for Black women and that Christian atonement doctrines are harmful to Black women. Womanist theology, she said, copes in the wilderness, struggles to survive, trusts in the wisdom of Black women, and embraces the ministerial ethic of Jesus. Rasmussen had begun his career as an expert on biblical ethics and Dietrich Bonhoeffer. Then in mid-career he responded to a global eco-catastrophe by making himself an expert in eco-ethics. Larry did not write about the environment, something external to us. He wrote with lyrical, ethical eloquence about things folding together from the inside out, stressing that the environment is not unsustainable. What is unsustainable is the modern way of life.[9]

I took to heart that Union had just lost these two giants to retirement. Then I lost my social ethics partner at Union, Emilie Townes, a few months before I got there. An eminent womanist scholar and teacher, Emilie teased me that my eighteen years of teaching at K amounted to "very extended boot camp." But in April 2005 she told me that boot camp would have to suffice as preparation for sustaining Union's program in social ethics because she was moving to Yale Divinity School. There was plenty of grapevine talk at Union about why she left. I marveled with a touch of comic incredulity that no one said it was because YDS might be a better outfit. Belief in Union's special mission was strong at Union. My first incoming doctoral student, Eboni Marshall (Turman), formerly an Alvin Ailey dancer, was as distraught as I was by Emilie's departure; Eboni and I figured out Union's doctoral process together.

Jim Cone took only one doctoral student after 2004, but he worked with mine whenever they asked for it, which was often. He knew my work better than anyone; he loved to talk shop about his career and legacy; and a few months after I arrived, he told me that I was a rare candidate for his trust. We became each other's closest friend at Union. I also befriended Catherine Keller, an eminent feminist theologian whose work I analyzed in volume three of the liberalism trilogy. Catherine had grown up in a chaotic, cerebral, emotionally turbulent, and constantly relocating family, found her way to Whiteheadian theology and third-wave feminism, and in mid-career appropriated poststructuralist criticism. We bonded over my comprehension of her work, her deep capacity for friendship, and long dinners that moved fluidly from the very intellectual to the very personal and back again, with due attention to the everyday mundane. Catherine, however, taught at Drew University in Madison, New Jersey, so our meetings required calendar appointments. Jim and I interacted constantly, with lunches that sometimes stretched into dinner time and afterglows that ended in his living room.

He had earned his doctorate in 1965 as an exponent of Barthian theology. The following year the Black Power movement exploded into being and Jim was enthralled by it. The year after that, he decided that he was in the wrong field. Jim wrote articles that editors declined to publish and which he agreed were not very good. They meant nothing to him, so how could they be worth publishing? American theologians imitated the German and Germanic Swiss theologians they admired; somehow racism was not even a topic of theological discussion. By 1967, Jim was ready to quit theology. He contemplated a doctoral program in Black history and literature, until September, when Detroit burst into flames. Now it was too late to return to graduate school. Teaching at Adrian College in Michigan, Jim doubled down, not for the last time, on theology, writing the sensational books that founded Black liberation theology, *Black Theology and Black Power* (1969) and *A Black Theology of Liberation* (1970).[10]

Jim beheld these books with awed gratitude and satisfaction. He had poured out *Black Theology and Black Power* in a month, expounding Black Power radicalism as a Christian theologian. He found his voice and subject by unleashing the rage that surged through him. Otherwise, it might have killed him. Black Power, he wrote, used boycotts when necessary, demonstrations when necessary, and violence when necessary, repudiating the assimilationist dream of civil rights liberalism. Jim said it was ridiculous for White liberals to ask Black people to like them; Malcolm was "not far wrong when he called the white man 'the devil.'" King wrongly assumed that racial integration was the model of success, that White Americans believed in their democratic ideals, and that White supremacy would break when enough good people recognized the justice of the civil rights cause. Jim countered that White liberalism was deeply implicated in America's racist sickness and no part of the remedy. A trickle of Whites recognized their complicity in White supremacy and strove to abolish it, but Jim stressed that there were very few of them.[11]

C. Eric Lincoln, a polymathic Black scholar with a doctorate in social ethics from Boston University School of Theology, was Jim's mainstay in the early years. Lincoln taught at Clark Atlanta University in Atlanta, served as a visiting professor at Union, and in 1970 became the founding president of the Black Academy of Letters. He opened numerous doors for Jim, including at Union, and shortly after *Black Theology and Black Power* went to press, Lincoln told Jim to write another book, immediately, for his new series with Lippincott. Jim was flabbergasted—what was left to say? Lincoln waved him off, and Jim fell back on his training in systematic theology: if one approaches the doctrines from a self-consciously Black perspective, no doctrine remains as it was. *A Black Theology of Liberation* described the God of the Bible as a partisan, liberating power who calls Black people to liberation, not to redemptive suffering. If liberation is the essence of the divine nature, God is Black.

For Blacks, Jim wrote, evil is anything that arrests or negates liberation; salvation is liberation. For Whites, evil is normal life, benefiting from the privileges of whiteness; salvation would be the abolition of whiteness. Jim launched the revolutionary turn in American theology that privileged liberationist questions, contending that the validating test of Black theology is whether it reflects the experience of oppressed Black people and contributes to their liberation. He felt special gratitude for the second book and for Lincoln, since he hadn't known that this book was in him. He loved to tell the story. The first time that Jim regaled me with it was over lunch at Pisticci, the favorite hangout restaurant of Union faculty. We sat there all afternoon, the wait staff refilled our water glasses, after which they brought dinner menus, with no objection that we monopolized a busy table, since they knew who James Cone was.

Jim dismissed the many White theologians who said he was too emotional, angry, binary, and anti-White to write "real" theology, such as they wrote. He didn't care what they thought, so he rarely bothered with White critics. In the early 1970s, however, four Black religious thinkers shook him to his core. Religious historian Charles H. Long contended that theology is inherently the power discourse of a privileged class, defining cultural categories. Culture gives birth to religion, a name for the cultural structures through which human beings apprehend the holy, but theology is an imperialistic morphology not salvageable by emphasizing blackness. Black theology should not exist. Religious historian Gayraud Wilmore argued that Black theology should be a subordinate discourse under the non-Christian category of Black thought. He urged Black theologians to throw off Christian orthodoxy and to reject Cone's twofold conception of "Black" as something specific to Black people and a symbol covering all who are oppressed, since the symbol-option emptied Black oppression of a specific religious meaning. AME minister Cecil Cone, Jim's brother, said the only legitimate Black theology is steeped in African history and the High Holy God of African theism. Historian Vincent Harding eschewed theology as a European construct that misnames what matters—the rise of spirituality within the Black community. All four argued that Black religious thought is a deeper and richer tradition than Black Christian theology, contending that Jim was too dependent on European theology and Black Power politics. His conceptual categories were European, not African. He substituted radical politics for Black religion. His position was reactively defined by White racism, rendering liberation as the negation of whiteness.[12]

Once again, Jim faced an existential crisis about whether he was in the right field. He spent the early 1970s struggling with this question and his position. If liberation is the central motif of the gospel, he reasoned, it is surely possible for theology to be liberating. Definitional refutations miss the liberating power of biblical faith. Jim acknowledged, however, that his early works overly depended on Barth and Tillich and were insufficiently grounded in Black history. In *Spirituals and the Blues* (1972), he took a first pass at deepening his roots in African American culture. Then he saved his career in theology by writing *God of the Oppressed* (1975), which intertwined the liberation trope in Scripture and African American history. Jim still argued that God's revelatory act must be the basis of theology and that a single narrative line runs through the Bible to liberation theology. He preserved the authority of the Bible and a divine-human Jesus on neo-orthodox terms; thus, Jim rejected liberal theology for putting God in question, questing for the historical Jesus behind the gospel narratives, and allowing modern skepticism to set the agenda for theology. But he cut back on his Barthian warnings against beginning with human questions, and he doubled down on the Christian gospel, changing his position about redemptive suffering: suffering can be redemptive, he argued, when it is an aspect of the struggle for liberation. Like King, Jim interpreted redemptive suffering as a sign of the presence of Jesus in the world, while rejecting King's emphasis on integration, reconciliation, and nonviolence.[13]

There were many more adjustments for Jim to make after he wrote *God of the Oppressed*. He wrote essays that recalibrated his positions on feminism, socialist criticism, Latin American liberation theology, African theology, and the Global South, and he wrote a major work that explicated his debts to King and Malcolm. But for thirty years he stopped writing systematic theology, since there was no need to supersede *God of the Oppressed*. It superbly explicated the basic theological position that he expounded to the end of his days. Jim was justly proud of the book and the landmark status it attained. He saw no point in diminishing its stature by writing another book that said the same thing in updated response to deconstructionist, womanist, queer, and cultural-studies trends. If dissertation writers wanted to engage his position, they had only to read *God of the Oppressed*. Jim was a gatekeeper of his historic legacy. He collaborated with Wilmore to preserve the documentary history of Black theology, carefully surveyed his classes for doctoral candidates, and mentored most of the liberationist and womanist theologians that Union produced.[14]

He loved to talk about all of it, and he did not say, "This is in confidence." You had to discern which parts were confidential. Jim cut his ties to colleagues who embarrassed him by blabbing something he said that wasn't meant for public consumption. He felt embattled at Union, believing that its liberationist reputation was exaggerated, partly because he felt embattled. He could be extremely caustic, needing to vent, so he needed some trustworthy friends. Jim was nostalgic about his early-career friendship with Union theologian Paul Lehmann, who engaged him like few others before retiring in 1974. For seven years, Jim and I fantasized about luring Cornel West back to Union, until Union president Serene Jones pulled it off. I moved up in Jim's index of trustworthiness by keeping his confidences and not holding a grudge when he excoriated me. Sometimes he lashed me for not anticipating how he would feel about a doctoral candidate or an exam reader; how could I not know? His family life was a category unto itself. If you were high enough in his trust, Jim emoted expansively about his family, but to all others this subject was a closed book. Few people knew that he faithfully supported his divorced first wife, Rose Hampton Cone, and cared deeply about his sons, Michael and Charles, and daughters, Krystal and Robynn.

He had ready opinions about every book I had written, plowed through volume three on liberalism before it went to press, and teased that I was the only person who could compel him to read hundreds of pages of Whiteheadian philosophy. That book, *The Making of American Liberal Theology: Crisis, Irony, and Postmodernity* (2006), also analyzed other forms of liberal, liberationist, and postmodern thought. What I should write next was obvious to Jim, and to me. I was still giving anti-war talks, but the next book needed to serve the entire field of social ethics. There was no book that described the history of social ethics and made an argument about its future. I wrote *Social Ethics in the Making* (2009) to provide one, interpreting social ethics as an academic field, a tradition of ecumenical discourse, and a form of public intellectualism. My Niebuhr inaugural lecture gave a preview of it. Jim introduced me by observing that it required a mighty exception for him to give up a night of his sabbatical. I gave shout-outs to Becca, Chuck, Jimmy, and my former K colleague Romeo Phillips, whose Underground Railroad singing graced many Stetson Chapel services. The talk expounded on the social gospel basis of social ethics and the pitifully weak anti-racism of my field.[15]

I argued that the field of social ethics was invented in the 1880s by White, middle-class, reformist, ecumenical, Protestant, social gospel academics—William Jewett Tucker, Graham Taylor, Richard Ely, and above all, Harvard Unitarian theologian Francis Greenwood Peabody. It bore all the limitations in this description, yet the social gospel was a revolution in Christian thought that reached far beyond the tame progressivism of this group. It was revolutionary in Christian theology for contending that the church operated for centuries with the wrong hierarchy of topics. The social gospel recovered the social justice emphasis of Hebrew scripture and the centrality of the kingdom of God in the teaching of Jesus. It created the ecumenical movement, putting social justice on the agenda of the ecumenical churches. The social gospel that arose in predominantly White churches had a reformist mainstream that changed what Christian ethics was about and a socialist flank that linked the capitalist system to racism, militarism, sexism, and imperialism. More important, there was a Black social gospel with reformist and radical flanks of its own. It combined the abolitionist faith in the God of the oppressed with an explicit political agenda to abolish lynching by federal statute and enforce the Fourteenth and Fifteenth Amendments. It enlisted churches in the struggle for racial justice, co-founded protest organizations opposing America's racial caste system, and devised its own theologies of social salvation, creating a new abolitionist politics and theology.[16]

I described AME cleric Reverdy Ransom as the quintessential Black social gospel founder, ranged over methodological debates and Niebuhr, and lingered over liberationist critiques of the social gospel and Niebuhr. I argued that Niebuhr did not worry about the disciplinary standing of his field or share the fixation of the social ethical founders with social scientific validation; he ended up in social ethics because that was where liberal seminaries directly took up current social problems. He so towered over the field that he virtually defined what it was, teaching that society is a theater of perpetual struggles for power among competing interests.

The book version ranged over all the above plus Roman Catholic social teaching, biblical interpretation, confessional discipline, the ecological crisis, gay sexuality, womanist and feminist praxis, queer theory, militarism, imperialism, neoconservative ideology, postmodern carnival, and the distinction between theories of rights and theories of right order. It was hard to imagine in 2006 that the flood of books about empire would soon abate, replaced by books on the Obama phenomenon and the global financial crash. I dealt with the too-many-subjects problem in *Social Ethics in the Making* by weaving a thread about racism and economic justice throughout the book, emphasizing war, militarism, and methodological issues in the middle chapters, and emphasizing gender theory, gay sexuality, ecology, and postmodern criticism in the later chapters. My publisher, Wiley-Blackwell, said there was room for four pictures on the cover, so who should they be? Choosing seven would have been difficult. Selecting four was easy: Peabody, the founder; Ransom, the Du Bois figure of the Black social gospel; Niebuhr; and Beverly Wildung Harrison, the mother of feminist social ethics.

Bev had come up as a Presbyterian near St. Paul, Minnesota, earned a degree in religious education at Union in 1956, worked in campus ministry for five years, and took pride that she was not needy and did not get hurt feelings like the women she knew. She felt superior to other women for not being feminine, prizing the admiration of her male clerical peers. Being man-like helped Bev succeed in the male-dominated Presbyterian Church, but it stripped her of the female power she possessed, succeeding professionally by imitating something she was not. Her success felt phony to her, not being really hers. In 1963 she entered the doctoral program in social ethics at Union, studying under Roger Shinn and John C. Bennett, and felt acutely the demise of Niebuhrian realism. Union had seemed powerful in the mid-1950s. But Niebuhr retired in 1960 and the new Union had no idea what came after Niebuhrian neo-orthodoxy.[17]

Niebuhr's muscular Protestantism felt quaint to Bev, his language of transcendent divinity and purpose no longer plausible. In 1966, Bennett appointed Bev as assistant dean of students and instructor in Christian ethics, though she had not completed her comprehensive exams. The following year she married a kindly gay man, James Harrison, while struggling with her conflicted feelings about herself and her job role. At first her job confirmed her belief that many female students at Union were too feminine and needy to survive the rigors of seminary. Bev eased them out of Union, in a difficult period at Union, when enrollment dropped from over 700 in the late 1960s to 456 in 1975. Gradually it occurred to her that perhaps women struggled at Union because they had better values than their male peers.

The movement for women's liberation taught Bev that her condescending attitude toward women was wrong and counter-productive, sabotaging the base of support for her work. She was granted tenure at Union in 1973, one year before she finished her doctorate, which offended Cone and numerous other faculty who protested that no one ever made an exception for them. Five years later, a spectacle controversy ensued over Bev's bid for promotion to full professor, now protesting that she had not authored a book. A full professor must be a book author. Union's board of trustees overrode an impassioned faculty campaign against her promotion, an unprecedented action that enraged many of her colleagues and left bitter feelings on both sides for many years. I had marched in armbanded support of Bev at Union's very tense commencement of 1978. Thirty years later her two essay collections, *Making the Connections* (1985) and *Justice in the Making* (2004) were staples of my courses.[18]

Social ethicist Carol S. Robb thankfully made available, in *Making the Connections*, Bev's pioneering lectures and essays on anger, love, social theory, misogyny, homophobia, and the Equal Rights Amendment. The best Harrison book, *Justice in the Making*, came five years after her retirement in 1999, superbly edited by her doctoral graduates Elizabeth M. Bounds, Pamela K. Brubaker, Jane E. Hicks, Marilyn J. Legge, Rebecca Todd Peters, and Traci C. West. It collected essays on the tasks of feminist liberation ethics, working within liberal Protestant traditions, and political economics, interspliced with interviews on these three subjects. It sparkled with Bev's signature themes: Justice is right-related community. Feminism works best as a form of strategic essentialism that affirms female subjectivity as a standpoint. Alienated power—evil—is a real force in the world that cuts us off from reciprocal relationships. Abortion is moral or not only in context, not as a discrete deed. Social ethics at its best is socialist, as it was for Union stalwart Harry Ward, Bev's favorite social ethicist. The divine, which she called "godding," is the Power of relation, not being itself.

Bev was furious when Union tabbed me for the Niebuhr chair. I told her I agreed with her: Any of her doctoral graduates would be better than me, and placing another hetero-White-male in the Niebuhr chair was dubious at best. This apology was sincere and perhaps slightly helpful. For many years afterward I was deeply grateful that Bev's beloved partner, feminist theologian Carter Heyward, was kind and generous with me whenever we met. Another field colleague who was close to Bev took the opposite tack, cutting me with periodic reports that Bev still seethed about Union and me. I hope Bev realized during the seven years that passed between my arrival and her passing that I did my upmost to lift up her legacy in social ethics. These were the years in which queer theology acquired movement status as an affirmative discourse, moving past the defensive phase. Bev had important affinities with it, but she recoiled during her last years at Union at the prevalence of French deconstruction in queer theory and academic feminism, calling it a new form of academic captivity. Bev said there are two places where academics can learn what they need to learn about struggling for justice: "Grassroots activism together with the rough-and-tumble of actual global networking." She was a social justice warrior who judged that her feminist and queer successors were becoming too comfortable in the neoliberal academy. I centered my course "Social Ethics as Social Criticism" on her two essay collections and two pillar texts of womanist ethics, *Black Womanist Ethics* (1988), by Katie Cannon, and *Womanist Ethics and the Cultural Production of Evil* (2006), by Emilie Townes.[19]

All four founders of womanist theology were doctoral graduates of Union—Williams, Cannon, Jacquelyn Grant, and Kelly Brown Douglas. Cannon had moved reluctantly from Hebrew Bible to social ethics. At Union she flourished in her new field because her extraordinary mentor, Harrison, urged her to expound the moral wisdom she knew from growing up Black and female in Kannapolis, North Carolina. Social ethics needed what she knew, not more books about Barth and Niebuhr.

Cannon argued that Black women have no experience of the self that ethics textbooks describe—the person bearing a wide capacity for moral agency who prizes White values of individuality and autonomy. To internalize White values is to legitimate the power that Whites hold over Blacks, thereby worsening the cycle of humiliation. In racist America, she said, the game is rigged against African Americans who try to climb a career ladder. Even when they adopt White individualism, they are put down anyway. Moreover, suffering is not a choice or a desirable norm for African Americans, especially for Black women. Suffering is a repugnant everyday reality to overcome.[20]

Katie was surprised when I told her that her work was essential to how I taught social ethics. She had scars from her battles with what she called "golden boy mindguards" in the academy, and she took a dim view of the deconstructionist turn in the academy, writing that there are far worse things to oppose than essentializing a racial or gender identity. In my living room she said it strongly to a gathering of students: womanism was born in the refusal of Black women to choose between their racial and gender identities. Being Black and female were profoundly and equally important to her. Katie said that if young Black women favored hip-hop, hybrid identities, queerness, and poststructuralist jargon, she would not tell them they had a moral obligation to be womanists, but *please* don't call yourselves post-womanists, a term that repulsed her. What matters is to actualize the self-naming sensibility that defines womanism, not to show up those who came before you.

For nine years I was the only ethicist at Union, mentoring up to seventeen doctoral students at a time and wishing for a partner. In my first year we conducted a targeted search for a womanist or Black feminist scholar and were turned down in succession by Traci West and Cannon. Traci stayed at Drew University, and Katie remained at the other Union Theological Seminary in Richmond, Virginia, which was later renamed Union Presbyterian Seminary. The fact that Traci and Katie were Union alums worked against us, since they were steeped in the good and bad of intense, combative, financially strapped Union. Union's fractious culture produces graduates who sometimes balk at returning to the site of painful memories. In my second year we took second passes at Traci and Katie, who still said no thanks; this time Katie added that her wounds from her Union years were deep.

We moved to the upcoming middle generation, offering the position to Stacey Floyd-Thomas, then of Brite Divinity School in Fort Worth, Texas. Stacey thought about it for months before saying no, which crushed me. She was trained by Cannon at Temple University, was a powerhouse teacher and scholar, and would have flourished at Union. Working with her would have been a godsend for me. But Stacey made the right choice, waiting for Vanderbilt to come through with positions for her and her religious historian spouse, Juan Floyd-Thomas. In my third year, desperate not to fail again, we aimed for a junior level appointment, choosing one of our recent graduates, Melanie Harris, still resisting the evidence that Union might be more appealing to someone not from Union. Melanie grappled with her choices and memories for months before opting to stay at Texas Christian University in Fort Worth. There were two other finalists for this position during my years of flying alone. One was before the financial crash of 2008 terminated faculty searches everywhere; the second came a few years after the crash; I went all-out for both candidates and failed both times to persuade Union to extend an offer, so my solo flying continued.

I nurtured doctoral students with delight and gratitude, undeterred by lacking a colleague in ethics. It helped that ethics is part of the theology field at Union, and that I also took candidates in theology. In those years we averaged eight new doctoral admits per year. I pulled two or three of my applicants through the arduous selection process every year, most in ethics, and some in theology. My field colleagues—Cone, Christopher Morse, Korean ecumenist Chong Hyun Kyung, Catholic theologian Roger Haight, and later, interfaith theologian Paul Knitter—wholly supported me, while some colleagues in other fields winced at my overlong advisee list. They were entirely justified in their wariness, but the high quality of our candidates in ethics and theology won out, to the immense credit of the Union faculty. My colleagues kept voting to give me new doctoral students, and I welcomed all of them gleefully. In my early years they included Nkosi Du Bois Anderson, Malinda Berry, Chloe Breyer, Ian Doescher, Babydoll Kennedy, Jeremy Kirk, David Orr, Tracy Riggle, Keun-Joo Christine Pae, Dan Rohrer, Gabriel Salguero, Charlene Sinclair, Joe Strife, Eboni Marshall Turman, Rima Vesely-Flad, Colleen Wessel-McCoy, Demian Wheeler, Todd Willison, and Jason Wyman.

The coming of my empty nest years freed me to fill my calendar with speaking engagements. Union did not have faculty secretaries, so I had travel mishaps until I learned to manage my calendar. I did not hire a publicist or join a speaker bureau, which left me free to have no minimal fee. Speaking at churches, activist organizations, and universities was a ministry to me, and I spoke for whatever a group could afford, which was often nothing beyond the travel expense. Usually I spoke from a bare-bones outline or winged them altogether. Lectures and sermons containing detailed data had to be written out, and sometimes a host required a written text, so I have a few manuscripts from those years. But most of the time I trusted my ability to wing it.

Middle-aged women audited my classes, I met others in New York City churches, and in both contexts, I awkwardly accepted invitations to lunch. I felt unready for dates, so I was polite and opaque through lunch and did not follow up with second lunches, except with a fellow Episcopal priest who explained to me the ways of the local diocese. The bishop of New York rejected my request to be transferred to his diocese because I lacked a congregational assignment. The small-minded rudeness of this policy stunned me. I had a national ministry, speaking in churches every Sunday. I wanted an ecclesiastical home but had come to the wrong diocese for that, so I accepted my homelessness and became habituated to it.

Meanwhile a Union auditor railed at me a few days after our lunch, "I just want to shake you!" This was a helpful notice that I had become a waste of time. I begged off from additional lunches, my birthday of March 2006 arrived, and I meant to pay it no mind, reading mid-term papers after dinner at home. But my first empty-nest birthday nagged at me. I surprised myself by rushing downtown to see whatever Broadway show might be available at the discount center in Times Square. It turned out to be *Doubt*, John Patrick Shanley's parable about moral uncertainty. Walking home from Times Square, and missing Sara on this familiar route, I thought about the shaking comment. Indeed, what was I waiting for? Somebody *should* shake me.

A week later, my life turned a corner at a café meeting with a female physical trainer, Eris Benzwie McClure, who worked out at the same gym as me. The gym trainers treated her as a friend and colleague, though she was not an employee of the gym. I had no expectation as we met for coffee, but four hours later I was still there, realizing by the three-hour mark that this meant something. Eris had a vulnerable radiance that enthralled me. We told our stories, and hers was spellbinding.

Eris was the firstborn of a Holocaust survivor couple, and an early citizen of newborn Israel. Her father Albert Hirschorn was born in 1918 in Przemysl, Poland and moved with his family the next year to Berlin, where Albert's brother Martin was born in 1921. Their father, Julius Hirschorn, was a wine merchant, and their mother, Helena Eisen Hirschorn, had a formidable sister named Lasha Eisen who spoke eight languages and worked as a nurse in New York City. In 1933, when Hitler rose to power, the two Hirschorn brothers were blond, blue-eyed, ardent Jewish Zionists. Their father believed they could get by in Nazi Germany by passing as Culture Protestants. The brothers and their Aunt Lasha knew better. Lasha was caustic about her brother-in-law and his political conservatism, opining that her sister married badly.

In 1934, Lasha financed Albert's getaway to the British-ruled Palestinian Territory. Three years later, she whisked Martin to safety in London. Her willingness to pay for Martin's schooling exempted him from having to qualify as one of the 10,000 Jewish German children allowed to enter England as students. Albert worked as an actor for the Habima Theater in Tel Aviv and adopted the Hebrew form of his name, Benzwie. Martin worked as a chemical and mechanical engineer during World War II and was denied entry to the British Army. Many Hirshorn relatives in Poland and neighbors in Germany perished in the Holocaust. Albert and Martin never learned how their mother died; their father was killed by the German Army in the house of a Catholic priest. In 1947, Lasha invited Martin to live with her in her Third Avenue apartment; somehow, she always had money. Lasha was acidic and severe, scary-mean to many, but devoted to Martin. Her apartment was adjacent to an elevated railway and its deafening noise, so Martin launched a noise control company on a shoestring budget, the Industrial Acoustics Company.[21]

Eris' mother, Hanna Nussbaum Benzwie, was the daughter of a judge in the Labor and Finance Court of Berlin, Meinhold Nussbaum, and his wife, Anna Nussbaum. Meinhold Nussbaum was also the ringleader of the Zionist movement in Nuremberg. In 1923 he visited Palestine, returning to Germany with figs and sugar cane, but lamented that he could not support his wife and four daughters there. For the next ten years his stately villa in the suburb of Ebensee was the hub for

Nuremberg Zionists. Every Sunday afternoon they convened at his home for salon-style socializing. Hanna Nussbaum and her sisters were pelted with stones and viciously slurred as "stinking Jews" at school and in the streets. On April 1, 1933, the Nazis proclaimed an economic boycott of Jewish-owned businesses; Nazi storm troopers swarmed the streets, blocking the entrances to stores; and Hanna's family hurriedly fled Germany, taking the next train the next day to Switzerland. They proceeded through Italy to Palestine, where Meinhold Nussbaum studied for the British bar and his daughters undertook agricultural schooling to prepare for life in a kibbutz. He opened a legal office in Tel Aviv and drafted restitution claims and legislation for exiled Jews in Palestine; later he served as head of the legal department of the Israel Purchasing Mission, for which he negotiated with German Chancellor Konrad Adenauer on behalf of Holocaust victims and their families. In 1953, Meinhold Nussbaum was killed by an oncoming car, perhaps murdered, while crossing a street in Cologne, Germany, while carrying out the controversial Reparations Agreement. The first Israeli plane to touch German soil retrieved his body, and he was awarded a state funeral.[22]

This story of persecution, genocide, homeless survival, refugee Zionism, and settler colonialism was a very heavy burden to inherit. Eris cringed at the atmosphere of violence and embattlement that permeated her childhood in Tel Aviv, recoiling especially at the anti-Arab hostility she heard daily. The Nussbaum family had high social standing in Israel and was long on business and academic achievers. Albert Benzwie cofounded the Kameri Theater in Tel Aviv in 1944 and moved up socially in 1948 by marrying into the Nussbaum family. He was a bohemian producer of avant-garde plays skewering fascism, ordinary bourgeois life, and, according to Eris, anything not-depressing. Meanwhile Martin Hirschorn thrived on his aunt's affection, made a fortune as a noise control engineer and entrepreneur, and was parsimonious with his needy older brother. There arose a family narrative about high-achieving status on the Nussbaum side, new wealth on the Hirschorn side, Hanna as the Nussbaum outlier who did not excel in school and then married downward, and Albert, to the acute embarrassment of his daughter, perpetually depending on his brother for money.

Eris grew up with these stories and under their immense weight. The epic narrative about the Holocaust and Zionism was too much for a sensitive girl averse to big talk about ideology, harsh talk about Palestinians, and her father's loudness. It was not that her parents admonished her to conform to a society she didn't like. Eris felt neglected by her parents in a country where she didn't belong. Albert Benzwie was a big talker who ignored his daughter, brushed her away at theater parties, and alienated her. Hanna Benzwie was a caring mother, but no exception to Eris' central lament about her childhood: "I never had any guidance." At home, Eris pleaded to be left in her room; at school recess, she hid in the bushes; in 1958, when Eris was nine years old, her family moved to New York City, which traumatized her. Overwhelmed in New York and later in West Hartford, Connecticut, she was thrown sink or swim into schools where she did not speak the language. At home she was as unhappy as ever, caught between a bombastic father who embarrassed and ignored her and a seemingly lost mother trapped in a bad marriage, suburban Connecticut, and vague confusion.

Eris raised herself, striving to be like her WASP classmates in West Hartford. She was rebellious, depressed, and difficult at home, unlike her friendly younger brother Michael, so she got much less from being a Benzwie than he did. Hanna resented that Eris did not want a Jewish identity. To Hanna, being Jewish was a given, the story of her life, with no need of religion. To Eris, the family's non-religiousness negated any reason to retain the cultural shell of Judaism. Hanna retained a strong feeling of kinship with Israel that Eris never had and did not want. On both issues, there was wounded feeling between Hanna and Eris laced with incredulity on both sides.

In her high school years in Hartford, Eris was perceived as a self-confident beauty, which amazed her years later. Her classmates did not fathom that she lacked their sense of belonging. Their recollections of her at reunions and on Facebook always shocked her: "I was popular?" Her undergraduate experience at three colleges was a nightmare blur that she could not bear to talk about, so many years passed before I heard anything about it. Eris moved to New York City in hopes of a singing career, landing a job at Manhattan Center in the music industry, where she worked on the 1972 Deutsche Grammophon recording of the Metropolitan Opera production of Georges Bizet's *Carmen*. There she befriended conductor Leonard Bernstein, mezzo-soprano Marilyn Horne, and Bernstein's sound engineer John McClure. Bernstein and Horne were superstars with gregarious personalities, McClure was quiet and modest, and Eris commenced a romantic relationship with McClure, an Oberlin College dropout and self-taught recording engineer for Columbia Records who had worked up to an elite producer. McClure recorded the nine Beethoven symphonies with Bruno Walter, produced thirty recordings with Igor Stravinsky, and produced nearly two hundred recordings with Bernstein, notably the nine symphonies of Gustav Mahler.

There was a twenty-year age difference between Eris and McClure, who had three sons and a daughter from his two previous marriages. McClure had won three Grammy Awards with Stravinsky and Bernstein when he brought Eris into Bernstein's inner circle; three years later, in 1975, he and Eris were married. Eris had always wanted a father figure and McClure stayed youthful through her. She helped McClure and Bernstein—"Lenny" to his friends—access the rock and roll culture that was second nature to her. Lenny was hard on McClure but warmly flirtatious with Eris. Eris absorbed Lenny's love of Mahler, indulged the praise he heaped on the Beatles, urged him that the Rolling Stones were better, helped to edit the book version of his Norton Lectures at Harvard, and negotiated his fraught personal life, which included a succession of gay lovers, his rocky marriage with actress Felicia Montealegre Bernstein, and the confusing fact that Lenny smooched her persistently.

Bernstein had skyrocketed to fame in November 1943 by substituting at the last minute for Bruno Walter with the New York Philharmonic, wowing the crowd at Carnegie Hall. He was profusely creative and expansive, a genius by any standard, with enormous achievements. He also roadblocked his highest ambitions as a composer by composing in multiple genres, cramming his calendar with conducting, recording, and television commitments, and struggling with himself. Eris watched all of it play out during Lenny's late-midlife crisis. She thrilled at watching him conduct, especially the Mahler and Beethoven symphonies, especially in Vienna and Munich. He lost himself ecstatically in the music, emoting and swaying and gesticulating. He identified passionately with Mahler, a Czech Jewish outsider who made his renown as a conductor. Lenny adored Mahler's wrongly denigrated symphonies. He won over the crusty Vienna Philharmonic on this subject, surpassing Walter in lifting Mahler to the high canonical standing he deserved. Sometimes Eris held Lenny's scotch and lighted cigarette in the wings, or supervised his performance rituals. She winced that Lenny routinely berated McClure while charming the musicians with an us-versus-him shtick. Lenny had no boundaries, so Eris fended off his wet kisses, his tongue down her throat, and his addiction-fueled roughness. Many insiders believed Bernstein was a straight-out gay man married to an elegant and devoted actress who balanced him out. Eris wondered if "bisexual" better described the man who came on to her like he did.

Eris entered Bernstein's world just after he commenced a romantic relationship with music professional Tommy Cothran and during the period that Lenny's *Mass* got a poor response that wounded him. Cothran supervised the early performances of the *Mass;* Eris had a cordial friendship with Felicia and a close friendship with Tommy; and in 1973 Eris witnessed Bernstein's spectacular performance of Mahler's Second Symphony with the London Symphony Orchestra at a highly demanding site for recording, Ely Cathedral in England. This famous recording epitomized the warmly romantic sound-ideal that McClure developed in close collaboration with Bernstein, sometimes called "sonic bloom." The following year, performing for the Israel Philharmonic Orchestra, Lenny made a secret beach getaway with Eris, McClure, and Tommy on camelback to Gaza. Afterward the government harshly grilled Eris at the airport in Tel Aviv, demanding to know why she had not served in the Israeli Defense Force. She and McClure barely made it to Bernstein's next booking in London, and Eris took no more return trips to Israel.

An apartment fire in 1974 drove Eris and McClure to move in with Lenny and Felicia at their Park Avenue apartment. For two weeks, Eris witnessed close-up the tensions between Lenny and Felicia over his relationship with Tommy that drove Felicia in July 1976 to a Tommy-or-me ultimatum. Bernstein chose Tommy, living with him until February 1977, when he reconciled with Felicia just before she was diagnosed with cancer. Lenny cared for Felicia until she died in 1978. He was exuberantly gay afterward, running through romantic relationships with young musicians, and remaining friends with Tommy, as did Eris, until Tommy died of AIDs in 1986. Later there was a Hollywood biopic starring Bradley Cooper as Bernstein, which Eris panned for failing to convey Bernstein's intense intellectualism and Jewish religiosity. The Lenny she knew could wax for hours on music history, philosophy, religion, cultural trends, and politics, especially Mahler, Leibniz, Arthur Schopenhauer, death, the death of tonality, and the Lefty politics he shared with Felicia, and the Felicia she knew was a far more vibrant personality than the character played by Carey Mulligan.

McClure ran the sound system for the Broadway show *Camelot*, whereby Eris befriended actor Richard Burton and his wife Susan Burton. McClure recorded Pink Floyd's *The Wall*, whereby Eris met everyone in Pink Floyd and befriended guitarist David Gilmour. Lenny and McClure introduced Eris to a slew of famous conductors, whom she ranked on a scale of kindly friendliness. Seiji Ozawa was number one, André Previn ranked far down at the other end, and she avoided facetime with the scary-severe Herbert von Karajan.

Eris began to fall out with McClure over his restless accumulation of diversions he couldn't afford. He piled up debts on a farmhouse in Vermont, a tractor and snowmobile, a small boat succeeded by a big boat, and a West Side apartment, all in addition to heavy alimony and child support payments. He was constantly anxious about his debts but couldn't resist trading up to the next recreational plaything. He wanted to be a rock producer but was unwilling to pursue the schmoozing and fundraising that were necessary for it. McClure shunned the New York City party scene and minimized his personal time with Bernstein, preferring his tractor-riding privacy in Vermont. He and Eris drifted apart over the debts, the big boat, his drinking, his reclusiveness, and arguing about them, divorcing after twelve years of marriage. McClure moved on to his fourth wife, and Eris sorely regretted that she had no work of her own or self-identity.

In her last years with McClure, Eris landed a designing job with Ralph Lauren. She rummaged through thrift stores, bought piles of shirts, and tore them apart alongside Lauren himself, plotting new designs. She was very good at it, but Lauren irked her by calling her one of his slaves, so Eris went into styling, another field in which she rummaged through thrift stores in search of the right item. Stylists coordinate outfits for models and actors, provide fashion advice for clothing brands, and choose props and accessories for photo, television, and film shoots. Eris had an eye for it that nearly took her to the top of the field shortly after her marriage ended. She won a high-profile job to direct a major project, nervously showed up for the first organizational meeting, and had a total meltdown, stalking out of the meeting in tears, which ended her career in styling. She hurtled downward into a devastating depression, devoured by the gaping hole in her psyche that blocked and shamed her.

She had never felt loved and didn't know who she was. Eris didn't blame McClure, while regretting that she allowed herself to depend utterly upon him. She had felt this way her entire life. Marrying McClure was just a bad idea that allowed her to hide from herself while she met a fascinating parade of high-end performers. Bernstein had once told Eris during a garden walk that she was strong and would be all right, whereas he was less sure about McClure. Eris savored these words for twenty years, wondering what her friend Lenny saw in her, disbelieving that he was right. She was deeply wounded and was now paying for the years that she had not dealt with herself.

She told this story with breathtaking candor and beauty. I was enthralled by her and it, admiring the contrast to my best-face-forward lunch dates. Hers was not a rear-view mirror story of triumph. Eris said her "raging anxiety and obsessions" had blocked her from the career and relationships she should have had, she had never filled the God-shaped hole in her psyche, and she had recently become a physical trainer, encouraged by her trainer friend Gigi Barlowe. The reference to the God-shaped hole was my first clue to the crucial part of her story, which Eris held to the end. It pointed to something beyond the clinical therapy that she had obviously done—a twelve-step program. Eris said she had done many years of intense work in Al-Anon. She spoke at Al-Anon meetings across New York City and knew as many famous people from Al-Anon as she knew from traveling the world with Lenny.

I learned that Al-Anon is a mutual-help group for people coping with alcoholic friends or family members that facilitates therapeutic work more broadly on addictive relationships and co-dependency. Al-Anon members share with each other the lessons they learn from practicing the twelve steps: confessing powerlessness, believing in a Power greater than oneself, giving one's life to the care of God according to one's understanding of God, conducting a moral inventory, confessing one's exact wrongs, cultivating the willingness for God to amend one's defects of character, asking God to do it, identifying the persons whom one has harmed, making direct amends to them when possible, continuing the personal inventory, praying for divine wisdom and power, and being spiritually awakened by practicing the steps. Now I comprehended the "guidance" regret that Eris expressed so poignantly, grasping that she had a lived faith. Her spirituality explained what I was experiencing in her presence. Eris was, and is, a luminous practitioner of twelve-step religion, with a rare and beautiful openness. We could have talked for another four hours but agreed instead to resume later.

We have resumed ever since. I had previously assumed that any romantic partner of mine would be a Christian, or a social justice activist, or an intellectual/academic, the three things that define me. But I fell in love with someone who was none of these things. My world and world-view were too foreign to Eris for her to feel overwhelmed by either one; she often burst out laughing at the strangeness of my progressive seminary world. I was a non-complainer who never told anyone when I was ill or feeling down. Eris thought that was the epitome of ridiculousness. What did I get from it? How had anyone ever put up with me? To Eris, my stoicism was bad-only, being unhealthy and pointless. She liked my shyness to a point, except it was absurdly excessive. She told her mother incredulously, "When a waiter brings him the wrong order, he quietly eats it!" Worst of all, as she told her therapist, "He has to be prodded to speak!" The therapist advised Eris that I was a very poor candidate for changing, so she had to decide whether she could live with a quiet type who lived in his head. This wise counsel made possible the happiness of my later life. Eris and I are devoted to each other in ways that reflect the gracious gift of love between us. In our early years together, she accompanied me to Berkeley and Claremont, California; to Durham and Highlands, North Carolina; to Lancaster and Philadelphia, Pennsylvania; and to venues across Germany and England, bringing light and love to lecture destinations I had previously raced through.

The United States had far more colleges, universities, and kinds of Christianity than she had imagined. In the car, we feasted on the blue notes and chord progressions in bluesy rock and roll. Eris chose most of the music, usually the Rolling Stones or U2, though sometimes she reached for a Rachmaninoff piano concerto before I did. I diversified the carfare with Johann Sebastian Bach, and bluesy jazz, especially Sarah Vaughan, and my longtime favorites in the Beethoven-Brahms-Mahler-Tchaikovsky canon, above all, the glorious *Ein deutsches Requiem* of Brahms. It surprised me that Eris didn't remember the Bernstein-Mc-Clure recording of *West Side Story*, until we learned that it occurred in

1985—the beginning of a dark time for her. We lingered in California because Eris blessedly had to see Joshua Tree and Palm Springs. In the Deep South she made two culture-shocked cellphone calls to her brother, feeling more Jewish and liberal than ever.

In Germany and England, she had favorite haunts to revisit. Eris loved Germany, especially Berlin and Frankfurt, where she made tenderly careful calls to her mother, respecting why Hanna Benzwie could barely stand to hear it. In Eris' favorite country, England, we toured Oxford and various conference centers, traipsed across London, and spent an especially delightful week at Gladstone's Library in Hawarden, where I lectured alongside the distinguished Oxford theologian Keith Ward, enjoying his splendid company. The locals confused me by claiming to live in Wales, and I thought they were just embarrassed to live in England, until I belatedly consulted a map. Hawarden, indeed, is in Wales. Along the way, Eris and I forged a love union that is the transcendent blessing of my later life.

Four months after I met Eris, Anson Biggs breathed his last. The following year we lost Brenda's brother John Biggs, and the year after that we lost Grace Biggs. I preached all the eulogies, and Sara drove from Kalamazoo each time, the saddest memories of her college years. For fifteen years, Grace lived with the terrible knowledge that both of her children would probably die before she did. John had two heart attacks and suffered from alcoholism; he also took wonderful care of his parents in his last years, while living in their basement. Grace and Brenda, for all the turbulence between them, were very much alike in defying afflictions and pushing forward. Both were wisecrackers with a load of sarcasm and a keen sense of the absurd. Four months before Grace died, walking the hallways at Country Meadows Nursing Home in Bethlehem, she cracked up Sara and I with edgy comments about nursing homes and falling apart: "You know, I can't make friends here. These people are so old." We said, "But Grace, you're eighty-eight years old. These people are your age." She shot back, "I know, but I have to mix it up. I can't relate to a bunch of old people." Grace was like Brenda in having a gift for friendship, but her friends had died, or moved away, and being the last of her family to die threw her into a sorrow for which there is no cure.

7

INTO THE OBAMA ERA

The early years in which I taught at Union and Columbia were the same in which neoliberalism lost its glow of triumph and the skyrocketing figure of Barack Obama inspired hopeful talk about a post-racial future. I had been immersed for three years in foreign policy debates about intervention when I moved to New York. Completing my third volume on liberal theology was a sideline compared to the talks I gave on militarism, preemptive war, counterterrorism, empire, and Empire. The occupations of Iraq and Afghanistan went badly, which set off a Reinhold Niebuhr revival just as the Obama phenomenon took off. In the academy there was a great deal of talk about neoliberal Empire replacing old-fashioned empire, with customary exaggeration. A generation grew up that knew not the Cold War, discovered that neoliberalism works only for a handful at the top, and witnessed the White nationalist backlash that later elected Donald Trump. Contrasting mass movements triggered each other while the world hurtled toward eco-apocalypse and into it.

New York Times columnist David Brooks, political scientist Andrew Bacevich, and a few of my guild friends stoked the Niebuhr revival by setting Niebuhr's realism against the militaristic extremism of Niebuhr-quoting neocons. Obama, a once-in-a-lifetime political talent, told Brooks in April 2007 that Niebuhr was his favorite philosopher. The following month *New York Times* religion writer Peter Steinfels asked me how my approach compared to Niebuhr's. I said my work is shaped by all three of the social ethical paradigms that came out of Union: the social gospel commitment to a love ethic of social justice, Niebuhr's critique of social gospel idealism and pacifism, and the liberation perspectives advocating the abolition of domination. Steinfels inquired about the U.S. occupation of Iraq; I said the United States should be planning how to get out of

Iraq, minimize the bloodshed, and build structures of collective security instead of babbling nonsense about prevailing there. Steinfels asked if this was a Niebuhrian or anti-Niebuhrian position; I said it was neither. I am not a Niebuhrian realist because realism thwarts any Christian or moral claim that conflicts with the national interest. But I persistently think with and through Niebuhr.[1]

It was hard not to fall into policy-wonk talk when these were the subjects. I plunged audiences into the deep weeds of U.S. American foreign policy, analyzed global hot spots and challenges, and argued that U.S. leaders had to stop inflaming anti-American feelings in the Middle East, an objective they once cared about even at the height of the Cold War. Obama, in my view, was the candidate best suited for it, though I opposed Obama's proposal to escalate by perhaps double the present force total of thirty-two thousand in Afghanistan. Doubling down in Afghanistan was a dangerous game no matter how shrewdly Obama played it to his political advantage.

The Soviets had invaded Afghanistan in 1979, wreaked colossal destruction, got stuck in a quagmire, and staggered on for eight years. They tried a new constitution, leader, and policy of reconciliation, all of which failed until they found a better Soviet leader, Mikhail Gorbachev, who faced up to reality and got out. I reflected that Afghanistan might not have descended into a civil war had the Soviets departed in the early 1980s. By 1987, a civil war was inevitable, which gave birth to al-Qaeda. The moral of the story: whenever an occupying power staggers along, it merely delays the inevitable, runs up the casualties on both sides, empowers its enemies, and disgraces itself. I allowed that the United States had a vital interest in preventing al-Qaeda from securing a haven in Afghanistan, which didn't require fifty thousand troops. On the other hand, it would require three hundred thousand troops to wage hearts-and-minds counterterrorism across the nation. Any escalation in Afghanistan, I argued, would only yield more of it with no idea of how to get out.[2]

This was a graveyard-of-empire subject that I flogged reluctantly but dutifully. Obama benefited from the antiwar movement despite not being in it, much like John Kerry in 2004. Obama had been a state lawmaker in Illinois in October 2002 when he derided the coming Iraq war as a "dumb war," but the following summer he fretted that he may have harmed his political prospects by doing so. In 2004 he declined to criticize Kerry for voting to authorize the Iraq war, which qualified Obama for the spectacle platform at the Democratic Convention that launched him. Then he made political hay off the position he took in 2002. The last thing I wanted to dwell upon as Obama waged his brilliant campaign for the presidency was his proposal to increase the Pentagon budget and double down in Afghanistan. But I urged Lefty-progressive audiences to help wobbly politicians find their nerve; it was a loser for us to censure ourselves out of fear of undermining the Democrats. I never had any illusion that Obama was a Lefty-progressive, but I did regard him as a redeemer candidate. Maybe this country still had a chance to save itself.[3]

Arriving at this two-thirds mark of a talk was usually my cue for a personal word leading to a close about belatedly fulfilling Martin's Dream. My Christian identity was far more fraught for broadly progressive audiences than it had been in the 1980s and 1990s. I had not felt obligated in those years to de-scarify audiences about my religious faith, though I wore a clerical collar only at Episcopal worship services. Any group that invited me knew that I was a Christian theologian, so I rarely said any self-conscious word about it.

That was no longer a tenable approach. Generation X and the coming Millennials had not grown up in a religious faith, never heard of the social gospel, and identified Christianity solely with the political Right. My audiences in the United States were increasingly similar in this respect to those I addressed on lecture tours in Germany and England, with the ironic difference that I was usually invited to Germany and England by church-based theological faculties in universities. In Europe, secularization ran deeper, but theology remained a university subject. Wherever I went, I explained that the formative figures who inspired me had a spiritual impulse that was deeper than their politics. MLK was foremost among them. All faith traditions, I said, must become known for caring about the poor, the excluded, the vulnerable, and a ravaged Earth.

Italian Marxist philosopher Antonio Negri and American literary theorist Michael Hardt made an academic splash by contending in *Empire* (2000) and *Multitude* (2004) that globalization renders old forms of imperialism obsolete. Globalization itself, they argued, is the ruling empire of the twenty-first century—a new type of global sovereignty based on the network power of transnational corporations, the global financial class, and compliant national governments. Hardt and Negri argued that globalization-as-empire nullifies democratic theory by undermining the capacity of states to channel economic forces and practice just procedures. On their telling, two progressive theoretical orientations and two conservative ones dominated what remained of democratic theory: social democracy, liberal cosmopolitanism, Old Right nationalism, and neoconservative nationalism. Social democracy is a weak throwback to the age of nation-based class conflict. Liberal cosmopolitanism is sophisticated and relevant but lacks transformative power. Old Right nationalism gets certain things right in a bad way. Neoconservatism is repugnant all the way down.[4]

Social democrats Paul Hirst and Grahame Thompson viewed globalization as a threat to democracy best combated by fortifying the sovereignty of states and gaining democratic political control over the economy. Liberal cosmopolitans David Held and Mary Kaldor viewed globalization as a generally good thing that enhances economic growth, encourages nations to get along with each other, and liberates individuals and groups from the rule of nation-states. On this optimistic view, globalization fosters democracy when it is managed by cosmopolitan internationalists with liberal values. Old Right nationalists Samuel Huntington and Patrick Buchanan condemned globalization for shredding traditional values, curbing national sovereignty, exporting the worst parts of U.S. American culture, and igniting imperial wars. Hardt and Negri said that each of these groups had one commendable point, while the neocon devotion to American domination was utterly bad, the exact opposite of the radical, bottom-up, participatory democracy on a world scale that is needed. The hope of the world is that a global multitude of postmodern hybrid identities is creating a new world society through its various struggles against Empire. A global democracy is possible, created by a unified global people, the multitude.[5]

Union and Columbia students got a strong dose of the Hardt and Negri books in my courses. Their analysis made a huge impact in the academy because it fostered interdisciplinary conversation about the neoliberal tsunami impacting everyone. Hardt and Negri aptly described how globalization changed empire into something far more fluid, intertwined, and trans-governmental than the old state-centered imperialisms. Neoliberal Empire replicates the universality-without-boundaries order of the old imperialism while transforming sovereignty into a global system of diffuse national and supranational institutions. I pushed back, however, that Hardt and Negri exaggerated the demise of national governments, and there is no substitute for democratic politics that wrests control over economic power. The motley crew Leftism of Hardt and Negri over-relies on protest politics, lacking a strategy that scales up.

Hardt and I spoke at a symposium at which I objected that he and Negri ignored democratic socialism. Their discussions of Social Democracy referenced only the Social Democratic parties that integrated into neoliberalism. Their discussions of socialism referenced only the neo-Leninist vanguard traditions that called for revolutionary purity and the abolition of the state. I said the democratic socialist vision of economic democracy is not as wild a dream as the one conjured by Hardt and Negri of postmodern multitudes discovering and producing their oneness on the way to global democracy. What if a successor to Norman Thomas or Martin Luther King Jr. were to galvanize a mass movement with a democratic socialist vision of justice? Hardt graciously replied that he agreed about democratic socialism and would welcome a resurgence of it.[6]

Meanwhile the Obama phenomenon hurtled past the analogies for it. Obama launched an early run for the presidency because massive throngs of White liberals and moderates urging him to run could not be put off. I went full-bore for Obama, turning most of my road lectures into Obama talks and writing articles about his campaign. Obama put everything on the line in the Iowa Democratic Caucus, figuring rightly that if he won in Iowa, his numbers would pop everywhere, Black voters would stop hedging against disappointment and move to his camp, and he would beat Hillary Clinton for the nomination. If he lost in Iowa, he was finished. In his victory speech on a magical night in Iowa, he claimed a promise-and-fulfillment relation to the civil rights movement, inviting all to help him redeem King's dream for America. Reaching this far, rhetorically, was for special occasions only; Obama needed the votes of people who had limited tolerance for such talk. But this was a special night not to be wasted. Thus, he called Americans to a freedom movement linking America's struggles against British tyranny and Axis fascism to its own history of bondage and exclusion. The same hope that braved fire hoses in Birmingham and beatings in Selma led him to Iowa. My Episcopal ethicist friend Bill Danaher and I watched this peroration while running on treadmills at the Society of Christian Ethics conference at the downtown Atlanta Hilton. We choked back tears requiring no words of commentary.[7]

This idea that the bridge in Selma led to Obama's campaign was always there, though he played it down most of the time. On March 13, 2008, ABC News dug up select jeremiads by Obama's pastor, Jeremiah Wright, which set off a psychodrama that engulfed Obama's campaign. Four days later, Obama delivered a dramatic speech on race at the National Constitution Center in Philadelphia that leveraged his considerable capacity to channel the feelings of different sides. That night I spoke to a buoyant crowd at the Vatican of liberal Protestantism, New York City's Riverside Church, where enthusiasm for Obama was sky-high. For the next six weeks I walked a daily tightrope along with Jim Cone, Michael Eric Dyson, James Forbes, Melissa Harris-Perry, Obery Hendricks Jr., and Cornel West. We were pro-Wright and pro-Obama, anxious to refute attacks on the Black church, and fearful that the journalists who called us would miss the nuance of a quote.[8]

Then on April 28, 2008, at the National Press Club, Wright blew up his relationship with Obama and our tightrope dance. The speech itself went fine, ending with an eloquent close on the Afrocentric, multicultural, liberationist theology of reconciliation that Wright preached at Trinity Church in Chicago. But question time came and Wright recoiled at being cornered with do-you-repudiate questions. The National Press Club had no standing to tell him who his friends should be, and his tart replies concerning Obama conveyed zero interest in helping Obama. Wright's tone of derision repelled Obama; it felt like a deliberate attempt to sabotage his candidacy. He was finished with Wright, fretting for the next week that Wright destroyed his campaign. Then Obama won North Carolina by fourteen points, which put him on a straight path to the nomination.[9]

At Union the Wright episode was deeply painful. Support for Obama was heartfelt and nearly universal at Union. Normal Union contentiousness melted in our classrooms. I worried that my public advocacy for Obama might be squelching our usual scrappy back-and-forth in class, but colleagues said no, they were experiencing the same thing. Obama's historic candidacy overrode the policy differences that some of us had with Obama. What did evoke bitter comments about Obama in my classes was his renunciation of Wright. Jeremiah Wright is an iconic figure in the Black church and Black theology. He built Trinity Church into a powerhouse of Afrocentric Christianity and founded the Samuel DeWitt Proctor Conference, every year the highlight event for our

Black students. At Union, Obama's treatment of Wright underscored the distinction between politics and cultural authenticity. A mere political victory would be empty, especially if it yielded sellout politics. Liberation at the level of spirit and community, on the other hand, is inherently redemptive. From a Black theology perspective, Wright's cultural authenticity was rock-of-ages certain, and Obama's was dubious at best. Swallowing Wright's exclusion was a bitter pill.

Shortly after Obama accepted the Democratic nomination for president the reckoning came for ten years of unhinged greed in the mortgage market. Your bank had resold your mortgage to an aggregator who bunched it up with thousands of other subprime mortgages, chopped the package into pieces, and sold them as corporate bonds. Your mortgage payments paid for the interest on the bonds until the whole casino crashed, after which Obama helped the Bush administration obtain its massive bailouts of September and October 2008. Had Obama not been a key political player in the bailout, he might have been less obsequious to Wall Street after he became president. As it was, he was co-opted before he began. Obama put his economic policy in the hands of Timothy Geithner, the Federal Reserve Bank of New York president who cut the bailout deals, and Lawrence Summers, who helped Bill Clinton tear down the Glass-Steagall banking wall. Geithner became Treasury Secretary, and Summers chaired the National Economic Council.

That was a sickening omen to many of us who had worked hard to elect Obama. Something precious was already slipping away before Obama was inaugurated in January 2009—the hope that he might change the system. Meanwhile Obama's election flooded Black communities with elation. There was a sizable gap already between political-Left progressives who reeled at Obama's appointments and the Black churches and radio stations that countenanced no criticism of Obama. Black communities granted Obama a pass for appointing only one Black member to his senior cabinet, Eric H. Holder Jr. as attorney general, and for slighting Black interest groups.

The progressive Left gasped with revulsion when Obama stocked his cabinet and staff with Wall Street insiders, Republican defense officials, and retreads from the Democratic establishment. Cornel West, who had spoken for Obama sixty-five times during the campaign, sometimes appearing with him, was prominent among the repulsed. Obama rudely brushed off West shortly after he was elected. Meanwhile Cornel teamed in January 2009 with Union's new president, Serene Jones, and me to teach a course at Union titled "Christianity and the U.S. Crisis." Students called it "the Mega-course." Every week we packed an overflow crowd of students and public auditors into James Chapel, taught for three hours, and followed up with three hours of receptions, schmoozing, dinners, and doctoral seminars. Serene had moved from Yale Divinity School to Union just before the bankers crashed the financial system. Cornel taught at Princeton and was already calling Obama "the Johnny Mathis of American politics," meaning the early Mathis, the tamely calculated crooner. I had spent the past year studying the spectacular growth of the derivatives market, especially the credit-default swaps in which parties bet in a completely unregulated market on whether a borrower would default. In 1998 the total value of credit-default contracts was $144 billion; by 2008 it was $62 trillion, the heart of the crash.[10]

So many plugged-in bankers, investors, brokers, and traders rode the financial lunacy of the neoliberal heyday for all it was worth, caught in the terribly real pressure of the market to produce constant short-term profits. Speculators gamed the system and regulators looked the other way. Mortgage brokers, bond bundlers, rating agencies, and corporate executives made fortunes selling bad mortgages, packaging them into securities, handing out inflated ratings, and putting the bonds on balance sheets. Serene, Cornel, and I did not believe there was only one crisis in January 2009. We highlighted multiple intersecting sites of injustice and exclusion, but the crisis we featured was the United States' worst economic crisis since 1933.

I gave detailed lectures on the systemic deflationary spiral exacting terrifying portfolio drops of thirty to forty percent. The national debt had tripled in eight years from $4 trillion to $12 trillion. The bill for Bush's recent bailouts exceeded $8 trillion, a figure half the size of the nation's economy. The banks had faked themselves out from knowing what their assets were worth, credit lines were frozen, the economy was losing up to 800,000 jobs per month, and the real economy of production was suffering structural damage. Income falls in a recession, which makes debt harder to bear, which discourages investment, which further depresses the economy, which leads to more deflation. I outlined the policy options that Obama's advisers were debating to deal with $2 trillion of toxic debt. One was to continue the cash-for-trash approach of Bush's Treasury Secretary Henry Paulson. Number two was to ramp up the insurance approach, ring-fencing bad assets by providing federal guarantees against losses. Number three was to create bad banks that soaked up bad debt. Obama and Geithner settled on an Aggregator Bank combining cash for trash with some elements of the bad bank model topped off with an auction scheme to find private buyers for the toxic debt.

I protested that the Geithner plan was obsequious to Wall Street. It coddled the banks and showered shareholders with taxpayer-funded gifts exceeding a trillion dollars. It was the most cumbersome and nontransparent option, paying huge bribes to private investors to buy the bad loans and toxic securities for more than they were worth. If we were going to bail out the banks with taxpayer money, where were the requirements to serve public needs? If we could create bad banks to soak up toxic debt, why not create good public banks to do good things? I spoke about making huge investments in green technology, infrastructure, high-speed trains, and education. We needed to scale back the U.S. military empire, break the economic oligarchy, restore progressive taxation, universalize Medicare, break the addiction to fossil fuels, and build a movement for economic democracy.

I argued that economic democracy begins by expanding the cooperative and social market sectors—producer and consumer cooperatives, cooperative banks, employee stock ownership plans, community land trusts, and community planning agencies—and that expanding these sectors is not enough. Cooperatives prohibit non-working shareholders, so they attract less outside financing than capitalist firms. They are committed to keeping low-return firms in operation, so they stay in business even when they can't pay competitive wages. They are committed to specific communities, so they are less mobile than corporate capital and labor. They smack of anti-capitalist bias, so banks don't like them. They maximize net income per worker rather than profits, so they tend to favor capital-intensive investments over job creation.[11]

Most of these problems are virtues, and the problematic aspects can be mitigated with tax incentives. But we also need forms of social ownership that facilitate democratic capital formation, have a greater capacity for scaling up, and are more entrepreneurial. Public bank models of economic democracy vest the ownership of productive capital through a mutual funded holding company or an outright public bank. The holding companies lend capital to enterprises at market rates of interest and otherwise control the process of investment. Equity shareholders, the state, and/or other cooperatives own the holding companies or public banks. This approach contains a built-in system of wage restraints and facilitates new forms of capital formation. It has nothing to do with nationalization, and investors still seek the highest rate of return. Economic democracy, I said, does not need a blueprint and does not rest on idealistic beliefs about human nature. It expands the social market in whatever ways make sense in specific communities to build a green economy.

Cornel observed that I had been giving this talk on economic democracy for twenty-five years and it was suddenly relevant! I did feel that this crisis must not be wasted. If we could spend trillions of dollars bailing out megabanks that cared only about themselves, why not create public banks to finance start-ups in green technology and provide financing for cooperatives that traditional banks spurn? It was no pipe dream in 2009. Union cut one of my lectures into two YouTube videos making the case that public banks could be financed by an economic stimulus package approved by Congress, or by claiming the good assets of the banks seized by the government at the end of every week of that period. Public television icon Bill Moyers devoted one episode of his PBS program, *Bill Moyers Journal*, to our class, at which Cornel said something we had not heard previously: Abraham Lincoln did not always agree with Frederick Douglass, but Lincoln listened to Douglass with respect. No one needed to explain the meaning of this anti-analogy. Meanwhile, Moyers introduced me: "His passion is economic democracy." That would have been spot-on, if tweaked: "His passion, on one side of his work, is economic democracy."[12]

The difference worked on me through four years of giving wonky road talks about economic policy, eco-economics, corruptions of empire, and the bruising politics of Obama's first term. In the classroom I never taught only social ethics. At Union my courses balanced social ethics and theology, and at Columbia these fields didn't exist, so I worked with graduate students in philosophy of religion and Euro-American religious history. My mainstay colleagues at Columbia were my friends Wayne Proudfoot and Mark C. Taylor; a few years later, my cherished friend Obery Hendricks joined us at Columbia, bringing his "guerrilla exegesis" brilliance. Wayne modeled how to teach our required Theory and Method courses, and I shared book-writing profusion with Mark, each of us asking the other about the one in the pipeline. Mark authored a major postmodern reflection on religion and culture, *After God* (2007), a luminous memoir of his near-death experience, *Field Notes from Elsewhere* (2009), and a vintage-Mark provocation calling for the abolition of tenure and academic fields, *Crisis on Campus* (2010). All had his signature blend of brilliance, playfulness, erudition, and cheek. In both academic contexts I ranged over broader ground than I covered on the road, where my Lefty-politics and progressive Christian audiences were eager to discuss the unfolding Obama era. I tried to put together a reader on my work for Columbia University Press but failed to produce a manuscript that felt like a real book. The first draft felt like a showoff display of my range, so I scaled back to my road lectures of that period on three broad topics within social ethics. *Economy, Difference, Empire: Social Ethics for Social Justice* (2010) had a centerpiece chapter on "Rethinking and Renewing Economic Democracy." The upshot was at least a book that hung together, albeit while reinforcing the Moyers-impression.[13]

Sara enrolled in 2008 at Columbia Theological Seminary in Decatur, Georgia, and I reveled in her experience of seminary-world. Two ecumenical Protestant summers in Nicaragua and one Presbyterian summer in Ghana had given her precious experiences of the church in Global South contexts. Then Sara got a strong seminary education that started with Greek, ranged over the standard Presbyterian curriculum, and relied on Shirley C. Guthrie's venerable textbook *Christian Doctrine* to prepare for ordination exams. She found a spirited gang of friends who were headed like her to the Presbyterian ministry. They were buoyant frequenters of bars and Mexican restaurants, and one of them, William Christians, blessedly became my son-in-law after he, Sara, Eris, and I shut down quite a few bars of our own. The Bitter End in Greenwich Village was our favorite. Will was a native of Birmingham, Alabama and a graduate of Auburn University who explained to me that the loathing-rivalry between Auburn and the University of Alabama is not analogous to the one I grew up with, Michigan versus Michigan State. Nothing could ever cause him to cheer for U-Alabama. In October 2010, Columbia Seminary ethicist Mark Douglas graciously hosted a Presbyterian Theological Educators symposium on *Social Ethics in the Making*. Sara and Will sat in the back, I gave a pro-and-con talk on Niebuhr, and Ronald Stone, Niebuhr's last doctoral protégé, couldn't bear the con parts. A dear friend to me, Ron teared up, his voice cracking, and declared: "Friends, Reinhold Niebuhr was a saint!"[14]

For six years, Jim Cone labored on a book that he named before he had written a single page, *The Cross and the Lynching Tree* (2011). Two things impelled him to write it: he had never clarified what he believed about the cross of Jesus, and a host of womanist theologians categorically rejected theologies of the cross and redemptive suffering. Delores Williams, who earned her doctorate under Tom Driver at Union in 1991 and joined the faculty that year, formulated the classic womanist critiques of liberation theology and atonement theory. Williams acknowledged that liberation theologians have one strand of the Bible that supports their position—God delivering the Hebrew slaves from bondage in Egypt and Jesus describing himself as the liberator of the poor and oppressed. But she highlighted a second tradition of Black American biblical appropriation that emphasizes female activity, plays down male authority, and revolves around Hagar—a female slave of African descent forced to be a surrogate mother. The Hagar story, Williams argued, parallels the African American female experience of being abused, raped, and forced to serve as sexual surrogates. It shows God helping Hagar to survive and to achieve a minimal quality of life by her initiative but has nothing to do with liberation.[15]

Taking seriously the Hagar tradition precludes any claim that God always works to liberate the oppressed. Williams stressed that the Bible takes slavery for granted, except when Hebrews are enslaved, and that Cone wrongly fixed on one strand of the Bible, looking past the fates of the oppressed of the oppressed in it. Liberation theology, she argued, does not fit Black women or work for them. It leaves them out, rendering them invisible. Moreover, if Jesus is saving for Black women, it cannot be as a surrogate or an example of sacrificial love. Jesus is saving only because he resisted being victimized, providing a model of resistance. He came to show people how to live, not to be crucified for their sake. Nothing in the cross is redeeming; it is an image of defilement. The same God who did not will the condemnation of Black women to surrogate slavery did not will the execution of Jesus. Jesus, Williams said, had a ministerial concept of salvation. He cast out demons, performed healings, called people to wholeness, and raised the dead. He conquered sin when he was tempted in the wilderness, not when imperial power slayed him on a cross. What is saving in Christianity is the ministerial life of Jesus and his resurrection.

Many womanists embraced this position. Cone stewed about it for years as he helped womanists obtain academic positions and wrote supportive blurbs for their books. It felt to him that they were making up a gospel of their own that refashioned the way-of-Jesus moralism of liberal theology. He could be scathing about the criticism he received from womanists, as Williams knew, so he and Williams had a frosty relationship. They did not like each other because each felt disrespected by the other. It was a relief for Cone when Williams retired in 2004 and subsequently refused to have anything to do with Union. He began to enjoy Theology Field meetings again, and to think about a capstone theological book. Jim chafed at reading term papers in which womanism was described as an advance beyond liberation theology; meanwhile he surveyed his classes for prospective Black theologians. In 1994 he had picked out Raphael Warnock, a Union student working at Abyssinian Church in Harlem as a youth pastor, for the doctoral program. Warnock had everything that Jim looked for in a theologian—a strong identification with Blackness, humble beginnings, religious passion, intellectual acumen, teachability, and courage. But he sharply disappointed Jim by heading into ministry, planning a dissertation that criticized the academic focus of Black liberation theology, and not finishing it until 2006.[16]

I heard a great deal about all three things during my first two years at Union. Jim planned to retire soon, while viewing anxiously the prevailing trends in the field. The theologian he most respected, and to whom he felt closest, was Kelly Brown Douglas, except for everything she said about the cross, on which she modified only slightly the rejectionist position of Williams, Katie Cannon, and Emilie Townes. That was another reason to write a capstone book—even Kelly Douglas told students there is no redemption in the cross.

Jim started on a book that related the cross of Jesus to the lynching trees of the United States. Staring at the pictures of tortured Black victims was too much to bear on a weekly basis. Writing about them was slow and labored. On numerous occasions, he had to push aside the manuscript. He was always reading whatever I wrote, so it was hard for me not to ask about his writing progress; he could tell me only so many times that he was proceeding "like a turtle." But Jim kept returning to the manuscript, called by youthful memories of hearing about the cross of Jesus. There were more hymns, gospel songs, spirituals, prayers, testimonies, and sermons about the cross than about anything else. They conveyed that Jesus was a friend of oppressed people who knew about their suffering. Jesus achieved salvation for "the least of these" through his solidarity with them, even unto death. Black Christians, like Jesus, did not deserve to suffer. But keeping faith in Jesus was the one thing that Black Christians possessed that Whites could not control or take from them. Black Christians gleaned from the suffering of Jesus that God was with them in their suffering.

The only White theologian that Jim taught was Niebuhr. This Niebuhr-exception puzzled many students over the years, since Niebuhr's anti-racism was temporizing, and his writings were strewn with slurs about the supposed cultural backwardness of Black Americans. Jim recoiled at Niebuhr's racist asides but treasured the cross theology that Niebuhr culled from the Lutheran tradition, and he noted that Niebuhr at least had a record of condemning racial bigotry, unlike most White theologians of his time. Niebuhr caught the tragedy and beauty of the cross—its terrible, paradoxical, and sublime blend of horror and redemption. He said the cross is the "supreme symbol of divine grace," bearing a "terrible beauty" that can only be expressed poetically. Jim said it requires "a powerful religious imagination to see redemption in the cross, to discover life in death and hope in tragedy."[17]

Suffering is not redemptive, but suffering can be *made* redemptive when oppressed people struggle against it in the name, way, and spirit of Jesus. Jim argued that only those who stand in solidarity with the oppressed can embrace the cross of Jesus. He believed, like MLK, that God's loving solidarity transforms even the hideous ugliness of imperial crucifixion and American lynching into occasions of liberating divine presence. Jim planned a concluding chapter that interrogated womanist theologians point by point and made his case. But as the manuscript took shape, he pulled back on the back-and-forth. It wasn't necessary to run through why he disagreed with Williams, a bit less with Douglas, considerably less with Joanne Terrell, and so on. By the time there was almost a book in hand, he opted for a brief summary of womanist criticism. Jim agreed with Williams that the gospel must not be preached in a way that encourages Black women to accept their surrogacy roles. Moreover, atonement theory and liberation theology are incompatible, so it's pointless to belabor the finer points of atonement theology. All atonement doctrines turn the gospel of Jesus into a rational concept that is explained by a theory of salvation. Even moral influence theory perpetuates the logic of surrogacy, at least implicitly.

Too much Black preaching, Jim acknowledged, wrongly encourages Black women to suffer for others as Jesus suffered for them. But Black Christians were not wrong to fix on the cross of Jesus. He noted that womanist theologians Terrell, Jacquelyn Grant, and M. Shawn Copeland agreed with him, contending that the cross is central to the gospel faith and not detachable from it. The cross is the symbol of God's triumph over the powers of death, and a burden to be borne for the sake of liberation. I asked Jim near the end of his life how he might have ended the book had there not been any womanists who agreed with him. He paused, said he would have made the same argument, but would have found it harder to finish the book. He paused again: *"Much harder."* He was indebted to womanists for prodding him to write his best book in decades, which felt, at the time, like the capstone to his career—until a brutal succession of killings triggered a mass movement proclaiming that Black Lives Matter.

Obama escalated the war in Afghanistan and expanded America's military empire. He watered down the financial reform bill as it moved through Congress, accepting carve-outs for corporate users of derivatives and opposing proposals to force banks to spin off their trading operations in derivatives. He killed a crucial amendment to the financial reform bill that would have imposed sensible limits on the size of megabanks. He took a passive approach to health-care reform legislation, letting a Democratic Congress write the bill, and refused to press for a public option. He put off immigration reform for a later time that did not come and broke a campaign promise by extending Bush's tax cut for the rich. Conciliation was not merely Obama's default mode, as some of us had worried in 2008. It was his chief operating mode.

Meanwhile Obama triggered a ferocious, titanic, vindictive backlash merely by living in the White House and doing his job. Every day that he served he made the nation look better than it was, which Donald Trump keenly grasped while putting it differently. Fox News and an unhinged Right-blogosphere stoked the backlash, expanding the market for a best-selling conspiracy literature. A skyrocketing Tea Party movement claimed that Obama's stimulus bill was a socialist takeover of America; somehow it was outrageous to prevent the nation from reliving 1932. Impassioned rallies demanding, "I want my country back" began shortly after Obama was inaugurated. More than one-fourth of the U.S. American population claimed to believe that Obama was a Muslim, a Socialist, not born in the United States, not a legitimate president, and sought to impose Sharia law throughout the world. The books and Right-blogosphere had sloppy lists of bad things that Obama supposedly believed, plus competing narratives about how he and his White lefty allies defrauded the nation. His entire presidency was a conspiracy to destroy America.[18]

The birther movement rang this alarm for two years before Trump joined it in 2011. It had no basis whatsoever besides racism and backlash hysteria, being too blatant to be called a dog whistle. Trump became a major political player by lauding the birther movement and stumping for it. He flirted with the idea of running for president, shooting to the top of the prospective Republican field, but wasn't ready to mount a campaign. He was impressed at how quickly he ascended and how easy it was. All he had to do was play to the rage and not get outflanked in doing so.

Many of us who had worked to elect Obama felt caught between our disappointment in his tepid politics and our revulsion at what he was up against. Cornel fell out dramatically, blistering Obama as "a black puppet of corporate plutocrats" who took pride in heading America's killing machine. Friendships were frayed and broken over this reaction, notably between Cornel and Michael Eric Dyson. Black churches and Black-community radio stations bristled at any criticism of Obama, especially since he was constantly attacked by the political Right. I spoke on many Black radio stations, always pressing a critique of Obama's meliorism while respecting the aversion of radio hosts and audiences to any criticism of Obama.[19]

These were the years that I road lectured on all-things-Obama while writing *Kantian Reason and Hegelian Spirit* (2012). My books on myth, Barth, and liberal theology had offered glimmers of an argument about the logic of post-Kantian idealism in modern theology. Now I made the argument in a book that was as large-scale and detailed as it needed to be, contending that Kant is the unavoidable figure in modern philosophy and religious thought. The culture of materialism was winning in philosophy until Kant argued that powers of mind are creative in producing experience. His doctrine of intellectual intuition opened the door to post-Kantian objective idealism, and the key to his system, its vicious ironies notwithstanding, was his belief in the emancipating power of freedom.

Kant laid the groundwork that Schelling, Schleiermacher, Hegel, and Kierkegaard took over and refashioned, all with vast legacies of their own. Modern theology cannot be understood, I argued, without comprehending Kant's critical idealism and the maze of responses to it.[20]

Kant conceived nature as a mere instrument or medium of moral action, subordinate to the striving of a moral subject, deriving its value from ethical ends imposed upon it. Schelling, Schleiermacher, and Hegel fashioned post-Kantian idealisms conceiving nature as an end in itself worthy of spiritual appreciation. On this view, Kant's dichotomy between form and content yielded a strangely abstract philosophy that knew only appearances. Schelling and Hegel appropriated Spinoza's concept of substance—that which is in-itself and is conceived through itself—by describing the absolute as the in-itself not depending on anything else. Substance must be infinite, because anything less than the whole of all things would depend on something outside itself. I argued that Schleiermacher understood religion better than Kant and Hegel, but he wrongly described feeling as unmediated. The bad parts of Hegel are terrible, but he broke open the deadliest assumptions of Western thought by conceiving being as becoming, subjectivity as intersubjective and social, and God as spiraling relationality that embraces all otherness and difference. God is the intersubjective whole of wholes, irreducibly dynamic and relational, saving whatever can be saved in the tragic slaughterhouse of history.[21]

My first draft of *Kantian Reason and Hegelian Spirit* began with the history of racist science in which Kant and Hegel were players before I made a case for what is salvageable from post-Kantian idealism. Then I rewrote the book to build up to a full-orbed discussion of racist ordering. Kant and Hegel heightened the customary pathological racism of their time and civilization. Kant said that Whites had soared so far past all others that the concept of a degree-difference no longer applied to them. The advance of the White race toward enlightened cosmopolitan perfection was carrying it beyond race. Hegel prattled that Africa proper was too barbaric to be of any historical interest; only North Africa interested him, and only because the Phoenicians, Romans, Vandals, Byzantine Romans, Arabs, and Turks successively colonized it.[22]

Swedish zoologist Carl Linnaeus (1707–1778), the founder of modern taxonomy, divided *Homo sapiens* into European, Asiatic, American, and African groups. Kant smelled the crackpot science in the burgeoning "race research" of the 1770s, telling his classes it was more of a game than a true science. He opposed the polygenesis theory that human beings derive from numerous independent stocks, which did not stop him from teaching that some "races" are superior to others, the human species consists of the White, Negro, Hun, and Hindustani races, and there must be a way to distinguish between race and species. Kant reasoned that all four "races" must have been prefigured *in potentia* in the first human beings, the stem genus; the lost prototype must have carried the seeds of all four races, and it surely resembled the White race, since Whites were superior to all others. No race had any chance, Kant told his students, of thwarting the global dominion of race-transcending White people. Only Whites were educable in the sciences and had a capacity for abstract concepts.[23]

Charles Darwin refuted holdover advocates of polygenesis by showing that all species of organisms evolve through the natural selection of minute and inherited variations that increase the ability to compete, survive, and reproduce. Darwin described the natural environment as doing the selecting or modifying, although he didn't know the mechanism by which traits are passed on, since he didn't know about genetics or genetic mutation, the source of natural variation. His theory was revolutionary for teaching that all species are related and gradually evolve over time, and evolution relies on (genetic) variations within groups that modify the physical characteristics (phenotype) of organisms. I stressed that Darwin was a straightforward believer in White superiority and male superiority, ranking human groups hierarchically from the "savage" to the "civilized," which gave ballast to an already thriving measuring industry devoted to determining the scientific basis of something presumed to be terribly important, racial difference.[24]

Scientists fixed on skin color, facial angles, jaws, skull size, and cranial bumps, to no avail. Some of the greatest scientists of the late nineteenth century were major players in this enterprise, especially German Social Darwinist zoologist Ernst Haeckel, who coined the biological terms anthropogeny, ecology, phylum, and phylogeny. Haeckel taught that the environment acts directly on organisms, yielding new races; the survival of a race depends on its interaction with its environment; and the superior race is best described as Mediterranean man, a more precise marker than Caucasian. My first draft began with the philosophy and science story, arguing that we must take from Darwin and Haeckel what is true in them, and purge what is toxically bad. The same thing is true of Kant and Hegel. Then I recast the book to build up to this conclusion.

Kantian Reason and Hegelian Spirit had gone into press on February 24, 2011, when Princeton University held a conference on "The Niebuhrian Moment, Then and Now: Religion, Democracy, and Realism." I gave an academic talk on "Relational Justice: Rights, Right Order, and the Principles of Justice" that registered my Niebuhr pro-and-con arguments. Princeton ethicist Eric Gregory read a paper by his ethicist colleague Jeff Stout that excoriated Obama as a liar and a fraud. Eric gamely read aloud a text he would not have written, and Cornel West, seated next to me, was delighted with every blistering word. I reiterated one of my pro arguments about Niebuhr, which applied to our political moment: Niebuhr was deeply political, accepting that being morally responsible in politics often requires lesser-bad choices that prevent the triumph of something worse. Moreover, the upcoming election presented more than the usual lesser-bad calculation because Obama was a pretty good president in some ways, while Republicans had lurched to their worst place ever.

The conference was ringing in my head three days later as I commuted to Trinity College in Hartford, Connecticut. Jimmy Jones had hooked me in 2009 to teach at Trinity on Mondays, so every Sunday night I whisked from wherever I was to Hartford. Should I write a book geared to the 2012 election? Was there time to do it? On the way to Hartford, I mapped out *The Obama Question* (2012). There were reflective chapters on Obama himself, centerpiece chapters on "Saving Capitalism from Itself" and "Timidly Bold Obamacare," a stand-alone chapter on "Moral Empire and Liberal War," and a financial follow-up chapter on "Banks and Budgets." I was still questioning whether I had time to write it when I lectured on Kant's idealism on March 27 at All Souls Church (Unitarian Universalist) in New York City. This was one of my home bases, where I spoke many times. My friends at All Souls were skilled at diverting me to politics, and the conversation veered from Kant to Obama. That night on the commute to Hartford I resolved to write the Obama book. Most of it was in hand by July 2011 when I took Eris and Sara, the proofs for the Kant-Hegel book, and two lecture outlines with me to the Chautauqua Institution in Chautauqua, New York.[25]

Sara had recently graduated from seminary and was applying for ministry positions. I had spoken at Chautauqua for a week in 2008 and Eris was determined this time not to miss the mainline Protestant Disneyland in the Finger Lakes region, notwithstanding that the three of us would be jammed into a tiny single room. The ludicrous debt ceiling extortion of July-August 2011 was underway, which had to play out before I could finish *The Obama Question*. We were immersed in the daily back-and-forth between Obama and House Speaker John Boehner, and appalled. Republican leaders, the Tea Party base, and the Republican contenders for president wanted to give yet another tax cut to corporations and the rich, which would worsen the debt, and to save money on the backs of the poor and disabled—slashing food stamps and welfare, turning Medicare into a voucher program, reducing Medicaid to block grants, and abolishing so-called Obamacare, the Affordable Care Act. They wanted to cut or abolish the capital gains tax and all taxes on interest, dividends, and inheritance. Republican leaders forced Democrats to come to them in making huge budget cuts, only to walk away from historic deals in fits of extremism, which strengthened their leverage. Meanwhile the growing base of the party thrived on conspiracy-pornography about America's first Black president.

The Obama Question argued that Obama should have been better, since he never planted a flag and fought, but it was too soon to give up on him. In some ways he represented the United States far better than it was, as the wildly toxic opposition to him demonstrated. The Republican rout in the 2010 midterm elections was partly on us for expecting too much of a redeemer politician as cautious as Obama. At Chautauqua, I patched debt ceiling updates into the Obama manuscript while looking further down the road from Kant, Hegel, and Obama. Jim had plied me for years to write the Black social gospel history, waving off my qualms that I was not the one who should do it: "For God's sake, Gary, it's your obsession. Just start writing it." He also put it negatively: "How can you write so much about Hegel? People are dying!" A multivolume work on the Black social gospel would require an elaborate framework. At Chautauqua, I lectured on Reverdy Ransom and Benjamin Mays, and my friend Joan Brown Campbell, now the religion director at Chautauqua, regaled us with stories about the glory days of the NCC in the civil rights movement.

Meanwhile an anarchist Internet organization called U.S. Day of Rage and a mostly anarchist social media network named Anonymous called protesters to occupy Zuccotti Park near Wall Street in September. The first few days of Occupy Wall Street were chaotic, sparsely attended, and disappointing, though new people joined every day. The decision-making body of Occupy, the NYC General Assembly, consisted of anarchists making no demands and refusing to be identified as leaders. They identified with the leaderless revolutionaries of the ongoing Arab Spring protests that spread across North Africa and the Middle East. A breakthrough occurred on Saturday, September 24, when eighty-seven protesters marching to Union Square were arrested, garnering major media coverage. Occupy spread to more than 50 cities and became a global sensation. I gave numerous Occupy talks within and outside New York City, wrote cover articles for the *Christian Century* and *America*, and encouraged New York City churches to join the spectacle protest near Wall Street.[26]

Occupy Wall Street was a mighty blast against the regime of severe inequality imposed by neoliberalism. It was a moment to imagine that we could break the dominance of Wall Street, invest in a green economy, democratize economic power, and replenish besieged communities. Occupy renamed Zuccotti Park as Liberty Square. There were many young anarchists among the founders, plus anti-globalization veterans, religious activists, Alinsky-style organizers, radical democracy activists, and late-coming waves of traditional progressive organizations and unions. There were tensions between smartly dressed professionals and students showing up after work or class, and hardcore types who slept there for weeks. Deodorized drop-ins tried not to wince at the odor and messiness of the occupation, while the live-in protesters were quick to detect wincing and discomfort. There were hard words between democratic Left activists, many from DSA, and anarchists who insisted that trying to change the system through electoral politics is pointless and corrupting. But the sheer diversity at Liberty Square exemplified that people from nearly all walks of life were disgusted with the system and with typical liberal attempts to reform it.

At Union, Occupy suffused our day-to-day and spilled into the classrooms. Forty-five Union students served as Protest Chaplains at Liberty Square. They struggled to stay awake during class, the faculty supported them, and I spoke at satellite events in lower Manhattan churches that germinated into the second phase of Occupy. The second phase came sooner than we wanted, after police armed with riot gear cleared Zuccotti Park in November. Churches stepped up as supportive communities and meeting sites. Occupy Faith, the religious wing of Occupy, organized Truth Commissions focused on home foreclosures. Judson Church, Trinity Church Wall Street, West Park Presbyterian, and Park Slope Methodist were the heart of the religious solidarity work. Occupy responded with appropriate moral outrage to severe inequality and injustice. That mattered more than all its shortcomings.

A tipping point had been reached. People were fed up with being downsized and humiliated, after which came a rush of new movements for immigration justice, a raised minimum wage, anti-racism, equality, ecojustice, and the rights of First Nation peoples—the Dreamer movement, Fight for $15, Black Lives Matter, the Bernie Sanders campaign, and the Dakota Access Pipeline protests. For twenty years, the neoliberal slogan "There is no alternative" had shut down critiques of neoliberalism. Now, TINA lost its shutdown power. There had damned well better be an alternative to severe inequality and destroying the planet.

I turned sixty years old in the same month that my Kant-Hegel and Obama books came out. Aside from watching very slow runners pass me in the park, I felt no different than I had at fifty or forty. I hit the lecture circuit harder than ever, giving as many theological talks as possible amid a blizzard of political talks. Many churches asked for a bit of both on Friday-Saturday followed by two Sunday sermons interspersed with an Adult Education group—my favorite kind of engagement. I accepted whatever fee was customary at large churches and usually spoke at smaller churches for no fee. Lectures at universities yielded invitations from nearby churches or the other way around. Many engagements began with a query asking if it was true that I spoke for free; often the caller puzzled that I had no publicity agent, was not on Facebook, had no website, and did not Tweet.

Two blessed afternoons of that period stand out, and both brought me back to First Presbyterian Church in Kalamazoo. On March 18, 2012, my activist friends in Kalamazoo marked an Iraq War anniversary and the publication of *The Obama Question* by filling First Presbyterian for a talk on ongoing perpetual wars. Paul Clements, a political scientist at Western Michigan University, was the lead organizer. Every pew contained treasured friends, the sea of friends and memories washed over me, I started calling out friends in the front rows, and broke down. Fortunately, I had anticipated that I might need a manuscript in Kalamazoo. It got me back on track and I clung to it. There was a book-signing in the reception hall after the discussion, but two-thirds of the crowd stayed in the pews and chanted for more discussion, so I hustled through the book event and returned to the sanctuary. From there I proceeded to a conference at Princeton Theological Seminary on the history of Princeton Seminary and wondered if I would ever be able to return to Kalamazoo. There is such a thing as feeling too blessed by a community to return to it.

But on January 22, 2013, I returned to First Presbyterian to preach at Sara's ordination service. She had accepted a call at Pine Island Church in Kalamazoo, a half-hour from Will Christians' first call at First Presbyterian Church in Decatur, Michigan. The crowd was sure to be too large for Pine Island, so the Presbytery ordained Sara in Brenda's sanctuary. I said that Sara is much like Brenda and not like Brenda. The mark of one who lives in the Spirit is the loving and gracious capacity to care for others. Sara has it deeply, like her mother—identifying with others, wanting always to help them hear God's Spirit speaking to them. Like her mother, she overflows with theological imagination. On the other hand, Sara is sentimental, nostalgic, and a risk-taker. The previous summer, she backpacked across Europe by herself, something her parents never, never would have done. Many of our friends were there, and this time I didn't worry that I might be seeing them for the last time. With Sara and Will located in Southwest Michigan, there were many more Kalamazoo visits to come.

For seven months between these Kalamazoo afternoons, I repaid a debt to Jon Sisk, the Senior Executive Editor of Rowman & Littlefield. Jon had fulfilled his pledge to fast-track *The Obama Question*, so I submitted to the beck and call of his two favorite bookers, appearing on two or three media outlets per day. Many were wholly enjoyable, and some were inspiring. But I was thrilled when the touring ended because the last three months consisted mostly of Right-wing radio stations. They described themselves as Christian or Family stations, but Right versus Left was the point since they almost never treated me as a fellow Christian. I stuck to one stratagem on these shows: picture a fifteen-year-old in their audience whose only idea of Christianity is White Christian nationalist and exemplify an alternative. A few maxims anchored me: Stay in character. Don't take the bait. Stay in your lane. Sometimes during a drivetime call-in, I reminded myself that if only one young listener out there was reachable for me, it was worth the onslaught. After the election of November 2012, I happily returned to my no-booker orbit of schools, churches, and conferences. *Kantian*

Reason and Hegelian Spirit won the PROSE Award of the Association of American Publishers, and for a while the theology invitations almost balanced the political ones, blessedly to me.

Meanwhile I received a spate of targeted search offers from seminaries and universities. Each became an occasion to count my blessings at Union, and each helped me to feel slightly less guilty about not doing enough to uphold Union's reputation. I never leveraged an offer to get something I wanted at Union, or even told Serene about them, though sometimes she knew from the grapevine. One offer that excited my parents would have taken me out of theology, a non-starter for me. Two offers gave me pause, and both recurred a year later. The kind of school that tempted me was a seminary with a strong social ethical tradition like Union's and a stronger Christian anchor than Union's. I had no interest in teaching at a secular university aside from my work at Columbia. I love to teach students who are on the path to ministry or whose faith impels them into social justice work. We got a diminishing stream of ministry-track students during my years at Union, but Union is in my head and heart like no other school. We rebranded as an interfaith seminary before it was true and adjusted rapidly to the rush of students from non-Christian faiths and no faith who enrolled. My gifted doctoral advisees of my later years at Union—Romy Felder, Hilly Haber, Neonu Jewell, Kelly Maeshiro, Anthony Jermaine Ross-Allam, Zachary Royal, Isaac Sharp, Aaron Stauffer, and Arvind Theodore, plus two others close to me who were not quite my advisees, Jamall Calloway and Irene Preetha Prasannakumar, made me grateful every day that I stayed at Union.

So, we never learned if my New York City partner could live somewhere else. Eris professed to believe that she might be able to do it, and I was dubious. Her band of elderly trainees dwindled, and she compensated by turning her thrift-store avocation into a store on Etsy called ErisVintage. Eris had survived the 1990s by becoming street smart and speaking at Al-Anon groups. She was a thrifter from her years in design and styling long before she turned her collection of jewelry, dresses, and handbags into an Etsy store. My awareness of thrift stores soared from being with her. Wherever I lectured, I looked for them, imagining a getaway cottage in a quaint location with a view, which we never bought. New York City became my home, through Eris, in a way that it never would have been left to my bumpkin self.

For four years I taught on the side at Trinity College, until 2013, and for three years after that I did the same thing at Harvard Divinity School. The schedule varied in different semesters, but the usual model was to arrive on Sunday night, teach on Monday, and hustle home to my day job. I had taught at Trinity because I couldn't say no to Jimmy Jones; then I got used to it. Trinity students were much like K students except Trinity had perennial drama over raucous behavior in its Greek societies. HDS was teetering on dropping social ethics. David Hempton, a church historian and dean at HDS, said that HDS might make a new hire at the junior level, or might not. In the meantime, was I willing to keep social ethics going? HDS had invented social ethics. To me, losing it at HDS would be a calamity for the field. I usually taught two classes at HDS, where I loved the students and classes and belatedly accrued some savings. HDS students were more academic than Union students, less committed to activism, and expressed more anxiety about feeling "safe" in the classroom. They asked many questions about scholarly trends, unlike Union, and few had backgrounds in social justice organizing, very much unlike Union. Social ethics is essential to Union's identity, but I could see why it was hanging by a thread at HDS.

In 2013 and 2014 I lectured for a week to seven hundred ecumenical activists gathered at the January Adventure conferences in St. Simon's Island, Georgia. In 2013 I lectured on social ethics and politics alongside the great biblical scholar Walter Brueggemann, who regaled the crowd with his customary blend of exegesis, humor, and prophetic ethical spirit. The following year I lectured on theology alongside biblical scholar Marcus Borg in his last venue of this kind. Every day, it seemed, there was a book signing before we commenced lecturing; perhaps the trauma magnified my sense of the frequency. The line on the left, for Walter and Marcus, was always very long. My line on the right was usually a modest affair, and some of my folks lined up just to talk. Walter claimed that he planned to get off the lecture circuit; he had retired with a new spouse to Cincinnati and didn't need to be writing lectures. He said it twice and I laughed both times, as a truly retired Walter is unimaginable. Marcus was as sharp and engaging as ever, but dying of the chronic scarring lung disease that ended his life the following January. He didn't room with the rest of us at Epworth by the Sea because he was not going to be deprived of smoking and drinking in his last months of life. By then I was stunned that my own mortality alarm bells were ringing loudly.

For many years, I had been working at a killer pace, so I didn't perceive the HDS sideline as an escalation, and in truth it wasn't. But in September 2013 in Cambridge, I learned that I was breaking down. Very labored running was my first symptom. The first time it hit me was on a Sunday night along the Charles River in Cambridge, one of my favorite routes. It seemed to come from nowhere and I bulled through it. Running in Central Park and Riverside Park became equally difficult—what the hell? There was also a distinctive headache, not explosive like a migraine, more like head-in-a-vice.

Four minutes into a doctor's appointment, I registered 250 over 120 for hypertension, three more readings were similar, and my life changed. I passed to the care of a specialist who told me confidently that many excellent medications existed; it was just a question of finding the right one. We tried one that failed, a second one that knocked me down with dizziness, and a third one that didn't work either. Mercifully, we tried Losartan, which pulled me back from way-up-there danger, except I was allergic to it. We reran the cycle, modified with combinations of half and quartered pills, none of which worked, while I zoomed back to the danger zone. Two years of this yielded a chastened verdict. My doctor observed that I was an exceptional case for combining extremely high numbers with failed treatment without stroking out, at least not yet. It was better to accept the consequences of taking a medication to which I'm allergic than to stroke out. Losartan has saved my life, thus far, though in Tübingen, Amsterdam, and San Diego I had warning shots that bolted up my arm to the back of my neck and throbbed for thirty minutes like the Big One. Each attack occurred two hours before a lecture that I anticipated with delight. I don't know why speaking engagements in pleasant far-off locales trigger them. Meanwhile, as far as we know, I will cope for the rest of my days with a medication that is toxic for me.

Shortly before this book entered the page-proof stage, I read a student's term paper that discussed my lecture of November 2015 on "James Luther Adams and the Spirit of Liberal Theology." I retrieved it on YouTube to recall what I had said. There were no surprises in the content; it was one of my standard fare lectures on post-Kantian idealism in modern theology. What stunned me was the kinetic presentational flow.

Who was this person so present and high-spirited in the video? He looked nothing like the violently ill person I remember of that period.

In the nine years that Losartan has since given me, I have published three books on the Black social gospel tradition, two books on European and U.S. American democratic socialism, a constructive work of philosophical theology, a book on U.S. American liberal theology, a book on the history of Anglican theology, and this memoir. All the others are doorstopper tomes exceeding five hundred pages. All are capstone works that I wrote in a health emergency. All convey, often explicitly, my contention that "Christianity" is a name for the many ways that story-shaped Christian communities have interpreted the original Jesus movement and constructed doctrines that make Christian experience intelligible. All these books were possible because Eris and I are a love union that works, looking out for each other and being grateful for each other. Her story is that she always wanted someone who loved her, and finally found one in an unlikely Christian Left intellectual. My story is that I was never good enough to justify my existence, and then lucked into a partner who looked out for me. Eris' greater beauty is inward, the great blessing of my later life.

I was desperate to write *The New Abolition* (2015) and felt a flood of relief when it went to press. Getting volume one on the Black social gospel out of my head and into a book was the high point of my academic career. I had feared that the book I cared most about would go unwritten. My scruple that a White scholar is not the best for it was correct, but I lingered there too long, now into the years of a health crisis. The relief and gratitude that I felt upon completing the proofs for that book top everything else in my career. If I stroked out a week later, there would still be a book making my case that the Black social gospel paved the way to MLK and liberation theology and is our most valuable religious tradition. Jim and I had our longest Pisticci lunch-dinner ever when *The New Abolition* went to press. I cannot repeat the overly generous things he said. I kept looking away from his intent gaze, embarrassed by praise as always, except more so. But he began by saying, "My friend, you have done it."

1   Jack Dorrien, DeTour High School; DeTour, Michigan, 1949.

2   Virginia Hank, DeTour High School; DeTour, Michigan, 1949.

3 Gary Dorrien
(GD), Midland
Trailer Park; Midland,
Michigan, 1953.

4 GD, Midland
Trailer Park, Midland,
Michigan, 1954.

FOREST SCHOOL
1957 - 1958

5 GD, Forest School; Bay County, Michigan, 1958.

Father's 6-59 Day

6 GD, Greg Dorrien, Jack Dorrien, and Andy Dorrien; Bay County, Michigan. Father's Day, 1959.

7 The Dorrien brothers at Alma College: from left, **front**: Eric and Mike; **back**: GD, Greg, and Andy; Alma, Michigan, 1972.

8 Jack and Virginia Dorrien; Midland, Michigan, 1978.

9   GD and Brenda L. Biggs, with Bishop Wilbur E. Hogg; ordination at
St. Andrew's Episcopal Church, Albany, New York, 1982.

10   Dorrien-Biggs ordination gathering: **from left**, Greg Dorrien, Jack
Dorrien, Virginia Dorrien, Eric Dorrien, GD, Brenda Biggs, Anson Biggs,
Grace Biggs, and Mike Dorrien; Albany, New York, 1982.

11   Sara B. Dorrien and Brenda Biggs; Kalamazoo, Michigan, 1988.

12   GD with Jürgen
Moltmann, Kalamazoo
College; Kalamazoo,
Michigan, 1988.

13   GD with Brenda Biggs and Skipper; Kalamazoo, 1998.

14   Sara Dorrien singing "Maybe," Kalamazoo Children's Chorus, 2000.

15 GD with Sara Dorrien on the Brooklyn Bridge, New York City, 2010.

16 GD with Eris McClure on the Brooklyn Bridge, New York City, 2010.

17   Seminary graduation: from left, Eris McClure, Sara Dorrien, GD, Robyn
Hampton Dorrien, Virginia Dorrien, and Greg Dorrien, Columbia Theological
Seminary; Decatur, Georgia, 2011.

18 GD Grawemeyer Award Lecture, Louisville, Kentucky, 2017.
Photograph by Jonathan Roberts, Louisville Theological Seminary.

19 GD with Cornel West, Nkosi Du Bois Anderson, and James Cone, Union
Theological Seminary; New York City, New York, 2017.
Photograph by Adam Crocker.

20 Eris McClure and GD, sunset in Traverse City, Michigan, 2018.

21 Baptism of Nicholas: from left, front: Patty Christians, Sara Dorrien-Christians, baby Nicholas Christians, and Eris McClure; back: Will Christians and GD, 2019.

22 Front: Clara Christians, Nicholas Christians, and Evie Christians; back: Sara Dorrien-Christians and Will Christians, 2023.

8

TWILIGHT SURGE

In the 1880s and 1890s, a stream of Black Methodist and Baptist ministers pressed a desperate question: what would a new abolitionism be? Abolitionism and the Civil War had come and gone, Reconstruction had come and been forsaken, and a mania of racist terrorism descended on Black Americans. The United States imposed a racial caste system lacking any parallel in the post-slavery Americas. Lynching backstopped the Black Codes, the 14th and 15th Amendments were eviscerated in most of the South, and a post-Confederate grievance mythology about a Lost Cause grew into a civil religion. The penalties for disputing any aspect of Jim Crow were swift and lethal. Baptist minister William Simmons, AME Zion minister Alexander Walters, and AME minister Reverdy C. Ransom enlisted churches to join political struggles against all of it. Mostly they failed. The Afro-American League folded, the Afro-American Council had a few good years before Booker T. Washington hijacked it, and the Niagara Movement of W. E. B. Du Bois sputtered and collapsed.

The founders of the Black social gospel kept pressing for an activist social justice religion. What was needed was precisely a new abolition fired by gospel faith. They taught that God cares about the poor, the excluded, the oppressed, and the kingdom of God. They preached about equality, democracy, righteousness, and Jesus loving all the children. Not to enter the social and political struggle for justice was to betray Jesus. In *The New Abolition: W. E. B. Du Bois and the Black Social Gospel* (2015), I argued that four schools of Black social gospel contention arose in the late nineteenth century.[1]

A large band of bishops and church leaders accepted Booker T. Washington's program of economic uplift and political accommodation, teaching that Black Americans would get their rights by learning a trade and winning the good will of White society. The second group embraced the Black nationalist colonialism or cultural nationalism of AME bishop Henry McNeal Turner and Episcopal cleric Alexander Crummell, while others such as Baptist cleric Sutton Griggs and AME anti-lynching crusader Ida B. Wells were culturally nationalist with one foot in the political liberationist camp. The third group consisted of neo-abolitionists and socialists who said there is no substitute for waging a political struggle for justice and liberation. Most of them operated in the orbit of Du Bois, notably Ransom, AME minister Richard R. Wright Jr., Presbyterian cleric Francis J. Grimké, Episcopal socialist clerics Robert Bagnall and George Frazier Miller, Congregational minister Byron Gunner, and Baptist ministers James R. L. Diggs and Peter James Bryant; others included Baptist socialist clerics George W. Woodbey and George W. Slater Jr. The fourth group mediated the rivalry between Du Bois-style militancy and Washington-style realism, contending that both were indispensable to building a civil rights movement. Leading figures in this group included Walters, Baptist cleric Adam Clayton Powell Sr., Congregational ministers Henry Hugh Proctor, and Baptist educators Nannie H. Burroughs and Lucy Wilmot Smith. For some in the fourth group, the founding of the NAACP in 1909 and the subsequent fading of Washington rendered moot the both/and equation, while others stuck to it for the rest of their lives.

I drew this frame at the outset of *The New Abolition*. Six conventions thwarted the Black social gospel from being recognized as a tradition at all, let alone a great one: (1) It consisted in the early twentieth century of only a handful of ministers. (2) Black churches were too self-centered, conservative, and preoccupied with survival to advocate a social justice agenda. (3) The social gospel was a White Progressive movement that avoided the racial justice issue. (4) Reverdy Ransom and Adam Clayton Powell Sr. were marginal figures who had little impact. (5) Religious intellectuals were irrelevant by the end of the nineteenth century. (6) Reinhold Niebuhr shredded the social gospel, so there's no usable history there.

I refuted the regnant conventions: (1) There were many Black social gospel advocates and leaders. (2) They inveighed assiduously against the provincialism problem. (3) They applied the justice activism of the social gospel to the racist evils of American society. (4) Ransom and Powell were sensational figures who reached as far as they could. (5) The convention about religious intellectuals was a prejudice of secular historians. (6) Niebuhr brilliantly skewered idealistic and pacifist strains of the social gospel, but his polemics misrepresented the social gospel and obscured his own debts to it. I argued that Black churches have always been widely diverse theologically, politically, culturally, and socially, united by only one thing—opposition to racism. Many of them *are*, and always have been, very conservative. But this fact accentuates the importance of the Black social gospel.

The idea that churches must be involved in political struggles for justice to be faithful to the gospel is disputed in every generation. Those who affirm it are always a minority. Walter Rauschenbusch refused for most of his career to employ the term "social gospel." There is no legitimately Christian non-social gospel, he protested; why should he concede otherwise by adding a redundant adjective? Rauschenbusch bowed to convention only near the end of his life, in 1917, lamenting that a non-social gospel was the norm. Those who dissented from it, like him, had to wear a special name. The founders of the Black social gospel confronted the same problem in a far more oppressive context. The Black church was mostly averse to social justice activism despite having been born liberationist. Those who preached about building protest organizations were always a minority. The tradition they forged is the greatest one we have in the United States, the moral epicenter of American religious thought and politics.

Far from having no subject, or only a sliver of a subject, I had to negotiate the profuse complexity of the Black social gospel. My chief concern was to establish this category, contending that Martin Luther King Jr. did not come from nowhere. But I also expanded the category beyond the line leading from Ransom and Wright to Mordecai Johnson and Benjamin E. Mays to King and Pauli Murray. Here I took a different tack than my closest reader urged upon me. Jim Cone exhorted me to define the subject narrowly and squ-e-e-e-ze it—until he saw what came of tracking the four schools of thought *and* the specific line that led to King and Murray. To focus only on the group surrounding Du Bois would have yielded a parade of males, the forerunners of the very male group that surrounded King in the Southern Christian Leadership Conference. The women in this story who broke the grip of male domination and presumption had to be creative, stubborn, independent, and tough, building new organizations and working with religious communities that denied women the right to lead.

I did not render Du Bois as a Christian against his will, but I pushed back against the many Du Bois scholars who are tone-deaf to his deep, vibrant, yearning spirituality. Du Bois had a powerful religious wellspring and a practical version of the social gospel. In his blistering Commencement Address in 1940 at Wilberforce University, he said that Christianity rightly understood is about sympathy and unselfishness, giving your life for others in sacrificial struggle. Wilberforce, he charged, inculcated a pious dogmatism that thwarted the ethical struggle for justice, "a miserable apprehension of the teaching of Christ." Du Bois elsewhere tweaked 1 Corinthians 13 on faith, hope, and love, contending that work, love, and sacrifice are saving, "and the greatest of these is sacrifice." The highest praise he ever conferred on anyone was for Karl Marx, "a colossal genius of infinite sacrifice and monumental industry." The early Du Bois conceived the divine in Hegelian fashion as the outward-reaching Spirit of freedom. The later Du Bois conjured a Black baby Jesus in his essay "The Second Coming," an adult Black Jesus in his scathing essay "Jesus Christ in Texas," and a hymn in which the Buddha walked with Christ. In his last years, though he drifted to the pro-Communist Left, Du Bois still wrote about saving "the tattered shreds of God."[2]

Many readers of his time had no doubt that Du Bois had a spiritual sensibility. They caught that a religious, arguably Christian passion lay behind his furious attacks on unworthy ministers and church dogmatism. They discerned that he agreed with them about the Black church, even if he didn't go to church: nothing compared to the Black church as a source of inspiration, hope, solidarity, identity, belonging, entertainment, moral language, and transcendence. Any justice movement worth building had to share in the life of the Black church, speaking its language of struggle, hope, sacrifice, love, and redemption.

I argued that Du Bois soared above all others in explaining what was happening in the world—the central problem of the twentieth century was the color line. In 1875 the European powers controlled one-tenth of the African continent. By 1900 they had devoured nearly the entire continent. Du Bois said the European powers learned a lesson from their own slave-trading systems: the pillage and rape of Africa could be called something else if Black people were less than human. English social critic

John A. Hobson, in *Imperialism* (1902), said that capitalism had reached the stage at which it depended on imperial plunder. The flow of finance capital to far-off lands ratcheted up the clash between empires. The political democracy of the colonizing powers was supposedly the answer to the terrible problems of inequality, exploitation, and oppression, yet as democracy spread, so did the rule of might. Du Bois said democracy and imperialism grew together because White workers shared the spoils of exploiting people of color. The capitalist class yielded to the unions for as long as capitalists found new markets to exploit, but most of this new wealth rested on the exploitation of Asians, Africans, South Americans, and West Indians. The only solution to this miserable picture was for the labor and socialist movements to reach all the way to the poorest and excluded, not stopping with White workers.[3]

There are bad things in Du Bois to reject. His Talented Tenth trope was snobby and elitist, which yielded some baleful passages about Black moral degeneracy. He had early flirtations with romantic imperialism and Social Darwinism, and he treated women badly, beginning with the shabby treatment he handed out to his wife Nina Gomer Du Bois and to Ida Wells. On these counts, exalting Du Bois must go only so far. But if I were limited to one author for the rest of my days, I might well choose Du Bois, boring into nooks and crannies of his vast corpus that always yield rewards.

On July 17, 2014, New York City police officer Daniel Pantaleo strangled to death an unarmed Black man named Eric Garner with a banned chokehold on a sidewalk in Staten Island. He had suspected Garner of selling single cigarettes from packs lacking tax stamps. Garner denied selling loose cigarettes, Pantaleo wrestled him to the ground, several officers helped to pin Garner to the ground, Garner pleaded "I can't breathe" eleven times, and the medical examiner ruled his death a homicide. At Union we waited with tense, fraught, wary vigilance to see if a state grand jury would press criminal charges against Pantaleo and his fellow officers.

On August 9, 2014, an unarmed Black man named Michael Brown was gunned down by police in the streets of Ferguson, Missouri. His body lay uncovered on the street for four hours. His blood poured onto the pavement. Ferguson sparked an historic eruption. Traci Blackmon, a United Church of Christ pastor in nearby Florissant, spoke to the moment, judging that Ferguson erupted because Brown's blood oozing for hours on the street made a statement about the value that America places on Black life. She said Brown's blood exposed the eagerness of White Americans to regard a teenaged Black man as the other to be feared. His blood displayed the widespread White American assumption that Black men are always guilty. It cried out against the racism that criminalizes and dehumanizes Black bodies. It unveiled the chasm between young people and an out-of-touch church. It showed how race and poverty and hopelessness intersect on American streets. Above all, Blackmon said, the blood of Michael Brown exposed the insidious effects of racism "that are intrinsic to the very fiber of our nation's being."[4]

On December 4, 2014, a Richmond County grand jury voted not to indict Pantaleo. At Union we mobilized the seminary community to join massive demonstrations downtown that carried on for weeks and spread to many cities. Many of us at Union were out there every night chanting "I can't breathe," keeping our distance from the police. On the night after the grand jury decision, I swung by Jim's apartment to work on him: "Jim, if you're ever going to join a demonstration, tonight's the night. Think what it would mean to our students if you joined them." He waved me off: "You go; you'll feel better." Joining an outdoor protest where he might be vulnerable was something that Jim never did. He owed that to no one. Demonstrating was for people who needed to feel better and who believed that demonstrating might do some good. That night I walked behind a student carrying a sign that said, "James Cone was right." We had to be out here because James Cone had been right about how White supremacy defends itself.

The following year, Jim, ethicists Thelathia Nikki Young and Peter Paris, and I spoke at an American Academy of Religion (AAR) forum in Atlanta on "Ferguson and Beyond: Race and Niebuhrian Ethics in the Age of Obama." Jim was scathing about Niebuhrian ethics: Reinhold Niebuhr never risked anything for a Black person; he had no moral authority in addressing the issue of racism, and neither did the Reinhold Niebuhr Society, the sponsoring organization of this program. Near the end of the session, a young academic in the standing-room section asked if any of us had anything hopeful to say. Jim shot me a look conveying that I was to filibuster while he thought of something. I talked about protest organizations old and new that were working together in New York City, until Jim indicated that he was ready, took the microphone, paused, and said: "We have a gospel. The gospel has something to say to us." That was it. Pay attention to Luke 4 and Matthew 25. Try to imagine living by the gospel.

My health crisis fueled a gush of capstone books and road lectures. Cornel West had come home to Union in 2012, but he and I were on the road so much that we had to communicate through our students, seeing them but not each other. Then in 2016 we lost Cornel again, this time to Harvard, and I cursed myself for the time not spent with him. My first two books on the Black social gospel were written much closer together than it looks. I had been preparing all my life to write *Breaking White Supremacy: Martin Luther King Jr. and the Black Social Gospel* (2018). It poured out of me, so Yale University Press put off the production process to create some separation from *The New Abolition*, after which I missed the next publication window by failing to secure permission for a picture of Benjamin Mays. My hypertension was so bad while I finished *Breaking White Supremacy* that I assumed I would never write volume three. If I had time for one more book, it would be on European democratic socialism, but I was teetering on disability termination and didn't expect to complete any more books. I would have ended *Breaking White Supremacy* with a much shorter chapter had I believed there would be a volume three. As it is, that book ends with a rush of feeling about the Black social gospel that registers something unsaid about the author.[5]

In mid-November 2016, two weeks after Donald Trump won the White House, I learned that *The New Abolition* had won the Grawemeyer Award and that I was being audited by the IRS. I puzzled over the IRS news while speaking at the AAR Conference in San Antonio, Texas, where we Union folk beamed that our leader, Serene Jones, served that year as president of AAR. Upon returning to New York, I spent night after night tearing apart my tax returns for 2014 and 2015, spreading rows of receipts across the dining room table, trying to find whatever it was that triggered an audit. I couldn't find anything, didn't trust the tax service to help me, and fell into a traumatized fright caused by not sleeping and not knowing. One morning in early December, I awoke unable to speak, producing only a whisper. Maybe laryngitis? Audit day came and an IRS official spent an hour tracking my road lecture expenses, his countenance slowly changing as my figures checked out. Finally, he asked, "What happened here?" Soon after he pulled back from the rows of receipts, he saw it. For two years my tax form preparer had classified my Harvard income as speaking fees, which confused the IRS and me. Two days later, a vocal cord specialist had bad news—this was auto-immune total paralysis in my right cord, not laryngitis.

For two months I whispered in class, helped by a boom box. I canceled a slew of speaking engagements and contemplated a suddenly ended career. It stunned me to go down just as Trump moved into the White House. A specialist who mostly treats Broadway singers tried to inflate the paralyzed cord with injections, reducing the distance that my good cord had to stretch to produce a sound, which didn't work. She tried a second round, failing on the first six attempts to poke into the paralyzed cord. It was unbearable torture. I was ready to give up, but she persisted and succeeded, and I regained half a voice. My first event with the new voice, on January 31, 2017, was the premiere of Martin Doblmeier's superb film, *An American Conscience: The Reinhold Niebuhr Story*. Cornel and I spoke at the premiere, he shot me a worried look, and I said this cringy voice is an occasion of thanksgiving because a week ago I couldn't speak. We discussed the film, Niebuhr, and especially, the crisis of U.S. American civilization in which we were immersed, confronted by a Donald Trump presidency. Three months later I was still grateful but embarrassed during Grawemeyer week in Louisville. I apologized at the first two lectures for inflicting this voice on everyone present. If it gets worse, I asked, please raise your hand and I will reach further down. Sara and Will, now pastors in Memphis, Tennessee, urged me to stop apologizing—my voice wasn't *that* bad; the apologies were worse. So I am finishing my career with a squeaky half-voice that isn't *that* bad.

Catherine Keller produced during this period a magnificent tapestry of apophatic Neo-Platonist mysticism, deconstructionist musings on the impossible, and Whiteheadian feminism titled *Cloud of the Impossible* (2014). Drawing on the fifteenth-century theologian Nicholas of Cusa, she took Jacques Derrida and Gilles Deleuze where they didn't want to go, into outright theological reflection on the "cloudy edges" of the impossible. Nicholas, she argued, was like Whitehead in being an experimental theorist of a non-oppositional binary dynamic—God is creating and creatable. The upshot of being moved by the moving manifold might be that God feels us through our feelings of God. However, Catherine allowed that only Whitehead went that far, not Nicholas, who assumed the Neo-Platonic One of Christian theism.[6]

Catherine recast Whitehead's idea that creativity drives God's becoming in response to the becoming of the world. Whitehead conceived the divine as a real entity in the process of creativity. Charles Hartshorne said Whitehead should have described God as a real society of occasions, not an entity. Catherine fashioned a theopoetic process theology in which the Whiteheadian divine—the lure of novel possibility—is a metaphor of entanglement. The divine becoming is the actualization of an indeterminate creativity. The many become one, and are increased by one, but this one is just one among many others, unfolding as a singular event by enfolding in the universe. What matters, Catherine said, is how we *do* God, not what we say about God. We had dinners that plunged into her forays into Nicholas, Deleuze, and Whitehead. Sometimes we replayed Whitehead versus Hegel or compared current Catherine to prepoststructuralist Catherine. On occasion a nearby diner guffawed at overhearing us, which Catherine usually didn't notice. She was immersed in the great constructive project of her later career, after which she plunged into eco-political theology.

Meanwhile Jim was buoyed by his long-delayed reckoning with James Baldwin and then by the Black Lives Matter movement. For the past decade he had swung up and down about theology, cultural trends, and retiring, fearing that he was losing his enthusiasm for teaching. It troubled him that theologians no longer wrote systematic theologies that grappled strenuously with the doctrines. One evening in his living room, Jim pulled down his copy of Emil Brunner's tome *The Mediator* (1934), opened it to one of his underlined pages, and asked me plaintively, "Gary, why don't theologians write like this anymore? Brunner dug into the doctrines! His books were rigorous and substantive!" Jim was justly proud of the theologizing that lit up his books *A Black Theology of Liberation* and *God of the Oppressed*. It thrilled him to add to these works *The Cross and the Lynching Tree*, which became his favorite among his books. But every year he read term papers that dismissed systematic theology as an antiquated enterprise, and papers that quoted Victor Anderson criticizing him.

A social ethicist and theologian at Vanderbilt, Anderson contended that Cone's Black theology was a reductive reaction against the White world that wrongly ontologized an essentialized Blackness. Being Black was not the story of Anderson's life. He was also gay, queer, postmodern, aesthetically attuned to the grotesque, and steeped in poststructuralism and Chicago School liberal theology. He had been hurt in his youth by the Black church, so he was allergic to hymnody about it. It took Anderson many years to throw off the message that he should hate himself for being most of the things he was, plus not Black enough. He contained too many worlds to feel included in Cone's unitary description of an ontologized Blackness, a mirror-image opposite of whiteness that ascribed qualities of being to Blackness. Victor refused to acclaim the Blackness that whiteness created. He said so powerfully at the outset of his career, in *Beyond Ontological Blackness* (1995).[7]

Every year, this book was a fresh discovery to Union students who identified with it and needed to talk about it. Victor had a deep integrity and defended his position eloquently, but he exaggerated Cone's essentialism, brushing past Cone's contention that he ontologized blackness only in a cultural sense of the term reflecting qualities of Black being-in-the-world. To Jim, ontological blackness was about fighting off oppression and having the courage to be, not about reifying race. He realized, however, why his distinctions cut no ice with Anderson. Often on the last page of a student's paper, Jim wrote back that Victor Anderson had his experience and James Cone had his experience. That was a version of Jim's mantra to Union students: work out your own perspective based on your own experience. For a while, Jim said that *The Cross and the Lynching Tree* was his last book. Then he reread Baldwin, Black Lives Matter arose in July 2013, and Jim began to talk about one more book, which he called "the Baldwin book."

Baldwin had long spoken to him more than any writer, helping him to sing his theological blues. But Jim felt unqualified to teach Baldwin's novels and social criticism. In 2011 the Cathedral Church of Saint John the Divine, an Episcopal colossus twelve blocks from Union, asked Jim to speak at Baldwin's induction into the Poet's Corner. He told the Cathedral gathering that people who read Baldwin become better human beings. Saying it aloud, at this site, broke Jim's paralysis about teaching Baldwin. He began to say that his trinity was Martin, Malcolm, and James, and he taught a course featuring Baldwin keynotes: a writer writes out of one thing only—one's own experience; Whites are the sickest people on earth; the church is the worst place to learn about Christianity (so Baldwin left the church); but every artist has a religious motivation (as Baldwin said of himself). Jim protested that most Baldwin scholars snuff out the fire in his work, sliding around the severe things he said about Whites. The fire was what enthralled Jim. Many students were appalled at Baldwin's trope that beauty is revealed in Black suffering. Jim replied that rationally there is no beauty or redemption in Black suffering, but Baldwin's art was theological, seeing the beauty in Black tragedy with the eyes of faith. Jim had never thought self-consciously about his own literary artfulness until he taught the Baldwin course. The Baldwin book didn't quite come together, but it morphed into a memoir, *Said I Wasn't Gonna Tell Nobody* (2018), which paid attention to the beauty of Baldwin's sentences and Jim's own.[8]

Jim wrote that he heard the cry of Black blood in 1967 and never stopped hearing it: "White people didn't hear it then, and they still don't hear it now. They are deaf to the cry of black blood. Yet black people will not be silent as our children are thrown in rivers, blown into eternity, and shot dead in the streets. Black Lives Matter!" He finished the manuscript on December 1, 2017, just before he learned that cancer would soon take him away. Jim was grateful to have had his say. He welcomed a select stream of guests to his apartment, reminiscing about his life. His daughter Robynn Cone came every day; Serene Jones and Kelly Brown Douglas were mainstay caregivers; and Jim gratefully trusted his editor friend Robert Ellsberg with his last book. Ellsberg published Jim's entire corpus at Orbis Books; now Jim's memoir got the same line-by-line care that Ellsberg devoted to *Martin & Malcolm & America* and *The Cross and the Lynching Tree*. On one occasion, Jim held aloft as I entered his copy of *Breaking White Supremacy*, a lunch topic of the past two years. It evoked his fond remembrance of writing the Martin-Malcolm book.[9]

Very near the end of his life, Jim asked me about Vincent Lloyd, a prolific Black theologian at Villanova University. I told him about Lloyd's new book, *Religion of the Field Negro* (2018), which made a framing argument about the history of Black theology. Lloyd said Black theology in its original phase was theological and social critical, making strong claims about God, Christ, the judgments of God, and the idolatry of White theology. The second phase began when secularism and its conjoined twin, multiculturalism, crept into Black theology, reducing it to one of many ways to pluralize theology. Black theology lost its nerve. It was not very theological anymore, being more concerned to pass secular and multicultural tests of civility and diversity. Historicists, feminists, womanists, postmodernists, and secular religious studies scholars played the leading roles in taming Black theology, but even Cone went along with relativizing critiques that stripped his early work of its power. The third phase, Lloyd argued, commenced with the rise of Black Lives Matter. It has no theological exemplars, but they are surely coming, because Black Lives Matter is closer to the Black Power moment than anything that existed between 1975 and 2010.[10]

"Hmmm," Jim said. "There's something to it, isn't there? What do you think?" I said this frame certainly describes something familiar but doesn't do enough sorting to accomplish what frames are supposed to do. Phase one is terribly brief, phase two is almost the entire history of Black theology lumped together in all its variations, and phase three is a blank space. But I added that Jim's forthcoming memoir was more like his first two books than any of the others. "Yes," he said, "that's what I mean. There *is* something to it." On April 28, 2018, we lost him. I eulogized him on April 30 at Union's memorial service. Eight days later, Raphael Warnock eulogized him at the funeral service at Riverside Church, declaring that to measure Cone's significance in modern theology, we must distinguish between "BC and AC." Theology was one thing Before Cone, and something very different After Cone.

I fought off a crushing sadness as we lost him, while giving talks at places that normally would have delighted me: Grosse Pointe War Memorial Association in Grosse Pointe Farms, Michigan; Morehouse College in Atlanta, welcomed by the great Lawrence Edward Carter Sr.; Corpus Christi Parish in New York City; Mason Temple in Memphis, Tennessee, on the 50th anniversary of MLK's "I've been to the Mountaintop" farewell; Duke Divinity School in Durham, North Carolina, where theologian J. Kameron Carter told me he was leaving the faculty; Mercer University in Macon, Georgia, hosted by the distinguished ethicist David Gushee; Loyola University in Chicago, where moral theologian Hille Haker and I bonded over post-Hegelian philosophy; Iliff School of Theology in Denver, where I savored an afternoon with my treasured hermano Miguel de la Torre; Ludwig-Maximilians-Universität München in Munich, Germany, where I feasted for four days with German, Scandinavian, British, and North American theologians; and the

Royal Netherlands Academy of Arts and Sciences in Amsterdam, Netherlands, where a hypertension bolt shook me to my core. I was habituated to a hypertension headache and my daily blast of allergic reaction to Losartan. In Amsterdam I realized that putting up with both did not pull me out of red-zone danger.

Most of my lectures in 2018 sang the song of *Breaking White Supremacy* that the civil rights movement of the King era was incomparably beautiful, daring, traumatic, and searing in U.S. American history. The movement abounded with noble visions, resounded with magnificent rhetoric, ended in nightmarish despair, and does not end. It put on global display the ravages of racism and racial caste in the United States. It sang and preached and marched for a better world. MLK became a global icon by assailing his country's racism, condemning its economic injustice, opposing its war in Vietnam, standing with the poor and oppressed, expounding a vision of liberation, and being assassinated for doing so. I said that to me, this story surpasses all other American stories because it is the passion narrative of our time. Yet this greatest of American stories no longer makes its own way. It must be retold in ways that accentuate why it was so radical and disruptive.[11]

Whenever a group let me choose the subject, I opted for MLK, setting the Black social gospel against the White nationalism pouring out of the White House. At Iliff, however, the faculty asked for a talk about my work as a whole. In Munich the subject was liberal theology. Theologian Jörg Lauster introduced me to the conference as "the pope of liberal theology." I gave a liberal-liberation talk, my emphasis on social justice surprised the newcomers to my work, and Lauster observed that the fire of Christian socialism still burned in me, whereas he and his German colleagues wrote theology "that describes things in clever ways." At the Netherlands Academy, the subject was historicism as an interdisciplinary concept; I argued that theologians historicized their subject ahead of the academic curve, which set up theology for an anti-historicist reaction before postmodern criticism seeped into every field.[12]

I hauled to these locales the galley proofs of my book on European socialism. In Munich I received the disappointing message from my luminous friend and editor Jennifer Banks that her colleagues at Yale University Press had decided against my title for the book, *Imagining Democratic Socialism*. This was the title that I assumed on every page

of the book. It captured the forward-looking imaginary of the historic
socialist project, evoked the Bernie Sanders movement in U.S. American
politics, and accentuated the line distinguishing democratic socialism
from Social Democracy. To Jennifer's colleagues, these were disqualifying
factors. My title smacked too much of the current political moment and
my politics, so they opted for a tame history title, *Social Democracy in
the Making* (2019).[13]

I have never denigrated Social Democracy and its achievements, but
democratic socialism is the real thing, a vision of radical democratic self-
determination. *Social Democracy in the Making* pressed on the difference,
telling a complex story about multiple European traditions including
intertwined traditions of secular and religious socialism. The founding
socialist traditions conceived it as producer cooperatives or cooperative
guilds. I argued that as soon as socialists imagined guilds that modified
the self-government of cooperatives, there were two kinds of socialism.
Then they debated whether government should finance the cooperatives
or guilds, which yielded the specter of state socialism. Some contended
that nothing socialist is possible without strong industrial unions, so con-
tentions arose over different kinds of syndicalism.

By the late nineteenth century, there were many kinds of socialism.
The fierce conflict between Marxists and Anarchists in the First International destroyed it. There were six kinds of Marxism alone that variously
interpreted Marx as a syndicalist; an anarcho-syndicalist utopian; a radical democrat; a two-track reformist revolutionary; a Communist; and a
guild socialist. There were Marx-lite forms of these types, plus the Fabian
tradition, which said that none of this theorizing was necessary. All that
socialists needed was for the civilizing growth of democratic government
to proceed on its present course to the socialist state, building a collective
technocratic government that (Fabian) experts would manage.

Historically, Marxism played the leading role in reducing the idea of
socialism to collective ownership, and Fabian socialism played the second
leading role in a very different way. I analyzed Marx's signature arguments, contending that he brilliantly dissected the factors of production
in capitalism and the structural capitalist tendency to generate crises of
overproduction and crash, and that his dogmatic determinism, catastrophe mentality, and doctrine of proletarian dictatorship wrecked immense
harm. Marx developed his theory during an era in which democracy was

merely a form of government, and thus of low importance to him. His denigration of ethical reason obscured his moral wellspring. His fixation on collective ownership instilled a magical socialist dogmatism in which anti-racism, feminism, and all other reform causes were relegated to secondary status at best.

I lingered over the fateful history behind the self-conscious term "democratic socialism." Marxists contended that existing democracy was a bourgeois fraud; real democracy would emerge only from a proletarian revolution, after which there would be no need for a state. Democracy would come by making the state irrelevant, as Marxists believed, or by smashing the state, as anarchists believed. In 1889, Socialists founded the Second International, now excluding the anarchists. They still believed that socialist revolutions were inevitable wherever capitalism arose, but none had occurred, so they were forced to rethink what they were doing. Eduard Bernstein, in 1898, rocked the German Social Democratic Party by contending that socialists must not subordinate democracy and its reform causes to a catastrophe vision of deliverance or the demands of a left-wing dictatorship. Socialists had to be resolutely democratic on their way to achieving socialism, and not merely on tactical grounds. I detailed the pro and con of Bernstein, mostly favoring pro.[14]

Social Democracy in the Making abounded with historic figures and the movements they led. In England the cast of figures included Robert Owen; Anglican socialist founders Frederick Denison Maurice and John Ludlow; literary icons John Ruskin and William Morris; Fabians Sidney Webb, Beatrice Webb, and George Bernard Shaw; Labour Party leaders Keir Hardie, Ramsay MacDonald, Clement Attlee, and Hugh Gaitskell; guild socialists G. D. H. Cole and S. G. Hobson; Labour Party intellectuals E. F. M. Durbin, James Meade, R. H. Tawney, R. H. S. Crossman, and C. A. R. Crosland; and Anglican clerics Stewart Headlam, Charles Marson, Scott Holland, Charles Gore, Conrad Noel, and William Temple. Ludlow was a better founder of Christian socialism than Maurice for embracing the political and labor union struggle for it. Morris wrote brilliant propaganda and novels imagining a society of equals. The Fabians were fabulous pamphleteers who balefully acquired racist leaders. I played up the role of Christian socialists in the Labour Party and their opposition to Fabian technocracy, stressing that many were radicals who loathed the Empire, didn't go to Oxford, and fought for guild socialism.

Two troikas stood out from the two halves of a complex political history: Cole-Tawney-Temple, and Gaitskell-Crossman-Crosland. All negotiated the tensions between their socialist politics and political reality. Cole was an atheist who made a religion of libertarian guild socialism until Labour stopped funding it and he grudgingly accepted the party as it was. Tawney made a similar transition except with no drama, quietly retaining aspects of guild socialist theory while ascending to icon status in the Labour Party. Temple seemed like a contented Fabian until he refashioned guild socialism as a mutual fund strategy based on an excess profits tax. After the Labour Party founded the British welfare state, Gaitskell, Crossman, and Crosland imagined a post-Fabian socialism. They said that Labour socialism must transform the welfare state into a society defined by democratic socialist values. Programmatically, socialists needed to develop multiple modes of decentralized socialization, accept the mixed economy, and emphasize their ethical socialist ideals. Crossman cushioned the blow to Fabian pride by titling his movement reader *New Fabian Essays* (1952). Gaitskell won the party leadership in 1955 but Labour lost the 1959 election. Crosland wrote the bible of the revisionist movement, *The Future of Socialism* (1956), making detailed arguments for an expanded cooperative sector, cooperative-public partnerships, solidarity wage policies, and economic rights.[15]

Today this movement is remembered for discrediting Fabian orthodoxy, not for creatively rethinking democratic socialism. The revisionists brimmed with ideas but lacked the big idea to replace the one they discredited. They said forcefully and correctly that the Fabian mentality was too bureaucratic and managerial. Fabian socialism, though remarkably successful, convinced too many people that socialism is about nationalizing the economy. Replacing this belief with a richer, ethical, culturally pluralistic, decentralized, and radically democratic socialism would take a generation—or so the Gaitskell revisionists said. Democratic socialists have labored ever since to theorize pluralistic economic democracy and to build movements for it.

I have made only slight contributions to economic democracy theory and built nothing for it, so I respect the British socialists for accomplishing more on both fronts. Democratic ownership is a complex idea encompassing a variety of rights. Social control of enterprises can mean government-directed public management representing the community at the local, regional, or national level; or cooperative worker management based on individual ownership in which each member owns one share in the enterprise; or cooperative worker management in which workers own a firm collectively as a group; or a blend of public and cooperative models. Social rights to income can mean that the surplus of the enterprise accrues to the public through a local, regional, or national government agency, or to the members of a cooperative enterprise, or to a blend of both. These sets of rights do not have to be assigned in the same way, so various combinations are possible. Many theorists minimize the complexity problem by opting for exclusively public or cooperative control combined with a similar right to income—centralized public management combined with public surplus appropriation, or cooperative worker management combined with worker appropriation.

I believe it is better to mix the cooperative and public models, accepting the complexity problem with the recognition that specific contexts determine which model works best. As a general principle I favor cooperative worker ownership over government ownership because cooperatives achieve direct, democratic, humane, interpersonal self-determination at the firm or guild level. But cooperatives tend to be inward-looking and have trouble scaling up. Public ownership usually works better than cooperatives in industries and enterprises with large economies of scale or extensive externalities, and it pays greater heed than cooperatives to the needs of society. Capitalist firms readily scale up because they have structural incentives to grow under conditions of constant returns to scale. When costs per item are constant, capitalist firms are predisposed to grow to increase profits. Doubling the size of a capitalist firm doubles its profit. Cooperatives maximize share income per worker, not total profits, so they don't automatically expand production when demand increases. Unless sizable economies of scale are involved, cooperatives have little to gain by doubling the size of their enterprises. A cooperative hardware store run by thirty people will have the same per-worker share income as one run by sixty people.

We need innovative forms of social ownership that scale up and serve the needs of sustainable communities. Mutual fund models that place a holding company between the state and the enterprise management vest the ownership of productive capital, creating a firewall of protection from state coercion while mitigating the risk-aversion of cooperatives.

Economic democracy and ecologic survival are linked by the necessity of creating alternatives to the capitalist fantasy of unlimited growth. The economy is physical. The global market destroys self-sufficient local cultures, replacing them with commercial monocultures that destroy sustainability and worsen inequality. Without a fundamental change in how we live, the earth is condemned to overheat, choke on its waste, exhaust its resources, and turn on its human destroyers. The link between economic democracy and the struggle for sustainable communities is a matter of life and death for the entire planet.

My hypertension bolt in Amsterdam was a turning point. My calendar for the succeeding year, 2019, was full, but in Amsterdam I vowed to get off the every-week road in 2020. Then Sara gave birth to Nicholas Christians in January 2019, and I had a magnificent new reason to save my health. That year I spoke at Christ Church in Cranbrook, Michigan, an Episcopal landmark pastored by my friend Bill Danaher; Brick Presbyterian Church in New York City, which asked for a talk on Karl Barth; All Souls Church in New York City, one of my home bases; Christ Church in Grosse Pointe, Michigan, an Episcopal landmark near Cranbrook; Middle Collegiate Church in New York City, another home base, pastored by the spectacular Jacqui Lewis; Westminster Presbyterian Church in Charlottesville, Virginia, where I gave four addresses in the shadow of the Unite the Right Rally of 2017; St. Stephen Presbyterian Church in Fort Worth, Texas, delivering three R. W. Jablonowski Lectures; St. Charles Avenue Presbyterian Church in New Orleans, inaugurating the Lupberger Lectures on Reformed Theology; Fountain Street Church in Grand Rapids, Michigan, which asked for a lecture and sermon on its history of liberal religion; and Marsh Chapel, Boston University, commemorating MLK and the UN Declaration on Human Rights. My non-church favorites that year were at Arizona State University in Tempe, Arizona; the African American Museum in Dallas, Texas; Boston University; Baylor University in Waco, Texas; Brite Divinity School in Fort Worth; Left Forum in New York City; Columbia University; Lehigh University in Bethlehem, Pennsylvania; the AAR Conference in San Diego, though bolt number three was no joke; and Oldenburg University in Oldenburg, Germany. Above all, Union convened a symposium on *Social Democracy in the Making*, a blessed occasion for me in the company of Serene, Kelly, and political historian Geoffrey Kurtz.

Sometimes I got an audience that just wanted to talk about Trump's latest eruption. I kept Trump talk to a minimum, fixing instead on the history that produced Trump, the countervailing history of Black freedom struggle, and the road ahead. Relating then to now was imperative, which for me was a volume three subject, the conclusion of the Black social gospel trilogy that I was committed to writing. But knowing that I was in trouble drove me to write two books smacking of capstone summation: *In a Post-Hegelian Spirit: Philosophical Theology as Idealistic Discontent* (2020), and *American Democratic Socialism: History, Politics, Religion, and Theory* (2021).[16]

In a Post-Hegelian Spirit mined Kant, Schleiermacher, and Hegel on the creative power and contradictions of subjectivity, sifting critiques of the post-Kantian tradition. It reclaimed Kant's ideas that reason and will are inseparable, reason is essentially an activity, and freedom is the unfathomable groundless ground of the moral law within us. It embraced Schleiermacher's thesis that religion is about feeling the whence, mystery, and infinity of one's life and the world, a deeper wellspring than moral duty. It danced with Hegel on being as becoming, consciousness as the social-subjective relation of spirit to itself, and salvaging what can be salvaged from the carnage of history. I argued that the valuable parts of Kant, Schleiermacher and Hegel are worth the digging and sifting it requires to recover them for religious thought.

Everything that Kant said about transcendental idealism was subjective idealist, which did not unify the manifold of intuition or make sense of beauty, organic relations, and the wholeness of nature. So he employed a doctrine of intellectual intuition in the *Critique of Pure Reason* and returned to it in the *Critique of Judgment*, treating it skittishly both times because it subverted his sense of being in rational control. To follow through takes some daring, as does Kant's principle that all human beings must be treated as ends in themselves, on which he grievously did not follow through. Kant deepened the contradictions of subjectivity by placing the conflicts between autonomy and heteronomy, freedom and determinism, reason and sensibility, a priori and a posteriori, universality and particularity, and objectivity and subjectivity *within* human subjects. The *Critique of Judgment*, mediating Kant's binary oppositions, described intellectual intuition as a form of inner teleology in which means and ends are internally and reciprocally related. Each means and end becomes itself in and through the other, and neither can be itself apart from the other. Every work of art contains an interplay between the whole and the parts, creating a type of unity that promotes and sustains differences. The inner reciprocity of parts and wholes is a kind of teleology, a form of internal purposiveness.

This idea launched the post-Kantian revolution that threw off Kant's restraints, embracing the upshot of inner teleology: there is a Kantian basis for the principle of constitutive relationality. Identity is differential, not oppositional. Romanticism was about transforming the world into a work of art. Schleiermacher put it theologically for the ages: true religion comes from spiritual feeling, a felt relation to the source of life, a sense of the spirit of the whole. The world is the totality of being, to which all judgments ultimately refer. God is the idea of the unity of being, to which all concepts ultimately refer. For all the ridicule that Hegel heaped upon Schleiermacher for theologizing about his feelings, they theorized the same distinction between *Empfindung* (sensibility) and *Gefühl* (feeling): sensibility is a product of sensations received in a mode of immediacy, while feeling is an act of consciousness as such that integrates sensations in a reflected totality. The differences between Schleiermacher and Hegel mostly favor Schleiermacher, but I argued that Schleiermacher and Hegel were more alike than not, and that Hegel theorized a distinctly profound process theodicy.[17]

Hegel carried forward Kant's idea of the intersubjective forms of experience, cribbing a post-Kantian ontology of love from Schelling and Friedrich Hölderlin. Then he developed a theology of Spirit fitting his discovery of social subjectivity: God is the intersubjective whole of wholes—spiraling relationality that embraces all otherness and difference. God's infinite subjectivity is an infinite intersubjectivity of holding differences together in a play of creative relationships not dissolving into sameness. Hegel and Whitehead similarly fashioned fluid, temporal, holistic, open, intersubjective, reconciling visions. I treasure Whitehead for developing the greatest metaphysical system of the twentieth century, an organic vision geared to relativity physics. But Whitehead's God is not a creator, not Triune, and not moved by ideal subjectivity to enter the suffering and otherness of the world.[18]

Hegel's immanent Trinity—God's self-othering—is a *condition* of empirical relations. Contrary to orthodoxy, the economic Trinity subsumes the immanent Trinity. *In a Post-Hegelian Spirit* argued that Hegel gave difference its due by replacing abstract identity with recognition. His triad of logic-nature-spirit has no absolute primacy, founding, or grounding. Each element of triadic mediation assumes the middle position and is mediated by the others, and the third term is never the same as the first. Hegel described the divine as the luminosity in which colors are discriminated, a holistic Trinitarian spiral of concentric relations—Creator within Redeemer within Spirit. Absolute knowledge, on Hegel's conception, is philosophical eros, the restless desire for wisdom and love of it, not the absoluteness that countless creeped-out interpreters describe. Those of us who theorize Hegel's self-transformative logic in religiously musical fashion—Stephen Crites, Molly B. Farneth, Hille Haker, Peter C. Hodgson, Thomas A. Lewis, Andrew Shanks, Mark C. Taylor, Robert R. Williams—conceive the absolute as radically relative and dynamic. Barth and Emmanuel Levinas, equating the absolute with anti-relative absoluteness, contended that God is only God as the Wholly Other not-something of radical exteriority, the other side of the abyss between creatures and God. But the infinite of Wholly Other transcendence is another finite, limited by its own exteriority. The Hegelian whole encompassing otherness is actually infinite. To know being is to know it as infinite.[19]

But the bad parts of Hegel are terrible. He threw away the two greatest strengths of religious idealism: its emphasis on ethical subjectivity and its insistence that all thinking about God is inadequate, a mere pointer to transcendent mystery. Hegel had overreaching confidence in his concepts, to put it mildly. He conceived philosophy as a superior mode of knowing, leaving no room for the apophatic intuition of God as the holy unknowable mystery of the world. He recycled racist conventions with casual conceit, drifting in his later career to the stuffy political right, and shunned those who burned for social justice, finding them boorish company. He sublimated God and selves into a logical concept that seemed to drain both of personality, meanwhile ridiculing Schleiermacher for theologizing about feeling. Hegel rolled his assumption that religion has a unitary history and his conviction that Christianity is the consummate religion into a toxic mythology of European superiority topped off by Prussian superiority. Everything that critical theory, deconstructionist criticism, and decolonial theory are about has some root in Hegel, usually in a way that does not favor him.

I take for granted that I don't have true concepts, and neither did Hegel or Whitehead. Metaphysical reasoning is a groping in the dark, taking a stand in the stream of one's experience, employing metaphors, symbols, and analogies to relate different aspects of experience to each other and to signify things beyond our grasp. *In a Post-Hegelian Spirit* recycled my lecture trope that a wholly realistic theology would be a monstrosity—a sanctification of mediocrity, inertia, oppression, domination, exclusion, and moral indifference. Christianity is inherently idealistic in imagining a divine unity of thought and being, but an idealistic theology lacking a sense of tragedy, real-world oppression and exclusion, and the danger of its own prideful intellectualism would be worse than the worst theological realism. The idealism that matters to me is liberationist—privileging the critique of oppression, linking tragedy with the struggle for justice, expressing ethical discontent, and admitting what it does not know.

I do not believe in a substantive self that possesses thoughts and purposes, but I refuse to doubt that I think my thoughts and will my purposes. Persons feel and think; there is no thought without attention, an act of will; and thought is an act performed with a motive, which implies feeling. Mind is a unity of feeling and willing in which feeling feels other feeling, every act of willing has an object, and one's moral experience implies a moral continuity. I take for granted, with Augustine and Meister Eckhart, that anything I understand is not God, and with Tillich that all God-language is symbolic. At the same time, I believe that religious thinking must be fired by a passion for truth. I do not spurn metaphysical audacity, for faith is a form of daring.

In a Post-Hegelian Spirit registered that Hegel is distinctly important and alien to me, and that Tillich's theological socialism is deep in me and a subject of regret. Marx and Kierkegaard scored against Hegel by emphasizing the situation of the knower, with no hope of reconciliation. Postmodernists score against Hegel by skewering ontology, but anti-ontology is still a form of ontology, mirroring what it repudiates, with no basis for claiming to know anything. Hegel had a better idea by relating God and the world dialectically, preserving unity and difference with a tragic sensibility that caught the infinite love-anguish of Calvary. Love, the moving power of life, the desire to reconcile the estranged, is greater than power and justice, as Hegel and Tillich contended. Therefore, separation cannot be ontologically ultimate.[20]

My deep regret about Tillich is that he basked in the applause of the U.S. American empire after he became an American, ridiculing social gospel socialists who battled in social justice and anti-colonial movements. In his head, Tillich remained a religious socialist imbued with Marxian dialectic. In real life, he spurned the civil rights movement, defended the U.S. American empire whenever it had an interest at stake in the Global South, and mocked those who battled for "lost" causes, deriding them as ethical idealists wasting their time. Marxism gave Tillich a rationale for doing nothing for social justice, since the Cold War created a political void contested only by idealists. My exemplars of that generation are the religious idealists who pulled the ecumenical movement into global solidarity struggles for social justice and decolonial reordering: Mordecai Johnson, Benjamin Mays, Howard Thurman, Martin Luther King Jr., Pauli Murray, Myles Horton, and Walter Muelder. It's the left wing of the Black social gospel and its White allies. To them, struggling for justice was not optional depending on the likelihood of success or whether they felt like it.

I was still writing *In a Post-Hegelian Spirit* when I rummaged through boxes of Socialist Party, DSOC, and DSA files that I had saved for decades, laying the research foundation for *American Democratic Socialism*. There was no political and intellectual history of the U.S. American democratic socialist tradition. Bernie Sanders was making another run for the Democratic nomination for president. The Democratic Party was trying hard to hold off an upsurge of democratic socialism in its ranks. DSA was conducting bruising debates about how, or if, it should make a dirty break from the Democrats. I argued that the United States has the richest cultural history of democratic socialism in the world, and a substantial intellectual and political history in which Christian socialism has been more important than scholarship on this subject conveys. But the United States did not have a real labor movement back when it mattered. It just had unions, most of them racist, sexist, nativist craft unions that divided workers from each other, fatally truncating the kind of socialism that was possible in the United States.[21]

European socialists poured into the U.S. after the liberal revolutions of 1848 were put down and socialists had to flee. German American socialists founded the Socialist Labor Party in 1877 along with a smattering of native-born anarchists and Marxists. Christian socialism sprawled across the nation in the 1880s and 1890s, often taking a Populist form. Soon after the Socialist Party was founded in 1901 it was a wondrous stew of radical democrats, neo-abolitionists, Marxists, Christians, Populists, feminists, trade unionists, industrial unionists, Single Taxers, anarcho-syndicalists, and Fabians. Jewish New Yorkers from Russia and Russian Poland espoused a universalistic creed in Yiddish. Rebellious tenant farmers in Oklahoma, red populists in Texas, syndicalist miners in Colorado and California, and Socialists across the Midwest and West built a sprawling network of periodicals, summer camps, and state parties. The first great hope of industrial unionism, the Knights of Labor, founded by Christian socialists, got pulled into more strikes than it could handle, learning bitterly that state governments stood ready to smash them. This pitiful story recurred over and over. Workers pulled together, struck for their rights, took beatings from hired thugs, cheered when government forces showed up, and discovered to their horror that the government did not come to curb the violence.

Many have argued that socialism would have floundered in the United States regardless of its problems with unions and the political system because it was no match for America's open borders, prosperity, and upward mobility. Certainly, many U.S. American workers feared that socialism would prevent them from getting ahead. But the United States had more than enough suffering and exploitation to create a surging socialist movement. The number one problem for U.S. American socialists was that divide and conquer worked in the United States. Workers were turned against each other, pitting native-born workers in the craft unions against unskilled immigrant workers and excluding Black Americans and women. U.S. American unions were founded separately from political parties and became part of the system of political control represented by the two-party system. Socialist union leaders stumped for a socialist labor party, but never topped 38 percent in the AFL.

Eugene Debs, the iconic founding leader of the Socialist Party, was the apostle of a true way that found strength in its socialist purity. I described it as a redemption strategy soaked in the idioms of American revivalism. Being a romantic U.S. American individualist made Debs a fabulous campaigner. He loved the workers, and they loved him back, but he excoriated the AFL and refused to work with reform movements, which made it hard for workers to join his party. Debs spurned the strategy that worked in England—forming a coalition party of the

Democratic Left—after which his party was destroyed in 1917 and 1919. The Socialists bravely opposed World War I and paid a horrific price for it, viciously persecuted by the government. Then the meteor of world Communism crashed into the party and blew it apart. The Debs heyday ended in shattered despair, yielding the dismal run-up to Norman Thomas Socialism.

Thomas was the landmark figure of the generation that preceded mine. He epitomized the social gospel of the early twentieth century that played a vital role in the socialist movement. He rose to the top of the party because most of its native-born intellectuals joined the stampede to war and he offered a noble contrast to patriotic gore. Then he tried valiantly to renew the democratic socialist idea. Thomas loved the United States to the point of believing it could expunge its vicious parts. At least, he believed it up to World War II, after which he said that his life was a series of crushing disappointments. *American Democratic Socialism* accentuated the pathos of Thomas' career *and* the noble warrior role that he played to the end of his days, pleading with New Left radicals not to hate their country. I never heard Thomas in person, but Michael Harrington was a fount of Thomas-lore, and many of our older comrades spoke of Thomas only with reverence.

When *American Democratic Socialism* moved into the 1970s, I registered my personal involvement in the struggles of the democratic Left with stagflation misery, the Reagan trauma, and the 1990s nadir. The book drove to the Sanders campaigns of 2016 and 2020, the rise of the next star of the democratic Left, Alexandria Ocasio-Cortez, and the Green New Deal. It went into production at Yale University Press in February 2020, just as Sanders seized the lead for the Democratic nomination and just before COVID-19 officially reached pandemic status. It felt precarious on both counts to meet the publishing deadline, but YUP's extensive editing process allowed a few galley tweaks. I assumed that the Democratic establishment would find a way to stop Bernie. My galley draft registered this assumption while reserving a slender hope that Massachusetts senator Elizabeth Warren might find a lane between Sanders and the five moderate Democrats they were opposing, which didn't happen.

Bernie had inveighed against corporate greed and inequality for decades before mass movements for social justice were possible again. In

1990 he won Vermont's lone seat in the U.S. House of Representatives as an independent democratic socialist. In 2006 he moved up to the U.S. Senate, already forging a career lacking any parallel in Left politics. In December 2010, Bernie held forth on the Senate floor for eight and a half hours. He had no prepared text; he had only scraps of various speeches and a determination to see how long he could last. All were wrapped around a basic storyline. In the 1970s, he observed, the top 1 percent of earners took home 8 percent of all income. In the 1980s they earned 12 percent. By the end of the 1990s they were getting 18 percent. By 2007 they were up to 24 percent. Sanders pleaded, "How much more do they want? When is enough enough? Do they want it all?" Greed is a sickness, he said, much like addiction. The 1 percent is addicted to greed: "I think this is an issue we have to stay on and stay on and stay on."[22]

Bernie has the virtue of relentlessly staying on. I love him for it. In 2016 he ran the greatest electoral campaign ever waged by a U.S. American democratic socialist, winning twenty-two primaries and caucuses in his contest with Hillary Clinton for the Democratic presidential nomination. I stressed that Bernie conceives democratic socialism as a compound of six rights: the right to universal health care, a living wage, a complete education, affordable housing, a clean environment, and a secure retirement. He got through the entire campaign without being asked a single time about worker ownership or public ownership, which was fine with him, content to fight for economic rights that Social Democrats achieved in Europe in the 1950s. Bernie speaks in one-key-only, the universalist humanism of the social democratic Left, so he sadly did not break through to Black and Latinx communities. But he deserves eternal credit for inveighing relentlessly against America's ever-worsening inequality.

His first run for president ignited a membership gusher in DSA that had climbed to 60,000 when he ran again in 2020. Bernie terrified the party establishment by tying for first place in Iowa, winning the New Hampshire primary, and crushing the field in the Nevada caucus. The Democratic establishment and corporate media shrieked with sky-is-falling alarm, pleading that regular Democrats and Wall Street Democrats had to consolidate before Sanders ran away with the nomination. South Carolina was next, fortunately for former Vice President Joe Biden. He had never won a primary, in three presidential nominating candidacies, until he vanquished Sanders in South Carolina. The waters parted for Biden as four moderate candidates and Warren dropped out, clearing his path to the nomination. Fear of Bernie and fear of a Trump reelection drove the field to consolidate with breathtaking speed.

In March 2020 I flew twice to Memphis to teach adult education classes at Sara's congregation, Idlewild Presbyterian Church. On the second flight home from Memphis, on March 8, 2020, I held my breath through O'Hare Airport, bracing for COVID-19. The world changed with stunning, sweeping, devastating brutality. COVID overwhelmed New York City hospitals and piled up bodies in makeshift morgues. It surged across the nation while Trump sprayed his news conferences with a firehose of lies and self-congratulation. Black and Brown Americans suffered the worst, as usual, while health-care workers struggled heroically to save as many lives as possible. Americans who didn't know what it's like to live in a state of hypervigilance got a taste of it. Feelings of anxiety, fear, and vulnerability that many Black and Brown Americans experience as normal life became, for a while, the daily bread of nearly all Americans.[23]

In the academy, those of us who lacked any experience of online teaching got an emergency baptism in it. I was grateful that Union was six weeks into its winter semester before our classes were driven online; we knew each other before we were forced to adjust. Those were days of tenderly careful inquiries about how students were faring and where they had relocated, or not. My doctoral advisee Aaron Stauffer had been slated to return to Union to defend his outstanding dissertation on the experience of sacred value in community organizing. Instead, he corralled his adviser and committee into a Zoom conference, my first one, which I undertook in a Fremont, Ohio hotel room. Then I hosted Zoom gatherings in my mother's bedroom in Midland, Michigan, where Eris and I retreated for most of the spring.

My father had died the previous December, we had not yet conducted a memorial service, and my mother was processing her grief and loss. It was strangely serendipitous to be driven together in this dreadful time. She recalled her growing up, dating my dad, studying at Marquette, getting married, moving to mid-Michigan, raising five boys, becoming a legal secretary, suffering Andy's searing death, running an establishment-Republican legal office, witnessing the White nationalist turn in the Republican Party, grandparenting three girls, and coping with an alcoholic husband, who did not help her try to enroll him in the Cree. My mother was a great storyteller who had never been alone except for one year of college, on which she still waxed vividly. It alarmed her when my dad retired at sixty-two and commenced drinking. Now he had no reason not to blotto himself. Not even golf was important enough to curb the drinking, though he beat his age a few times in his seventies, scrambling for pars, until he started drinking on the back nine. My dad lost his golf refuge and much of his brain matter to alcohol. His messy behavior got him expelled from his golf group and fell hard on his sons—Greg as a prominent public figure in Midland; Mike as the father of an adolescent daughter, Anna; and Eric as a County Commissioner living a block from our parents' home on Lambros Drive.

My mother had wanted a taste of the life she had missed. She could have joined Dave Camp's Congressional staff in Washington, DC, but my dad refused to go. Politics was not the issue; my parents were middle-road Democrats at the national level and swing voters closer to home. The issue was that his golf retirement in Midland familiarity could not be disrupted. Had I known of my mother's dream, I would have urged her to leave him behind, hoping to jar him from his selfishness. She knew it, so she didn't tell me. Now she imagined the life in DC that she could have had, crying at the thought of it, for me an echo of long-ago sessions with her college yearbook. My mother had feared that her boys would disown her if she divorced our dad. It was never true of any of us, and we told her so. Yet the love that my parents held for each other trumped everything else. Neither of them could have tolerated living without the other for more than a week. He had said so emphatically to me. She agreed: "I know it hurt you boys, the way your dad and I sniped at each other. But all that fighting didn't detract from our love for each other. We thrived on the fighting. I miss it so much, and him. I loved him through all the parts that were terrible and painful."

Mike was divorced during the early weeks of COVID and moved with Anna to Midland to live with my mother, so Eris and I spent the summer of 2020 in the tiny Hank family lodge in Goetzville in which my mother had grown up. Our cell phones were useless, the television accessed three channels, and the lush forest scenery was magnificent. We went for walks every day in the magnificence, fending off giant blackflies that dive-bombed into our heads. Eris found a remarkably good thrift store in nearby Cedarville, where well-off vacationers in the

Les Cheneaux Islands drop off their hand-me-downs. Sometimes it was possible in the parking lot to pick up one bar of cell phone service. There I accessed the Internet, on the good days, via an open Wi-Fi line from a shutdown hair salon across the road. While Eris rummaged for dresses and jewelry alongside fellow masked thrifters, I scoured the archives of the *Atlanta Constitution* and the *Washington Post* for stories about Andrew Young.

It seemed that I had not picked a good summer to begin my third volume on the Black social gospel, *A Darkly Radiant Vision: The Black Social Gospel in the Shadow of MLK* (2023). It required a complex frame with an elaborate bibliographical base, but I was at Grandma's house in a global pandemic with a trunk-load of books. All I could do was design the frame and write the book's simplest chapter. We were far from any cities, university libraries, Wi-Fi hotspots, Black Americans, or Democrats. Sublime vistas of forests and lakes were interrupted by Trump flags, Trump billboards, and pickup trucks festooned with TRUMP. Yoopers dearly love Trump for voicing their resentments. Most of my Yooper relatives are Trump supporters, as is my brother Eric, for whom Democrats are the party of affirmative action, open borders, gun control, and woke elitism that betrayed people like him. The only Biden sign that Eris and I saw was in Sault Ste. Marie, where I ventured twice to make extensive downloads powered by the thrilling sight of four-bar access. It helped that I usually knew what I was looking for, because I came of age following Young's political career.[24]

Young moved from the SCLC to the U.S. Congress to the United Nations to the mayoralty of Atlanta to the boards of major corporations. He and Jesse Jackson stood out among the King disciples who applied King's vision to political realities of the post-MLK shadow years. To Young's surprise, he became the first of King's lieutenants to run for office, taking the path that won the biggest spotlight, until Jackson surpassed him. Entering the political realm could be construed as winning the right to moral authority, or as squandering it. Young's successful political career and Jackson's longtime drive to win insider status in the Democratic Party dramatized this tension. I relived in the thrift store parking lot how I had felt when Young was elected to Congress, pushed for investments in Atlanta, stirred controversy at the UN, and turned Atlanta into a global corporate showcase. The Young chapter was nearly finished when the summer faded. By then I had the frame worked out for what became *A Darkly Radiant Vision*.[25]

At Union and Columbia, we geared up for another strange semester, teaching students who had never stepped on campus. Many of my colleagues had summer homes where they remained, but Eris and I had nothing like that, and her mother was confined to a COVID-quarantined nursing home in New York City. I got used to Zoom classes and conferences, even Zoom socializing. In November 2020, Sara and Will announced that the baby they were expecting was going to be two girls. I had fretted through Sara's pregnancy with Nicholas, being prone to meltdown over any threat to Sara, so this was worse. At the thirty-week mark in May 2021, Sara called us to Memphis, knowing that birth-day for Evelyn and Clara was imminent.

We delayed for one day because Hanna Benzwie had died at 101 years of age. Hanna had endured longer than she wanted, even brushing off a bout with COVID. Just before I conducted the memorial service, Sara counseled me firmly, "Dad, be present at the service. I will be ok." Hanna got the loving remembrance of her long, feisty, caretaking, remarkable life that she deserved, memorialized by her son Michael, daughter Eris, daughter-in-law Laurie Lieberman, nephew Michael Hirschorn, grandson Joshua Benzwie and his partner Raine Manley, granddaughter Ashley Benzwie and her partner Stephan Olson, and honorary grandson Benjie De Groot. Her life had taken her from Germany to Palestine to Egypt to Italy—serving in the British Army during World War II—to Israel to the United States, landing in a society she viewed with puckish gratitude and curiosity. As reparation for losing her home and childhood, Hannah had received as an adult a monthly check of $65 from the German government. I observed that she came alive whenever we asked about her early life, which was not often enough, since we tended to fix on the mundane. Being a Holocaust survivor made Hanna Benzwie allergic to the frivolous.

The next day, on May 24, 2021, the girls were born just as Eris and I landed in Memphis. Evie came first, ready to be seen; extracting Clara required an emergency Caesarian. Each little one weighed almost four pounds, and scary details of the entire drama were doled out to me over the summer. There were nearly two months of preemie care in the Neonatal Intensive Care Unit. We had weeks of anxiety that both girls, especially Clara, were prone to stop breathing. They had different personalities from the beginning—Evie sweet and trusting, and Clara intense. More adorable than these little girls one cannot get. Meanwhile Eris and I had three sublime months of singing, climbing, swinging, hide-and-seeking, "Singing in the Rain," see-sawing, roughhousing, Blippi-watching, sliding, and cavorting with Nicholas, creating a magical world with a toddler born with sparkling humor. At the end of the summer, we rented a car in Memphis, where a student working at the front desk had one of my books. We talked for a few minutes, and Eris beamed with delight. Afterwards in the car she explained, "I wasn't sure that you could still talk like a professor."

American Democratic Socialism came out during our summer in Memphis. It was adorned with a generous quote from Michael Eric Dyson that I heard every time I was introduced that fall. One interviewer asked me how it feels to be described in such terms; mercifully he rescued our discussion from my stammering. *A Darkly Radiant Vision* went to press that fall and I turned to a long-delayed book on the history of American theological liberalism, *The Spirit of American Liberal Theology* (2023). Essentially it is a condensed summary of the liberalism trilogy, but nearly everything in it is newly written and many things in it are wholly new, including the twenty years of theology that succeeded volume three. My argument about the Black social gospel is amplified; my post-Hegelian liberal-liberation perspective is on the table; my Union colleagues Roger Haight, Paul Knitter, and John Thatamanil are featured near the end; my brilliant former advisee Demian Wheeler is mentioned twice; and being reduced to one book helped me to feature the argument that I pressed in the trilogy only in volume three: the most abundant, diverse, and persistent tradition of liberal theology is the one that blossomed in the United States and is still refashioning itself.[26]

There were periodic reminders as I wrote the book that my previous pass at this subject labored through grieving trauma and pulled me through it. The U.S. American tradition of liberal theology holds a special place in my feeling for giving me a cascade of creative, thoughtful, energetic, flawed, very and wonderfully human theologians to live with and write about. I wrote *The Spirit of American Liberal Theology* under the strongest feeling of well-being of my career, grateful to count every member of our faculty as a friend, especially Tim Adkins-Jones, Sarah Azaransky, Eileen Campbell-Reed, David Carr, Cláudio Carvalhaes, Sam Cruz,

Karenna Gore, Roger Haight, Tara Chong Hyung Kyung, Brigitte Kahl, Aliou C. Niang, Su Yon Pak, Jan Rehmann, Greg Snyder, John Thatamanil, and Mary Boys. Four others will have to endure extra comment.

Andrea White joined the Union faculty in 2015. A third-generation womanist theologian endowed with brilliance and deep goodness, including an oversupply of taking-care-of-you care, she taught for six years at Emory University in Atlanta before we landed her. Andrea is as shyly introverted as I am, but puts herself out there anyway, needing to do something with all that care. It takes a very special person to be the one whom I would call without hesitation for advice, to share an anxiety or hurt, to talk shop, or just to stay in touch. The friendship that I have with Andrea is graciously beautiful in a way that I had not expected to experience after leaving Kalamazoo.

Kelly Brown Douglas joined the Union faculty in 2017. A founder of womanist theology and a prominent womanist theologian, she taught for sixteen years at Goucher College in Towson, Maryland before she came to Union to run the Episcopal Divinity School at Union. I had assigned Kelly's books for many years in classes; we shared a conference platform in January 2016 at Trinity Church Wall Street; and I was thrilled when EDS at Union landed her. Kelly asked me to teach the history of Anglican theology, for centuries a parade of White supremacy and empire. I dove into Anglican history and a scholarly project on it, she soared as a public theologian by launching an extraordinary podcast called *Just Conversations*, and we bonded as friends. Kelly's radiant witness has grown only stronger in her later career, recently at a self-standing EDS and its online programs. She is showing the church and the field of theology how theological education must change to have a future worth saving.

Serene Jones and Cornel West are cherished friends to me of longer standing. Serene grew up in the Barth-Niebuhr Calvinism of her father Joe Jones, a Disciples of Christ theologian. She joined the Yale faculty in 1991 upon earning her doctorate at Yale; I taught her book *Feminist Theory and Christian Theology* (2000); and in November 2003 she and I spoke at a session of the Society of Biblical Literature in Atlanta. Serene deftly analyzed John A. T. Robinson's patchwork of theologies in his book *Honest to God* (1963) and moved to a personal close on faith, daring to inspire a gathering of academics. There was a light in Serene, which I remembered in 2007 when I played an assertive role in Union's presidential search. Several months into the search, we had a short list dominated by friends of mine, and Serene had not applied. We debated whether asking her to consider it was too far-fetched. Serene had academic nirvana at Yale, with four appointments. What chance did we have? The first time that I spoke with her about it, in November 2007 at AAR in San Diego, we talked for three hours, and she had five questions. The next time she had twenty-five questions in a longer conversation that looped around the Columbia campus and ended at a diner. Hope was rising. Near the end she said, "Gary, the Union presidency is the only position in this country that could lure me from Yale."[27]

I have befriended every president-boss I've had, so it was doubly predictable that Serene and I would be friends. But Serene is a special person whose friendship was immediately high up on the list of things I care about. On the road, former Yale students serving as pastors pulled me aside to congratulate Union on stealing her away, often adding that she was the best teacher they ever had. In 2009, Serene organized our mega-course trio with Cornel, and in 2014, she mercifully ended my only-status at Union by appointing a search committee that brought a superb social ethicist, Sarah Azaransky, to the Union faculty. Serene has been a brilliant president of Union, a visionary who loves the work and pours herself out for Union, teaching us that theology is the place and story through which you ask about the meaning of your life and world. She is creative, brave, resilient, and a loving soul. In 2021, she and I served on the Bonhoeffer Chair search that lured Cornel back to Union. This time, Cornel and I thwarted the ships-passing tendency by getting on each other's schedules, even as he ran for President of the United States.

Breaking bread with Cornel is a public event on the way to the restaurant, throughout the meal, and getting home. Passersby and nearby diners need a moment with him, a Facebook picture, and often, to tell him their story. He is unfailingly, exceedingly gracious to one and all, asking them how it's going and urging them to stay strong. Strangers throng to him wherever he goes and he thrives on it, always on, responding to the world around him, and is never not dressed in that funeral suit, ready to be carried out. I urged him not to run for the presidency, at least in swing states, but he knew that his crowds would not vote for an establishment Democrat. Cornel is an American Original, containing multitudes, like the American Originals he treasures—Frederick Douglass, Walt

Whitman, Herman Melville, W. E. B. Du Bois, James Baldwin, Martin
Luther King Jr., Toni Morrison, and jazz saxophonist John Coltrane. He
admires apostles of one truth, like Ida B. Wells, but favors the multitude-
containers who are blessed, like him, with expansive love and creativity.

In 2024 he gave the most bluesy Gifford Lectures ever delivered,
extolling "jazz-soaked" artists and thinkers who respond to nihilism,
anxiety, oppression, denigration, and catastrophe with gritty courage and
love. Cornel intertwines the genealogical, existential, and pedagogical
registers. He mines Homer, Aeschylus, Sophocles, Sappho, and Euripides
for tragic wisdom; excavates Erasmus on folly and Anton Chekhov on
meaninglessness; and laments that White American literature abounds
with pursuits of innocence, Melville notwithstanding. Cornel's lifeblood
is the Black American tradition of soulful, funky, freedom-loving artists,
thinkers, and activists; sometimes he spends an entire semester squeezing out the tragic wisdom in Du Bois' *Darkwater* or Baldwin's *The Price
of the Ticket* (1985). As he says, "I belong to a people with a history
of responding to trauma and catastrophe with love and courage and
joy." This blues-soaked faith is epitomized by Du Bois' *Souls of Black
Folk* (1903), Morrison's *Beloved* (1987), and Coltrane's four-part suite *A
Love Supreme* (1965). But Cornel really lights up when he riffs on Curtis
Mayfield, the gentle genius of funky soul.

In the spring of 2023, Cornel, Serene, and I reprised our course on the
U.S. Crisis with a stronger interfaith and ecological slant than last time.
The only carry-over author from last time was Reinhold Niebuhr. Cornel prized the semi-Marxist Niebuhr who wrote *Moral Man and Immoral
Society*. Serene stressed that Niebuhr's *Nature and Destiny of Man* is a quintessential work of Reformed theology. I clarified to this highly engaged class
that I was not the one who assigned Niebuhr, much as I treasure him. It
was the other two who said that we must read Niebuhr.

Our students appreciated Niebuhr's powerful emphasis on the class
struggle and his blistering critique of middle-class idealism. They puzzled
that the author of *Moral Man* ended up in the Democratic Party establishment and that someone as cynical as Niebuhr could be a Christian
theologian. I reprised my road-lecture theme that Niebuhr was not as
cynical as he seems on the page. He was a passionate personality who
took his Christ-following passion for justice for granted. In the 1930s
he described love as the content of an impossible ethical ideal. Later he

demonized Soviet Communism and dropped his emphasis on economic justice, yet Niebuhr also described love, rightly, as the motive force of the struggle for justice. The meaning of justice is determined in the inter-action of love and situation, through the mediation of the regulative principles of equality, freedom, and order. Love is uncalculating concern for the dignity of persons; as such it asserts no interests. But because love motivates concern for the dignity of persons, it motivates a passion for justice overflowing with interests and requiring principles of justice. To Niebuhr, the Christian love ethic was the point, the motive, and the end, despite having no concrete social meaning. Since he followed Jesus, he had to take responsibility for society's problems, even if Jesus did not. In Niebuhr's own way, which always grappled with paradoxes, he was rooted in, and sought to be faithful to, the love ethic to which the Word of the gospel called him.[28]

On the road I meet pastors and activists who say they are frightfully lonely. I practice the ministry of encouragement: "I see you; I appreci-ate you; please hang in there; we need you." The loneliness has haunted me through decades of preaching in declining congregations and buck-ing-up the peace and justice activists. The liberal Protestant churches that founded the social gospel and ecumenical movements never out-grew their ethnic families of origin or replaced themselves. In the late 1950s they acquired a self-conscious name, "the mainline," just before the name became misleading. In the mid-1960s their demographic fate began to show; in the 1970s they plunged off a cliff. The steep fall of the Protestant mainline was a catastrophe for American society. Liberal Protestant churches were, and still are, devoted to intellectual freedom and the public good. They engage in every kind of public work except direct political advocacy, practicing a distinct form of civic engagement that cares for the commons and emphasizes the complexities of moral responsibility and citizenship in a pluralistic society. Flawed as they were, and are, these custodians of America's moral culture at least espouse the values of civility, inclusion, personal freedom, equality, and pluralism, virtues that now make them appear quaint.

One school of thought on this subject is nostalgic for the 1950s hey-day when Protestant leaders forged a national ecumenical church, the National Council of Churches. A second school contends that the NCC heyday was illusory, an impressive façade built upon sand. Another school argues that acquiring the mainline name marked the beginning of the end of the historic Protestant denominations. A fourth school contends that liberal Protestantism achieved a self-negating cultural victory by identifying with bourgeois culture; in essence, the mainline provided religious cover for bourgeois liberalism to the point that it succeeded in making itself dispensable. Each of these interpretations describes a piece of the truth. Today, church life is cratering across the United States except for the Pentecostal traditions and an aggressive White Christian nationalism. The capacity of liberal Protestants and progressive Catholics to sustain what they love in their traditions—the best meaning of the term "conservative"—has badly eroded. Thousands of congregations that were barely surviving before Covid are closing down and selling their buildings. Even the pastors of strong congregations talk mostly about their struggles and loneliness, not about how great they're doing.[29]

My generation of liberal Protestant theologians dispensed in the 1980s with the terms "mainline" and "liberal Protestant," self-identifying as progressive Christian or ecumenical Christian. Today, progressive theologians tend to be highly individuated, thinking our own thoughts, while progressive Christian communities and institutions work in a coalitional style, speaking in the voice of an improvisational ensemble. Our communities instill an ethos of inclusive civility that is usually allergic to developing strong leaders. Progressive Christians tend to bristle when someone presumes to lead us or speak for us. Many of us are not nostalgic for the heyday of the mainline because it was a Christendom project living off the spoils of racial and cultural privilege and the American empire. We seek to build cooperative communities that are ecumenical, multicultural, egalitarian, intersectional and eco-feminist, nurturing the variety of spiritual gifts.

I had hoped that the insurrection of January 6, 2021 at the U.S. Capitol and the second impeachment of Donald Trump by the U.S. House of Representatives would break the power of Trumpism in U.S. American politics. Trump was impeached in the House for inciting the insurrection, after which the U.S. Senate voted 57-43 in favor of conviction, falling short of the required two-thirds for conviction. It seemed that he had undermined his domination of the Republican Party. Surely the party would return to policy-based conservatism or at least a cleaned-up version of Trumpism. Instead, Trump only grew stronger in the evangelical

Right, to the point that he trounced the field of 2024 Republican candidates without bothering to debate them.

Democracy is at risk in the severity of American inequality, the ubiquity of culture war, the hateful nationalistic rhetoric that demonizes migrants, and the new normal, for many, of refusing to accept the outcomes of elections they lose. Liberal democracy, a nineteenth-century Progressive fusion of two contrasting political philosophies, is riddled with problems inherent in its founding. But it names precious rights to individual freedom and democratic self-governance that today are imperiled. We cannot shred them and get something better. We can only qualify for something better than the existing liberal democracy by building upon the rights it established.

In 2022 I joined my friends Aaron Stauffer and Charlene Sinclair in vowing to create an organization that brings together organizers, pastors, and academics. Aaron is a former IAF organizer, Charlene served at the time of our founding as chief of staff of Race Forward, and both had written dissertations with me on organizing. We resolved to bring together organizers, pastors involved in organizing, academics who teach social ethics and related subjects, and people with a foot in two or more of these camps to forge new friendships, discuss strategy and trends, workshop their scholarship, conduct advocacy on issues, and counteract frontline loneliness. In July 2022 we convened a two-day gathering of twenty-five founders. The following January we conducted two sessions at the Society of Christian Ethics conference in Chicago, inaugurating an annual tradition of meeting at SCE. The following July we held a weeklong gathering in Nashville and agreed on a name, SEED (Social Ethics Energizing Democracy). By then we had forty members and two new steering committee leaders: Peter Laarman, a former director of Progressive Christians Uniting in Los Angeles, and Allyn Maxfield-Steele, co-executive director of the Highlander Research and Education Center in New Market, Tennessee. The early gatherings were buoyantly constructive; the Nashville gathering displayed why this group is novel.

Community organizing organizations are notoriously fractious with each other, habituated to fighting each other for funding and standing. Asking organizers to work with academics is no picnic either, since organizers often hold negative views of the academy, academics are prone to act like academics, and the commitment of organizers to building bases of power in local communities has little place in the academy. We came to Nashville to defy the usual organizing tradeoffs. Democracy in the USA, we said, always fragile and imperiled in the first place, has entered a new period of acute crisis. White Christian nationalism plays a major role in the mounting danger. Climate change is driving millions of desperate people from places that are no longer habitable. Ranged against a toxic tide of authoritarian nationalism, we see faint and fragmented resistance movements. We need stronger counter-narrative voices in the work of social justice organizing, and we need to resource those on the front lines doing the work.

The "we" in Nashville was constantly questioned and contested. We had leaders representing over twenty organizations, including Abolitionist Sanctuary, Faith in Action (formerly PICO), Gamaliel, and the Poor People's Campaign. We were careful not to bring together organizers whom we knew to be antagonistic toward each other, but we had too many organizing traditions in the room not to generate ample "who are we" contention. There were working groups on economic democracy, nonviolent resistance, and pedagogy, workshops on public education projects, and programs on catalyzing critical consciousness, working within churches, and organizing in Nashville. We convened at historic Nashville sites of social gospel praxis: American Baptist College, Clark Memorial United Methodist Church, Edgehill United Methodist Church, Scarritt Bennett Hall, and Vanderbilt Divinity School. We acknowledged the sheer difficulty of uniting organizers, clergy, and academics. The discussion of nonviolence was so volatile it threatened to blow up our entire enterprise.

To some of our members, Gandhi-King nonviolent resistance is a spiritual way of life. To some it is an important strategy to be employed as far as it works. To some, any reference to nonviolent norms or strategy is triggering, offensive, and at best, outdated. We heard from members who have been driven by White nationalist violence into a hypervigilant state of fight-or-flight, determined to beat down antagonists. We also heard from members who feel trapped by intimate intrafamilial violence that is even harder to talk about. Feelings were hurt, appeals were made not to take criticism personally, and new friendships were forged. The academics tried not to act like academics, but never enough for the organizers. The academic-organizer binary was named, queried, deconstructed, reasserted, and lamented. The fact that many in the room were fully both did not dispose of the binary. In Chicago our group was new and exuberant. In Nashville it got real.

There ought to be a group at SCE that reaches out to social justice organizers and includes them, and now there is one. There ought to be courses in seminaries that train future pastors and activists in organizing, and SEED is developing them. Social ethics was founded in the 1880s to do this work. It was the wing of the social gospel that operated in the academy, seeking to link the academy to reform movements. Rebuilding this tradition of scholar-activism within SCE and theological education links both to their own histories. The academy is sometimes a valuable site of social justice work, though mostly not. Some organizers value public intellectualism and rigorous analysis, and many do not, especially if it has any connection to the academy. SEED is built to stay the course with no illusions about the difficulties of working together.

I have less confidence in the future of DSA. The Sanders campaign of 2016 set off a rush of new democratic socialists into DSA, which impelled various kinds of ultraleft sectarians to join too. Neo-Leninists and semi-anarchists clash with each other about ideology while agreeing that DSA must disavow its social democratic legacy and its coalition work with liberals. Today, DSA has a Communist Caucus, something unthinkable to founders like me. DSA has groups that campaign to expel Alexandria Ocasio-Cortez every time she fails one of their litmus tests. Many of my friends have resigned in despair, believing that the organization we founded is hopelessly ruined or lost. If they prove to be right, I will have to join them in sorrow, but meanwhile my longtime friend Maxine Phillips and I remind our old friends that actual democratic socialists still overwhelmingly out-number the ultraleft sectarians in DSA, and they include many of the best organizers that Generation Z has produced.

The SEED gathering in Nashville had reached its final day when I received the crushing news that Eric had suffered a severe stroke in Mid-land. His left side was almost entirely paralyzed. We rallied to him as he endured grueling months of surgery and rehab. My mother was foremost, as always, among the family caregivers, until she suffered a brokenhearted stroke. It was her first experience of failing to will-power herself through a crisis. There followed weeks of shuttling between Eric and my mother. I caught pneumonia in the only nursing home that would take Eric, my mother mercifully recovered enough to return home, the pneumonia persisted, Eric opted for the living room of his home, and my mother moved in with him, resuming her role as the irrepressible family caregiver. We are a diverse bunch bonded deeply by mother love and brother love. My mother had begun to recover in October 2023 when the world rocked with the horrible news that Hamas had massacred nearly 700 Israeli civilians and 70 foreign nationals, and killed over 370 Israeli soldiers, in southern Israel. I crashed emotionally at the worst possible moment, knowing what was coming in Gaza. My usual orbit of congregations and schools called for a sermon, a class, or a talk, and for five weeks I begged off from all of them. I was too drained by illness and despair to offer the help for which congregations were pleading. It was late November before I crawled back to saying what I've always said.

Two historic peoples with rival narratives must find a way to share the land and respect each other's right to self-determination and safety. You cannot brutally oppress any people anywhere without driving them to desperate rebellion. Palestinian children are as precious as Israeli children and no less deserving of a decent future. Christians must atone for the bigotry against Jews and Muslims that caused so much of the trauma in Israel and Palestine. I still believe all these things. But the dream of a two-state solution lies shattered across Israel and Palestine. The occupied West Bank, as I write in June 2024, may be slipping into outright annexation, and Gaza is unspeakably ravaged, its people slaughtered, its homes, schools, universities, and hospitals pulverized by Hellfire missiles and two thousand-pound-bombs. One-third of Gaza has been razed, relief aid is blocked, starvation is rampant, and even the refugee camps have been firebombed. The Palestinians have nowhere to go, yet the purpose of squeezing the West Bank and making Gaza unlivable is to drive them out.

The Oslo Accords of 1993 were supposed to deliver a Palestinian state by 1999. Instead, Israeli settlers doubled from 200,000 to 400,000 while the Oslo process crumbled over settlers, the second Intifada, Jerusalem, secure borders, and above all, the right of return. Two decades of vicious cynicism ensued in Israel-Palestine. Contrasting forms of river-to-the-sea conquest ascended on each side, each determined to drive the other into the sea. Then Hamas struck in October 2023 and Israel responded by destroying Gaza. There are no words for the agony of Gaza. There is only the imperative of stopping the carnage, defending the right of

Palestinians and Israelis not to be terrorized, taking a stand against ethnic cleansing, and refusing to finance it.

On April 11, 2024 I was awarded the Gandhi, King, Mandela Peace Prize at the cavernous Martin Luther King Jr. Chapel of Morehouse College. I spoke in the morning and afternoon and received the prize for my life's work at an evening celebration conducted by my eminent friend Lawrence Carter, Morehouse president David Thomas, and my dear friend Eboni Marshall Turman, now a social ethicist at Yale. Even my previous appearances at Morehouse had not prepared me for the waves of feeling that washed over me through the day and evening. My notecard said at the top, "Find the words." I surely failed, but perhaps my feeling came through.

The next week Columbia became the epicenter of nationwide campus protests against the carnage in Gaza. Many Union students joined the protest encampments, which were forcefully shut down by the New York City police at the behest of the Columbia administration. Serene eloquently condemned the shutdowns and was thanked by the entire faculty for doing so. On other issues pertaining to Israel-Palestine, however, our faculty held a wide range of views. I led the faculty through five days of tense discussions that produced a public statement expressing what we could agree upon. It was a grueling experience that made me more grateful than ever that we are a band of colleagues and friends.

My book *Anglican Identities* (2024) came out that week, threading a story about the making of Anglican logos idealism, imperial whiteness, and commonweal ecumenism. For forty years, one section of my library had grown relentlessly while I periodically pared back all the others. The Anglican section sprawled across the room, spilled into the hallway, infiltrated other categories, and filled storage boxes marked "A," awaiting what became my Anglicanism book. It was published just before I spoke at the Wake Forest University Baccalaureate in Winston-Salem, North Carolina, where my friend Corey D. B. Walker, the dean of the Divinity School, is building a powerhouse of Black religious scholarship. Corey and I converse in a shorthand based upon our shared love of the Black social gospel tradition.

No ethical conviction that religious people bring to social justice causes is unique to them, but it often helps to have a religious faith. I noticed long ago that the stalwart-types often have a spiritual wellspring that keeps them going. The political Left can be as toxic and mean as the

political Right. Some sectors of the Left are prone to demonize opponents, and some are virtually defined by their self-righteousness and dogmatic truculence. Religious progressives, though no less prone to these
moral failings as everyone else, bring to social justice causes our language
and practices for the experiences of being faithful, not victorious, and
of being saved by something greater than ourselves and our efforts. We
strive, reason, socialize, and play through the symbolic forms by which
we glimpse who we are in the world. Individual reasoners have not made
up the symbols by which we find our identity and make sense of it. The
symbols and practices emerge through processes of birth, differentiation,
association, grace, suffering, death, and reconciliation.

The odyssey aspect of my life overlaps the story of grace. I am the
toddler who was flogged to be perfect and was told that he would surely
graduate from college. I am the eight-year-old who scoured ditches and
fields for waterlogged baseballs and longed to whisk away on a train. I am
the nine-year-old who fixed on the crucified God and puzzled at being a self,
the ten-year-old who pleaded for a move over from Union Road, and the
middle schooler who discovered that being a sports star did not ward off the
bullies. I am the ninth grader who memorized chunks of *Crusader Without
Violence* and idolized MLK, the eleventh grader who devoured the writings
of James Baldwin, and the twelfth grader who acquiesced to Duane Lehman, who always recruited the quarterback. Mr. Carey had played for Alma
College, so I landed at a college that should have been out of reach for me.
My mother turned out to be right that college is a place to reinvent yourself.
There my yearning for a life-giving worldview overtook my sports-perfec-
tionism, though I remained very much a product of Bay County.

It thrilled me to learn how the Platonic forms of being, sameness, and
difference passed into Christianity as God's thoughts via the founding
Neoplatonist, Plotinus. If the Hellenization of Christianity was a major
problem for Christian theology, as I heard on my first day of college, it
was imperative to dig into the problem, and right away. My broken heart
threw me into a brutal depression that had waited for me since toddler
years, yet the life of the mind lifted me above it. I fixed on academic fields
that grappled with big questions, debated what might be true, queried
how we know anything, explained how society got the way it is, and
imagined a just society. I had no career plans, nor hardly any thoughts

about a career. It was the subject matter that caught me: Who am I? What do I believe? What is worth struggling for?

My wonderment at the mystery of "I am myself" led me to thinkers who wrestle with the puzzles of subjectivity. Fixing on Immanuel Kant did not feel like something I had chosen because he was the unavoidable modern thinker, audaciously proposing to unify reason and experience. Kant's doctrine of intellectual intuition scared him, so he inadvertently set off the post-Kantian gusher that refused to subordinate intuition to the concept. I was deeply a post-Kantian by the end of my college years, believing that concepts and intuition fuse in acts of imagination. My senior thesis on Marx highlighted the influence of Hegel on Marx, and my thesis on Karl Rahner highlighted the influence of Kant and Heidegger on Rahner. I was feeling my way toward Christian social ethics and economic democracy, on one side, and post-Kantian philosophy and theology, on the other side. Both involved dances with Hegel that became increasingly conflicted, enabling, and complex, and both propelled me into intellectual history.

At Alma College, I thought Hegel was a post-Kantian theorist of a *Gestalt* of consciousness who delivered philosophy from Kantian dualism by rendering Kant's transcendental ego as the idea of Mind in general, the unifying principle of consciousness. That wasn't wrong—Hegel did describe a logical process of Spirit dividing itself, opposing itself to itself, and restoring its unity by returning to itself, which he described as the solution to the problem of the Kantian ego. But it was Hegel's Christianity that caught me, something deeper than an argument about Kantian dualism: Christianity is a picture story about Spirit pouring itself into the world and embracing the suffering of the world. Any theory of existence that bypasses the mind and its experiences of anguish and freedom is too blinkered. At Harvard, Dieter Henrich confirmed my religious affinity for Hegel by showing that Hegel founded his concept of Spirit on Christian love as the principle of unification. The Hegel scholarship of the 1980s pressed further along this line by stressing the significance of recognition in Hegelian Geist. The keynote was Hegel's *I ch, dass Wir, und Wir, dass Ich ist* in the *Phenomenology of Spirit:* "'I' that is 'We,' and 'We' that is 'I.'" The 'I' exists concretely as self-recognition in others, not as the "I am I" that Fichte derived from Kant.[30]

The Kantian transcendental ego is an abstraction from Spirit, which first emerges as intersubjective recognition. Spirit is the process of self-abandonment and finding selfhood in the other, becoming intersubjective as the *Gestalt* of the world, not only of consciousness. I concurred with Kierkegaard that the self is a relation that relates itself to itself, and I treasured him for contending that life is absurd unless the self becomes grounded in the Power that posits it. But Kierkegaard claimed that one knows one's unique individuality within and together with one's self. His polemic against Hegelian sociality discarded Hegel's deeply Christian focus on apprehending the divine in the self-likeness and suffering of others. God is the transfiguring power of an emergent intersubjectivity symbolized by Christ, the paradigm of infinite love revealed in the infinite anguish of Calvary. Once I landed in the academy and found myself teaching Hegel to college students, I asked them to keep in mind two things: (1) There are many ways to interpret Hegel because he was elusive and complex, developing multidimensional concepts that translators couldn't translate. But (2), if you remember only one thing about Hegel, make it the I that is a We and the We that is an I.

This has been a decidedly I-We-We-I memoir. I have never been interested in myself except as a participant in relationships and movements. I am far more interested in friends and loved ones, social justice causes, and intellectual trends than in myself, and I am painfully aware that my-self is a shy loner saved only by the love and grace of others. So now I have written a memoir that runs long on friends, causes, and intellectualism and short on how I carried brutal depression through my college years, why I had to be alone after we lost Andy, why Brenda is the main figure of chapters 4 and 5, and so on.

A reviewer chided me that the middle chapters vividly describe Brenda's sermons without citing my own. There was never a chance that I would quote my own sermons. Serene was surprised to learn about my singing: "We never heard that at Union—what happened?" Sorry, I was a reluctant performer even in my singing years, and now I'm down to one cringey vocal cord. Kelly wondered about the eighteen years that I handled every harassment charge at Kalamazoo College: "Did you burn out on that kind of ministry?" In a word, yes. Another reviewer exhorted me not to begin the last chapter with six pages on the history of the Black social gospel. But nothing was more personal for me than struggling to finish *The New Abolition*, the book of mine that I care most about. Then I wrote *Breaking White Supremacy* with no expectation of completing it. I am ineffably grateful for a beloved partner who stuck with me through years of raging illness and a compulsion to write the Black social gospel history.

I surely overcompensated for lacking self-confidence and needing to justify my existence. In my school years I had to be called upon to speak in class, after which I stumped for years as an organizer for solidarity causes that mercifully required no talking about myself. There I found a call to ministry that led to an academic calling, where I drew out the quiet types in class, knowing they usually have something to say, if only someone draws them out. When I moved to Union, I befriended a perceptive trustee, Doug Ames, who said he hoped that wearing Reinhold Niebuhr's name would enable me, but he feared it would drag me down. Doug perceived that my overcompensating was bound to fall short.

So I failed over and over to cut back on road lecturing. I light up when provided with a class or a crowd. During the worst years of my health drama, I relied completely on adrenalin-fueled lighting-up. Then I managed to cut back only because COVID-19 broke my self-justifying rush to the next speaking venue and the next one, and I had a loving partner who was ready for twilight years. Eris, a bluesy soul steeped in Holocaust-survival family trauma, is prone to observe incredulously, "Somehow you are actually happy." Exactly right. My life is buoyed by joyous gratitude at being blessed by loved ones, and by work that I love. I hope this memoir has told an interesting story about the theological, broadly intellectual, and social justice struggles of my generation in which I have been privileged to be a participant.

On the road, at Columbia, and even at Union, I meet people for whom Christianity is a ruined word. They ask me nicely, or with puzzlement, or hostility, why I am a Christian. I try to explain that I was drawn long ago into the spirit and way of Jesus, which draws me like a magnet into its gravitational force. I was caught by the gospel picture of the divine Word entering the world. I am held by the subversive peace and grace of Christ, the meaning of suffering, the challenge to oppose every form of exploitation and violence, the willingness to give my life to others, and the promise of new life that it brings. These experiences shape my understanding of how I should live. To say with Paul that faith, hope, and love remain, these three, doesn't mean the evidence is in their favor. It means they remain, they abide, regardless of the evidence.

Faith is trust and commitment. Hope gives you courage, helps you face another day. Love makes you care, makes you angry, throws you into the struggle. I need all the faith, hope, and love I can get, and I cannot get any of it on my own. Only through the ties of faith and love with others that grace my life do I have any capacity for hope. We are not in control, so it isn't up to us to make history come out right. In drawing closer to the divine, we are thrown into work that allows others to share in the harvest, which is enough. Love divine calls out from created things the love for which all things are created to be, pouring through all the processes of life across all boundaries, exceeding what we understand. We enter the mystery of the divine by its grace, beginning in faith with that which transcends faith and draws it forth.

NOTES

1 Over from Union Road

1 L. D. Reddick, *Crusader without Violence* (New York: Harper & Row, 1959).

2 Martin Luther King Jr., *Stride toward Freedom: The Montgomery Story* (New York: Harper & Brothers, 1958).

3 James Baldwin, *The Fire Next Time* (New York: Dial Press, 1963); Baldwin, *Go Tell It on the Mountain* (New York: Knopf, 1953); Baldwin, *Nobody Knows My Name* (New York: Dial Press, 1961); John Steinbeck, *The Grapes of Wrath* (New York: Viking, 1939); Steinbeck, *East of Eden* (New York: Viking, 1952).

4 Henry Grady Weaver, *The Mainspring of Human Progress* (1st ed., 1947; rev. ed., New York: Foundation for Economic Freedom, 1953).

5 C. S. Lewis, *Mere Christianity* (London: Geoffrey Bles, 1952); John R. W. Stott, *Basic Christianity* (Grand Rapids: Eerdmans, 1958).

6 Ralph Waldo Emerson, *The Portable Emerson*, ed. Mark Van Doren (New York: Viking, 1963); William James, *The Varieties of Religious Experience: A Study in Human Nature* (London: Longmans, Green, 1902); John Dewey, *Democracy and Education* (New York: Macmillan, 1916); Dewey, *A Common Faith* (New Haven: Yale University Press, 1934).

7 Jim Stick, "Dorrien Hurls No-Hitter for Berryhill 165," *Midland Daily News*, July 20, 1970, quote.

8 G. W. F. Hegel, *Phenomenology of Mind*, trans. J. B. Baillie (London: Macmillan, 1910).

2 Alma College

1 W. T. Jones, *A History of Western Philosophy: The Classical Mind* (New York: Harcourt, Brace & World, 1969); Jones, *A History of Western Philosophy: The Medieval Mind* (New York: Harcourt, Brace & World, 1969).

2 Immanuel Kant, *Foundations of the Metaphysics of Morals*, trans. Lewis White Beck (1785; Indianapolis: Bobbs-Merrill, 1969); Kant, *Critique of Practical Reason*, trans. Lewis White Beck (1788; Indianapolis: Bobbs-Merrill, 1958).

3 Immanuel Kant, *Critique of Pure Reason*, trans. Norman Kemp Smith (1781; London: Macmillan, 1933).

4   G. W. F. Hegel, *Phenomenology of Mind*, trans. J. B. Baillie (London: Macmillan, 1910).

5   J. N. Findlay, *Hegel: A Ree-xamination* (London: George Allen, 1958); Alasdair MacIntyre, ed., *Hegel: A Collection of Critical Essays* (Garden City, N.Y.: Anchor Books, 1972); Alexander Kojéve, *Introduction to the Reading of Hegel*, trans. James H. Nichols Jr. (New York: Basic Books, 1969); Herbert Marcuse, *Reason and Revolution: Hegel and the Rise of Social Theory* (2nd ed., London: Routledge & Kegan Paul, 1941).

6   G. W. F. Hegel, *Science of Logic*, trans. A. V. Miller (London: George Allen & Unwin, 1969); Gary Dorrien, *Kantian Reason and Hegelian Spirit: The Idealistic Logic of Modern Theology* (Chichester, UK: Wiley-Blackwell, 2012), 159–242; Gary Dorrien, *In a Post-Hegelian Spirit: Philosophical Theology as Idealistic Discontent* (Waco, Tex.: Baylor University Press, 2020).

7   F. H. Bradley, *Appearance and Reality: A Metaphysical Essay* (Oxford: Oxford University Press, 1893); Bradley, *Essays on Truth and Reality* (Oxford: Oxford University Press, 1914); Bernard Bosanquet, *The Principle of Individualism and Value* (London: Macmillan, 1912).

8   Bertrand Russell, *The Principles of Mathematics* (Cambridge: Cambridge University Press, 1903); Alfred North Whitehead and Bertrand Russell, *Principia Mathematica*, 3 vols. (Cambridge: Cambridge University Press, 1910, 1912, 1913); G. E. Moore, "The Refutation of Idealism," (1903), and Moore, "The Nature and Reality of Objects of Perception" (1905–1906), repr. in Moore, *Philosophical Studies* (London: Routledge & Kegan Paul, 1922), 1–30, 31–96; Ludwig Wittgenstein, *Tractatus Logico-Philosophicus* (London: Kegan Paul, Trench, Trubner & Co., 1922); Rudolf Carnap, *Der logische Aufbau der Welt* (Berlin: Weltkreis, 1928); A. J. Ayer, *Language, Truth, and Logic* (1936; 2nd ed., New York: Dover, 1952); Ayer, ed., *Logical Positivism* (New York: Free Press, 1959); Carnap, *Logical Foundations of Probability* (Chicago: University of Chicago Press, 1950).

9   Ludwig Wittgenstein, *Philosophical Investigations*, trans. G. E. M. Anscombe (London: Blackwell, 1953); Immanuel Kant, *Universal Natural History and Theory of the Heavens* (1755), trans. Stanley L. Jaki (Edinburgh: Scottish Academic Press, 1981); John Stuart Mill, *Utilitarianism, with Critical Essays*, ed. Samuel Gorovitz (Indianapolis: Bobbs-Merrill, 1971); Mill, *On Liberty*, with *The Subjection of Women* and *Chapters on Socialism*, ed. Stefan Collini (Cambridge: Cambridge University Press, 1989).

10 Talcott Parsons, *The Structure of Social Action* (New York: Free Press, 1937); Parsons, *The Social System* (New York: Free Press, 1951); Parsons and Edward A. Shils, *Toward a General Theory of Action: Theoretical Foundations for the Social Sciences* (Cambridge, Mass.: Harvard University Press, 1951).

11 John Bright, *A History of Israel* (Philadelphia: Westminster, 1959; 2nd ed., 1972); Bernhard W. Anderson, *Understanding the Old Testament* (Hoboken, N.J.: Prentice-Hall, 1957).

12 Ernst Bloch, *Das Prinzip Hoffnung*, 3 vols. (Frankfurt: Suhrkamp Verlag, 1954, 1955, 1959); Jürgen Moltmann, *Theologie der Hoffnung* (5th ed., Munich: Christian Kaiser Verlag, 1965; trans. James W. Leitch, London: SCM Press, 1967); Thomas J. J. Altizer and William Hamilton, *Radical Theology and the Death of God* (Indianapolis: Bobbs-Merrill, 1966); Altizer, *The Gospel of Christian Atheism* (Philadelphia: Westminster, 1966).

13 Friedrich Schleiermacher, *On Religion: Speeches to Its Cultured Despisers* (1799), trans. Richard Crouter (Cambridge: Cambridge University Press, 1993).

14 Walter Rauschenbusch, *Christianity and the Social Crisis* (New York: Macmillan, 1907). This is my tightest summary of a book I have summarized many times, notably in Gary Dorrien, *Social Ethics in the Making: Interpreting an American Tradition* (Chichester, UK: Wiley-Blackwell, 2009), 94–97.

15 James H. Cone, *Black Theology and Black Power* (New York: Seabury Press, 1969); Cone, *A Black Theology of Liberation* (Philadelphia: J. B. Lippincott, 1970). I have previously told a shorter version of this story in Dorrien, *In a Post-Hegelian Spirit*, xii.

16 Walter Mischel, *Personality and Assessment* (Mahwah, N.J.: Lawrence Erlbaum Associates, 1968); Mischel, "Toward a Cognitive Social Learning Reconceptualization of the Personality," *Psychological Review* 80 (1973): 252–83; Albert Bandura, *Social Learning Theory* (Englewood Cliffs, N.J.: Prentice-Hall, 1971); B. F. Skinner, *Beyond Freedom and Dignity* (New York: Bantam Books, 1971).

17 Karl Barth, *Der Römerbrief* (Bern: G. A. Baschlin, 1919); Barth, *The Epistle to the Romans*, trans. of 6th ed., Edwyn C. Hoskyns (London: Oxford University Press, 1933); Barth, *The Word of God and the Word of Man*, trans. Douglas Horton (New York: Harper, 1928); Barth, *Church Dogmatics: The Doctrine of the Word of God*, I/1, trans. G. T. Thomson (Edinburgh: T&T Clark, 1936); Barth, *Church Dogmatics: The Doctrine of God*, II/1, trans. T. H. L. Parker (Edinburgh: T&T Clark, 1957); Barth, *Church Dogmatics: The Doctrine of Creation*, III/1, trans. J. W. Edwards, O. Bussey, and Harold Knight (Edinburgh: T&T Clark, 1958).

18 Paul Tillich, *Systematic Theology*, 3 vols. (Chicago: University of Chicago Press, 1951, 1957, 1963); Tillich, *Theology of Culture*, ed. Robert C. Kimball (New York: Oxford University Press, 1959); Tillich, *The Protestant Era*, trans. James Luther Adams (London: Nisbet, 1951).

19 Paul Tillich, *The Courage to Be* (New Haven: Yale University Press, 1952); Tillich, *Biblical Religion and the Search for Ultimate Reality* (Chicago: University of Chicago Press, 1964); Tillich, "Die religionsgeschichtliche Konstruktion in Schellings positiver Philosophie, ihre Voraussetzungen und Principien" (doctoral dissertation, University of Breslau, 1910); Friedrich W. J. Schelling, *Vorlesungen über die Methode des academischen Studium* (Stuttgart: J. G. Cotta, 1830).

20 Reinhold Niebuhr, *Moral Man and Immoral Society: A Study in Ethics and Politics* (New York: Charles Scribner's Sons, 1932); Niebuhr, *Nature and Destiny of Man*, 2 vols. (New York: Scribner's, 1949); Niebuhr, *The Irony of American History* (New York: Scribner's, 1952); Niebuhr, *Christian Realism and Political*

Problems (New York: Scribner's, 1953); Niebuhr, "Communism and the Protestant Clergy," *Look* 17 (November 17, 1953): 37.

21   Michael Novak, "Needing Niebuhr Again," *Commentary* 54 (September 1972): 52–61; Novak, "Reinhold Niebuhr: Model for Neoconservatives," *Christian Century* 103 (January 22, 1986), 69–71; Paul Ramsey, "Farewell to Christian Realism" (1966), repr. in Ramsey, *The Just War: Force and Political Responsibility* (Lanham, Md.: University Press of America, 1983 [1968]), 487–88; James Nuechterlein, "The Feminization of the American Left," *Commentary* 84 (November 1987), 43–47.

22   Karl Marx, *Capital: A Critique of Political Economy* (vol. 1, 1867, 3rd ed., trans. Samuel Moore and Edward Aveling; Chicago: Charles H. Kerr, 1906); Karl Rahner, *Geist in Welt: Zur Metaphysik der endlichen Erkenntnis bei Thomas von Aquin* (Innsbruck: Rauch, 1939); 2nd ed., rev. Johannes B. Metz, Munich: Kösel-Verlag, 1957; English ed., *Spirit in the World*, trans. William Dych (New York: Herder and Herder, 1968).

23   Robert Paul Wolff, *Kant's Theory of Mental Activity* (Cambridge, Mass.: Harvard University Press, 1963); Norman Kemp Smith, *A Commentary to Kant's Critique of Pure Reason* (2nd ed., 1923; repr., Atlantic Highlands, N.J.: Humanities Press, 1962).

24   Karl Marx, *Writings of the Young Marx on Philosophy and Society*, ed. L. Easton and K. Guddar (New York: Doubleday, 1967); Marx, *The German Ideology* (1845), in *Karl Marx: Selected Writings*, ed. David McLellan (Oxford: Oxford University Press, 1977), 159–92; Marx, *A Contribution to the Critique of Political Economy* (1859), trans. S. W. Ryazanskaya (New York: International Publishers, 1999).

25   Martin Heidegger, *Being and Time*, trans. John Macquarrie and Edward Robinson (New York: Harper & Row, 1962); Heidegger, *An Introduction to Metaphysics*, trans. Ralph Manheim (New Haven: Yale University Press, 1959); Edmund Husserl, *Ideas: General Introduction to Pure Phenomenology*, trans. W. R. Boyce Gibson (London: George Allen & Unwin, 1976); Husserl, *The Phenomenology of Internal Time-Consciousness*, ed. Martin Heidegger, trans. James S. Churchill (Bloomington: Indiana University Press, 1964).

26   Joseph Maréchal, *Le point de départ de la métaphysique*, 2nd. ed., 5 vols. (Brussels: L'Edition universelle; Paris: Descleé de Brouwer, 1944–1949); *A Maréchal Reader*, ed. and trans. Joseph Donceel (New York: Herder and Herder, 1970); Rahner, *Geist in Welt*; Rahner, *Schriften zur Theologie*, 9 vols. (Einsiedeln: Benziger Verlag, 1959–1970); Rahner, "Christianity and the Non-Christian Religions," *Theological Investigations*, 23 vols. (London: Darton, Longman & Todd, 1966), 5:115–34; Thomas Aquinas, *Summa Theologica*, 5 vols., trans. Fathers of the English Dominican Province (Westminster, Md.: Christian Classics, 1920).

27   Michael Harrington, *The Other America: Poverty in the United States* (New York: Macmillan, 1993); Harrington, *Toward a Democratic Left: A Radical Program for a New Majority* (New York: Macmillan, 1968); Harrington,

Socialism (New York: Saturday Review Press, 1972); Harrington, *Fragments of the Century* (New York: Saturday Review Press, 1973).

3 Harvard–Union–Princeton–Brenda

1   Mary Daly, *Beyond God the Father: Toward a Philosophy of Women's Liberation* (Boston: Beacon, 1973).

2   Mary Daly, *The Church and the Second Sex* (1968; 2nd ed., New York: Harper & Row, 1975); Daly, *Beyond God the Father*, quotes. This section on Daly and Rosemary Radford Ruether adapts material from Gary Dorrien, *Economy, Difference, Empire: Social Ethics for Social Justice* (New York: Columbia University Press, 2010), xviii–xix, 289–94.

3   Rosemary Radford Ruether, *Disputed Questions: On Being a Christian* (Nashville: Abingdon, 1982), 17–29; Ruether, *Women and Redemption: A Theological History* (Minneapolis: Fortress, 1998), 220–21; Ruether, "Beginnings: An Intellectual Autobiography," in *Journeys: The Impact of Personal Experience on Religious Thought*, ed. Gregory Baum (New York: Paulist, 1975), 34–56; Ruether, "Robert Palmer: First the God, Then the Dance," *Christian Century* 107 (February 7–14, 1990): 125–26; Ruether, *The Church against Itself: An Inquiry into the Conditions of Historical Existence for the Eschatological Community* (New York: Herder and Herder, 1967), 234–35; Ruether, *The Radical Kingdom: The Western Experience of Messianic Hope* (New York: Paulist, 1970).

4   Rosemary Radford Ruether, *New Woman, New Earth: Sexist Ideologies and Human Liberation* (New York: Seabury Press, 1975), 89–133; Ruether, *Faith and Fratricide: The Theological Roots of Anti-Semitism* (New York: Seabury Press, 1974); Ruether, "Motherearth and the Megamachine: A Theology of Liberation in a Feminine, Somatic and Ecological Perspective," *Christianity and Crisis* 31 (April 12, 1972): 267–73, repr. in Ruether, *Liberation Theology: Human Hope Confronts Christian History and American Power* (New York: Paulist, 1972), 115–26; Ruether, *Disputed Questions*, quote 53.

5   Norman Thomas, *A Socialist's Faith* (New York: Norton, 1951), 9–21; Martin Luther King Jr., "The Bravest Man I Ever Met," *Pageant* (June 1965), repr. in Cornel West, ed., *The Radical King* (Boston: Beacon, 2015), 225–34. For my analyses of Thomas and Harrington, see Gary Dorrien, *American Democratic Socialism: History, Politics, Religion, and Theory* (New Haven: Yale University Press, 2021), 207–328, and 343–453.

6   H. John McDargh, *Psychoanalytic Object Relations Theory and the Study of Religion: On Faith and the Imaging of God* (Lanham, Md.: University Press of America, 1983).

7   Robin W. Lovin, *Christian Faith and Public Choices: The Social Ethics of Barth, Brunner, and Bonhoeffer* (Philadelphia: Fortress, 1984); Lovin, *Reinhold Niebuhr and Christian Realism* (Cambridge: Cambridge University Press, 1995); Gary Dorrien, "The Christian Socialist Difference: Moral Realism, Robin Lovin, Reinhold Niebuhr, and Democratic Socialism," chapter 1 in *The*

Future of Christian Realism: International Conflict, Political Decay, and the Crisis of Democracy, ed. Dallas Gingles, Joshua Mauldin, and Rebekah L. Miles (Lanham, Md.: Lexington Books, 2023), 3–20.

8   Nicholas Wolterstorff, *Reason within the Bounds of Religion* (Grand Rapids: Eerdmans, 1976); Kenneth Baynes, *The Normative Grounds of Social Criticism: Kant, Rawls, and Habermas* (Albany: State University of New York Press, 1992).

9   Willard Van Orman Quine, *From a Logical Point of View* (Cambridge, Mass.: Harvard University Press, 1953); Quine, *Word and Object* (Cambridge, Mass.: MIT Press, 1960); Quine, *Ontological Relativity and Other Essays* (New York: Columbia University Press, 1969); Stanley Cavell, *Must We Mean What We Say?* (Cambridge: Cambridge University Press, 1958); John Rawls, *A Theory of Justice* (Cambridge, Mass.: Harvard University Press, 1971).

10 Mark C. Taylor, *Erring: A Postmodern A/theology* (Chicago: University of Chicago Press, 1984); Taylor, *After God* (Chicago: University of Chicago Press, 2007); David S. Pacini, *The Cunning of Modern Religious Thought* (Philadelphia: Fortress, 1987); Stephen N. Dunning, *Kierkegaard's Dialectic of Inwardness: A Structural Analysis of the Theory of Stages* (Princeton: Princeton University Press, 1985).

11 George E. Rupp, *Christologies and Cultures: Toward a Typology of Religious Worldviews* (The Hague: Mouton, 1971); Rupp, *Culture-Protestantism: German Liberal Theology at the Turn of the Twentieth Century* (Missoula, Mont.: Scholars, 1977); Rupp, *Beyond Existentialism and Zen: Religion in a Pluralistic World* (New York: Oxford University Press, 1979); Gary Dorrien, *The Word as True Myth: Interpreting Modern Theology* (Louisville: Westminster John Knox, 1997).

12 Dieter Henrich, *Between Kant and Hegel: Lectures on German Idealism*, ed. David S. Pacini (Cambridge, Mass.: Harvard University Press, 2003), 15–64. This section glosses my discussion in Gary Dorrien, *In a Post-Hegelian Spirit: Philosophical Theology as Idealistic Discontent* (Waco, Tex.: Baylor University Press, 2020), 70–72.

13 Immanuel Kant, *Kritik der reinen Vernunft: Werke in sechs Bänden, Band 2* (1781; Cologne: Könemann Verlagsgesellschaft, 1995); Kant, *Kritik der Urtheilskraft: Werke in sechs Bänden, Band 4* (Cologne: Könemann Verlagsgesellschaft, 1995); Kant, "Welches sind die wirklichen Fortschritte, die die Metaphysik seit Leibnizens und Wolf's Zeiten in Deutschland gamacht hat?" ("What Real Progress Has Metaphysics Made in Germany since the Time of Leibniz and Wolff?" [1804]), ed. Friedrich Theodore Rink, in *Kant's handschriftlicher Nachlass, Band VII*, ed. Gerhard Lehmann, in *Kant's gesammelte Schriften*, ed. Königlich Preussiche Akademie, 29 vols. (Berlin: Georg Reimer Verlag, 1910–1942), 20:311.

14 Henrich, *Between Kant and Hegel*, 46–64, 279–315; Dieter Henrich, "Formen der Negation in Hegels Logik," in *Seminar: Dialektik in der Philosophie Hegels*, ed. Rolf-Peter Horstmann (Frankfurt: Suhrkamp Verlag, 1978), 213–29.

15 Josef Sudbrack, *Spiritual Guidance*, trans. Peter Heinegg (New York: Paulist, 1983).

16 Paul Tillich, "Christentum und Sozialismus," *Das neue Deutschland* 8 (December 1919): 106–10; Tillich and Richard Wegener, *Der Sozialismus als Kirchenfrage: Leitsätze von Paul Tillich und Richard Wegener* (Berlin: Gracht, 1919), in Tillich, *Gesammelte Werke*, 14 vols. (Stuttgart: Evangelisches Verlagswerk, 1962–1975); Tillich, "Kairos," *Die Tat* 14 (August 1922): 330–50; Tillich, "Masse und Religion," *Blätter für religiösen Sozialismus* 2 (1921): 1–7, 9–12; Tillich, "Die Theologie als Wissenschaft," *Vossische Zeitung* 512 (October 30, 1921): 2–3; Tillich, "Religiöse Krisis," *Vivos voco* 11 (April–May 1922): 616–21; Tillich, *Das System der Wissenschaften nach Gegenständen und Methoden* (Göttingen: Vandenhoeck & Ruprecht, 1923); Tillich, "Zur Klärung der religiösen Grundhaltung," *Blätter für religiösen Sozialismus* 3 (December 1922): 46–48; Tillich, "Basic Principles of Religious Socialism" (1923), in *Political Expectation*, ed. James Luther Adams, trans. James Luther Adams and Victor Nuovo (New York: Harper & Row, 1971), 58–88.

17 John Patrick Diggins, *Up from Communism: Conservative Odysseys in American Intellectual History* (New York: Harper & Row, 1975).

18 Raymond E. Brown, *The Gospel According to John*, 3 vols. (New York: Doubleday, 1970).

19 Pius XIII, *Divino afflante Spiritu* ("The Divine Inspiration of the Holy Spirit," 1943) (Vatican City: Libreria Editrice Vaticana, 1943); Vatican Council II, *Dei verbum* ("Word of God: Dogmatic Constitution on Divine Revelation," 1965), in *Vatican Council II: The Conciliar and Post Conciliar Documents*, 2 vols., ed. Austin Flannery, O.P. (Northport, N.Y.: Costello, 1996), 1:750–64; Raymond E. Brown S.S., "Historical-Critical Exegesis of the Bible in Roman Catholicism," in *Contemporary Catholic Theology*, ed. Michael A. Hayes and Liam Gearon (New York: Continuum, 1998), 25–39.

20 James H. Cone, *God of the Oppressed* (New York: HarperCollins, 1975); Gustavo Gutiérrez, *A Theology of Liberation* (Maryknoll, N.Y.: Orbis Books, 1973).

21 G. W. F. Hegel, *Phenomenology of Spirit*, trans. A. V. Miller (Oxford: Oxford University Press, 1977); Cornel West, *Prophesy Deliverance! An Afro-American Revolutionary Christianity* (Philadelphia: Westminster, 1982).

22 Michael Harrington, *The Vast Majority: A Journey to the World's Poor* (New York: Simon & Schuster, 1977).

23 G. A. Cohen, *Karl Marx's Theory of History* (Princeton: Princeton University Press, 1978); Cohen, "Forces and Relations in Production," in *Analytical Marxism*, ed. John Roemer (Cambridge: Cambridge University Press, 1986), 11–22; John Roemer, "New Directions in the Marxian Theory of Exploitation and Class," in Roemer, *Analytical Marxism*, 81–113; Roemer, "'Rational Choice' Marxism: Some Issues of Method and Substance," in Roemer, *Analytical Marxism*, 191–201; Jon Elster, "Further Thoughts on Marxism, Functionalism, and Game Theory," in Roemer, *Analytical Marxism*, 202–20; Elster, *Making Sense of Marx* (Cambridge: Cambridge University Press, 1985). This discussion adapts material from Dorrien, *American Democratic Socialism*, 423–27.

24 James O'Connor, *The Fiscal Crisis of the State* (New York: St. Martin's Press, 1973), 13–39, 49–51, 82–96.

25 Claus Offe, *Berufsbildungsreform* (Frankfurt: Suhrkamp Verlag, 1975), 22–25; Offe, *Strukturprobleme des kapitalistischen Staates* (Frankfurt: Suhrkamp Verlag, 1973); Offe, "The Political Economy of the Labor Market," in Offe, *Disorganized Capitalism*, ed. John Keane (Cambridge, Mass.: MIT Press, 1985), 10–51; Offe, "Some Contradictions of the Modern Welfare State," in Offe, *Contradictions of the Welfare State*, ed. John Keane (Cambridge, Mass.: MIT Press, 1984), 147–61; Michael Harrington, *Twilight of Capitalism* (New York: Simon & Schuster, 1976), 307–12; Harrington, *Decade of Decision: The Crisis of the American System* (New York: Simon & Schuster, 1980), 80–106.

26 G. W. Leibniz, *Discourse on Metaphysics; Correspondence with Arnauld; Monadology*, trans. George Montgomery (La Salle, Ill.: Open Court, 1902); Leibniz, *Theodicy*, trans. E. M. Huggard (La Salle, Ill.: Open Court, 1985); Leibniz, *New Essays on Human Understanding*, trans. Peter Remnant and Jonathan Bennett (Cambridge: Cambridge University Press, 1982).

27 Gustavo Gutiérrez and Richard M. Shaull, *Liberation and Change* (Atlanta: John Knox, 1977).

28 Gibson Winter, *Elements for a Social Ethic: Scientific Perspectives on Social Process* (New York: Macmillan, 1966); Winter, *Liberating Creation: Foundations of Religious Social Ethics* (New York: Crossroad, 1981); Alfredo Fierro, *The Militant Gospel: A Critical Introduction to Political Theologies* (Maryknoll, N.Y.: Orbis Books, 1977).

29 Søren Kierkegaard, *The Point of View: On My Work as an Author; The Point of View for My Work as an Author; and Armed Neutrality*, trans. Howard V. Hong and Edna H. Hong (Princeton: Princeton University Press, 1998), 21–126.

30 Emil Brunner, *The Scandal of Christianity: The Gospel as Stumbling Block to Modern Man* (London: SCM Press, 1951).

31 James E. Loder, *Religious Pathology and Christian Faith* (Philadelphia: Westminster, 1966).

32 C. G. Jung, *Psychology and Western Religion*, trans. R. F. C. Hull (Princeton: Princeton University Press, 1984); Jung, *Symbols of Transformation*, trans. Gerhard Adler and R. F. C. Hull (Princeton: Princeton University Press, 1956); Sigmund Freud, *The Future of an Illusion*, trans. James Strachey (New York: W. W. Norton, 1961).

33 James E. Loder, *The Transforming Moment: Understanding Convictional Experiences* (New York: Harper & Row, 1981; 2nd ed., Colorado Springs: Helmers & Howard, 1989); John Macquarrie, *Principles of Christian Theology* (New York: Charles Scribner's Sons, 1966).

34 Wilder Penfield, *The Mystery of the Mind: A Critical Study of Consciousness and the Human Brain* (Princeton: Princeton University Press, 1975); Søren Kierkegaard, *The Sickness unto Death: A Christian Psychological Exposition for Upbuilding and Awakening*, trans. Howard V. Hong and Edna H. Hong (Princeton: Princeton University Press, 1980).

35   Jean-Paul Sartre, *Being and Nothingness: An Essay on Phenomenological Ontology*, trans. Hazel E. Barnes (New York: Philosophical Library, 1956); Sartre, *Essays in Existentialism*, ed. Wade Baskin (Secaucus, N.J.: Citadel Press, 1974).

36   William Temple, *Nature, Man, and God* (London: Macmillan, 1934).

4 Albany Activism

1   Lawrence S. Wittner, *Rebels against War: The American Peace Movement* (New York: Columbia University Press, 1969); 2nd ed., *Rebels against War: The American Peace Movement, 1933–1983* (Philadelphia: Temple University Press, 1984). This discussion adapts material from Gary Dorrien, *American Democratic Socialism: History, Politics, Religion, and Theory* (New Haven: Yale University Press, 2021), 429–30.

2   William Temple, *Nature, Man, and God* (London: Macmillan, 1934); Temple, *Christus Veritas: An Essay* (London: Macmillan, 1924); Temple, "The Divinity of Christ," in *Foundations: A Statement of Christian Belief in Terms of Modern Thought, by Seven Oxford Men*, ed. B. H. Streeter (London: Macmillan, 1912), 213–59; Temple, *Christianity and the Social Order* (Harmondsworth, Middlesex: Penguin, 1942); Temple, *The Church Looks Forward* (New York: Macmillan, 1944). This section adapts material from Gary Dorrien, *Anglican Identities: Logos Idealism, Imperial Whiteness, Commonweal Ecumenism* (Waco, Tex.: Baylor University Press, 2024), x–xi.

3   Alfred North Whitehead, *Process and Reality: An Essay in Cosmology* (New York: Macmillan, 1929), 27–54, 520–22; Whitehead, *Adventures of Ideas* (New York: Macmillan, 1933; repr., New York: Free Press, 1967), 175–190. This section adapts material from Gary Dorrien, *Kantian Reason and Hegelian Spirit: The Idealistic Logic of Modern Theology* (Chichester, UK: Wiley-Blackwell, 2012), 415–43.

4   Temple, *Nature, Man, and God*, 301–27.

5   Antonio Gramsci, *Selections from the Prison Notebooks*, ed. and trans. Quintin Hoare and Geoffrey Nowell Smith (New York: International Publishers, 1971), 5–23; Chantal Mouffe, *Gramsci and Marxist Theory* (London: Routledge & Kegan Paul, 1979), 155; Barbara Ehrenreich, "What Is Socialist Feminism?" in *Working Papers on Socialism and Feminism* (New York: New American Movement Pamphlet, 1976); Judith Kegan Gardiner, "Ambitious Moderation: Socialist Feminism in the NAM Years," *Works and Days* 28 (2010): 49–63; Stanley Aronowitz, "The New American Movement and Why It Failed," *Works and Days* 28 (2010): 21–33; Aronowitz, *The Crisis in Historical Materialism: Class, Politics and Culture in Marxist Theory* (New York: Praeger, 1981); Carl Boggs, *Gramsci's Marxism* (London: Pluto Press, 1976); Boggs, *The Two Revolutions: Gramsci and the Dilemmas of Western Marxism* (Boston: South End Press, 1984); Dorrien, *American Democratic Socialism*, 440–42.

6   Muriel James and Dorothy Jongeward, *Born to Win: Transactional Analysis with Gestalt Experiments* (Boston: Addison-Wesley, 1971); Eric Berne, *Games People*

Play: The Psychology of Human Relationships (New York: Grove, 1964); Fritz Perls, Ralph Hefferline, and Paul Goodman, *Gestalt Therapy: Excitement and Growth in the Human Personality* (Gouldsboro, Maine: Gestalt Journal Press, 1951).

7   Gary Dorrien, *The Democratic Socialist Vision* (Totowa, N.J.: Rowman & Littlefield, 1986).

8   Alasdair MacIntyre, *After Virtue: A Study in Moral Theory* (Notre Dame: University of Notre Dame Press, 1981); Michael Sandel, *Liberalism and the Limits of Justice* (Cambridge, Mass.: Harvard University Press, 1982).

9   Robert Bellah et al., *Habits of the Heart: Individualism and Commitment in American Life* (Berkeley: University of California Press, 1985); Michael Walzer, *Spheres of Justice: A Defense of Pluralism and Equality* (New York: Basic Books, 1983); Amitai Etzioni, *The Moral Dimension: Toward a New Economics* (New York: Free Press, 1988).

10   Harry C. Boyte, *CommonWealth: A Return to Citizen Politics* (New York: Free Press, 1989); Benjamin Barber, *Strong Democracy: Participatory Politics for a New Age* (Berkeley: University of California Press, 1984); Sheldon Wolin, *Politics and Vision: Continuity and Innovation in Western Political Thought* (Princeton: Princeton University Press, 1960); Wolin, *Democracy Incorporated: Managed Democracy and the Specter of Inverted Totalitarianism* (Princeton: Princeton University Press, 2008).

11   Elizabeth K. Minnich, *Transforming Knowledge* (Philadelphia: Temple University Press, 1991).

12   Ernst Breisach, *Historiography: Ancient, Medieval, and Modern* (Chicago: University of Chicago Press, 1983); E. Rozanne Elder and Susan M. B. Steuer, eds., *Catalogue of the Manuscripts in the Dom Edmond Obrecht Collection of Gethsemani Abbey* (Kalamazoo: Medieval Institute Publications, 2016); Franklin A. Presler, *Religion under Bureaucracy: Policy and Administration for Hindu Temples in South India* (Cambridge: Cambridge University Press, 1987).

5 Kalamazoo Heartbreak

1   Gary Dorrien, *Reconstructing the Common Good: Theology and the Social Order* (Maryknoll, N.Y.: Orbis Books, 1990).

2   Cornel West, *Prophesy Deliverance! An Afro-American Revolutionary Christianity* (Philadelphia: Westminster, 1982); West, *Prophetic Fragments: Illuminations of the Crisis in American Religion and Culture* (Grand Rapids: Eerdmans, 1988); Rosemary Radford Ruether, *Sexism and God-Talk: Toward a Feminist Theology* (Boston: Beacon, 1983); Michael Harrington, *Socialism: Past and Future* (New York: Penguin, 1989).

3   This section adapts material from Gary Dorrien, *A Darkly Radiant Vision: The Black Social Gospel in the Shadow of MLK* (New Haven: Yale University Press, 2023), 158 and 162.

4   Arjun Appadurai, *Worship and Conflict under Colonial Rule: A South Indian Case* (Cambridge: Cambridge University Press, 1981); Appadurai, *Modernity at*

Large: Cultural Dimensions of Globalization (Minneapolis: University of Minnesota Press, 1996); bell hooks, *Ain't I a Woman? Black Women and Feminism* (Boston: South End Press, 1981); hooks, *Feminist Theory: From Margin to Center* (Boston: South End Press, 1984); hooks, *Talking Back: Thinking Feminist, Thinking Black* (Boston: South End Press, 1989).

5   Amy Gutmann, *Liberal Equality* (Cambridge: Cambridge University Press, 1980); Nancy L. Rosenblum, *Another Liberalism: Romanticism and the Reconstruction of Liberal Thought* (Cambridge, Mass.: Harvard University Press, 1987).

6   Nancy Fraser, *Unruly Practices: Power, Discourse and Gender in Contemporary Social Theory* (Minneapolis: University of Minnesota Press, 1989).

7   Ronald Dworkin, *Taking Rights Seriously* (Cambridge, Mass.: Harvard University Press, 1977); Dworkin, *A Matter of Principle* (Cambridge, Mass.: Harvard University Press, 1985); Dworkin, *Law's Empire* (Cambridge, Mass.: Harvard University Press, 1986).

8   Russell Kirk, *The Conservative Mind: From Burke to Eliot* (Washington, DC: Henry Regnery Company, 1953).

9   Michael Walzer, *The Revolution of the Saints: A Study in the Origins of Radical Politics* (Cambridge, Mass.: Harvard University Press, 1965); Walzer, *Spheres of Justice: A Defense of Pluralism and Equality* (New York: Basic Books, 1983); Robert Nozick, *Anarchy, State, and Utopia* (New York: Basic Books, 1974).

10   Langdon Gilkey, *Naming the Whirlwind: The Renewal of God-Language* (Indianapolis: Bobbs-Merrill, 1969); Gilkey, *Reaping the Whirlwind: A Christian Interpretation of History* (New York: Seabury Press, 1981).

11   Langdon Gilkey, *Creationism on Trial: Evolution and God at Little Rock* (Minneapolis: Winston Press, 1985).

12   Jürgen Moltmann, *God in Creation: A New Theology of Creation and the Spirit of God*, trans. Margaret Kohl (London: SCM Press, 1985); Moltmann, *The Way of Jesus Christ: Christology in Messianic Dimensions*, trans. Margaret Kohl (London: SCM Press, 1990); Dorrien, *Reconstructing the Common Good*, quotes 95.

13   Dorrien, *Reconstructing the Common Good*, 127–59, quote 155.

14   José Míguez Bonino, *Christians and Marxists: The Mutual Challenge to Revolution* (Grand Rapids: Eerdmans, 1976); Míguez Bonino, *Toward a Christian Political Ethics* (Philadelphia: Fortress, 1983); Míguez Bonino, *Doing Theology in a Revolutionary Situation* (Philadelphia: Fortress, 1975); Míguez Bonino, "Historical Praxis and Christian Identity," in *Frontiers of Theology in Latin America*, ed. Rosino Gibellini (Maryknoll, N.Y.: Orbis Books, 1979), 269–73.

15   Gary Dorrien, *The Neoconservative Mind: Politics, Culture, and the War of Ideology* (Philadelphia: Temple University Press, 1993); Dorrien, *Soul in Society: The Making and Renewal of Social Christianity* (Minneapolis: Fortress, 1995).

16   Gary Dorrien, "Hanging in There for a Good Cause: Donald Shriver's Presidency at Union Theological Seminary," chapter 2, *Christian Ethics in Conversation: A Festschrift for Donald W. Shriver Jr.*, ed. Isaac B. Sharp and Christian T. Iosso (Eugene, Ore.: Cascade Books, 2020).

17 Dorrien, *Soul in Society*, 350–61; Stanley M. Hauerwas, "A Christian Critique of Christian America," in Hauerwas, *Christian Existence Today: Essays in Church, World and Living in Between* (Durham, N.C.: Labyrinth Press, 1988), 171–90; Hauerwas, "Christian Ethics in America (and the *Journal of Religious Ethics*): A Report on a Book I Will Not Write," in Hauerwas, *A Better Hope: Resources for a Church Confronting Capitalism, Democracy, and Postmodernity* (Grand Rapids: Brazos Press, 2000), 55–69; Hauerwas, "Christian Ethics and Advocacy," in *Ethics and Advocacy: Bridges and Boundaries*, ed. Harlan Beckley, Douglas F. Ottati, Matthew R. Petrusek, and William Schweiker (Eugene, Ore.: Cascade Books, 2022), 131–39; Gary Dorrien, "Social Ethics for Social Justice: The Legacies of the Social Gospel and a Case for Idealistic Discontent," in Beckley et al., *Ethics and Advocacy*, 106–30.

18 Michael Awkward, *Negotiating Difference: Race, Gender, and the Politics of Positionality* (Chicago: University of Chicago Press, 1995); Orlando Patterson, *Freedom in the Making of Western Culture* (New York: Basic Books, 1991); Robert N. Bellah, Richard Madsen, William M. Sullivan, Ann Swidler, and Steven M. Tipton, *Habits of the Heart: Individualism and Commitment in American Life* (Berkeley: University of California Press, 1985); Amitai Etzioni, *The Spirit of Community: Rights, Responsibilities, and the Communitarian Agenda* (New York: Crown, 1993); Etzioni, ed., *New Communitarian Thinking: Persons, Virtues, Institutions, and Communities* (Charlottesville: University Press of Virginia, 1995).

19 Darlene Clark Hine, *Black Women in White: Racial Conflict and Cooperation in the Nursing Profession, 1890–1950* (Bloomington: Indiana University Press, 1989); Martin E. Marty, *The One and the Many: America's Struggle for the Common Good* (Cambridge, Mass.: Harvard University Press, 1987); John B. Cobb Jr., *Sustainability: Economics, Ecology, and Justice* (Maryknoll, N.Y.: Orbis Books, 1992); Daniel C. Maguire, *The Moral Core of Judaism and Christianity: Reclaiming the Revolution* (Minneapolis: Fortress, 1993); Richard John Neuhaus, *The Catholic Moment: The Paradox of the Church in the Modern World* (New York: Doubleday, 1987); Robert C. Neville, *The God Who Beckons: Theology in the Form of Sermons* (Nashville: Abingdon, 1999); Hilary Putnam, *The Threefold Cord: Mind, Body, and World* (New York: Columbia University Press, 1999).

20 Kenneth Baynes, *The Normative Grounds of Social Criticism: Kant, Rawls, and Habermas* (Albany: State University of New York Press, 1991).

21 Iris Marion Young, *Justice and the Politics of Difference* (Princeton: Princeton University Press, 1990); Young, *Inclusion and Democracy* (Oxford: Oxford University Press, 2000).

22 Todd Gitlin, *The Twilight of Common Dreams: Why America Is Wracked by Culture Wars* (New York: Henry Holt, 1995); Richard Rorty, "Is 'Cultural Recognition' a Useful Notion for Leftist Politics?" *Critical Horizons* 1 (2000): 7–20; Judith Butler, "Merely Cultural," *Social Text* 15 (1997): 265–77; Nancy Fraser,

"From Redistribution to Recognition? Dilemmas of Justice in a 'Postsocialist' Age," *New Left Review* 212 (July/August 1995): 68–93.

23 Gary Dorrien, "Triangulating to the Right: Social Democracy in Europe and the United States," *Religious Socialism* (Summer 1999): 9; Dorrien, "Rethinking the Theory and Politics of Christian Socialism," *Democratic Left* (January 2000): 23–26.

24 Michael Eric Dyson, *Reflecting Black: African-American Cultural Criticism* (Minneapolis: University of Minnesota Press, 1993); Dyson, *Race Rules: Navigating the Color Line* (New York: Basic Books, 1996); Dorrien, *Darkly Radiant Vision*, 344–45.

25 Michael Eric Dyson, *Making Malcolm: The Myth and Meaning of Malcolm X* (New York: Oxford University Press, 1995).

26 Gary Dorrien, *The Word as True Myth: Interpreting Modern Theology* (Louisville: Westminster John Knox, 1997).

27 Gary Dorrien, *The Remaking of Evangelical Theology* (Louisville: Westminster John Knox, 1998); Dorrien, *The Barthian Revolt in Modern Theology* (Louisville: Westminster John Knox, 2000).

6 Over from Kalamazoo

1 Gary Dorrien, *The Making of American Liberal Theology: Imagining Progressive Religion* (Louisville: Westminster John Knox, 2001).

2 Gary Dorrien, "Hegelian Spirit and Holy Spirit: Theology, Myth, and Divine Transcendence," February 2001, Ann V. and Donald R. Parfet Distinguished Professor Inaugural Lecture, Kalamazoo College, Gary Dorrien Papers, Burke Library, Columbia University, New York.

3 Dorrien, *The Making of American Liberal Theology*.

4 This section contains capsule summaries of my arguments in Gary Dorrien, *Imperial Designs: Neoconservatism and the New Pax Americana* (Philadelphia: Temple University Press, 2004).

5 George W. Bush, State of the Union Address, January 29, 2002, Washington, D.C.: The White House.

6 Angelo Codevilla, "Victory: What It Will Take to Win," *Claremont Review of Books*, November 2001; Frank Gaffney, "The Path to Victory," *Claremont Review of Books*, Fall 2002, 10; Michael Ledeen, *The War Against the Terror Masters: Why It Happened; Where We Are Now; How We'll Win* (New York: St. Martin's Press, 2002); Norman Podhoretz, "The Path to Victory," *Claremont Review of Books*, Fall 2002, 11–12; Podhoretz, "In Praise of the Bush Doctrine," *Commentary* 114 (September 2002): 19–28.

7 Gary Dorrien, "Axis of One: the 'Unipolarist' Agenda," *Christian Century*, March 8, 2003.

8 Obery Hendricks Jr., *The Politics of Jesus: Rediscovering the True Revolutionary Nature of the Teachings of Jesus and How They Have Been Corrupted* (New York:

Doubleday, 2007); this section adapts material from Gary Dorrien, *A Darkly Radiant Vision: The Black Social Gospel in the Shadow of MLK* (New Haven: Yale University Press, 2023), 352–53.

9   Alice Walker, *In Search of Our Mothers' Gardens: Womanist Prose* (New York: Harcourt Brace Jovanovich, 1983); Delores S. Williams, "The Color of Feminism: On Speaking the Black Woman's Tongue," *Journal of Religious Thought* 43 (1986): 42–58; Williams, *Sisters in the Wilderness: The Challenge of Womanist God-Talk* (Maryknoll, N.Y.: Orbis Books, 1993); Larry L. Rasmussen, *Dietrich Bonhoeffer: Reality and Resistance* (Nashville: Abingdon, 1972); Rasmussen, *Earth Community, Earth Ethics* (Maryknoll, N.Y.: Orbis Books, 1996).

10   James H. Cone, *Black Theology and Black Power* (New York: Seabury Press, 1969); Cone, *A Black Theology of Liberation* (Philadelphia: J. B. Lippincott, 1970).

11   Cone, *Black Theology and Black Power*, quote 56.

12   Gayraud S. Wilmore, *Black Religion and Black Radicalism: An Interpretation of the Religious History of African Americans* (New York: Anchor Doubleday, 1973; 3rd ed., Maryknoll, N.Y.: Orbis Books, 1998); Charles H. Long, "Perspectives for a Study of Afro-American Religion in the United States," *History of Religion* 11 (August 1971): 54–66; Long, "Structural Similarities and Dissimilarities in Black and African Theologies," *Journal of Religious Thought* 32 (Fall/Winter 1975): 9–24; Gayraud S. Wilmore, *Black Religion and Black Radicalism* (Garden City, N.Y.: Doubleday, 1972); Cecil W. Cone, *Identity Crisis in Black Theology* (Nashville: African Methodist Episcopal Church, 1975); Cecil W. Cone, "The Black Religious Experience," *Journal of the Interdenominational Theological Center* 2 (Spring 1975): 137–39; Vincent Harding, "The Religion of Black Power," in *The Religious Situation, 1968*, ed. D. R. Cutler (Boston: Beacon, 1969); J. Deotis Roberts, *Liberation and Reconciliation: A Black Theology* (Philadelphia: Westminster, 1971; 2nd ed., Maryknoll, N.Y.: Orbis Books, 1994), 75–80; James H. Cone, *For My People: Black Theology and the Black Church* (Maryknoll, N.Y.: Orbis Books, 1984), 78–98.

13   James H. Cone, *The Spirituals and the Blues* (New York: Seabury Press, 1972); Cone, *God of the Oppressed* (New York: Seabury Press, 1975).

14   Gayraud S. Wilmore and James H. Cone, eds., *Black Theology: A Documentary History, 1966–1979* (Maryknoll, N.Y.: Orbis Books, 1979); Cone and Wilmore, ed., *Black Theology: A Documentary History, Volume 1, 1966–1979* (Maryknoll, N.Y.: Orbis Books, 1993); Cone and Wilmore, eds., *Black Theology: A Documentary History, Volume 2, 1980–1992* (Maryknoll, N.Y.: Orbis Books, 1993).

15   Gary Dorrien, *The Making of American Liberal Theology: Crisis, Irony, and Postmodernity* (Louisville: Westminster John Knox, 2006); Dorrien, *Social Ethics in the Making: Interpreting an American Tradition* (Chichester, UK: Wiley-Blackwell, 2009).

16   Gary Dorrien, "Social Ethics in the Making: History, Method, and White Supremacism," Reinhold Niebuhr Inaugural Lecture, January 30, 2007, Union

Theological Seminary, in Dorrien, *Economy, Difference, Empire: Social Ethics for Social Justice* (New York: Columbia University Press, 2010), 392–409.

17   Dorrien, *Social Ethics in the Making*, 421–37.

18   Beverly W. Harrison, *Making the Connections: Essays in Feminist Social Ethics*, ed. Carol S. Robb (Boston: Beacon, 1985); Harrison, *Justice in the Making: Feminist Social Ethics*, ed. Elizabeth M. Bounds, Pamela K. Brubaker, Jane E. Hicks, Marilyn J. Legge, Rebecca Todd Peters, and Traci C. West (Louisville: Westminster John Knox, 2004).

19   Katie Geneva Cannon, *Black Womanist Ethics* (Atlanta: Scholars Press, 1988); Emilie Townes, *Womanist Ethics and the Cultural Production of Evil* (New York: Routledge, 2006).

20   Jacquelyn Grant, *White Women's Christ and Black Women's Jesus: Feminist Christology and Womanist Response* (Atlanta: Scholars Press, 1989); Kelly Brown Douglas, *The Black Christ* (Maryknoll, N.Y.: Orbis Books, 1994); Katie G. Cannon, *Katie's Canon: Womanism and the Soul of the Black Community* (New York: Continuum, 1995); Dorrien, *Social Ethics in the Making*, 587–90; Dorrien, *Darkly Radiant Vision*, 279–83.

21   This section draws upon the author's conversations with Eris McClure, Martin Hirschorn, Hanna Benzwie, Michael Benzwie, and Michael Hirschorn, and upon Martin Hirschorn's memoir, *Can You Hear Me? Making the World a Quieter Place: My Life as an Unwitting Entrepreneur* (Bay Village, Ohio: Acoustical Publications, 2007), 4–78.

22   Jewish Telegraphic Agency, "Israel Legal Aide in Germany Dies after Automobile Accident," *JTA Daily News Bulletin*, September 14, 1953.

7 Into the Obama Era

1   Peter Steinfels, "Two Social Ethicists and the National Landscape," *New York Times*, May 26, 2007; David Brooks, "Obama, Gospel and Verse," *New York Times*, April 26, 2007.

2   Gary Dorrien, "Imperial Designs: Neoconservatism and the Iraq War," "Militaristic Illusions: The Iraq Debacle and the Crisis of American Empire," and "Empire in Denial: American Exceptionalism and the Community of Nations," in Dorrien, *Economy, Difference, Empire: Social Ethics for Social Justice* (New York: Columbia University Press, 2010), 214–39, 240–58, 259–88.

3   Barack Obama, October 2, 2002, "Transcript: Sen. Barack Obama's Speech against Iraq War," National Public Radio, January 20, 2009, https://www.npr.org/templates/story/story.php?storyId=99591469.

4   Michael Hardt and Antonio Negri, *Empire* (Cambridge, Mass.: Harvard University Press, 2000); Hardt and Negri, *Multitude: War and Democracy in the Age of Empire* (New York: Penguin, 2004).

5   Paul Hirst and Grahame Thompson, *Globalization in Question*, 2nd ed. (Oxford: Polity, 1999); David Held, *Democracy and the Global Order* (Stanford: Stanford

University Press, 1995); Mary Kaldor, *Global Civil Society: An Answer to War* (Cambridge: Polity, 2003); Samuel P. Huntington, *The Clash of Civilizations and the Remaking of World Order* (New York: Touchstone, 1996); Patrick J. Buchanan, *Where the Right Went Wrong* (New York: Thomas Dunne Books, 2005).

6   Dorrien, *Economy, Difference, Empire*, 284–85.

7   Gary Dorrien, *The Obama Question: A Progressive Perspective* (Lanham, Md.: Rowman and Littlefield, 2012), 42–46; Barack Obama, *The Audacity of Hope: Thoughts on Reclaiming the American Dream* (New York: Three Rivers Press, 2006); David Remnick, *The Bridge: The Life and Rise of Barack Obama* (New York: Vintage Books, 2011), 468–70; Obama, "Barack Obama's Caucus Speech," January 3, 2008, transcript, *New York Times*, https://www.nytimes.com/2008/01/03/us/politics/03obama-transcript.html; Mary Frances Berry and Josh Gottheimer, *Power in Words: The Stories behind Barack Obama's Speeches, from the State House to the White House* (Boston: Beacon, 2010), 134.

8   Brian Ross and Rehab El-Buri, "Obama's Pastor: God Damn America, U.S. to Blame for 9/11," ABC News, March 13, 2008, abcnews.go.com; Barack Obama, "On My Faith and My Church," *Huffington Post*, March 15, 2008, huffingtonpost.com; Obama, "Text of Obama's Speech: A More Perfect Union," *Wall Street Journal*, March 18, 2008, http://blogs.wsj.com/washwire; for another text, see Obama, "A More Perfect Union," March 19, 2008, www.latimes.com/news/nationworld, accessed March 8, 2011.

9   CQ Transcriptions, "Reverend Wright at the National Press Club," *New York Times*, April 28, 2008.

10   Gary Dorrien, "Breaking the Oligarchy: Globalization, Turbo-Capitalism, Economic Crash, Economic Democracy," in Dorrien, *Economy, Difference, Empire*, 143–67.

11   Gary Dorrien, "Rethinking and Renewing Economic Democracy," in Dorrien, *Economy, Difference, Empire*, 168–86.

12   Bill Moyers and Cornel West on *Bill Moyers Journal*, July 3, 2009, http://www.pbs.org/moyers/journal/07032009/profile.html; Chris Hedges, "The Obama Deception: Why Cornel West Went Ballistic," *truthdig*, May 16, 2011, www.truthdig.com.

13   Dorrien, *Economy, Difference, Empire*, ix–x.

14   Shirley C. Guthrie Jr., *Christian Doctrine* (Louisville: Westminster John Knox, 1994); Ronald H. Stone, *Politics and Faith: Reinhold Niebuhr and Paul Tillich at Union Seminary in New York* (Macon, Ga.: Mercer University Press, 2012).

15   James H. Cone, *The Cross and the Lynching Tree* (Boston: Beacon, 2011); Delores S. Williams, *Sisters in the Wilderness: The Challenge of Womanist God-Talk* (Maryknoll, N.Y.: Orbis Books, 1993); Williams, "The Color of Feminism," *Christianity and Crisis*, April 29, 1985, 164–65; Williams, "The Color of Feminism: On Speaking the Black Woman's Tongue," *Journal of Religious Thought* 43 (1986): 42–58.

16 Raphael G. Warnock, *The Divided Mind of the Black Church: Theology, Piety, and Public Witness* (New York: New York University Press, 2014); Kelly Brown Douglas, *The Black Christ* (Maryknoll, N.Y.: Orbis Books, 1994); Douglas, *What's Faith Got to Do with It? Black Bodies/Christian Souls* (Maryknoll, N.Y.: Orbis Books, 2005).

17 Reinhold Niebuhr, "The Terrible Beauty of the Cross," *Christian Century*, March 21, 1929, "supreme" and "terrible," 386; Cone, *Cross and the Lynching Tree*, "a powerful," 37; Gary Dorrien, *A Darkly Radiant Vision: The Black Social Gospel in the Shadow of MLK* (New Haven: Yale University Press, 2023), 328–33.

18 Hedges, "The Obama Deception," "a black puppet."

19 Gary Dorrien, *Kantian Reason and Hegelian Spirit: The Idealistic Logic of Modern Theology* (Chichester, UK: Wiley-Blackwell, 2012).

20 Friedrich Schleiermacher, *On Religion: Speeches to Its Cultured Despisers* (1799), trans. Richard Crouter (Cambridge: Cambridge University Press, 1988); F. W. J. Schelling, *System of Transcendental Idealism* (1800), trans. Peter Heath (Charlottesville: University Press of Virginia, 1978); G. W. F. Hegel, *Phenomenology of Spirit* (1807), trans. A. V. Miller (Oxford: Oxford University Press, 1977).

21 Immanuel Kant, *Akademie-Ausgabe of Kant's Gesammelte Schriften* (Berlin: G. Reimer, 1910–), XXV: 878; Kant, *Anthropology from a Pragmatic Point of View*, trans. Victor Lyle Dowdell (Carbondale: Southern Illinois University Press, 1978), 226–29; G. W. F. Hegel, *Lectures on the Philosophy of World History*, trans. H. B. Nisbet (Cambridge: Cambridge University Press, 1984), 170–74.

22 Dorrien, *Kantian Reason and Hegelian Spirit*, 530–67; Kant, *Akademie-Ausgabe of Kant's Gesammelte Schriften*, II: 429.

23 Charles Darwin, *On the Origin of Species* (London: John Murray, 1859); Darwin, *The Descent of Man* (New York: John Murray, 1874).

24 Dorrien, *The Obama Question*.

25 Gary Dorrien, "The Case against Wall Street," *Christian Century*, November 15, 2011; "Savvy Occupiers: An Interview with Gary Dorrien," *Christian Century*, November 15, 2011; "Occupy the Future: Can a Protest Movement Find a Path to Economic Democracy?" *America*, March 12, 2012; "Questions for Gary Dorrien: On the Ethical Roots and Uncertain Future of Occupy Wall Street," *America*, March 12, 2012; Dorrien, "What Kind of Country? Economic Crisis, the Obama Presidency, the Politics of Loathing, and the Common Good," *Cross Currents*, Spring 2012.

26 Gary Dorrien, *The New Abolition: W. E. B. Du Bois and the Black Social Gospel* (New Haven: Yale University Press, 2015).

8 Twilight Surge

1 Gary Dorrien, *The New Abolition: W. E. B. Du Bois and the Black Social Gospel* (New Haven: Yale University Press, 2015).

2 W. E. B. Du Bois, "The Future of Wilberforce University," *Journal of Negro Education* 9 (October 1940), "a miserable," 565; Du Bois, "The Joy of Living," in *Writings in Periodicals Edited by Others*, ed. Herbert Aptheker, 4 vols. (Millwood, N.Y.: Kraus-Thomson, 1982), "and the greatest," 129; Du Bois, "Marxism and the Negro Problem," *Crisis* 40 (May 1933), "a colossal," 103; Du Bois, "Credo," "The Second Coming," "Jesus Christ in Texas," and "A Hymn to the Peoples," in Du Bois, *Darkwater: Voices from within the Veil* (New York: Harcourt, Brace, 1920), 1–2, 60–62, 70–77, 161–62; Du Bois, "Untitled," in *Creative Writings by W. E. B. Du Bois*, ed. Herbert Aptheker (Millwood, N.Y.: Kraus-Thomson, 1985), "the tattered," 41. This section adapts material from Dorrien, *New Abolition*, 282–84.

3 W. E. B. Du Bois, "The African Roots of the War," *Atlantic Monthly* 115 (May 1915): 707–14; John A. Hobson, *Imperialism* (1902; repr., London: George Allen & Unwin, 1948).

4 Traci D. Blackmon, "The Blood Did It: Why Michael Brown's Death Was Different," *Sojourners*, September 12, 2014, quote, https://sojo.net/articles/faith-action/blood-did-it-why-michael-browns-death-was-different.

5 Gary Dorrien, *Breaking White Supremacy: Martin Luther King Jr. and the Black Social Gospel* (New Haven: Yale University Press, 2018).

6 Catherine Keller, *Cloud of the Impossible: Negative Theology and Planetary Entanglement* (New York: Columbia University Press, 2015).

7 Victor Anderson, *Beyond Ontological Blackness: An Essay on African American Religious and Cultural Criticism* (New York: Continuum, 1995).

8 James Baldwin, *The Fire Next Time* (1963), in *Collected Essays*, ed. Toni Morrison (New York: Library of America, 1998), "are probably," 326; Cone, *Said I Wasn't Gonna Tell Nobody* (Maryknoll, N.Y.: Orbis Books, 2018).

9 Cone, *Said I Wasn't Gonna Tell Nobody*, quote 171.

10 Vincent W. Lloyd, *Religion of the Field Negro: On Black Secularism and Black Theology* (New York: Fordham University Press, 2018), 5–38; I first recounted the Lloyd story in Gary Dorrien, *A Darkly Radiant Vision: The Black Social Gospel in the Shadow of MLK* (New Haven: Yale University Press, 2023), 482.

11 This section adapts material from Dorrien, *Breaking White Supremacy*, 1–2.

12 Gary Dorrien, "Breaking White Supremacy: Morehouse, MLK Jr., and the Black Social Gospel," Founders Day Keynote Address, Morehouse College, Atlanta, Ga., February 15, 2018; "*The New Abolition* and *Breaking White Supremacy:* Reflections on the Black Social Gospel," International Chaplains Association, Morehouse College, Atlanta, Ga., February 15, 2018; "The Radical King: Martin Luther King Jr. and the Black Social Gospel," Grosse Pointe War Memorial Association, Grosse Pointe Farms, Mich., February 24, 2018; Lenten Vespers Homily, Corpus Christi Parish, New York, N.Y., March 4, 2018; "Bearing the Cross in Memphis," I AM Mountaintop Conference, Mason Temple, AFSCME/COGIC, Memphis, Tenn., April 2, 2018; "The Radical King: Martin Luther King Jr. and the Black Social Gospel," Duke

Divinity School, Durham, N.C., April 3, 2018; "How I See Walter Rauschenbusch," Keynote Address, Conference on Walter Rauschenbusch, Mercer University, Macon, Ga., April 9, 2018; "Breaking White Supremacy, Then and Now," John Cardinal Cody/Richard A. McCormick Lecture in Moral Theology, Loyola University, Chicago, Ill., April 16, 2018; "Remembering James Cone," Chapel Service, Union Theological Seminary, New York, N.Y., April 30, 2018; "Reflections on My Current and Recent Work: *The New Abolition, Breaking White Supremacy, Imagining Democratic Socialism,* and *In a Post-Hegelian Spirit,* Iliff School of Theology and University of Denver, Denver, Colo., May 9, 2018; Keynote Address, International Conference on Liberal Theology, "Liberal Theology, Then and Now: Germany, Britain, and the USA," Ludwig-Maximilians-Universität München, Munich, Germany, July 18, 2018; Keynote Address, "Historicism as a Modern Theological and Philosophical Problem," International Conference on "Historicism as a Concept in the Humanities and Social Sciences, 1890–1980," Royal Netherlands Academy of Arts and Sciences, Amsterdam, Netherlands, August 31, 2018.

13 Gary Dorrien, *Social Democracy in the Making: Political and Religious Roots of European Socialism* (New Haven: Yale University Press, 2019). This section contains capsule summaries of my argument in this book.

14 Dorrien, *Social Democracy in the Making,* 147–216.

15 G. D. H. Cole, *Self-Government in Industry* (London: G. Bell, 1st ed., 1917; 5th ed., 1920); R. H. Tawney, *Equality* (New York: Harcourt, Brace, 1931); William Temple, *Christianity and the Social Order* (Harmondsworth, Middlesex: Penguin, 1942); R. H. S. Crossman, *Labour in the Affluent Society* (London: Fabian Society, 1960); Crossman, ed., *New Fabian Essays* (London: J. M. Dent, 1952); C. A. R. Crosland, *The Future of Socialism* (New York: Macmillan, 1956).

16 Gary Dorrien, *In a Post-Hegelian Spirit: Philosophical Theology as Idealistic Discontent* (Waco, Tex.: Baylor University Press, 2020); Dorrien, *American Democratic Socialism: History, Politics, Religion, and Theory* (New Haven: Yale University Press, 2021).

17 Dorrien, *In a Post-Hegelian Spirit,* 73–111, 113–64.

18 Alfred North Whitehead, *Process and Reality: An Essay in Cosmology* (New York: Macmillan, 1929). This section contains capsule summaries of my arguments in *In a Post-Hegelian Spirit.*

19 Stephen Crites, *Dialectic and Gospel in the Development of Hegel's Thinking* (University Park: Pennsylvania State University Press, 1998), 517–26; Robert R. Williams, *Tragedy, Recognition, and the Death of God: Studies in Hegel and Nietzsche* (Oxford: Oxford University Press, 2014), 360–69; Peter C. Hodgson, *Hegel and Christian Theology* (Oxford: Oxford University Press, 2005), 267–70; Andrew Shanks, *Hegel and Religious Faith: Divided Brain, Atoning Spirit* (London: T&T Clark, 2012), 6–7.

20 Paul Tillich, *Love, Power, and Justice: Ontological Analyses and Ethical Applications* (London: Oxford University Press, 1952).

21 This section contains capsule summaries of my arguments in *American Democratic Socialism*.

22 Bernie Sanders, *The Speech: On Corporate Greed and the Decline of the Middle Class* (New York: Nation Books, 2015), "how much," 73; "I think," 126. This section adapts material from the concluding chapter of Dorrien, *American Democratic Socialism*, 556–57.

23 This discussion adapts material from the preface to Dorrien, *American Democratic Socialism*, x.

24 Dorrien, *Darkly Radiant Vision*.

25 Dorrien, *Darkly Radiant Vision*, 491–99.

26 Gary Dorrien, *The Spirit of American Liberal Theology* (Louisville: Westminster John Knox, 2023).

27 L. Serene Jones, *Feminist Theory and Christian Theology: Cartographies of Grace* (Minneapolis: Fortress, 2000); John A. T. Robinson, *Honest to God* (London: SCM Press, 1963; 40th anniv. ed., Louisville: Westminster John Knox, 2003).

28 This was one of my set pieces for years before I finally recorded it in a book; see Gary Dorrien, *Economy, Difference, Empire: Social Ethics for Social Justice* (New York: Columbia University Press, 2010), 65.

29 Gary Dorrien, "The Protestant Mainline Makes a (Literary) Comeback," *Religion Dispatches*, August 5, 2013, https://religiondispatches.org/the-protestant -mainline-makes-a-literary-comeback/.

30 G. W. F. Hegel, *Phenomenology of Spirit*, trans. A. V. Miller (Oxford: Clarendon Press, 1977), 110, par. 177; Dieter Henrich, "Hölderlin und Hegel," in Henrich, *Hegel im Kontext* (Frankfurt: Suhrkamp Verlag, 1967), 26–27; H. F. Fulda, "Der Begriff des Geistes bei Hegel und seine Wirkungsgeschichte," ed. Joachim Ritter, vol. 3 (Stuttgart: Schwabe, 1971), 191–93; Robert Pippin, *Hegel's Idealism: The Satisfactions of Self-Consciousness* (Cambridge: Cambridge University Press, 1989), 35–41, 163–71, 175–88; Robert R. Williams, *Recognition: Fichte and Hegel on the Other* (Albany: State University of New York Press, 1992), 141–60; H. S. Harris, "The Concept of Recognition in Hegel's Jena Manuscripts," *Hegel-Studien Beiheft* 20 (Bonn: Bouvier Verlag, 1979), 229–48; Heinz Röttges, *Dialektik und Skeptizismus: Die Rolle des Skeptizismus für Genese, Selbstverständnis und Kritik der Dialektik* (Frankfurt: Athenäum Verlag, 1986), 149–56; Ludwig Siep, *Anerkennung als Prinzip der praktischen Philosophie* (Freiburg: Alber Verlag, 1979); Dorrien, *In a Post-Hegelian Spirit*, 122–27; see Italo Testa and Luigi Ruggiu, eds., *"I that is We, We that is I": Perspectives on Contemporary Hegel* (Leiden: Brill, 2016).

ACKNOWLEDGMENTS

The first draft of this memoir was in hand when my book *Anglican Identities: Logos Idealism, Imperial Whiteness, Commonweal Ecumenism* entered the page-proof stage at Baylor University Press in November 2023. I don't like to pitch proposals for books I haven't written, and I'm equally averse to competitive bidding and deadlines, so I nearly always put off the publisher issue until I have a first draft. A few days before the American Academy of Religion convened in San Antonio, I sent the memoir draft to my friend R. David Nelson, the director of Baylor University Press. Dave, assistant editor Cade Jarrell, and production manager Jenny Hunt had worked superbly with me on the Anglicanism book. One cannot get more friendly, supportive, and professionally skilled than they are. My first choice for the memoir felt obvious. If Dave wants the book, I thought, I will give no further thought to the publisher issue. I didn't expect to see him at AAR, but he came to a session where I spoke, telling me he wanted the book very much. That is a sweet memory for me as this book heads to the page-proof stage in June 2024, two months after *Anglican Identities* came out between two covers.

I am deeply grateful to Dave, Cade, and Jenny for the devoted care they gave to this book, and for the sheer enjoyment they conveyed in producing it. BUP graphic designer Elyxandra Encarnación put a stunning cover design on *Anglican Identities* that always receives rave reviews. Then she followed up by persuading me, fortunately, to put the tricycle picture on the cover of this book. Many thanks, Ely, you were right to wear me down! Thanks as well to copyeditor Evan Herrington and proofreader Simon Coll, who saved me from what-were-you-thinking howlers and indulged the signature style I fashioned long ago.

Since this book discusses most of the books I've written, it marks an occasion of gratitude for the many publishers and editors with whom I've worked. I have had only good experiences with publishers, and three of my previous editors—Stephanie Egnotovich at Westminster John Knox Press, Rebecca Harkin at Wiley-Blackwell, and Jennifer Banks at Yale University Press—became treasured friends to me. My well of gratitude runs deep for the back-and-forth I enjoyed with Stephanie on five books, with Rebecca on two books, and with Jennifer on five books. Whenever I advise students to consider book publishing as a career, I sing the praises of Stephanie, whom we lost too soon, of Rebecca, who got pulled upstairs out of the Religion division, of Jennifer, a truly wonderful friend and editor, and now, of Dave Nelson. I also owe a special debt of gratitude to Jonathan Sisk, the Vice President and Senior Executive Editor of Rowman & Littlefield, whose firm published *The Democratic Socialist Vision* when I was a diocesan priest and who personally fast-tracked *The Obama Question* when speed was essential. As an advocate for young scholars, I am grateful to Jon that Rowman & Littlefield and Lexington Books publish many books by scholars beginning their careers.

I shall end with a word about treasured friends whose names somehow did not come up in the text. Jennifer Jesse befriended me through liberal theology, persuaded me to love William Blake half as much as she does, and tried, bless her, to slow me down. Barbara Hiles Mesle, one-half of a golden couple, taught literature at Graceland University for many years while actually loving literature (especially Toni Morrison); then she added me to her long roster of friends. Cynthia Moe-Lobeda, a highly accomplished eco-feminist ethicist and activist, is teaching us how to teach organizing in seminary contexts. Mary Elizabeth Moore, a poet of eco-feminist process theology, brought me to Boston University School of Theology at the end of her outstanding eleven-year deanship. Alma College president Jeff Abernathy will complete the fifteenth and final year of his kindly, accomplished, and distinguished presidency in 2025. Blessings and thanks to all.

It was hard enough for me to restrict my mentions of students to my doctoral advisees, but if I make only two exceptions here at the end, they have to be Kirsten Lodal and Hortensia Gooding, for lighting up every classroom I ever shared with them.

I can only hope that my love of the faculty and students of Union Theological Seminary has come through in the text. Union is very much my home and milieu, "where faith and scholarship meet to reimagine the work of justice," as we say in the Union videos. I am deeply grateful for these unlikely years of twilight among beloved friends at the seminary that has my heart.

INDEX

A

Abernathy, Jeff, 300
Abolitionist Sanctuary, 266
Abraham, Spencer, 71
Adams, James Luther, 72
Adenauer, Konrad, 192
Adkins-Jones, Tim, 259
Adorno, Theodor, 96, 147
Affordable Care Act, 220
Afghanistan war, 201–3
Afro-American Council, 229
Afro-American League, 229
After God (Taylor), 211
After Virtue (MacIntyre), 117
AIDS Coalition to Unleash Power (ACT UP), 123
Ain't I a Woman (hooks), 129
Al-Anon, 197–98
Alcoff, Larry, 126
Alcoff, Linda, 126, 130, 147
Allen, Diogenes, 81–82
Allen, Scotty, 164
Alma College, 23, 25–53, 120–21, 270–71
Altimore, Frank, 19
Altizer, Thomas J. J., 39, 41
America magazine, 221
American Academy of Religion (AAR), 154, 234
An American Conscience: The Reinhold Niebuhr Story (documentary), 236
American Democratic Socialism: History, Politics, Religion, and Theory (Dorrien), 247, 251–53, 259

American Federation of State, County and Municipal Employees (AFSCME), 78
Ames, Doug, 273
Anarchy, State, and Utopia (Nozick), 132
Anderson, Bernhard W., 39
Anderson, Carol, 141
Anderson, Nkosi Du Bois, 189
Anderson, Victor, 237–38
Andrewes, Lancelot, 105
Anglican Identities (Dorrien), 269–70
Anglicanism, 104–6
Anglo-Catholicism, 106
Ann V. and Donald R. Parfet Distinguished Chair, 163–64
Anonymous, 220–21
Another Liberalism (Rosenblum), 130
Appadurai, Arjun, 129
Aquinas, Thomas, 45, 51–52
Arendt, Hannah, 119
Aristotle, 30–32, 34, 77, 117
Armstrong, Louis, 26
Arnold, Marigene, 127
Aronowitz, Stanley, 108
Attlee, Clement, 243
Augustine (Saint), 250
Awkward, Michael, 145–46
"Axis of One: The 'Unipolarist' Agenda" (Dorrien), 171
Ayers, A. J., 36
Aylward, Brian, 97
Azaransky, Sarah, 259, 261

B

Ba'alism, 59
Bacevich, Andrew, 201
Bach, Johann Sebastian, 155
Bagnall, Robert, 230
Baillie, J. B., 34, 78
Bainton, Edgar, 155
Bakhtin, Mikhail, 96, 147
Baldwin, James: Cone's analysis of,
    42–43, 237–39; Dorrien's analysis
    of, 19, 270; West's analysis of, 262
Bandura, Albert, 44
Banks, Jennifer, 241, 300
Baptist fundamentalism, 4
Barber, Benjamin, 118
Barlowe, Gigi, 197
Barth, Karl: Cone's work on, 180,
    182; Dorrien on, 40–42, 44–46,
    81, 152, 216, 249; Moltmann on,
    134–35; theology of, 65–66, 83,
    85, 187, 260
baseball, 22–24
Basic Christianity (Stott), 22
Basic Writings of Nietzsche, 95
Baynes, Ken, 63, 65–67, 74, 96,
    146–47
Bechet, Sidney, 26
Beecher, Henry Ward, 163
Beer, Samuel, 130
Bellah, Robert, 117, 145–46, 149
Beloved (Morrison), 262
Bennett, John C., 185–86
Bennett, William, 117
Benzwie, Albert (Hirschorn), 191–93
Benzwie, Ashley, 258
Benzwie, Hanna Nussbaum, 191–93,
    199, 258
Benzwie, Joshua, 258
Benzwie, Michael, 193, 258
Bergman, Ingmar, 19, 65
Berne, Eric, 112
Bernstein, Eduard, 243
Bernstein, Felicia Montealegre,
    194–96
Bernstein, Julius, 62
Bernstein, Leonard, 193–99
Berry, Malinda, 176, 189

Beyond God the Father (Daly), 57–58
Beyond Ontological Blackness
    (Anderson), 238
biblical scholarship: Dorrien on,
    38–39, 44–45, 48–49, 75–76;
    feminist theology and, 59
Biblical Theology movement, 133
Biden, Joe, 254–55
Biggs, Anson, 91–92, 96, 110–12,
    137, 157, 167, 199
Biggs, Brenda Louise: childhood of,
    89, 91; Dorrien's meeting with, 89;
    family conflict and, 111–12, 199;
    illness and death of, 138, 152–58,
    161, 163; at Kalamazoo, 135–36,
    138–40, 142, 147; marriage to
    Dorrien, 92; motherhood for, 119,
    123–24, 223; pastoral career of,
    90–92, 95–97, 101, 106, 110–16,
    121; pregnancies and miscarriages
    of, 110–11; sermons of, 272
Biggs, Grace Sorenson, 91–92, 96,
    110–12, 157, 167, 199
Biggs, John, 91, 157, 199
Biggs, Ryan, 167
Biggs, Taryn, 167
birther movement, 216
Black Americans, 150–51; church
    alliances with, 114–15
Black feminism, 129–30, 178–79,
    187–88, 231–32; *see also* womanist
    theology
Black Lives Matter movement, 215,
    237–40
Blackmon, Traci, 233–34
Black nationalism, 230
Black Power movement, 41–43, 180
Black social gospel, 166, 184–85,
    220, 227–35, 257–59, 269,
    272–73
Black theology, 42–43, 64, 181–84;
    Cone and, 212–15, 239–40
Black Theology and Black Power
    (Cone), 41, 180–81
A Black Theology of Liberation (Cone),
    41, 180–81, 237
Black Womanist Ethics (Cannon), 187

Blake, William, 300
Bloch, Ernst, 39
Blust, Ron, 20
Bob Seger System, 107
Boehner, John, 220
Boggs, Carl, 108
Bonhoeffer, Dietrich, 64, 179
Booty, John E., 101
Borg, Marcus, 225
Born to Win: Transactional Analysis with Gestalt Experiments (James & Jongeward), 112
Bosanquet, Bernard, 35
Bouck, Dale, 13
Bounds, Elizabeth M., 186
Boys, Mary, 260
Boyte, Harry C., 117–18, 145–46
Braden, Virginia, 17
Bradley, F. H., 35
Brandon, Nathaniel, 21
Breaking White Supremacy: Martin Luther King Jr. and the Black Social Gospel (Dorrien), 235, 239, 241, 273
Breisach, Ernst, 120
Breneman, David, 121
Breyer, Chloe, 189
Brickner, Balfour, 145–46
Bright, John, 38–39
British Anglicanism, 22
British philosophy, 35–36
Brody, Janet, 163
Brooks, David, 201
Brothers, Clifford, 97
Brown, Bob, 20
Brown, Delwin, 169
Brown, Jim, 11
Brown, Michael, 233–34
Brown, Raymond E., 75–77
Brubaker, Pamela K., 186
Brueggemann, Walter, 225
Brumson, April, 100
Brunner, Emil, 40, 84, 237
Bryan, Lawrence D., 128, 140–41, 162, 175
Bryant, Peter James, 230
Buber, Martin, 128
Buchanan, Pat, 204

Bultmann, Rudolf, 40, 52, 69–70, 76
Burke, Edmund, 132
Burke, Roxanna, 21
Burnham, James, 72–73
Burnkamm, Günther, 76
Burroughs, Nannie H., 230
Burtch, Duane, 20
Burton, Richard, 196
Burton, Susan, 196
Bush, George H. W., 167
Bush, George W., 167–73, 208
Bush Doctrine, 167
Bushnell, Horace, 163
Butler, Joseph, 105, 131
Butler, Judith, 148–49

C

Calloway, Jamall, 224
Calvin, John, 45
Camp, Dave, 175, 256
Campbell, Joan Brown, 172, 220
Campbell-Reed, Eileen, 259
Camus, Albert, 87
Cannon, Katie, 187–89, 213
Cantrell, Butch, 29
Capital (Marx), 49–51
Capital Area Council of Churches, 114
capitalism, Du Bois on, 232–33
Carey, Keith, 18–20, 29, 270
Carnap, Rudolf, 36
Caroline divinity, 105
Carr, David, 259
Carter, Jimmy, 78–79, 95, 98–99
Carter, J. Kameron, 240
Carter, Lawrence Edward S., 240, 269
Carvalhaes, Cláudio, 259
Case, Jenny, 175
Casey, Maureen, 98
Catalano, Eduardo, 71, 73
Cavell, Stanley, 66
Cekola, Gilda, 124
Channing, William Ellery, 163
Chapin, Dave, 25
Cheney, Dick, 167, 170
Chicago School of Theology, 141

Chong Hyun Kyung, Tara, 189, 260
Christian Century magazine, 171, 221
Christian Doctrine (Guthrie), 211
Christian ethics, 143–44, 179
Christianity: decline of progressivism
  in, 263–64; Dorrien's belief in, 227,
  273–74; Du Bois on, 232; feminist
  theology and, 57–60; philosophy
  and, 30, 34–35, 39
Christianity and the Social Crisis
  (Rauschenbusch), 41
Christians, Clara, 258–59
Christians, Evelyn, 258–59
Christians, Nicholas, 246, 258–59
Christians, William, 211, 223, 236,
  258
Christology, 104
Church, Forrest, 62–63
Church, Frank, 62–63
Church Dogmatics (Barth), 44–45
The Church and the Second Sex (Daly),
  58
Civil Rights Movement, 16–18, 53
Clarke, Maura, 99
Clements, Paul, 222
Clergy Leadership Network for
  National Leadership Change,
  172–73
Cleveland Browns, 11
Clinton, Bill, 139, 149–50, 161, 167,
  169, 208
Clinton, Hillary, 206, 254
Cloud of the Impossible (Keller),
  236–37
Cobb, John B., 145–46
Codevilla, Angelo, 169
Coffin, William Sloane, Jr., 172
Cohen, G. A., 79
Cole, G. D. H., 243–44
Coleridge, Samuel Taylor, 131–32
Coll, Simon, 299
Coltrane, John, 262
Columbia University, 210–11, 269
Commentary magazine, 47
Committee in Solidarity with the
  People of El Salvador (CISPES),
  99–101, 116, 171

CommonWealth: A Return to Citizen
  Politics (Boyte), 118
Communism, 46
communitarianism, 117–18, 130, 132
community organizing, 265–66
Concordia Seminary system, 54
Cone, Cecil, 181–82
Cone, Charles, 183
Cone, James: on Baldwin, 238–39; on
  Black social gospel, 231, 234–325;
  on Black theology, 41–43, 52, 64,
  212–15, 237–40; on cross of Jesus
  and womanist theology, 212–15;
  Dorrien's friendship with, 102, 227;
  feminist theology and, 58; Harrison
  and, 186; liberation theology and,
  149; on Niebuhr, 234; politics
  and, 206; on redemptive suffering,
  76–77, 151; social ethics and, 143;
  at Union, 81, 189, 213–14; writings
  of, 179–84
Cone, Krystal, 183
Cone, Michael, 183
Cone, Robynn, 183, 239
Cone, Rose Hampton, 183
Congress on Religion and Politics, 125
The Conservative Mind (Kirk), 131
Contribution to the Critique of Political
  Economy (Marx), 50–51
Conzelmann, Hans, 76
Cook, Richard, 138, 175
Cooney, Don, 126
Cooper, Bradley, 195
Cortés, Ernesto, Jr., 145–46
Cothran, Tommy, 195
Councilism, 124–25
COVID-19 pandemic, 255–56, 258
Cowell, Marcia, 156
Cox, Harvey, 72, 109
Crandall, Ralph, 4
Crisis on Campus (Taylor), 211
Crites, Stephen A., 249
Critique of Judgment (Kant), 50,
  64–65, 67–69, 243–44
Critique of Practical Reason (Kant),
  31–33, 67–69
Critique of Pure Reason (Kant),
  31–35, 37, 67–69, 243

Crosby, Stills, Nash & Young, 26
Crosland, C. A. R., 243, 244
The Cross and the Lynching Tree
    (Cone), 212–15, 237–39
Crossman, R. H. S., 243–44
cross-of-Jesus theology, 212–15
Crummell, Alexander, 230
Crusader without Violence (Reddick),
    16–18, 270
Cruz, Sam, 259
cultural leftism, 148–49
cultural nationalism, 230
Curtis, Phyllis, 156

D

Daly, Mary, 57–60
Danaher, Bill, 205, 246
*A Darkly Radiant Vision: The Black
    Social Gospel in the Shadow of MLK*
    (Dorrien), 257–59
Darkwater (Du Bois), 262
Darling, Billy, 96
Darling, Lisa, 96
Darwin, Bruce, 22
Darwin, Charles, 218–19
Davaney, Sheila, 174
Dean, William, 174
death-of-God theology, 39–41
DeBoer, Anne, 45
Debs, Eugene, 252–53
De Groot, Benjie, 258
Dei verbum (papal encyclical), 76
de la Torre, Miguel, 240
Deleuze, Gilles, 236–37
democracy, decline of, 264–65
Democratic Party, 43, 46–47, 53, 78,
    99–100, 114–15
democratic socialism, 116, 119, 125,
    241–43, 251–54
Democratic Socialist Organizing
    Committee (DSOC): Democratic
    party and, 78, 98; Dorrien's
    involvement in, 72, 77–78, 83, 88,
    96, 98–100; founding of, 60–62,
    150; limitations of, 107; New
    American Movement and, 108–9,
    116, 118

Democratic Socialists of America
    (DSA), 109, 115–16, 118, 149–50,
    221, 251, 254, 267
The Democratic Socialist Vision
    (Dorrien), 116, 119, 125
dependency theory, 135
Derrida, Jacques, 96, 126, 149, 236
Descartes, Rene, 31, 81–82
De Sica, Vittorio, 65
Dewey, Bob, 127
Dewey, John, 22, 30, 37, 117–18
Dews, Peter, 69
Dibelius, Martin, 76
Diggins, John Patrick, 72
Diggs, James R. L., 230
Dissent magazine, 148
Divino afflante Spiritu (Pius XII
    encyclical), 76
Doane Stuart School, 106–7, 119
Doblmeier, Martin, 236
Doescher, Ian, 189
Donaghy, Andy, 20
Donovan, Jean, 99
Donovan, Ray, 105
Dorrien, Andy: birth of, 5, 9;
    childhood of, 12, 14–16, 54–55;
    death of, 71–74
Dorrien, Anna, 256
Dorrien, Anne Rice, 3–7
Dorrien, Ellis, 3–4, 9–11
Dorrien, Eric, 13–14, 73–74, 175,
    256–57, 267–68
Dorrien, Greg, 9, 12, 14, 73–74,
    95–96, 167, 175, 256
Dorrien, Hope, 156, 167
Dorrien, John Ellis (Jack), 2–15,
    22–24, 49, 54, 73–74, 156,
    255–56
Dorrien, Kenneth, 6–7, 9
Dorrien, Mike, 13–14, 74, 175, 256
Dorrien, Ralph, 6, 8–9
Dorrien, Robyn Hampton, 156, 163,
    167
Dorrien, Sara Biggs: birth of,
    119; career of, 255; childhood
    of, 123–24, 137, 140, 148,
    163–67; children of, 246, 258; at
    college, 178; marriage to William

Christians, 223; mother's illness and death and, 154–58, 190, 199, 236; musical theater and, 174–75, 190; ordination of, 223; seminary education of, 211, 219–20

Dorrien, Virginia Catherine (Hank): beauty of, 49; early life of, 2–9; Gary Dorrien and, 96, 156, 255–56; as mother and caregiver, 15–16, 73–74, 267–68; Sara Dorrien and, 163

Dorrien, William, 3

Dos Passos, John, 72–73

Doubt (Shanley), 190

Douglas, Kelly Brown, 187, 213–15, 239, 246, 260, 272

Douglas, Mark, 211

Douglass, Frederick, 210, 261

draft lottery, 49

Drake, Tom, 20

Driver, Tom, 212

Du Bois, Nina Gomer, 233

Du Bois, W. E. B.: Dorrien's analysis of, 54, 229–32; on race and racism, 232–33; spirituality of, 231–32; West's study of, 262

Dufford, Bob, 155

Dukakis, Michael, 126

Dummett, Michael, 69

Dunning, Stephen, 66

Durbin, E. F. M., 243

Durkheim, Emile, 37

Dworkin, Ronald, 129, 131

Dykstra, Ivan, 29

Dykstra, Wesley, 29–34, 39–40

Dyson, Michael Eric, 129, 149–52, 206, 216, 259

E

Eastman, Max, 72

East of Eden (Steinbeck), 19

Eckhart, Meister, 250

economics, Dorrien on, 49–51, 78–79, 208–10, 244–46

Economy, Difference, Empire: Social Ethics for Social Justice (Dorrien), 211

Edwards, John, 172

Egnotovich, Stephanie, 163–64, 166, 300

Ehrenreich, Barbara, 108–9

Eisen, Lasha, 191

Elder, E. Rozanne, 120

Elements for a Social Ethic (Winter), 83

Ellsberg, Robert, 239

El Salvador, 99–100

Elster, Jon, 79

Ely, Richard, 184

Emerson, Ralph Waldo, 22, 163

Empire (Hardt & Negri), 203–5

Encarnación, Elyxandra, 299

Episcopalian church: decline of, 131–32; Dorrien's interest in, 81, 88–89, 101–4; Dorrien's ordination into, 104–6, 110

Episcopal Peace Fellowship, 110

The Epistle to the Romans (Barth), 44

Equal Rights Amendment, 58

Etzioni, Amitai, 117, 145

evangelical feminism, 89–90

evangelicalism, Dorrien family and, 4–5

F

Fabian socialism, 241–44

Fairbairn, Ronald, 63

Faith in Action, 266

Fajnzylber, Fernando, 135

Fanon, Frantz, 42

Farmer, James, 62

Farneth, Molly B., 249

Farrer, Austin, 82

Faulkner, William, 19

Felder, Cain Hope, 77

Felder, Romy, 224

Fellini, Federico, 65

feminist movements: *see* Black feminism, 129–30; Black social gospel, 231–32; evangelical feminism, 89–90; Harrison, Beverly Wildung, 185–86; socialist feminism, 108; theology, 57–60, 70, 186–87; womanist theology

Feminist Theory (hooks), 129

Feminist Theory and Christian Theology (Jones), 260

"Ferguson and Beyond: Race and Niebuhrian Ethics in the Age of Obama" (AAR forum), 234
Ferrer, Aldo, 135
Field Notes from Elsewhere (Taylor), 211
Fierro, Alfredo, 83
Financial Crisis of 2008–2009, 207–10
Firack, David, 5, 7
The Fire Next Time (Baldwin), 19
First Presbyterian Church Free Health Clinic, 139–40
The Fiscal Crisis of the State (O'Connor), 79
Floyd-Thomas, Juan, 189
Floyd-Thomas, Stacey, 189
Focus Institute, 101
Forbes, James, 172, 206
Ford, Ita, 99
foreign policy, Dorrien's discussion of, 201–2
form criticism, 76
Forsman, Deborah, 73
Foster, Kenny, 25, 44
Foucault, Michel, 96, 126, 149
Fragments of the Century (Harrington), 53
Frank, Andre Gunder, 135
Frank, Manfred, 69
Frankfurt school, 77
Frankl, Viktor, 145
Fraser, Doug, 78
Fraser, Nancy, 129–30, 148–49
Freedom in the Making of Western Culture (Patterson), 146
Frege, Gottlob, 35–36
French, Bill, 65
Freud, Sigmund, 84–85
Fuller, Lon, 63–64
The Future of Socialism (Crosland), 244

G

Gadamer, Hans Georg, 65–66, 83
Gaitskell, Hugh, 243–44
Galston, William, 117
Gamaliel, 96, 266

Gandhi, King, Mandela Peace Prize, 269
Gandhi, Mohandas K., 17
Gardiner, Judith Kegan, 108
Gardner, Freda, 84
Garner, Eric, 233
Gathje, Pete, 175
Gay, Ken, 13
gay activism, 63, 128
Gaza crisis, 268–69
Geithner, Timothy, 208–9
General Theological Seminary, 176–77
German idealism, 66–67
gestalt theory, 112, 270–72
Geyer, Edna Dorrien, 9–10
Geyer, Glen, 10
Geyer, Judy, 10
Geyer, Marybeth, 11
Gilkey, Langdon, 129, 133–34
Gilkey, Sonja Weber, 133–34
Gillespie, Dizzy, 26
Gitlin, Todd, 148
Givens, Jane, 156
globalization, 203–5
God in Creation (Moltmann), 134
God of the Oppressed (Cone), 77, 182–83, 237
Gooding, Hortensia, 300
Gorbachev, Mikhail, 202
Gore, Charles, 106, 243
Gore, Karenna, 260
Gospel According to John (Brown), 76
Gotbaum, Victor, 78
Go Tell It on the Mountain (Baldwin), 19
Graham, Guile, 48–49
Gramsci, Antonio, 108
Grant, Jacquelyn, 187
Grapes of Wrath (Steinbeck), 19
Gray, Bruce, 101–2, 104, 106
Green, T. H., 77
Green New Deal, 253
Green's Barber College, 6
Greer, Colin, 118–19
Gregory, Eric, 219
Griffin, Gail, 140
Griggs, Sutton, 230

Grimké, Francis J., 230
Groundwork of the Metaphysics of Morals (Kant), 31
Guatemala, 99
Gunkel, Hermann, 76
Gunner, Byron, 230
Guntrip, Harry, 63
Gushee, David, 240
Gustafson, James, 143
Guthrie, Shirley C., 211
Gutiérrez, Gustavo, 76–77, 82, 124, 149, 169–70
Gutmann, Amy, 129–30, 132

H

Haber, Hilly, 224
Habermas, Jürgen, 69, 147
Habits of the Heart (Bellah), 117, 146
Haeckel, Ernst, 218–19
Hagar tradition, 212
Haight, Roger, 189, 260
Haker, Hille, 240, 249
Hamilton, William, 39, 41
Handy, Robert, 75
Hank, Charlotte, 7
Hank, Edward, 4–5, 12
Hank, Leon, 5
Hank, Mary Jane (Moore), 4–5, 7–9
Hannay, David, 119
Hannay, Margaret, 119
Hardesty, Nancy, 90
Hardie, Keir, 243
Harding, Vincent, 182
Hardt, Michael, 203–5
Harkin, Rebecca, 300
Harold Baker Foundation, 29
Harrington, Michael, 53–55, 60–62, 78–80, 98, 107–9, 125, 150
Harris, Melanie, 189
Harrison, Beverly Wildung, 185–88
Harrison, James, 186
Harris-Perry, Melissa, 206
Hart, H. L. A., 63–64
Hartman, Jeff, 19
Harvard Divinity School, 57–75, 225–26
Hauerwas, Stanley, 143–44
Haverfield, Carol, 37

Haverfield, Roger, 29, 35–37, 40, 50
Hawkins, Coleman, 26
Hawkins, Karl, 26
Headlam, Stewart, 243
Healey, Richard, 108–9
Heckart, Jennifer, 176
Hegel, G. W. F.: Dorrien's study of, 23, 30–31, 37–38, 247–50; Du Bois and, 232; Kant and, 34–35, 37–38, 50, 81, 216–17, 270–72; liberalism and, 117; Marx and, 51; theology and influence of, 39–41, 52, 65–69; Tillich and, 46, 166; translations of, 77–78; Whitehead and, 237
"Hegelian Spirit and Holy Spirit: Theology, Myth, and Divine Transcendence" (Dorrien lecture), 164
Heidegger, Martin, 50–52, 69–70, 96, 147, 271
Held, David, 204
Hempton, David, 225
Hendricks, Obery, Jr., 172–73, 206, 210
Henrich, Dieter, 66–69, 81, 271
Herberg, Will, 72–73
Herrington, Evan, 299
Heschel, Abraham Joshua, 128
Heyward, Carter, 187
Hicks, Jane E., 186
Hilberry, Conrad, 127
Hill, Thomas, 43–44
Hine, Darlene Clark, 145–46
Hirschorn, Helena Eisen, 191
Hirschorn, Julius, 191
Hirschorn, Martin, 191–92
Hirschorn, Michael, 258
Hirst, Paul, 204
History of Israel (Bright), 39
A History of Western Philosophy (Jones), 29
Hobson, John A., 233
Hobson, S. G., 243
Hodgson, Peter C., 249
Hogg, Wilbur E., 97, 104–6, 110
Holder, Eric H., 208
Hölderlin, Friedrich, 69, 248

Holiday, Billie, 26
Holland, Scott, 106, 243
Holocaust memorials, 144–45
Honest to God (Robinson), 260
Hooker, Richard, 105
hooks, bell, 129–30
hope, Marxist/Christian philosophy of, 39
Hopkins, Peter, 175
Horne, Marilyn, 193–94
Horton, Myles, 251
Hough, Joe, 173–74, 176
Hubbard, Howard, 98
Humberto Romero, Carlos, 99
Hume, David, 32
Hunt, Jenny, 299
Huntington, Samuel, 204
Husserl, Edmund, 51

I

Iliff School of Theology, 174–76
Imperial Designs (Dorrien), 171–72
imperialism, Du Bois' discussion of, 233
Imperialism (Hobson), 233
In a Post-Hegelian Spirit: Philosophical Theology as Idealistic Discontent (Dorrien), 247–51
Industrial Areas Foundation (IAF), 96, 118
Inge, W. R., 106
Inglis, Laura, 88
Intervarsity Christian Fellowship, 22
Iosso, Christian, 88, 95, 172
Iraq war, 167–72, 202–3
Ireland, John, 155

J

Jackson, Jesse, 115, 123, 125–27, 172, 257
James, Muriel, 112
James, William, 22, 30
"James Luther Adams and the Spirit of Liberal Theology" (Dorrien lecture), 226–27

January 6, 2021 Capitol attacks, 263–64
January Adventure conferences, 225
Jarrell, Cade, 299
Jesse, Jennifer, 300
Jewell, Neonu, 224
Jewish Currents magazine, 109
Jewish Labor Committee, 62
Johnson, Lyndon, 17
Johnson, Mordecai, 231, 251
Johnson, Theresa, 163–64
Jones, James F., 162–63, 175, 184, 219–20, 225
Jones, Joe, 260
Jones, Serene, 183, 208, 224, 239, 246, 260–61, 269, 272
Jones, W. T., 29–30
Jongeward, Dorothy, 112
Jozwiak, Gary, 19
Jung, Carl, 85
Just Conversations (podcast), 260
Justice in the Making (Harrison), 186
Justice and the Politics of Difference (Young), 148

K

Kahl, Brigitte, 260
Kähler, Martin, 46
Kalamazoo College, Religion Department and, 140–41; *see also* Liberal Arts Colloquium Credit program (Kalamazoo College); Stetson Chapel, Dorrien at, 120–21, 123–28, 162–66, 174–77, 277
Kalamazoo Nonviolent Opponents to War, 171
Kaldor, Mary, 204
Kant, Immanuel: Dorrien's study of, 31–37, 41, 50, 218–19, 223–24, 247–48, 271–72; Hegel and, 34–35, 37–38, 50, 81, 216–17, 270–72; Henrich on, 66–69; on race, 218–19; social ethics and, 64–65; Tillich and, 45
Kantian idealism, 30–35, 50, 52, 67–69, 147

Kantian Reason and Hegelian Spirit (Dorrien), 216–19, 223–24
Kazel, Dorothy, 99
Keeley, Steve, 23–24
Kefauver, Estes, 14
Keller, Catherine, 179, 236–37
Kennedy, Babydoll, 189
Kennedy, Edward, 98
Kerry, John, 202–3
Kierkegaard, Søren, 44, 83–88, 147, 250, 272
Kimm, Kelsey, 148
Kimm, Kristen, 138
King, Martin Luther, Jr.: Black culture and, 150–51; Black social gospel and, 231, 251; Cone's discussion of, 180, 182–83; influence on Dorrien of, 16–19, 22, 40–41, 52, 123, 203, 241; March on Washington and, 62; SCLC and, 118; theology and, 146; West and, 262
Kirk, Annette, 131
Kirk, Jeremy, 189
Kirk, Russell, 129, 131–32
Klein, Melanie, 63
Klimpel, Charlene, 13
Klimpel, Dick, 13
Knights of Labor, 252
Knitter, Paul, 189, 259
Kramer, Larry, 123
Kramer, Ron, 123
Krauthammer, Charles, 169
Kristol, Irving, 47, 142
Kurtz, Geoffrey, 246
Kutz-Marks, Becca, 136, 156, 157, 161, 163–65, 175–76, 184
Kutz-Marks, Charles, 136, 175, 184
Kutz-Marks, Marie, 148, 165

L

Laarman, Peter, 265
LaFever, Windle, 20
Lahti, Terry, 175
Lamar, Robert C., 97–98, 111
Lange, Oskar, 121
Language, Truth, and Logic (Ayer), 36

La Plante, Marilyn, 128
Latin American liberation theology, 77, 82–83, 135–36, 149
Latiolais, Cecelia, 148
Latiolais, Christopher, 136, 147–48
Latiolais, Laura Packard, 136, 147–48, 156, 157, 163
Laud, William, 105
Lauren, Ralph, 196
Lauster, Jörg, 241
Law's Empire (Dworkin), 131
Ledeen, Michael, 169
Led Zeppelin, 26
Lee, Edward L., Jr., 121, 128
Lee, Gladys Dorrien, 9–11
Lefever, Ernest, 48
Legge, Marilyn J., 186
Lehman, Duane, 21, 270
Lehmann, Paul, 183
Leibniz, G. W., 32, 81–82
Leigeb, Randy, 20
Lemmon, David, 29, 37–38, 49–50, 52
Leo XIII (Pope), 76
Levinas, Emmanuel, 249
Lewis, C. S., 22
Lewis, Jacqui, 246
Lewis, Thomas A., 249
Liberal Arts Colloquium Credit program (LACC, Kalamazoo College), 127–29, 136, 141, 145, 161, 165–66, 177
Liberal Equality (Gutmann), 130
liberal theology, 40–41, 45, 133 163, 165, 174, 183, 226, 241, 259
liberalism, 47, 73, 117, 130–31; Cone's critique of, 180; decline of, 263–65
Liberalism and the Limits of Justice (Sandel), 117
liberation theology, 42–43, 46–47, 58–61, 77, 83, 119, 124, 135–36, 143, 149, 180–83, 185–86, 212, 214, 241
Lieberman, Laurie, 258
Lincoln, Abraham, 210
Lincoln, C. Eric, 180–81

Linde, Bill, 20
Linnaeus, Carl, 217–18
Lloyd, Vincent, 239–40
Loatman, Paul, 107
Lodal, Kirsten, 300
Loder, Arlene, 84–85
Loder, James E., 83–92
Loder, Kim, 84
Loder, Tamara, 84
logical atomism, 36
Long, Charles H., 181–82
Looking for Mr. Goodbar (film), 90
A Love Supreme (Coltrane suite), 262
Lovin, Robin, 63–65, 69, 73, 77
Ludlow, John, 243
Luke, Tracy, 42
Luther, Martin, 84
Lynch, Roberta, 109
Lynn, Fred, 71

M

Maatman, Jan, 124, 156, 163
Maatman, Vaughn, 124
MacDonald, Ramsay, 243
MacIntyre, Alasdair, 117
Macquarrie, John, 85, 86, 102
Maeshiro, Kelly, 224
Maguire, Daniel, 145–46
Mahler, Gustav, 193–94
Mailer, Norman, 19
The Mainspring of Human Progress
   (Weaver), 21
The Making of American Liberal
   Theology: Crisis, Irony, and
   Postmodernity (Dorrien), 183–84
The Making of American Liberal
   Theology: Idealism, Realism, and
   Modernity (Dorrien), 165
The Making of American Liberal
   Theology: Imagining Progressive
   Religion (Dorrien), 163–64
Making Connections (Harrison), 186
Making Malcolm (Dyson), 151
Malcolm X, 42, 151, 180
Manley, Raine, 258
Mannheim, Karl, 37
Mansbridge, Jane J., 117

Marable, Manning, 109
March on Washington (1963), 62
Maréchal, Joseph, 52
Marson, Charles, 106, 243
Marstin, Ron, 72
Martin, James Alfred, Jr., 81
Martin & Malcolm & America
   (Cross), 239
Marty, Martin E., 145–46
Marx, Karl: Dorrien's analysis of, 17,
   34, 38, 49–53, 250, 271, 353–54;
   Du Bois on, 232; philosophy and,
   39; socialism and, 72, 79–80;
   West's study of, 77
Marxsen, Willi, 76
Mass (Bernstein), 194–95
Massanari, Ronald, 29, 39–41, 45,
   50, 52
Mathis, Johnny, 208
Maurice, Frederick Denison, 243
Maxfield-Steele, Allyn, 265
Mayfield, Curtis, 262
Mays, Benjamin E., 166, 220, 231,
   235, 251
McClure, Eris Benzwie, 190–99,
   211–12, 224, 227, 255–59, 273
McClure, John, 193–99
McDargh, H. John, 63, 96
McDonald, Jim, 5
McDonald, Mickey, 177
McDowell, John, 69
McGill, Arthur C., 67
McGinnis, Blanche, 6
McGlasson, Paul, 140
McGovern, George, 42–44, 47
McGuckin, John, 174
Meade, James, 243
The Mediator (Brunner), 237
Meeks, Howard, 120–21
Meier, Deborah, 109
Meland, Bernard, 102–4, 141
Melville, Herman, 262
Mere Christianity (Lewis), 22
Merleau-Ponty, Maurice, 85
Mesle, Barbara Hiles, 300
Metcalf, Jim, 22, 54
Midland High School, 1, 18–22

Migliore, Daniel, 83
Míguez Bonino, José, 124, 129,
    135–36, 149
The Militant Gospel (Ferro), 83
Mill, John Stuart, 37
Miller, A. V., 77–78
Miller, David, 100–101
Miller, George Frazier, 230
Minard, Nick, 62
Minnich, Elizabeth, 118–19
Minot, Winthrop Gardner, 71
Mischel, Walter, 43
Missouri Synod Lutheran Church, 54
Moe-Lobeda, Cynthia, 300
Mollenkott, Virginia Ramey, 90
Moltmann, Jürgen, 39, 102, 124,
    129, 134–35
Mondale, Walter, 107, 115
Moore, G. E., 35–37
Moore, Mary Elizabeth, 300
Moore, Milt, 4
Moral Man and Immoral Society
    (Niebuhr), 64, 262
Morris, William, 243
Morrison, Toni, 262, 300
Morrissey, Karen, 21
Morse, Christopher, 81, 176, 189
Moyers, Bill, 210
Mueller, Walter, 251
Mulligan, Carey, 196
Multitude (Hardt & Negri), 203–5
Mumma, Keith, 164
Munger, Theodore, 163
Murnane, Jay, 98
Murray, John Courtney, 64, 143
Murray, Pauli, 231, 251
music, Dorrien's reliance on, 15–16,
    26–27, 65, 155, 157–58, 174,
    194–95, 198–99, 272

N

Nader, Ralph, 96
*Naming the Whirlwind: The Renewal
    of God-Language* (Gilkey), 133
National Council of Churches, 97,
    172–73, 263–64

Nature, Man, and God (Temple),
    88–89, 102
Nature and Destiny of Man (Niebuhr),
    262
Negri, Antonio, 203–5
Nelson, R. David, 299–300
*The Neoconservative Mind: Politics,
    Culture, and the War of Ideology*
    (Dorrien), 142–43, 146
neoconservatism: criticism of, 201;
    Dorrien on, 46–49, 53, 142–43,
    146; rise of, 64, 72–73, 142–46,
    167–71
neo-orthodoxy, 44–45, 133
Neuhaus, Richard John, 47–48, 145
Neville, Robert C., 145, 147
*The New Abolition: W. E. B. Du
    Bois and the Black Social Gospel*
    (Dorrien), 227, 229–33, 235, 273
New American Movement (NAM),
    108–9, 116, 118
New Fabian Essays (Crossman), 244
New Left, 46–47, 53, 62, 108, 118
Newton, Isaac, 32
*New Woman, New Earth: Sexist
    Ideologies and Human Liberation*
    (Ruether), 60
Niagara Movement, 229
Niang, Aliou C., 260
Nicaragua, 99–100
Nicholas of Cusa, 236–37
Niebuhr, H. Richard, 143
Niebuhr, Reinhold: anti-Communism
    of, 47; Cone on, 214, 234–35;
    criticism of, 185; Dorrien's analysis
    of, 17, 88, 219; Kirk's discussion
    of, 131–32; liberal theology and,
    166; Lovin's analysis of, 64–65;
    neoconservatism and, 142–43; neo-
    orthodoxy and, 41; retirement of,
    185; revival of, 201–2; social ethics
    and, 44, 184–85, 211–12; social
    gospel and, 48, 143, 231; theology
    of, 46–48, 133, 262–63
Niebuhr, Richard R., 73

"The Niebuhrian Moment, Then and
   Now: Religion, Democracy, and
   Realism" (conference), 219
Nietzsche, Friedrich, 17, 95–96, 147
Nisbet, Robert, 117
Nixon, Richard, 42, 47, 53–54
Nobody Knows My Name (Baldwin),
   19
Noel, Conrad, 106, 243
Nolan, Liz, 98
*The Normative Grounds of Social
   Criticism* (Baynes), 147
Noth, Martin, 76
noumena, 68
Novak, Michael, 47, 142
Nozick, Robert, 132
Nugent, Nancy, 22, 24–25
Nussbaum, Anna, 191–92
Nussbaum, Meinhold, 191–92
NYPIRG, 96

O

Obama, Barack, 201–3, 205–9,
   215–16, 219–20
The Obama Question (Dorrien),
   219–20, 222–23
object-relations theory, 63
Ocasio-Cortez, Alexandria, 253, 267
Occupy Wall Street movement,
   220–22
O'Connor, James, 79–80
Offe, Claus, 80
Olson, Stephan, 258
Operation Rolling Thunder, 17
Orbis Books, 239
Organization of Petroleum Exporting
   Countries (OPEC), 78
Orr, David, 189
O'Shaughnessy, Brian, 98
Oslo Accords (1993), 268–69
The Other America (Harrington), 53, 61
Owen, Bud, 11
Owen, Robert, 1, 243
Owen, John, 1
Owen, Rick, 1
Ozawa, Seiji, 196

P

Pacific Institute for Community
   Organizations (PICO), 96, 266
Pacific School of Religion, 169
Pacini, David S., 66
Pae, Keun-Joo Christine, 189
Palestine Liberation Organization
   (PLO), 109
Pannenberg, Wolfhart, 134
Pantaleo, Daniel, 233–34
Parfet, Don, 163
Paris, Peter, 234
Parker, Jim, 20
Parsons, Talcott, 37–38
Parsons Child and Family Center,
   96–97
Patterson, Orlando, 145–46
Paulson, Henry, 209
Peabody, Francis Greenwood, 184–85
Penfield, Wilder, 86–87
Penney, Darby, 100
Pennybacker, Al, 172
Perle, Richard, 167–68
Perls, Fritz, 112
Peters, Rebecca Todd, 186
Petrina, David, 19, 29
phenomena, 68
Phenomenology of Mind (Hegel), 23,
   34–35, 67–69, 77–78
Phillips, Maxine, 267
Phillips, Romeo, 127, 184
Philosophical Investigations
   (Wittgenstein), 36
philosophy, Dorrien's interest in,
   29–53, 66–69, 81–82
Piaget, Jean, 85
Pink Floyd, 196
Pippen, Robert, 147
Pius X (Pope), 76
Pius XII (Pope), 76
Plaskow, Judith, 128
Plato, 30–31, 35, 60, 68, 270
Plotinus, 30, 270
Plum, Milt, 11
Podhoretz, Norman, 47, 142, 169

Point of View for My Work as an Author (Kierkegaard), 83
Polanyi, Karl, 38
politics, Dorrien's interest in, 43–49, 53–55
Poor People's Campaign, 266
populism, 252
The Portable Nietzsche, 95–96
post-Kantian philosophy, 50–52, 67, 69, 102–3, 132, 166, 216, 219, 240, 247–51, 271, 272
Powell, Adam Clayton, Sr., 230–31
Powell, Colin, 170–77
Prassannakumar, Irene Preetha, 224
Preller, Victor, 150
Presbyterian Church USA, 97
Presler, Franklin, 120–21
Previn, André, 196
The Price of the Ticket (Baldwin), 262
Princeton Theological Seminary, 81–92, 223
Principles of Mathematics (Russell), 36
Process and Reality (Whitehead), 141
Proctor, Henry Hugh, 230
Protestant church, decline of, 263–64
Proudfoot, Wayne, 210–11
psychology, 43–44, 63, 83–85
Public Interest Research Group (PIRG), 96
public theology, 64
Pursel, Robert, 105–6
Putnam, Hilary, 69, 145–47

Q

queer theory, 148, 149, 185, 187, 188
Quine, Willard Van Orman, 66

R

Raber Bible Baptist, 4
Raboteau, Albert, 150
race and racism, 7–8, 16, 18, 41–43, 114–15, 118, 125–26, 129–30, 146, 149, 152, 180–83, 185, 188, 206–7, 217–19, 229, 229–35,

238–40, and 241; Du Bois on, 232–33
Rahner, Karl, 49–52, 271
Rainbow Coalition, 125
Ramsey, Paul, 47, 143
Rand, Ayn, 21
Randolph, A. Philip, 61–62
Ransom, Reverdy, 184–85, 220, 229–31
Rashdall, Hastings, 106
Rasmussen, Larry, 143, 178–79
rational-choice Marxism, 79
Rauschenbusch, Walter, 17, 40–41, 52, 77, 124, 143, 165, 231
Rawls, John, 63–64, 66, 130, 132
Reagan, Ronald, 98–100
Reaping the Whirlwind (Gilkey), 133
Reason within the Bounds of Religion (Wolterstorff), 65
Rebels against War (Wittner), 98–99
The Recliners (Band), 175
Reconstructing the Common Good (Dorrien), 135
Reddick, L. D., 16–18
Reflecting Black (Dyson), 150–51
Rehmann, Jan, 260
religion: Dorrien's commitment to, 2, 21–22, 33–34, 74, 121, 269–70; feminism and, 58; *see also* Christianity; theology
"Religion and the Common Good" (Dorrien lecture), 121
Religion of the Field Negro (Lloyd), 239
"Resisting the Permanent War" (Dorrien lecture), 169–70
The Revolution of the Saints (Walzer), 132
Ricardo, David, 50–51
Rice, Jim, 71
Ricoeur, Paul, 83
Riggle, Tracy, 189
Ritschlian Culture Protestantism, 45
Rizzuto, Ana-María, 63
Robb, Carol S., 186
Roberts, Tom, 13
Robinson, John A. T., 260

Roemer, John, 79
Rogers, William, 63
Rohrer, Dan, 189
Rolander, John, 71–73
Rolling Stones, 26
Romanaux, Paula Pugh, 124, 139–40, 175
Roman Catholicism: Dorrien and, 2–4, 7, 16, 49–52, 74–75; feminism and, 58, 98; social ethics and, 185
Romero, Óscar, 99
Roosevelt, Franklin D., 61
Rorty, Richard, 77, 148
Rosenblum, Nancy, 106
Rosenblum, Nancy L., 129–30
Rosenman, Mark, 118–19
Rosenzweig, Franz, 128
Ross, Mary Ellen, 63, 65
Ross-Allam, Anthony Jermaine, 224
Rowman & Littlefield, 223
Royal, Zachary, 224
Ruether, Rosemary Radford, 58–60, 70, 102, 117, 124–25, 149
Ruhle, Vern, 24
Rumsfeld, Donald, 167
Rupp, George, 67
Ruskin, John, 243
Russell, Bertrand, 35–37
Rustin, Bayard, 53, 62
Rutter, John, 155

S

Said I Wasn't Gonna Tell Nobody (Cone), 239
Salguero, Gabriel, 189
Samuel DeWitt Proctor Conference, 206–7
Sandel, Michael, 117
Sanders, Bernie, 251, 253–55, 267
Sanders, Earl, 13
Sanzoni, Letha, 90
Sartre, Jean-Paul, 87
The Scandal of Christianity (Brunner), 84
Scarrow, David, 127, 147–48
Schappes, Morris, 109

Schelling, Friedrich W. J., 46, 68, 166, 217, 248
Schleiermacher, Friedrich, 40, 45, 52, 133, 217, 247–48
Schmeichel, Waldemar, 121, 141
Schremp, Lorraine Hank, 74
Schremp, Wilbert, 74
Schutte, Dan, 155
Schuyler, George, 151
Schweiker, William, 65
Science of Logic (Hegel), 35, 69
Sczepanski, David, 1
"The Second Coming" (Du Bois), 232
secularization, 203
SEED (Social Ethics Energizing Democracy), 265–67
Seeley, Harriet, 110
Seger, Bob, 107
Selznick, Philip, 117
September 11, 2001 attacks, 165–66, 168
sexism, 58
Shachtman, Max, 47
Shanks, Andrew, 249
Sharp, Isaac, 224
Shaull, Richard, 82–83
Shaw, George Bernard, 243
Sheraw, Sheryl, 110, 112
Shinn, Roger, 185
Shklar, Judith, 130
Shriver, Donald, 143
Shriver, Peggy, 143
Simmons, William, 229
Sinclair, Charlene, 189, 265
Sisk, Jonathan, 223, 300
Skinner, B. F., 43
Slater, George W., Jr., 230
Smith, Adam, 50–51
Smith, Kathy, 127
Smith, Lucy Wilmot, 230
Smith, Norman Kemp, 50
Snyder, Greg, 260
Social Democracy, 295
Social Democracy in the Making (Dorrien), 242–44, 246–47
social ethics: community organizing and, 265–67; Dorrien's work in,

83, 143, 149, 184–85, 210–12,
  225; at Union, 179, 187–89
Social Ethics in the Making (Dorrien),
  184–85, 211–12
social gospel, 41, 143–44, 166,
  184–85, 201–2, 231; *see also* Black
  social gospel
socialism, 53, 61–62, 116, 241–44,
  251–53
Socialism (Harrington), 53, 61
Socialism: Past and Future
  (Harrington), 125
socialist feminism, 108
Socialist Labor Party, 251–53
Social Justice Center, 100, 106, 119
Society of Christian Ethics (SCE),
  265, 267
sociology, Dorrien's interest in, 37–38
Sojourners community, 89–90
sola scriptura biblicism, 44–45
Solberg, Jan, 127
Soley, Ginny, 89–90
Soley, Rob, 89–90
Sommers, Christina Hoff, 117
Sotherland, Pam, 136, 156, 161
Sotherland, Paul, 136
*Soul in Society: The Making and
  Renewal of Social Christianity*
  (Dorrien), 142–43
Souls of Black Folk (Du Bois), 262
Southern Christian Leadership
  Conference (SCLC), 118, 231
Spencer, John, 102–4, 141
Spheres of Justice (Walzer), 132
Spinoza, Baruch, 32, 81–82, 217
The Spirit of American Liberal Theology
  (Dorrien), 259–60
Spirituals and the Blues (Cone), 182
sports, Dorrien's interest in, 12–24,
  54–55, 71, 152
Spraetz, Clark, 20
Spraetz, Glenn, 20–21
Stanton, Elizabeth Cady, 163
Start, Lester, 127
Stauffer, Aaron, 224, 255, 265
Steinbeck, John, 19
Steinfeld, Peter, 88

Steinfels, Peter, 201–2
Stendahl, Krister, 75
Stetson Chapel, Dorrien at, 120–21,
  127–31, 136, 140–41, 144–45,
  161, 164–65, 177
Stills, Stephen, 26
Stone, Ronald, 211–12
Stoppert, Robert, 19, 22
Stott, John R. W., 22
Stout, Jeffrey, 150, 219
Strauss, David Friedrich, 67
Stravers, Cindy, 175–78
Stravers, Hannah, 175
Stravers, Nelleke, 175
Stravers, Xan, 175
Stride toward Freedom (King), 17, 19,
  41
Strife, Joe, 189
Students for a Democratic Society
  (SDS), 108
Sudbrack, Josef, 69–70
Sullivan, Harry Stack, 63
Sullivan, William, 117
Summa Theologica (Aquinas), 51
Summers, Lawrence, 208
Su Yon Pak, 260
Swanson, Robert, 42
Systematic Theology (Tillich), 45

T

Taking Rights Seriously (Dworkin),
  131
Talented Tenth, Du Bois' concept of,
  233
Talking Back (hooks), 129
Tawney, R. H., 243–44
Taylor, Charles, 117
Taylor, Gerald, 118
Taylor, Graham, 184
Taylor, Herb, 25
Taylor, Jeremy, 105
Taylor, Mark C., 66, 210–11, 249
Taylor, Randy, 97
Tea Party movement, 215–16
Temple, William, 81, 88–89, 101–4,
  243–44
Thatamanil, John, 260

Theodore, Arvind, 224
theology: Dorrien's study of, 22, 39–40, 49–5, 82–83; feminism and, 58; philosophy and, 66–67; *see also* religion
Theology of Hope (Moltmann), 39
A Theory of Justice (Rawls), 132
Thomas, David, 269
Thomas, Norman, 3, 61–62, 78, 116, 123, 253
Thompson, Grahame, 204
Thompson, J. Mark, 121, 127, 141
Thurman, Howard, 166, 251
Tillich, Paul: Christian myth and, 48–49; Cone's work on, 42, 124, 182; Dorrien's work on, 81, 102, 166, 250–51; Niebuhr and, 133; on religious socialism, 72; theology of, 40, 44–46, 52
Tinker, Tink, 175
Toller, Louis, 29, 38–39
Torrance, Thomas F., 85
Toward a Democratic Left (Harrington), 53, 61
Townes, Emilie, 179, 187, 213
Tractatus Logico-Philosophicus (Wittgenstein), 36
transactional analysis, 112
Transcendentalism, 22
Transcendental Thomism, 52
"Transformations of the Human Spirit" (Loder), 85–86
The Transforming Moment (Loder), 88
Trapp, Carolee, 21
Trapp, Walter, 21
Traschen, Francie, 100–101
Trinity College, 219–20, 225
Tristman, Dorothy, 99
Troeltsch, Ernst, 40, 133
Truffaut, François, 65
Trump, Donald, 215–16, 235–36, 247, 263–64
Tubman, Harriet, 89
Tucker, William Jewett, 184
Turman, Eboni Marshall, 179, 189, 269
Turner, Henry McNeal, 230

U

Understanding the Old Testament (Anderson), 39
Union Institute (Cincinnati), 118–19
unions: declining power of, 78–80; Dorrien's work with, 61–62, 78, 96, 99; history of, 252
Union Theological Seminary: Dorrien's appointment to, 173–74, 176–78, 184–90, 224, 299–301; Dorrien's early studies at, 74–81; faculty at, 260; politics and, 206–7; White supremacy protests and, 234
University Christian Movement, 70
Unruly Practices (Fraser), 130
Up from Communism: Conservative Odysseys in American Intellectual History, 72
U.S. Day of Rage, 220–21

V

The Varieties of Religious Experience (James), 22
The Vast Majority (Harrington), 78
Vatican Council II, 52, 59, 76
Vaughan, Sarah, 26
Vesely-Flad, Rima, 189
Vienna Circle, 36
Vietnam War, 17–18, 42–43, 46–48
von Karajan, Herbert, 196

W

Waite, Charlie, 13
Walker, Alice, 129, 178
Walker, Corey D. B., 269
The Wall (Pink Floyd), 196
Walser, Joseph, 29, 38–40
Walter, Bruno, 194
Walters, Alexander, 229
Walzer, Michael, 117, 129–30, 132, 149
Ward, Keith, 199
Warnock, Raphael, 213, 240
Warren, Elizabeth, 253, 255
Washington, Booker T., 229–30
Washington, James, 77

The Way of Jesus Christ (Moltmann), 134
Weaver, Henry Grady, 21
Webb, Beatrice, 243
Webb, Sidney, 243
Weber, Max, 37
Weckesser, Greg, 20
welfare state, 78–80
Wells, Ida B., 230, 233
Wessel-McCoy, Colleen, 189
West, Cornel: Cone and, 183; democratic socialism and, 109, 124–25; Dorrien's friendship with, 236, 260–62; Dyson and, 129, 150; Obama and, 206, 208–9, 216, 219; at Union, 77–78, 81, 208, 210, 235, 261
West, Traci C., 186, 188
Western Michigan University, 119–20, 124, 126, 178
Weston School of Theology, 70
Wheeler, Demian, 189, 259
White, Andrea, 260
White Christian nationalism, 266
Whitehead, Alfred North, 102–4, 141, 146, 236–37, 250
Whitman, Walt, 261–62
Wiesel, Elie, 144–45
Wilberforce University, Du Bois' address at, 232
Williams, Delores, 178, 187, 212–15
Williams, Preston, 63–64
Williams, Ralph Vaughan, 155
Williams, Robert R., 249
Willison, Todd, 189
Wilmore, Gayraud, 181–83
Winnicott, Donald, 63
Winpisinger, Bill, 78
Winter, Gibson, 83
Wittgenstein, Ludwig, 35–36
Wittner, Larry, 98–99
Wolff, Christian, 32
Wolff, Robert Paul, 50
Wolfowitz, Paul, 167
Wolin, Sheldon, 77, 118
Wolterstorff, Nicholas, 65
A Woman Called Moses (documentary), 89

Womanist Ethics and the Cultural Production of Evil (Townes), 187
womanist theology, 129–30, 178–79, 183, 187–88, 212–15
Woodbey, George W., 230
Woolcock, Jim, 25
The Word as True Myth (Dorrien), 67, 152
The Word of God and the Word of Man (Barth), 44
World Council of Churches (WCC), 135–36
world-process theology, 102–4, 141
Wright, Jeremiah, 206–7
Wright, Richard R., Jr., 230–31
Wurf, Jerry, 78
Wyckoff, Campbell, 84
Wyman, Jason, 189

Y

Yale Divinity School, 179, 260–61
Yoder, John Howard, 143–44
Young, Andrew, 257–58
Young, Iris Marion, 148–49
Young, Thelathia Nikki, 234
Young People's Socialist League, 99